Planning, Implementing, and Maintaining a Microsoft® Windows Server™ 2003 Active Directory Infrastucture (70-294)

Textbook

Wendy Corbin

PUBLISHED BY
Microsoft Press
A Division of Microsoft Corporation
One Microsoft Way
Redmond, Washington 98052-6399

Copyright © 2004 by Microsoft Corporation

All rights reserved. No part of the contents of this book may be reproduced or transmitted in any form or by any means without the written permission of the publisher.

Library of Congress Cataloging-in-Publication Data
Corbin, Wendy, 1965-
 MOAC Planning, Implementing, and Maintaining a Microsoft Windows Server 2003 Active Directory Infrastructure / Wendy Corbin, Kurt Hudson.
   p. cm.
  Includes index.
  1. Electronic data processing personnel--Certification.   2. Microsoft software--Examinations--Study Guides.   3. Microsoft Windows Server.   I. Hudson, Kurt.   II. Title.

QA76.3.C665 2004
005.4'47682--dc22   2004065172

Printed and bound in the United States of America.

1 2 3 4 5 6 7 8 9   QWT   8 7 6 5 4 3

A CIP catalogue record for this book is available from the British Library.

Microsoft Press books are available through booksellers and distributors worldwide. For further information about international editions, contact your local Microsoft Corporation office or contact Microsoft Press International directly at fax (425) 936-7329. Visit our Web site at www.microsoft.com/learning. Send comments to *moac@microsoft.com*.

Active Directory, Excel, Exchange, Microsoft, Microsoft Press, MSDN, PowerPoint, Windows, the Windows logo, Windows NT, and Windows Server are either registered trademarks or trademarks of Microsoft Corporation in the United States and/or other countries. Other product and company names mentioned herein may be the trademarks of their respective owners.

The example companies, organizations, products, domain names, e-mail addresses, logos, people, places, and events depicted herein are fictitious. No association with any real company, organization, product, domain name, e-mail address, logo, person, place, or event is intended or should be inferred.

This book expresses the author's views and opinions. The information contained in this book is provided without any express, statutory, or implied warranties. Neither the authors, Microsoft Corporation, nor its resellers or distributors will be held liable for any damages caused or alleged to be caused either directly or indirectly by this book.

Program Manager: Linda Engelman
Project Editor: Lynn Finnel
Technical Editor: Robert Lyon
Instructional Designer: Emily Springfield

ISBN 13: 978-0-470-64119-4

SubAssy Part No. X10-36045
Body Part No. X10-23988

CONTENTS AT A GLANCE

CHAPTER 1:	OVERVIEW OF ACTIVE DIRECTORY	1
CHAPTER 2:	IMPLEMENTING ACTIVE DIRECTORY	27
CHAPTER 3:	WORKING WITH ACTIVE DIRECTORY SITES	59
CHAPTER 4:	GLOBAL CATALOG AND FLEXIBLE SINGLE MASTER OPERATIONS (FSMO) ROLES	83
CHAPTER 5:	ACTIVE DIRECTORY ADMINISTRATION	111
CHAPTER 6:	SECURITY PLANNING AND ADMINISTRATIVE DELEGATION	139
CHAPTER 7:	INTRODUCTION TO GROUP POLICY	159
CHAPTER 8:	CONFIGURING THE USER AND COMPUTER ENVIRONMENT USING GROUP POLICY	183
CHAPTER 9:	MANAGING SOFTWARE	221
CHAPTER 10:	PLANNING A GROUP POLICY MANAGEMENT AND IMPLEMENTATION STRATEGY	251
CHAPTER 11:	ACTIVE DIRECTORY MAINTENANCE, TROUBLESHOOTING, AND DISASTER RECOVERY	281
CHAPTER 12:	UPGRADING AND MIGRATING TO WINDOWS SERVER 2003	311
APPENDIX:	DNS OVERVIEW	331
	GLOSSARY	349

TABLE OF CONTENTS

ABOUT THIS BOOK xiii
   Target Audience xiii
   Prerequisites xiii
   The Textbook xiii
   The Supplemental Course Materials CD-ROM xiv
      Readiness Review Suite Setup Instructions. xv
      eBook Setup Instructions. xv
   The Lab Manual xv
   Notational Conventions xvi
   Keyboard Conventions xvii
   Coverage of Exam Objectives xvii
   The Microsoft Certified Professional Program xix
      Certifications xx
      MCP Requirements xx
   About the Authors xx
   For MOAC Support. xxi
   Evaluation Edition Software Support xxii

CHAPTER 1: OVERVIEW OF ACTIVE DIRECTORY 1
   Active Directory's Functions and Benefits 2
      Centralized Resource and Security Administration 2
      Single Point of Access to Resources. 3
      Fault Tolerance and Redundancy. 3
      Simplified Resource Location 4
   Active Directory Schema 5
   Active Directory Components 7
      Organizational Units 8
      Domains. 8
      Trees 9
      Forests. 9
      Sites 11
      Naming Standards. 11
   Planning an Active Directory Implementation 13
      The Logical and Physical Structure 13
      The Role of DNS 14
      Windows Server 2003 Forest and Domain Functional Levels. . . 15
      Understanding and Comparing Active Directory Trust Models . . 21
   Summary 24
   Exercises 24
      Exercise 1-1: Logical Versus Physical Structure 24
      Exercise 1-2: Functional-Level Decision Making 25

Review Questions 25
Case Scenarios. 26
 Scenario 1-1: Rolling Out Windows Server 2003 26
 Scenario 1-2: Accessing Resources in More than One Network . 26

CHAPTER 2: IMPLEMENTING ACTIVE DIRECTORY 27

Requirements for Active Directory. 28
Sizing the Active Directory Database. 29
Pre-Installation Tasks. 29
The Active Directory Installation Process. 30
 Creating a Forest Root Domain. 31
Post-Installation Tasks. 39
 Verifying and Finalizing DNS Settings 39
 Adding a Second Domain Controller to the Forest Root Domain   45
Modifying the Active Directory Schema 46
 Installing the Schema Management Snap-in 47
Raising the Domain and Forest Functional Levels. 48
Establishing and Managing Trust Relationships 49
 Verifying Trusts 52
 Revoking a Trust 53
Creating and Deleting User Principal Names 54
Summary 56
Exercise 56
 Exercise 2-1: Planning for an Active Directory Installation 56
Review Questions 57
Case Scenarios. 58
 Scenario 2-1: Planning a Migration 58
 Scenario 2-2: DNS Naming. 58

CHAPTER 3: Working with Active Directory Sites. 59

Overview of Sites and Site Links 60
 Sites and the Replication Process 62
 Linked Multi-Valued Attribute Replication. 70
Implementing and Managing a Site Plan 70
 Creating the Site Structure. 71
 Managing Replication 73
Monitoring Replication. 75
 Dcdiag 76
 Repadmin. 76
 Replmon. 76
Summary 78
Exercise 78
 Exercise 3-1: Viewing Connection Objects 78

Review Questions 79
Case Scenarios. 80
    Scenario 3-1: Adding a New Facility to a Network 80
    Scenario 3-2: Improving Replication Efficiency 81

CHAPTER 4: GLOBAL CATALOG AND FLEXIBLE SINGLE MASTER OPERATIONS (FSMO) ROLES. 83

Understanding the Global Catalog 84
    Understanding the Functions of the Global Catalog 84
    Universal Group Membership Caching. 85
    Planning Global Catalog Server Placement 87
    Enabling a Global Catalog Server 88
Understanding FSMO Roles 89
    Domain-Specific Roles. 90
    Forest-Wide Roles 93
Placing FSMO Servers 94
Managing FSMO Roles. 100
    Transferring an FSMO Role. 102
    Seizing an FSMO Role 103
Summary 106
Exercises 106
    Exercise 4-1: Viewing Forest-Wide FSMOs 106
    Exercise 4-2: Using Repadmin 107
Review Questions 107
Case Scenarios. 109
    Scenario 4-1: Creating a Global Catalog and Assigning
    FSMO Roles 109
    Scenario 4-2: Developing a Contingency Plan for a
    failed FSMO 110

CHAPTER 5: ACTIVE DIRECTORY ADMINISTRATION 111

Understanding User Accounts 112
    The Administrator Account 112
    The Guest Account 113
Groups and Their Uses 114
Group Types 115
    Distribution Groups 115
    Security Groups 115
    Converting Group Types 116
Group Scopes. 116
    Domain Local Groups 116
    Global Groups. 117
    Universal Groups. 117
    Group Nesting. 119

CONTENTS

    Functional Levels and Group Scopes. 120
    Default Groups 120
    Local Groups 127
    Developing a Group Implementation Plan 127
Creating Users and Groups 128
    Using Batch Files 129
    Using CSVDE 130
    Using LDIFDE 131
    Using Windows Scripting Host 132
Summary 134
Exercises 134
    Exercise 5-1: Viewing Group Object Properties. 134
    Exercise 5-2: Exploring Special Identity Groups 135
Review Questions 135
Case Scenarios. 137
    Scenario 5-1: Administering Groups for Humongous Insurance .137
    Scenario 5-2: Evaluating Scripts. 138

CHAPTER 6: SECURITY PLANNING AND ADMINISTRATIVE DELEGATION. 139

Planning and Implementing Account Security. 140
    Education of Users 140
    Strong Passwords 141
    Using Smart Cards for Authentication 142
    Smart Card Benefits and Considerations. 143
    Enabling a User Account for Smart Card Authentication 144
    Administrator Account Security. 145
Planning an Organizational Unit Strategy. 146
    Representing the Company Model 147
    Delegating Administrative Responsibility 147
    Implementing Group Policies 147
    Hiding Objects 147
Creating an OU Structure. 148
    Using OUs to Delegate Active Directory Management Tasks . . 149
    Using Delegation Of Control Wizard. 150
    Verifying and Removing Delegated Permissions 152
Moving Objects Between OUs. 153
    Using Drag and Drop 153
    Using the Move Option 154
Summary 155
Exercises 155
    Exercise 6-1: Planning a Naming Standard and
    Password Strategy. 155
    Exercise 6-2: Moving Objects in Active Directory 156
Review Questions 156

Case Scenarios. 158
    Scenario 6-1: Planning Active Directory for Contoso
    Pharmaceuticals 158
    Scenario 6-2: Smart Card Implementation Proposal. 158

CHAPTER 7: INTRODUCTION TO GROUP POLICY 159

What is Group Policy? 160
Group Policy Benefits. 161
    User Benefits 161
    Administrator Benefits. 161
Understanding Group Policy Objects 162
    Local Group Policy Objects. 162
    Nonlocal Group Policy Objects 162
    Default Group Policy Objects 165
    Using Group Policy Object Editor. 166
    Group Policy Settings. 167
    Administrative Template Setting Options 169
    Group Policies and the Active Directory Structure. 171
    How Group Policies Are Processed 172
Summary 178
Exercises 178
    Exercise 7-1: Viewing and Comparing the GPC and
    GPT Folders 178
    Exercise 7-2: Finding Explanations for Administrative
    Template Settings 179
Rreview Questions. 180
Case Scenarios. 181
    Scenario 7-1: Determining Group Policy Placement 181
    Scenario 7-2: Understanding Group Policy Planning 182

**CHAPTER 8: CONFIGURING THE USER AND COMPUTER
ENVIRONMENT USING GROUP POLICY. 183**

Security Policies 184
    Account Policies 185
    Local Policies 189
    Event Log Policy 195
    Restricted Groups Policy 196
    System Services Policy 197
    Registry and File System Policies 198
    Wireless Network (IEEE 802.11) Policies. 198
    Public Key Policies. 199
    Software Restriction Policies 204
Folder Redirection 205
Offline Files 208

CONTENTS

Disk Quotas 210
Refreshing Group Policy 213
    Manually Refreshing a Group Policy 214
    Policy Processing Optimization 214
Summary 216
Exercises 217
    Exercise 8-1: Documenting Log File Settings 217
    Exercise 8-2: Finding Out More About Gpupdate 217
Review Questions 218
Case Scenarios. 219
    Scenario 8-1: Lucerne Publishing and Offline Files. 219
    Scenario 8-2: Smart Card Setup and Enrollment 220

CHAPTER 9: MANAGING SOFTWARE 221
The Software Life Cycle 222
Windows Installer 222
    Using Transform Files 223
    Repackaging Software 223
Implementing Software Using Group Policy 225
    Creating a Distribution Share 225
    Creating or Modifying a Group Policy Object. 226
    Using Software Categories. 227
    Configuring a Policy to Deploy Applications 227
    Adding Windows Installer Packages 231
    Setting Windows Installer Package Properties 232
Software Restriction Policies 236
    Default Security Level 236
    Software Restriction Rules. 237
    Using Multiple Rule Types 240
    Additional Options 240
    Implementation Recommendations. 242
Summary 244
Exercises 245
    Exercise 9-1: Using Msiexec to Deploy Software Applications
    and Patches 245
    Exercise 9-2: Viewing the Default Security Level 245
Review Questions 246
Case Scenarios. 247
    Scenario 9-1: Planning Group Policy Software Deployments . . 247
    Scenario 9-2: Consulting with Wide World Importers 248

**CHAPTER 10: PLANNING A GROUP POLICY MANAGEMENT
AND IMPLEMENTATION STRATEGY. 251**
Filtering Group Policy's Scope. 252
    Group Policy Permissions. 252
    WMI Filters 254

Introduction to Group Policy Management Console (GPMC). 256
    Installing GPMC 257
    Navigating with Group Policy Management. 257
    Determining and Troubleshooting Effective Policy Settings . . . 261
    Resultant Set Of Policy Wizard 262
    Using Group Policy Results and Group Policy Modeling. 265
    Using GPResult. 271
    Delegating Group Policy Administrative Control 272
Planning Group Policy Integration 276
Restoring Group Policy Integration 277
Summary 278
Exercises 278
    Exercise 10-1: Navigating with GPMC 278
    Exercise 10-2: Using GPResult. 279
Review Questions 279
Case Scenario 280
    Scenario 10-1: Planning GPOs for Tailspin Toys 280

CHAPTER 11: ACTIVE DIRECTORY MAINTENANCE, TROUBLESHOOTING, AND DISASTER RECOVERY 281

Maintaining Active Directory. 282
    Moving the Active Directory Database 284
Backing Up Active Directory 285
    Preparing to Back Up Active Directory 287
Restoring Active Directory 292
    Using the Replication Process 292
    Backup Utility Restoration Options 292
    Using Ntdsutil. 293
    Performing a Primary Restore. 293
    Performing a Normal Restore 294
    Performing an Authoritative Restore 295
Monitoring Active Directory and File Replication Services 297
    Understanding Event Logs 297
    Using System Monitor 298
Diagnosing and Troubleshooting Active Directory 305
System Services. 307
Summary 308
Exercise 309
    Exercise 11-1: Viewing System Services 309
Review Questions 309
Case Scenario 310

Scenario 11-1: Consulting for Margie's Travel 310

CHAPTER 12: UPGRADING AND MIGRATING TO WINDOWS SERVER 2003 . . . . **311**

Reasons to Upgrade or Migrate 312

Migrating and Upgrading Windows NT 4.0 to Windows Server 2003. 313

    Preparing to Upgrade. 313

    Upgrading the PDC 316

Migrating and Upgrading Windows 2000 to Windows Server 2003. 324

    Preparing for a Windows 2000 Upgrade 324

    Upgrading to Windows Server 2003 325

    Migrating from Windows 2000 to Windows Server 2003 326

Summary 328

Review Questions 329

Case Scenario 329

    Scenario 12-1: Restructing Wingtip Toys 329

APPENDIX: DNS OVERVIEW **331**

Name Resolution 331

    What Is Name Resolution?. 331

    What Is a Host Name?. 332

    Resolving Host Names 332

The Domain System (DNS). 333

    What Is a Domain? 334

    Understanding Domain Hierarchy Levels 336

    Understanding the DNS Name Resolution Process. 338

    Using Active Directory 340

    Combining Internal and External Domains 340

    Creating an Internal Root. 341

    Understanding DNS Server Types 342

    Creating Zones 344

Glossary 349

Index. 363

System Requirements 378

ABOUT THIS BOOK

Welcome to *Planning, Implementing, and Maintaining a Microsoft Windows Server 2003 Active Directory Infrastructure (70-294)*, a part of the Microsoft Official Academic Course (MOAC) series. Through lectures, discussions, demonstrations, textbook exercises, and classroom labs, this course teaches students the skills and knowledge necessary to help prepare you to take the Microsoft 70-294 exam. The 70-294 exam is one of the required core exams in the Microsoft Certified Systems Engineer (MCSE) certification track. You will work with Microsoft Windows Server 2003 Active Directory in planning, implementing, and maintaining forests, sites, domains, and organizational units that meet the accessibility, performance, and security goals of a business plan. In addition, you will learn to work with Group Policy to deploy software and configure a computer or user environment. Finally, you will learn troubleshooting techniques that are valuable to the maintenance of a corporate network environment.

TARGET AUDIENCE

This course is intended to meet the needs of individuals preparing for the MCSE Windows Server 2003 certification. In addition to providing coverage of the 70-294 exam objectives, this course provides comprehensive coverage of the skills necessary for people aspiring to obtain positions such as systems engineer, systems analyst, or high-level systems administrator on Microsoft Windows Server 2003.

PREREQUISITES

The prerequisite for this course is the completion of the course titled *Planning and Maintaining a Microsoft Windows Server 2003 Network Infrastructure (70-293)*, or equivalent knowledge of the skills presented in this course.

THE TEXTBOOK

The textbook content has been crafted to provide a meaningful learning experience to students in an academic classroom setting.

Key features of the Microsoft Official Academic Course textbooks include the following:

- Learning objectives for each chapter that prepare the student for the topic areas covered in that chapter.
- Chapter introductions that explain why the content is important.
- An inviting design with screen shots, diagrams, tables, bulleted lists, and other graphical formats that makes the book easy to comprehend and supports a number of different learning styles.

- Clear explanations of concepts and principles, and frequent exposition of step-by-step procedures.
- A variety of readeraids that highlight a wealth of additional information, including:
  - Note–Real-world application tips and alternative procedures, and explanations of complex procedures and concepts
  - Caution–Warnings about mistakes that can result in loss of data or are difficult to resolve
  - Important–Explanations of essential setup steps before a procedure and other instructions
  - More Info–Cross-references and additional resources for students
- Short, optional, hands-on exercises that break up lectures and provide a warm-up for more complex lab exercises.
- End-of-chapter review questions that assess knowledge and can serve as homework, quizzes, and review activities before or after lectures. (Answers to these questions are in the Textbook Answers document in the Answers Guide folder on the Instructor CD.)
- Chapter summaries that distill the main ideas in a chapter and reinforce learning.
- Case scenarios, approximately two per chapter, provide students with an opportunity to evaluate, analyze, synthesize, and apply information learned during the chapter.
- Comprehensive glossary that defines key terms introduced in the book.

THE SUPPLEMENTAL COURSE MATERIALS CD-ROM

This book comes with a Supplemental Course Materials CD-ROM, which contains a variety of informational aids to complement the book content:

- An electronic version of this textbook (eBook). For information about using the eBook, see the section titled "eBook Setup Instructions" later in this introduction.
- The Microsoft Press Readiness Review Suite built by MeasureUp. This suite of practice tests and objective reviews contains questions of varying complexity and offers multiple testing modes. You can assess your understanding of the concepts presented in this book and use the results to develop a learning plan that meets your needs.
- Installation scripts and example files for performing the hands-on exercises in the Lab Manual. These include files that demonstrate key concepts and illustrate a specific point, as well as files included for your convenience, such as scripts that can be used to reduce the amount of time you spend setting up your system to perform a particular exercise.
- An eBook of the *Microsoft Encyclopedia of Networking*, Second Edition.
- Microsoft PowerPoint slides based on textbook chapters, for note taking.

- Windows System Resource Manager, a feature of Microsoft Windows, that allows administrators to control how CPU and memory resources are allocated to applications, services, and processes. For more information or to install Windows System Resource Manager, open the Readme.htm file in the \WSRM folder.
- Microsoft Word Viewer and PowerPoint Viewer

A second CD contains a 180-day evaluation edition of Windows Server 2003 Enterprise Edition.

NOTE *The 180-day evaluation edition of Windows Server 2003 Enterprise Edition provided with this book is not the full retail product; it is provided only for the purposes of training and evaluation. Microsoft Technical Support does not support this evaluation edition.*

Readiness Review Suite Setup Instructions

The Readiness Review Suite includes a practice test of 300 sample exam questions and an objective review with an additional 125 questions. Use these tools to reinforce your learning and to identify areas in which you need to gain more experience before taking the exam.

▶ **Installing the Practice Test**

1. Insert the Supplemental Course Materials CD into your CD-ROM drive.

   NOTE *If AutoRun is disabled on your machine, refer to the Readme.txt file on the Supplemental Course Materials CD.*

2. On the User Interface menu, select Readiness Review Suite and follow the prompts.

eBook Setup Instructions

The eBook is in Portable Document Format (PDF) and must be viewed using Adobe Acrobat Reader.

▶ **Using the eBook**

1. Insert the Supplemental Course Materials CD into your CD-ROM drive.

   NOTE *If AutoRun is disabled on your machine, refer to the Readme.txt file on the CD.*

2. On the User Interface menu, select Textbook eBook and follow the prompts. You also can review any of the other eBooks provided for your use.

   NOTE *You must have the Supplemental Course Materials CD in your CD-ROM drive to run the eBook.*

THE LAB MANUAL

The Lab Manual is designed for use in a combined lecture and lab situation, or in a separate lecture and lab arrangement. The exercises in the Lab Manual correspond to textbook chapters and are intended for use in a classroom setting under the supervision of an instructor. However, they are also suitable for independent study under the supervision of an instructor.

The Lab Manual presents a rich, hands-on learning experience that encourages practical solutions and strengthens critical problem-solving skills:

- Lab Exercises teach procedures by using a step-by-step format. Questions interspersed throughout Lab Exercises encourage reflection and critical thinking about the lab activity.
- Lab Review Questions appear at the end of each lab and ask questions about the lab. They are designed to promote critical reflection.
- Lab Challenges are review activities that ask students to perform a variation on a task they performed in the Lab Exercises, but without detailed instructions.
- Troubleshooting Labs appear after a number of regular labs and consist of mid-length review projects based on true-to-life scenarios. These labs challenge students to think like an expert to solve complex problems.
- Labs are based on realistic business settings and include an opening scenario and a list of learning objectives.

Students who successfully complete the Lab Exercises, Lab Review Questions, Lab Challenges, and Troubleshooting Labs in the Lab Manual will have a richer learning experience and deeper understanding of the concepts and methods covered in the course. They will be better able to answer and understand the testbank questions, especially the knowledge application and knowledge synthesis questions. They will also be much better prepared to pass the associated certification exams if they choose to do so.

NOTATIONAL CONVENTIONS

The following conventions are used throughout this texbook and the Lab Manual:

- Characters or commands that you type appear in **bold** type.
- Terms that appear in the glossary also appear in **bold** type.
- *Italic* in syntax statements indicates placeholders for variable information. *Italic* is also used for book titles and terms defined in the text.
- Names of files and folders appear in Title caps, except when you are to type them directly. Unless otherwise indicated, you can use all lowercase letters when you type a filename in a dialog box or at a command prompt.
- Filename extensions appear in all lowercase.
- Acronyms appear in all uppercase.
- `Monospace` type represents code samples, examples of screen text, or entries that you might type at a command prompt or in initialization files.

- Square brackets [ ] are used in syntax statements to enclose optional items. For example, [*filename*] in command syntax indicates that you can type a filename with the command. Type only the information within the brackets, not the brackets themselves.
- Braces { } are used in syntax statements to enclose required items. Type only the information within the braces, not the braces themselves.

KEYBOARD CONVENTIONS

- A plus sign (+) between two key names means that you must press those keys at the same time. For example, "Press ALT+TAB" means that you hold down ALT while you press TAB.
- A comma (,) between two or more key names means that you must press the keys consecutively, not at the same time. For example, "ALT, F, X" means that you press and release each key in sequence. "Press ALT+W, L" means that you first press ALT and W at the same time, and then you release them and press L.

COVERAGE OF EXAM OBJECTIVES

The title is intended to support your efforts to prepare for the 70-294 exam. The following table correlates the exam objectives with the textbook chapters and Lab Manual lab exercises.

NOTE The Microsoft Learning Web site describes the various MCP certification exams and their corresponding courses. It provides up-to-date certification information and explains the certification process and the course options. See http://www.microsoft.com/learning/mcp for up-to-date information about MCP exam credentials for other certification programs offered by Microsoft.

Table I-1 Textbook and Lab Manual Coverage of Exam Objectives

MOAC 70-294 Objective Map	Textbook	Lab Manual
Planning and Implementing an Active Directory Infrastructure		
Plan a strategy for placing global catalog servers.	4	
Evaluate network traffic considerations when placing global catalog servers.	4	
Evaluate the need to enable universal group caching.	4	
Plan flexible operations master role placement.	4	
Plan for business continuity of operations master roles.	4	
Identify operations master role dependencies.	4	
Implement an Active Directory directory service forest and domain structure.	1, 2	2
Create the forest root domain.	2	2
Create a child domain.	2	2
Create and configure Application Data Partitions.	2	
Install and configure an Active Directory domain controller.	2	2

ABOUT THIS BOOK

Table I-1 Textbook and Lab Manual Coverage of Exam Objectives

MOAC 70-294 Objective Map	Textbook	Lab Manual
Set an Active Directory forest and domain functional level based on requirements.	1, 2	4
Establish trust relationships. Types of trust relationships might include external trusts, shortcut trusts, and cross-forest trusts.	1, 2	
Implement an Active Directory site topology.	3	3
Configure site links.	3	3
Configure preferred bridgehead servers.	3	3
Plan an administrative delegation strategy.	6	
Plan an organizational unit (OU) structure based on delegation requirements.	6	6
Plan a security group hierarchy based on delegation requirements.	6	
Managing and Maintaining an Active Directory Infrastructure		
Manage an Active Directory forest and domain structure.	1, 2	All labs
Manage trust relationships.	1, 2	12
Manage schema modifications.	1, 2	5
Add or remove a UPN suffix.	2	5
Manage an Active Directory site.	3	3
Configure replication schedules.	3	3
Configure site link costs.	3	3
Configure site boundaries.	3	3
Monitor Active Directory replication failures. Tools might include Replication Monitor, Event Viewer, and support tools.	3, 11	3
Monitor Active Directory replication.	3	3
Monitor File Replication service (FRS) replication.	11	
Restore Active Directory directory services.	11	11
Perform an authoritative restore operation.	11	11
Perform a nonauthoritative restore operation.	11	
Troubleshoot Active Directory.	11	11
Diagnose and resolve issues related to Active Directory replication.	11	
Diagnose and resolve issues related to operations master role failure.	11	
Diagnose and resolve issues related to the Active Directory database.	11	11
Planning and Implementing User, Computer, and Group Strategies		
Plan a security group strategy.	5	
Plan a user authentication strategy.	5	
Plan a smart card authentication strategy.	6, 7	
Create a password policy for domain users.	6, 8	8
Plan an OU structure.	1, 6	
Analyze the administrative requirements for an OU.	6	

ABOUT THIS BOOK

Table I-1 Textbook and Lab Manual Coverage of Exam Objectives

MOAC 70-294 Objective Map	Textbook	Lab Manual
Analyze the Group Policy requirements for an OU structure.	7, 8	
Implement an OU structure.	6	6
Create an OU.	6	6
Delegate permissions for an OU to a user or to a security group.	6	6
Move objects within an OU hierarchy.	6	6
Planning and Implementing Group Policy		
Plan Group Policy strategy.	7, 8, 9, 10	TS Lab B
Plan a Group Policy strategy by using Resultant Set of Policy (RSoP) Planning mode.	10	
Plan a strategy for configuring the user environment by using Group Policy.	7, 8, 9	TS Lab B
Plan a strategy for configuring the computer environment by using Group Policy.	7, 8, 9	TS Lab B
Configure the user environment by using Group Policy.	8	8
Distribute software by using Group Policy.	9	9
Automatically enroll user certificates by using Group Policy.	8	
Redirect folders by using Group Policy.	8	8
Configure user security settings by using Group Policy.	8	8
Deploy a computer environment by using Group Policy.	8, 9	8, 9
Distribute software by using Group Policy.	9	9
Automatically enroll computer certificates by using Group Policy.	8	
Configure computer security settings by using Group Policy.	8	8
Managing and Maintaining Group Policy		
Troubleshoot issues related to Group Policy application deployment. Tools might include RSoP and the gpresult command.	10	10
Maintain installed software by using Group Policy.	9	9
Distribute updates to software distributed by Group Policy.	9	
Configure automatic updates for network clients by using Group Policy.	9	
Troubleshoot the application of Group Policy security settings. Tools might include RSoP and the gpresult command.	10	TS Lab C

THE MICROSOFT CERTIFIED PROFESSIONAL PROGRAM

The MCP program is the best way to prove your proficiency with current Microsoft products and technologies. The exams and corresponding certifications are developed to validate your mastery of critical competencies as you design and develop, or implement and support, solutions using Microsoft products and technologies. Computer professionals who become Microsoft certified are recognized as experts and are sought after industrywide. Certification brings a variety of benefits to the individual and to employers and organizations.

MORE INFO For a full list of MCP benefits, go to http://www.microsoft.com/learning/itpro.

Certifications

The MCP program offers multiple certifications, based on specific areas of technical expertise:

- **Microsoft Certified Professional (MCP)** In-depth knowledge of at least one Windows operating system or architecturally significant platform. An MCP is qualified to implement a Microsoft product or technology as part of a business solution for an organization.

- **Microsoft Certified Systems Engineer (MCSE)** Qualified to effectively analyze the business requirements for business solutions and design and implement the infrastructure based on the Windows and Windows Server 2003 operating systems.

- **Microsoft Certified Systems Administrator (MCSA)** Qualified to manage and troubleshoot existing network and system environments based on the Windows and Windows Server 2003 operating systems.

- **Microsoft Certified Database Administrator (MCDBA)** Qualified to design, implement, and administer Microsoft SQL Server databases.

MCP Requirements

Requirements differ for each certification and are specific to the products and job functions addressed by the certification. To become an MCP, you must pass rigorous certification exams that provide a valid and reliable measure of technical proficiency and expertise. These exams are designed to test your expertise and ability to perform a role or task with a product, and are developed with the input of industry professionals. Exam questions reflect how Microsoft products are used in actual organizations, giving them real-world relevance.

- Microsoft Certified Professional (MCP) candidates are required to pass one current Microsoft certification exam. Candidates can pass additional Microsoft certification exams to validate their skills with other Microsoft products, development tools, or desktop applications.

- Microsoft Certified Systems Engineer (MCSE) candidates are required to pass five core exams and two elective exams.

- Microsoft Certified Systems Administrator (MCSA) candidates are required to pass three core exams and one elective exam.

- Microsoft Certified Database Administrator (MCDBA) candidates are required to pass three core exams and one elective exam.

ABOUT THE AUTHORS

The textbook, Lab Manual, pretest, testbank, and PowerPoint slides were written by instructors and developed exclusively for an instructor-led classroom environment.

Wendy Corbin, the author of the textbook, has 12 years of technology teaching experience that includes corporate, private, and academic instruction. Ms. Corbin began her career in technology as an end-user applications trainer and Certified Novell Instructor for a national computer training company. After adding MCSE courses to her instructional skill set, she moved on to work for a systems integrator as a network engineer and technical consultant. Currently, Ms. Corbin is the Department Chair for Computer Networking at Baker College in Auburn Hills, Michigan. In addition, she works as an independent network engineer whenever possible. This enables her to bring real-world skills and scenarios to the classroom by sharing her field experiences. Ms. Corbin holds a Bachelor of Arts degree from Oakland University in Rochester, Michigan, and she is pursuing a Masters of Science degree in Information Technology with a concentration in Network Architecture and Design from Capella University. Her technical certifications include Microsoft MCT, MCSE, and MCP + I; Novell CNI and CNE; and Cisco CCNA and CCAI. Wendy lives in Sterling Heights, Michigan, with her husband, Gary, and their two wonderful children, Joshua and Allegra. Their unconditional love, support, and encouragement are appreciated more than they will ever know.

Kurt Hudson, the author of the Lab Manual, pretest, testbank questions, and PowerPoint slides, is an instructor, author, and consultant for computer technologies. In recent years, he has concentrated on the areas of computer networking, Active Directory, integrating UNIX and Microsoft Windows, and computer security. Kurt regularly teaches summer programs at Northern Arizona University in Flagstaff, Arizona. He also has taught several courses through Microsoft Research for several other universities throughout the United States.

Kurt has earned many technical certifications, including MCSE, MCSA, MCT, CCNA, Security+, A+, Network+, i-Net+, and CTT+. He also has a graduate degree in Business Management (Masters of Management) from Troy State University in Troy, Alabama. Kurt has authored many books on computer-related topics and contributed to numerous other publications.

Kurt appreciates the hard work and dedication of his co-author Wendy Corbin. He is also tremendously grateful for the thorough assistance of Robert Lyon with the labs and setup document. Kurt's colleague, Terry Bright helped with the testbank as well as the labs for this publication. Kurt is also blessed to have a wonderful and understanding wife, Laura, who has endured his working late nights and weekends for several stressful months on this project.

FOR MOAC SUPPORT

If you have any problems regarding the use of this book's CD-ROM, you should first consult with your instructor. If you are using the CD-ROM at home or at your place of business and need additional help with the practice files, contact Wiley Technical Support at:

http://higheredwiley.custhelp.com

where you can view our Knowledge Base of frequent questions, Chat live with an Agent, or submit a question.

Please note that product support is not offered through the above.

EVALUATION EDITION SOFTWARE SUPPORT

The 180-day evaluation edition of Windows Server 2003 Enterprise Edition provided with this textbook is not the full retail product and is provided only for training and evaluation purposes. Microsoft and Microsoft Technical Support do not support this evaluation edition. For information about issues relating to the use of the evaluation edition, go to the Support section of the Microsoft Press Web site (*http://www.microsoft.com/learning/support/*).

For online support information relating to the full version of Windows Server 2003 Enterprise Edition that might also apply to the evaluation edition, go to *http://www.microsoft.com/learning/support/*. For information about ordering the full version of any Microsoft software, call Microsoft Sales at (800) 426-9400 or visit *http://www.microsoft.com*.

CAUTION The evaluation edition of Windows Server 2003 Enterprise Edition should not be used on a primary work computer.

CHAPTER 1
OVERVIEW OF ACTIVE DIRECTORY

Upon completion of this chapter, you will be able to:

- Describe the Active Directory directory service and its functions and benefits.
- Understand the Active Directory schema and identify object classes and attributes.
- Describe the components of Active Directory, including forests, sites, domains, domain trees, and organizational units (OUs).
- Understand Active Directory's naming standards and their significance.
- Determine the logical and physical structure of a network.
- Understand the role of the Domain Name System (DNS) in an Active Directory environment.
- Understand and assess the domain and forest functional levels according to the needs of an organization's network environment.
- Understand the trust models used by Active Directory and their role in resource accessibility.

Before you can plan, implement, and maintain an Active Directory infrastructure, you must first understand all of the foundational concepts. This chapter introduces you to these concepts, including the new terminology and features that you will need to understand. In particular, this chapter explores the structural elements of Active Directory, forest and domain functional levels, and the trust models used by Microsoft Windows Server 2003.

ACTIVE DIRECTORY'S FUNCTIONS AND BENEFITS

Active Directory, the directory service in Windows Server 2003, is the main repository for information about network users and resources. A *directory service* is a tool that allows businesses to define, manage, access, and secure network resources, including files, printers, people, and applications, for a group of users. Without the efficiency of a directory service, businesses of today would have difficulty keeping up with demands for fast-paced data exchange. As corporate networks continue to grow in complexity and importance, more is required from the networks that facilitate this business automation. Active Directory uses a **domain controller** to manage access to network services. A domain controller is a server that stores the Active Directory database and authenticates users with the network during logon. Each domain controller actively participates in storing, modifying, maintaining, and replicating the Active Directory database information that is stored on each domain controller in a file named NTDS.dit. Domain controllers automatically replicate with other domain controllers in the same domain to ensure that the Active Directory database is consistent.

Active Directory is designed to allow for scalability by handling organizations of any size, from small businesses to global enterprises. In fact, the version of Active Directory used in Windows Server 2003 operating systems has been successfully tested at one billion objects. The major benefits of the high-powered Active Directory directory service include:

- Centralized resource and security administration
- Single logon for access to global resources
- Fault tolerance and redundancy
- Simplified resource location

Centralized Resource and Security Administration

Active Directory provides a single point from which administrators can manage network resources and their associated security objects. An organization can decide to administer Active Directory based on an organizational or business model, or according to the types of functions being administered. As an example, an organization could choose to administer Active Directory by logically dividing the users according to the departments in which they work or by their supervisory structure.

Active Directory can simplify the security management of all network resources and extend interoperability with a wide range of applications and devices. Management is simplified through centralized access to the administrative tools and to the Active Directory database of network resources. Interoperability with prior versions (downlevel clients) of Microsoft Windows is available in Windows Server 2003 through the use of functional levels.

When Active Directory is installed and configured, management of the database is performed using specific tools that can administer network services, resources, and security at a detailed level. These administrative tools can be accessed from any domain controller in the network or from a workstation having these administrative tools installed. Administrative tasks can also be completed with a properly configured handheld device that uses the PocketPC operating system and an administrative Terminal Server session. The following are several administrative tools that are added to the Administrative Tools folder when a Windows 2003 member server or Windows 2003 standalone server is promoted to a Windows 2003 Active Directory domain controller:

- Active Directory Users And Computers
- Active Directory Domains And Trusts
- Active Directory Sites And Services

These administrative tools are described in this textbook. As concepts are introduced, we will associate tools with the tasks for which they are used. This will allow you to build your administrative knowledge at a manageable pace.

Single Point of Access to Resources

Prior to the introduction of directory services into corporate networks, all users were required to log on to many different servers for access to a variety of different resources. This required users to enter their authentication information multiple times, and an administrator had to maintain duplicate user accounts on every server in the organization. Imagine how enormous the management task would be if the network had 10 servers and 500 users per server. The administrator would have to create and maintain 5000 user accounts, along with all of the associated security assignments.

By contrast, Active Directory provides a single point of management for network resources. Active Directory uses a single sign-on to allow access to network resources located on any server within the domain. The user is identified and authenticated by Active Directory, and once this process is complete, single sign-on is now available to the user to provide access only to the network resources that are authorized for the user according to his or her assigned roles and privileges within Active Directory.

Fault Tolerance and Redundancy

A system is said to be fault tolerant if it is capable of responding gracefully to a software or hardware failure. In particular, a system is considered fault tolerant when it has the ability to continue providing authentication services after a domain controller failure. A redundant (or duplicate) solution allows the system to continue operating without any adverse effects being noticed by the user.

Active Directory builds in **fault tolerance** through its multi-master domain controller design. In a Windows Server 2003 environment, Active Directory provides fault tolerance using a **multi-master replication** system, where multiple servers, installed as domain controllers, share a common database. Redundancy is provided because all domain controllers are equal in a multi-master environment, and changes can be made from any domain controller. When changes occur at one domain controller, those changes are replicated to all other domain controllers in the domain. This ensures that all domain controllers have consistent information about the domain. The database can be referred to as "loosely consistent," which means that, until all domain controllers have replicated (converged), each domain controller will contain slightly different copies of the database, and following replication, they will all contain the same information as shown in

Figure 1-1. Since the entire database is duplicated on all domain controllers, if one domain controller fails, it is still possible for authentication and resource access to take place via another domain controller.

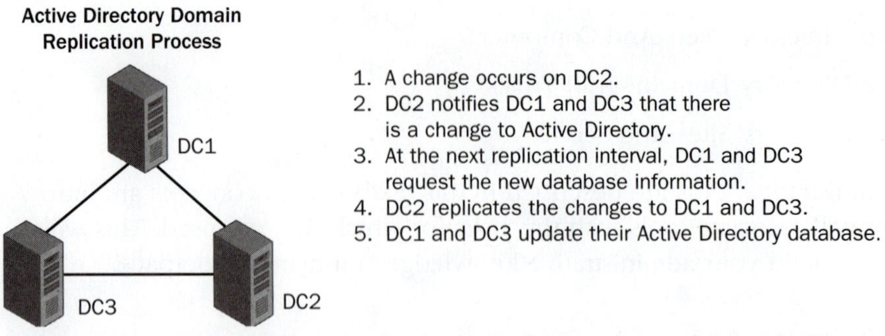

Active Directory Domain Replication Process

1. A change occurs on DC2.
2. DC2 notifies DC1 and DC3 that there is a change to Active Directory.
3. At the next replication interval, DC1 and DC3 request the new database information.
4. DC2 replicates the changes to DC1 and DC3.
5. DC1 and DC3 update their Active Directory database.

Figure 1-1 The Active Directory replication process

> **CAUTION** **Single Domain Controller Domains** Single domain controller environments do not provide fault tolerance and redundancy as described here. Microsoft recommends installing more than one domain controller in every domain.

Simplified Resource Location

Imagine you are a user in a 10-server environment, where every server has a different set of resources that facilitate how you do your job. If you were in this situation, having to know which server provides each resource would not be an enviable task. Active Directory facilitates resource searching by allowing resources to be published on the network. Publishing an object allows users to gain access to network resources by searching the Active Directory database for the desired resource. This search can be based on the resource's name, description, or location. The values to enter into a search are included as values in the object's attributes. For example, a shared folder can be found by clicking the appropriate search button using My Network Places in Microsoft Windows 2000 Professional, Microsoft Windows XP, or Microsoft Windows Server 2003.

Figure 1-2 shows the Find Shared Folders dialog box in Microsoft Windows XP. The search criteria entered include the scope of the search, cohowinery.com, the name of the shared folder, data, and any keywords that might be used to find the folder. Generally, the scope of the search can be configured by the user based on his or her desired search parameters. Both the shared folder name and keyword information do not need to be present. The more information provided in the search, the more specific the results. For example, if the word *accounting* is used as a keyword for 100 folders, the search returns 100 results. The user will then have to narrow the results further in order to find the desired folder. It should be understood that the ability to perform a search is controlled by the permissions defined in Active Directory for the user. As is true with all tasks, permissions may also be revoked at any time.

> **NOTE** **Resource Location** Note that the physical location of the resource is transparent to the user. The administrator decides which server is the best choice for storing and maintaining resources based on other requirements, such as storage space or processing abilities of the host server.

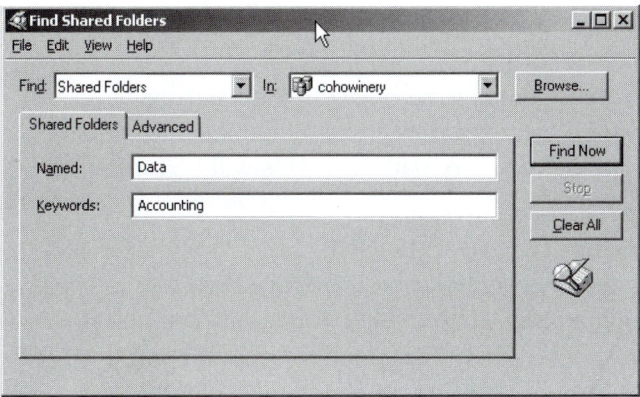

Figure 1-2 The Find Shared Folders dialog box

ACTIVE DIRECTORY SCHEMA

Every resource in Active Directory is represented as an **object**, and each object has specific attributes. Active Directory objects define different levels of resources within the Active Directory structure. In Active Directory, each object is defined in a **schema**. A schema is a master database that contains definitions of all objects in the Active Directory—it is the Active Directory. There are two parts to the schema, **object classes** and attributes. Each object that is represented in Active Directory—for example, the user John and the printer Laserprinter—is an instance of the object classes User account and Printer, respectively. It is important to remember that these object classes and their associated attributes are logical mappings and constructs within the structure of Active Directory itself. They are not the actual objects themselves, only "images" of these real objects.

Each object class in the schema is further defined according to a list of attributes that make the object class unique within the database. The list of attributes is defined only once in the schema, but the same attribute can be associated with more than one object class. Some attributes are required for the object to be created, such as a user account logon name, while other attributes, such as street address and phone number, provide additional details that can be published for user and administrative purposes.

When Active Directory is installed, a number of object classes are created automatically. Some of these object classes include:

- Domain
- User account
- Computer
- Printer
- Group
- Shared folder
- Shared drive

All object classes have a common set of attributes that help to uniquely identify each object within the database. Some of these common attributes are listed here:

- **A unique name**   This name identifies the object in the database. A unique name is given to the object upon its creation and includes references to its location within the directory database. This will be further explained later in this chapter.

- **A globally unique identifier (GUID)**   The GUID is a 128-bit hexadecimal number that is assigned to every object in the Active Directory forest upon its creation. This number does not change even when the object itself is renamed.

- **Required object attributes**   These attributes are required for the object to function. In particular, the user account must have a unique name and a password entered upon creation.

- **Optional object attributes**   These attributes add information that is not critical to the object in terms of functionality. This type of information is "nice to know" as opposed to "need to know." An example of an optional object attribute would be a phone number or street address for a user account.

Figure 1-3 shows an example of the attributes for a user account.

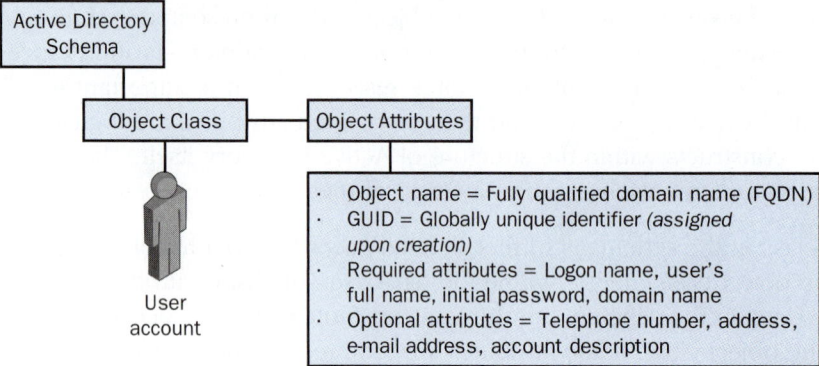

Figure 1-3   User object and attributes

As we will see, the schema can be modified to include additional objects and attributes when necessary. Each object in the schema is protected by **access control lists (ACLs)** to enable only authorized administrators to access and modify the schema. ACLs are implemented by the administrator and used by the directory to keep track of which users and groups have permission to access specific objects and to what degree they can use or modify them. For example, if JSmith needs to be able to delete a file in a shared folder, JSmith's user object must appear on the shared folder's ACL. In addition, the permission associated with JSmith's object for this folder must include the ability to delete a file from this shared folder.

> **NOTE**   **Adding the Active Directory Schema snap-in**   The Active Directory schema can be managed using the Active Directory Schema snap-in. It does not exist by default in the Administrative Tools folder. The snap-in must be manually added. The steps to do this will be covered in Chapter 2, "Implementing Active Directory."

ACTIVE DIRECTORY COMPONENTS

Active Directory consists of a number of hierarchical components. These components allow for flexibility with regard to design, scalability, administrative strategy, and the security of the network. **Organizational units** that have **parent/child relationships** with one another form the main hierarchy. As the hierarchy is formed, organizational units can be nested in other organizational units, which in turn form parent/child relationships. These parent/child relationships play an important role in the functionality of Active Directory permissions. Because some of the components of the hierarchy can be changed and scaled to fit a future design while others are more difficult to change after the initial configuration, a clear plan for the parent/child relationships of the organizational units must be defined prior to installing Active Directory.

Each component in Active Directory can be categorized as either a **container object** or a **leaf object**. A container object is a holder of other objects, either additional child containers or leaf objects. A leaf object cannot contain other objects and usually refers to a particular resource such as a printer, folder, or user. To begin, let's discuss the following container objects:

- OUs
- Domains
- Domain trees
- Forests
- Sites

Figure 1-4 depicts a simple Active Directory structure that includes a parent domain, cohowinery.com, and a child domain, north.cohowinery.com. The IP Site element window will be explained in subsequent sections of this chapter.

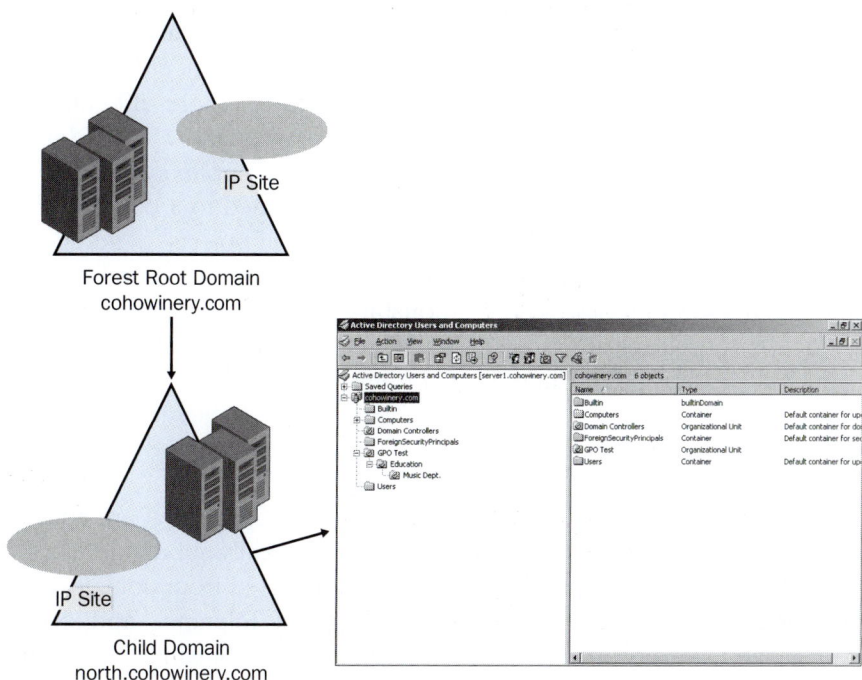

Figure 1-4   Simple Active Directory structure

Organizational Units

At work or at home, we use containers to hold and organize things according to some kind of plan that makes them easier to locate when necessary. Active Directory allows for organization of objects in the same manner. An *organizational unit* is a container that represents a logical grouping of resources that have similar security guidelines. The OU structure can reflect the logical structure of the organization by modeling the company's organzational chart depicting employees and their respective departments, or by organizing users according to their resource needs. For example, all users that have similar resource needs can be placed in an OU for ease of management if this best supports the business needs of the organization. Security applied to the OU is by default inherited by all child objects of the container, thereby simplifying management. Administration of an OU can be delegated to a supervisor or manager and thus can allow that person to manage the day-to-day resource access. This is referred to as **delegation of administration**. Each container or OU can be created with custom security guidelines in mind, allowing for detailed administrative control.

OUs can contain the following objects:

- Users
- Groups
- Contacts
- Printers
- Shared folders
- Computers
- OUs
- InetOrgPerson

Although it is possible to create a nested OU structure containing a number of parent/child relationships, you must consider that, if nested too deeply, these subsequent relationships can make the administration of OUs more difficult. In fact, Microsoft recommends an OU structure that is not more than 10 levels deep. Increasing the number of nested relationships adds to the complexity of permission and group policy **inheritance**. Any permissions assigned to a parent container are by default inherited by all child containers and leaf objects. In addition, troubleshooting user problems with regard to resource access can become cumbersome when a number of nested relationships can affect what the user is allowed to do. Group policies are a major part of securing and managing Active Directory and will be detailed in Chapters 7 through 10.

Domains

A **domain** is a logical grouping of network resources and devices that are administered as a single unit. A domain can contain OUs that logically subdivide users and resources. The information within the domain is replicated from domain controller to domain controller to provide redundancy, fault tolerance, and load balancing for Active Directory. You might use more than one domain for a variety of reasons. For example, suppose your company has separate business units or is separated by distances. In this case, you might want to create separate domains to cut down on the replication and authentication traffic that would be required to maintain a consistent environment. A domain also functions as a security boundary because access to domain objects is controlled by ACLs, which include a list of users with permissions to an object. Each domain uses a separate set of ACLs and policies that apply specifically to the resources within the domain. The administrator can create policies that control the environment for the entire domain at this level and can have these policies flow down to each container and resource within the domain.

Domains can contain the following objects:

- Child domains
- OUs

Like OUs, a domain can contain other sub-domains, or **child domains**. This allows for the creation of a hierarchical network in which all objects are related to their parent objects. The first domain created in a Windows Server 2003 domain is referred to as the **forest root domain**. All subsequent domains that share the name of the parent domain are considered child domains.

Trees

A domain **tree** is a grouping of domains that have the same parental hierarchy and share part of the name of the parent domain. Each tree contains a *domain family*. A domain family consists of the parent domain and all child domains. All domains within a domain tree share a contiguous name space. Consider an example where the company Coho Winery, Inc., has several divisions scattered across the United States. If the company installed the root domain as cohowinery.com to match its registered DNS name, each division would then be installed as a child domain of cohowinery.com and retain the cohowinery.com suffix as a part of its name. For example, if there were three divisions of Coho Winery, Inc., with the names Northern, Southern, and Central, the domain names would be northern.cohowinery.com, southern.cohowinery.com, and central.cohowinery.com, respectively. If one of the divisions (child domains) had a subdivision, its entire parental suffix would be appended to the name of the subdivision, for example, redgrape.central.cohowinery.com. Figure 1-5 shows an example of this tree structure.

Forests

One or more Windows 2003 trees is defined as a **forest**. A forest is the highest level in the Active Directory domain hierarchy. Administrative security implemented at the forest level flows down through the hierarchy to all domain trees below. In a forest, Active Directory uses **directory partitions** to store and replicate information. These partitions divide the database into manageable pieces that separate forest-wide information from domain-specific information. In order for all domains in the forest to be able to share and replicate information, they must have common partitions. The forest-wide directory partitions include the **schema** and **configuration** partitions. They are defined as follows:

- **Schema partition**   Contains the rules and definitions that are used for creating and modifying object classes and attributes.
- **Configuration partition**   Contains the replication topology and other configuration data that must be replicated throughout the forest.

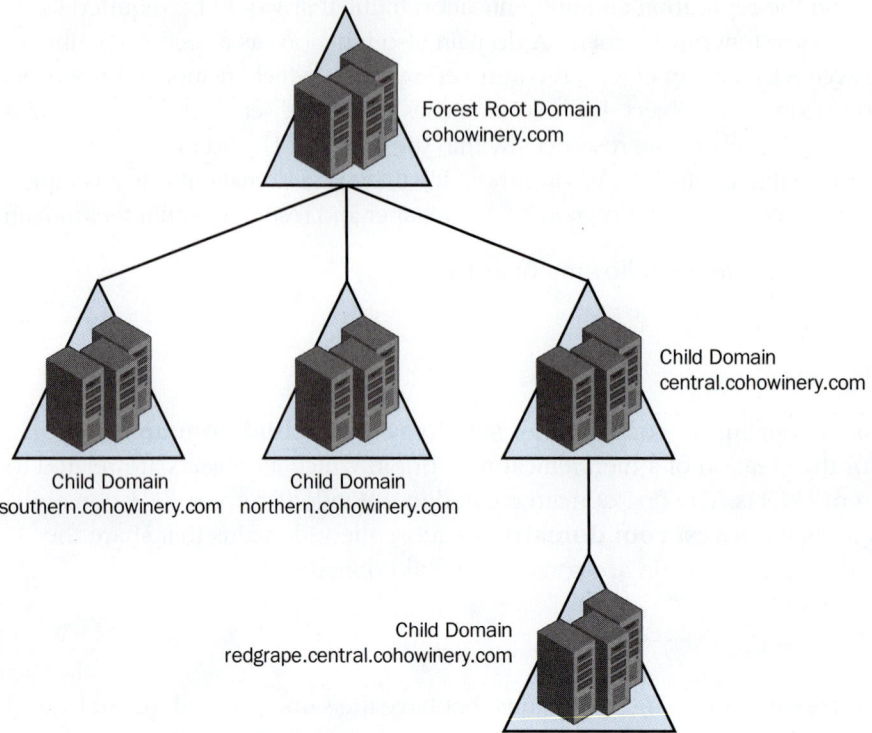

Figure 1-5 Coho Winery, Inc., tree structure

In addition, all domains must have domain-specific information that is replicated to all domain controllers within a domain. This directory partition is referred to as the **domain partition** which contains all of the objects within the local domain.

Windows Server 2003 introduces a fourth partition type, the **application partition**. The application partition allows administrators to control what information is replicated and to which domain controllers. This results in greater flexibility and better control over replication performance.

Although not considered as a formal partition, the **global catalog** must also be replicated to each domain. In contrast to the domain partition, the global catalog does not replicate to all domain controllers; rather, it replicates only to domain controllers designated specifically to hold the global catalog. These domain controllers are known as global catalog servers. Global catalog servers will be discussed in detail in Chapter 4, "Global Catalog and Flexible Single Master Operations (FSMO) Roles."

Figure 1-6 depicts a forest and the placement of directory partitions as discussed here. Notice that the trees have different DNS names.

> **NOTE** **Forest Root Names** Forest root names most often reflect the registered Internet domain name of the company. Although Windows Server 2003 allows for domain renaming, it is best to start with the registered DNS name if at all possible. Changing a domain name can be a nontrivial process since all references to the domain must also be changed.

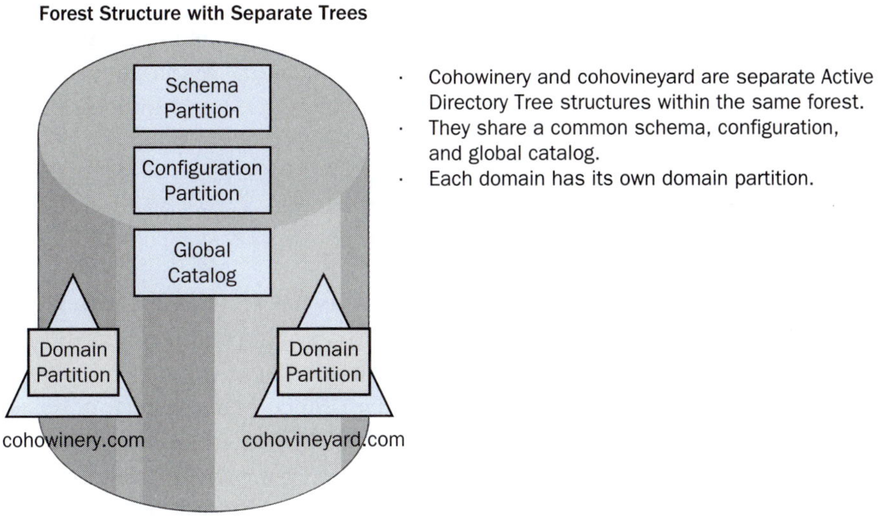

Forest Structure with Separate Trees

- Cohowinery and cohovineyard are separate Active Directory Tree structures within the same forest.
- They share a common schema, configuration, and global catalog.
- Each domain has its own domain partition.

Figure 1-6 Multiple tree forest structure

Sites

A **site** is defined as one or more IP subnets that are connected by fast links. In most circumstances, the LAN constitutes a site. Sites are created to facilitate the replication of Active Directory information. All domain controllers within the same site replicate information at regular intervals, while domain controllers at external sites replicate less frequently. As discussed previously, all trees in a forest share a common schema, configuration, and global catalog. This information is replicated among all domain controllers in the forest.

Sites are used to optimize replication. Within a site, the **knowledge consistency checker (KCC)** is responsible for assisting in this optimization by creating and maintaining the replication topology. The KCC does its job based on the information provided by the administrator in the Active Directory Sites And Services snap-in. Administrators can add connections and force replication in particular situations, but the KCC can generally take care of all replication topology issues. The Active Directory Sites And Services snap-in is located in the Administrative Tools folder of the domain controller.

> **MORE INFO** Replication, the KCC, and Active Directory Sites And Services
> Chapter 3, "Working with Active Directory Sites," covers the KCC, replication, and the use of the Active Directory Sites And Services snap-in.

Naming Standards

Active Directory's scalability and integration capabilities result from the use of industry standards for naming formats and directory functions. **Lightweight Directory Access Protocol (LDAP)** was developed in the early 1990s by the **Internet Engineering Task Force (IETF)** to facilitate the implementation of **X.500** in
e-mail. X.500 is the standard that defines how global directories should be structured and includes the hierarchical specifications. Since then, LDAP has become

an industry standard that enables data exchange between directory services and applications. The LDAP standard defines the naming of all objects in the Active Directory database and therefore provides a directory that can be integrated with other directory services such as Novell Directory Service (NDS) and directory-enabled applications such as Microsoft Exchange.

> **MORE INFO** **LDAP Standard** *For further information on the objects defined by LDAP, search for RFC 1779 and RFC 2247 on the Internet using a search engine.*

Domain Name System (DNS) is commonly known as the service that provides **Uniform Resource Locator (URL)** resolution for accessing a Web site on the Internet. In Windows Server 2003, DNS is used to provide name resolution for computers and services within the Active Directory domain. Since Active Directory relies heavily on DNS, Active Directory domain names follow the same naming standards as DNS. For example, if Coho Winery, Inc., has registered cohowinery.com as its DNS name, the first domain in Active Directory will be installed as cohowinery.com. As discussed previously, all other child domains and objects will be appended with the suffix of cohowinery.com.

Access to all directory objects happens through LDAP. For this reason, it is necessary to understand how objects are referenced in Active Directory. Consider the following example in Figure 1-7.

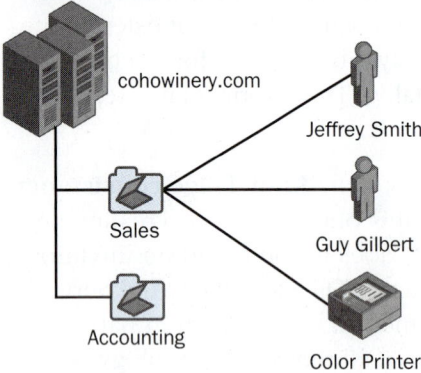

Figure 1-7 Cohowinery.com domain, OUs, and leaf objects

Two types of names can be used to reference an object, its **distinguished name**, or full name, and its **relative distinguished name**, or common name. When a distinguished name is used, an object in the directory structure shown in Figure 1-7 is referenced by its complete name using the entire hierarchical path. The hierarchical path begins with the lowest object in the tree and includes all parent objects up to and including the root of the domain. LDAP defines the naming attributes that identify each part of the object's name. Table 1-1 lists these attributes.

Table 1-1 Active Directory Object Classes and Naming Attributes

Object Class	LDAP Naming Attribute	Definition of Naming Attribute
User or any leaf object	cn	Common name
Organizational unit object	ou	Organizational unit name
Domain	dc	Domain components, one for each part of the DNS name

When Figure 1-7 is used as a reference, JSmith has a distinguished name as shown here:

cn=JSmith,ou=sales,dc=cohowinery,dc=com

The relative distinguished name for JSmith is simply JSmith or the common name equivalent.

The naming attributes listed in Table 1-1 are not required within most management tools. However, these naming attributes are an important part of understanding how Active Directory distinguishes between common names, and they can be used with certain advanced command line utilities. For example, suppose you need to restore an object using Active Directory Restore mode and the ntdsutil command. The ntdsutil command requires the administrator to use the complete name to reference the object that is to be restored. In this situation, using the proper naming syntax is critical to accomplishing the desired restore. Using Active Directory Restore mode and the ntdsutil command will be discussed and practiced in Chapter 11, "Active Directory Maintenance, Troubleshooting, and Disaster Recovery."

In addition to understanding the significance of DNS and LDAP in Active Directory name formats, it is important to understand the use of **User Principal Names (UPNs)** in Windows Server 2003. UPNs follow the format *username@companyname.com*.

This convention provides a simple solution to a complex domain structure, where it can be difficult to remember the distinguished name. It also provides an opportunity for consistency between the user's e-mail name and his or her logon name.

> **NOTE** UPN Implementation Reference   More detail on UPNs and the planning and implementation of them will be discussed in Chapter 2, "Implementing Active Directory."

PLANNING AN ACTIVE DIRECTORY IMPLEMENTATION

"Failing to plan is planning to fail." You may have heard this phrase before. The meaning can be applied to any project, whether it is large or small. Specifically in Windows Server 2003, there are several key areas that should be thoroughly reviewed prior to implementation. Although a high-level design has most likely already been created with business goals in mind, the planning phase is necessary to ensure a smooth deployment. Planning an Active Directory implementation involves having a detailed understanding of the design components and how they are to be configured. It is the planner's responsibility to make sure that all aspects of the proposed design can be achieved. Developing a solid implementation plan can be accomplished by gaining a full understanding of the following Active Directory elements:

- The logical and physical structure of the plan
- The role of DNS
- Windows Server 2003 forest and domain functional levels
- Active Directory trust models

Each of these is discussed in the following sections.

The Logical and Physical Structure

The logical structure includes the overall Active Directory structure of forests, domains, and OUs. As part of the implementation plan, the logical structure should be closely examined with regard to business needs, security, resource accessibility, and ease of administration. Most logical structures reflect the organization's business model. Users and resources are grouped in domains and OUs according to resource needs, location, department, or even security guidelines.

Security goals are met through the logical structure's design by using domains and OUs as natural groups. These container objects allow for ease of administration and accessibility boundaries. For example, if all users in a particular domain need to have a consistent desktop environment, a domain group policy can be implemented to achieve this goal. Through the concept of inheritance, all users in the domain receive the settings invoked by the policy. A policy can also be put into place to serve as a security mechanism, blocking users' ability to run programs from the command prompt. The same concept can be used with respect to OUs. A policy or security setting can be applied to the OU, and it will affect all user accounts within that container.

> **MORE INFO** Group Policy Implementation   A detailed discussion of Group Policies and their implementation will be covered in Chapters 7 through 10.

Administrative goals can also be met with the help of a sound logical structure. For example, departments and divisions can have administrative control over their resources and users through the **Delegation of Administration** feature. Delegated administrative control can be customized to allow full control or task-based control within the container.

> **MORE INFO** Delegation of Administration   Chapter 6, "Security Planning and Administrative Delegation," will cover delegation of administration in detail.

Recalling that sites are simply an object containing one or more IP subnets, the physical structure of the network takes into consideration the physical links and the connectivity between the sites. Each physically separate location is typically placed on a separate site. Planning the site implementation takes into account which sites need to communicate with one another. The physical structure also reflects how data and information will travel on the network and which servers are responsible for certain network services. This is different from the previously described logical structure, which is more concerned with the administrative and management model of users and resources.

Do Exercise 1-1 now to work with logical and physical planning.

> **MORE INFO** Site Planning and Implementation   The planning and implementation of sites will be covered in Chapter 3, "Working with Active Directory Sites."

The Role of DNS

DNS is a distributed database that provides name resolution services for an Active Directory domain. DNS is the foundational requirement for Active Directory; Active Directory cannot be installed without it. The forest name structure follows DNS naming standards and allows for a hierarchical, distributed, and scalable network. In most modern networks, TCP/IP is the primary protocol used to communicate between systems. All devices on an IP network use a unique number to identify themselves and their location on the network. This is called an **IP address**. IP addresses are four octets long and are commonly expressed in dotted decimal notation such as 192.168.10.1. One way of accessing a resource is by knowing its IP address. However, when a computer system identifies resources using 32-bit numbers, accessing a resource by using its IP address would be cumbersome at best. In addition to an IP address, all computers are given a logical host name upon installation. Although the host name helps us to define a device's location or purpose, it needs to be translated into a value that computers can understand. This is why we need DNS. DNS provides a solution by mapping a computer's host name to an IP address. When a computer's host name is referenced, DNS provides the translation of the host name to an IP address, thereby allowing the traffic to be routed appropriately to the correct destination.

DNS and Windows Server 2003

In addition to providing computer host name–to–IP address mappings on the network, DNS plays a much larger role in the functionality of Active Directory. Windows Server 2003 uses DNS to provide a locator service for clients on the network. The locator service provides direction for clients needing to know which server does what. For example, if a user were attempting to log on to the network, the locator service would provide the client with the host name and IP address of the closest domain controller. Network services such as the Netlogon service might not always be provided by the same server. In fact, in most networks, more than one server in the environment provide a specific service. Fault tolerance, load balancing, and redundancy are among the reasons for setting up even a small network with multiple servers. As the implementation is planned, services can be spread across multiple systems with or without Active Directory on each server. These services can include authentication, e-mail, printing, file sharing, and other pertinent tools to assist in creating a productive work environment. Each server that is hosting a particular service will register with DNS to facilitate resolution by a client. For example, when a client requests e-mail, a query is made to DNS for the name and IP address of the mail server. After the request is processed, the client is directed to the appropriate computer hosting the e-mail application.

Windows Server 2003 has a specific service that must be supported by DNS for the Active Directory infrastructure to function properly. This service is as follows:

- **Support for SRV records**   SRV records are locator records within DNS to provide a mapping to a host providing a service. For example, a client requesting access to Active Directory via the logon process would need to locate an Active Directory server. This query would be resolved by the appropriate SRV resource record.

In addition to the required support of SRV records, DNS has the ability to support dynamic updates. This feature is described here:

- **Dynamic updates**   Dynamic updates permit DNS clients to automatically register and update their information in the DNS database. When a domain controller is added to the forest, the SRV and A records are added dynamically to the DNS database to permit the locator service to function. Dynamic DNS provides a convenient method to assist in keeping the database current. However, some security-minded companies will disable this ability so that changes to the database cannot be made without administrative intervention.

During the installation of Active Directory, DNS parameters need to be supplied if you want to use an existing DNS server. If an Active Directory–compliant DNS server is not supplied, DNS can be installed as part of the Active Directory installation process.

> **MORE INFO**   SRV and Dynamic Update RFCs   More information on SRV records can be found in RFC 2782. RFC 2136 further explains dynamic updates. DNS is explained in detail in Appendix A of this book.

Windows Server 2003 Forest and Domain Functional Levels

Forest and domain functional levels are designed to offer flexibility. The versioning mechanism within the operating system controls the Active Directory features based on the domain controllers that are present on the network. There are some features in Active Directory that cannot be activated until all domain controllers in a forest are upgraded to the Windows Server 2003 family. Similarly, there are certain features that require all domain controllers in the domain to be upgraded to the Windows Server 2003 family.

As corporate enterprises determine the need for expansion and updates to their networks, they typically do not plan to upgrade the entire network all at once. The upgrade strategy usually depends on the size of the network and the impact an upgrade will have on production. Microsoft has considered the fact that not all organizations will upgrade all of their domain controllers to the Windows Server 2003 family simultaneously. Instead, it is expected that many organizations will migrate gradually based on the need and desire for the new functionality. The domain and forest functional levels are explained here.

Domain Functional Levels

Four functional levels are available that are domain specific. Functionality specified by a particular level affects only that domain. This allows different domains within the forest to be at different phases in the process of transitioning to Windows Server 2003. The domain functional levels include:

- **Windows 2000 mixed** This level allows for backward compatibility with Microsoft Windows NT 4.0 and Microsoft Windows 2000.
- **Windows 2000 native** This level allows for backward compatibility with Microsoft Windows 2000.
- **Windows Server 2003 interim** This level provides an upgrade path to Windows Server 2003 for Microsoft Windows NT 4.0 domains.
- **Windows Server 2003** This level provides the highest functionality and does not provide any backward compatibility with older operating systems.

The default is set to Windows 2000 mixed. This level provides functionality with pre–Windows Server 2003 domain controllers (see Figure 1-8). Adding Windows Server 2003 domain controllers to an existing Windows NT 4.0 or Windows 2000 network provides new Active Directory enhancements, but it does not allow for full feature support until the domain is raised to the Windows Server 2003 level. The domain functional levels provide a tiered approach to the available enhancements. As domain functionality is advanced, support for older domain controllers becomes more restrictive in exchange for Windows Server 2003 Active Directory enhancements.

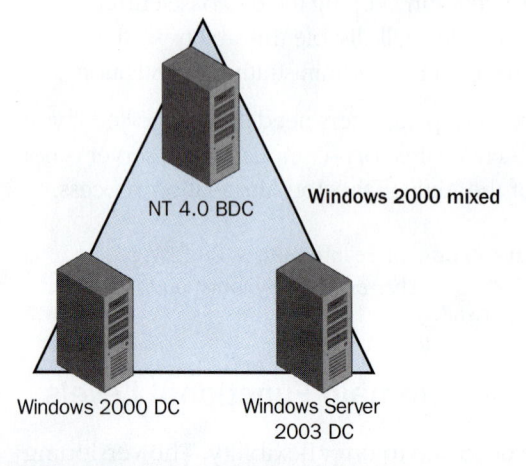

Figure 1-8 Windows 2000 mixed

As shown in Figure 1-8, domains with a functional level set to Windows 2000 mixed can contain Windows NT 4.0, Windows 2000, and Windows Server 2003 domain controllers. This is similar to the support that is offered in Windows 2000 mixed networks. This level is the most flexible, although it offers only the following additions to Active Directory functionality in the domain:

- **Install From Media** A new feature that allows servers to be promoted to domain controllers using a backup replica from another domain controller.

- **Application Directory Partitions** A new feature that allows a separate replication partition for application data that does not need to be globally available. The feature allows greater control over replication placement and scopes.

- **Enhanced User Interface** A feature that includes drag and drop and saved queries.

Figure 1-9 depicts a Windows 2000 native environment that advances from Windows 2000 mixed by no longer supporting Windows NT 4.0 domain controllers. This is a one-way conversion in that once the transition is made to Windows 2000 native, it is irreversible. Reverting to Windows 2000 mixed would require a reinstallation of the entire Active Directory domain. Windows 2000 native includes the following Windows Server 2003 features:

- **Group Nesting** Allows Global Group objects to become members of other group objects.

- **Universal Groups** Adds members from multiple domains within the forest.

- **sIDHistory** Keeps the Security Identifier (SID) of an object that was migrated from another domain.

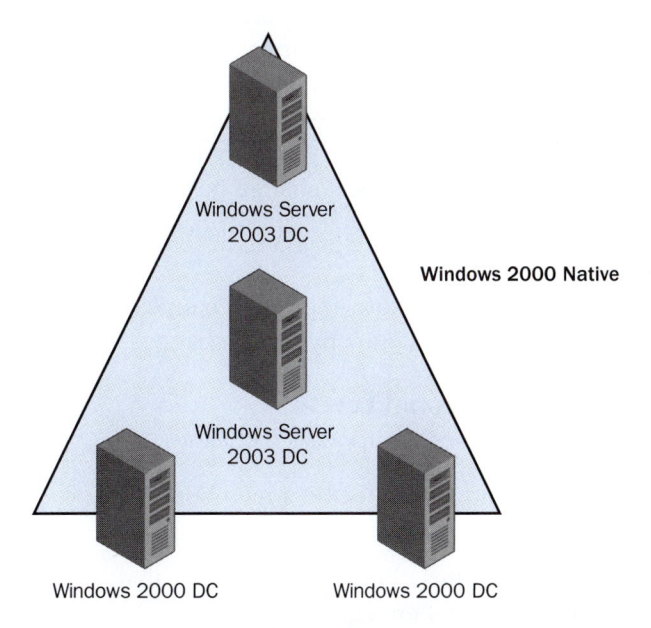

Figure 1-9 Windows 2000 native

Figure 1-10 illustrates the next domain functional level in Windows Server 2003 interim. Its main purpose is to provide a migration path for organizations that contain only Windows NT 4.0 domains. Windows 2000 domain controllers are not able to participate in this domain functional level. It includes only the Windows 2000 mixed functional level features.

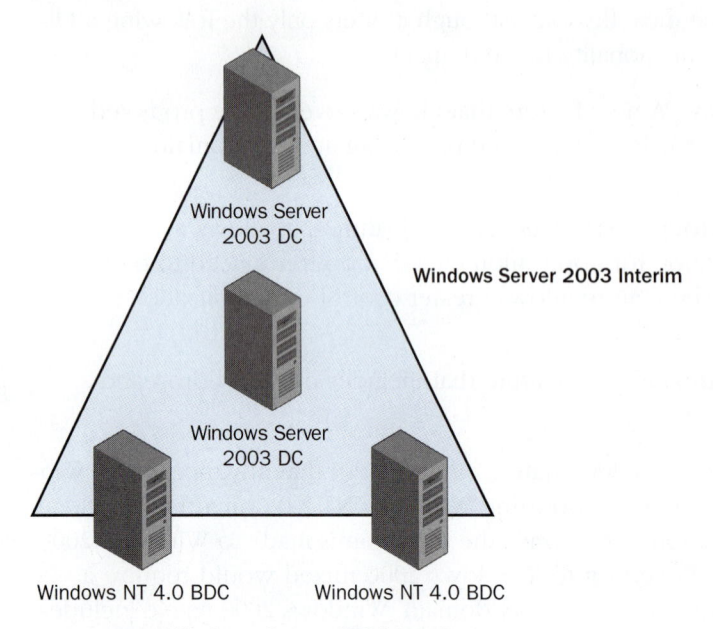

Figure 1-10 Windows Server 2003 interim

Windows Server 2003 interim is the highest domain functional level and can contain only Windows Server 2003 family domain controllers. All Windows 2000 native features are available, in addition to the following:

- **Replicated lastLogonTimestamp Attribute**   Allows logon tracking of computers and users within the domain.

- **User password on inetOrgPerson**   As defined in RFC 2798, it can be used as a security principal just like the user object, and it is helpful when migrating from other LDAP directory services such as Novell Netware. The password attribute can be set as effective in the same manner as the **unicodePwd attribute** on a user object. The unicodePwd attribute on a user object is created using administrative privileges. It cannot be read. To modify this attribute, either you can use a typical change password operation or it can be scripted, ensuring that there are appropriate calls for the old password and new password fields.

- **Domain renaming**   Allows for greater flexibility in design changes for situations such as mergers, acquisitions, and company name changes.

Requirements for Raising Domain Functional Levels

Raising the domain functional levels has a number of important guidelines, as follows:

- To raise the functional level of a domain, you must be a member of the Domain Admins group.

- The functional level of a domain can be raised only on the server that holds the Primary Domain Controller (PDC) emulator role.

- The functional level of a domain can be raised only if all domain controllers in the target domain are running supported versions of the operating system.

- Raising the functional level is an irreversible procedure.

Table 1-2 provides a summary of the domain functional levels and the included features.

Table 1-2 **Summary of Domain Functional Levels**

Domain Functional Level	Supported Operating Systems	Windows Server 2003 Features
Windows 2000 mixed	Windows NT 4.0 Windows 2000 Windows Server 2003	Install From Media Application Directory Partitions Enhanced User Interface
Windows 2000 native	Windows 2000 Windows Server 2003	All mixed features and the following: Universal Groups Group Nesting SID History
Windows Server 2003 interim	Windows NT 4.0 Windows Server 2003	Same as Windows 2000 mixed
Windows Server 2003	Windows Server 2003	All Windows 2000 native features and the following: Replicated lastLogonTimestamp attribute User password on inetOrgPerson Domain rename

Forest Functional Levels

In terms of progression, forest functional levels are treated similarly to domain functional levels. Advancing from a lower to a higher functional level is a one-way process that cannot be reversed. Domain functional levels can be independent of other domains in the forest. However, since domains are child containers of a forest, the forest functional level applies to all domains contained within that forest.

There are three levels of forest functionality. They include Windows 2000, Windows Server 2003 interim, and Windows Server 2003. Windows 2000 is the default forest functionality enabled when the first Windows Server 2003 domain controller is introduced into the network. Just as in Windows 2000 mixed domain functionality, Windows 2000 forest functionality supports domain controllers running Windows NT 4.0, Windows 2000, and Windows Server 2003. The Windows 2000 forest functional features include:

- **Install From Media**   This is the same feature that was described in the Windows 2000 mixed domain functional level. It allows servers to be promoted to domain controllers using a backup replica from another domain controller.

- **Universal Group Caching**   This is the ability to log on to a domain at a remote site without having a global catalog server in that site.

- **Application Directory Partitions**   Like the Windows 2000 mixed domain functionality, this allows a separate replication partition for application data that does not need to be globally available. It allows greater control over replication placement and scopes.

Windows 2003 interim functionality is available for existing Windows NT 4.0 networks as a migration path that allows for a gradual transition to Windows Server 2003. Windows 2000 domain controllers are not permitted to join this forest type. Supported features include all Windows 2000 forest functionality features in addition to the following:

- **Improved Inter-Site Topology Generator (ISTG)**   ISTG is the process used to initiate the creation and management of the replication topology between sites. In Windows 2000, this feature was limited by the number of sites in the forest. In Windows Server 2003, this feature scales to allow a greater number of sites.

- **Linked Value Replication** This feature allows group membership changes to be treated individually during replication. Prior to Windows Server 2003, any changes to the membership of a group triggered replication of the entire group. The improved replication process results in lowered bandwidth and processing utilization and less possibility of lost updates.

The highest forest functional level is Windows Server 2003. This requires that all domain controllers have Windows Server 2003 installed. Before raising the forest functional level, it is important to ensure that support is no longer required for non–Windows Server 2003 domain controllers. Raising the forest functional level is an irreversible procedure, as is raising the domain functional level. The Windows Server 2003 forest functional level includes all Windows Server 2003 interim features in addition to the following:

- **Dynamic Auxiliary class objects** A new schema modification option that provides support for dynamically linking auxiliary classes to individual objects. Prior to this functionality, an auxiliary class object could be linked only to an entire class of objects.

- **User objects can be converted to InetOrgPerson objects** The InetOrgPerson object is used by non-Microsoft LDAP directory services such as Novell. This new base object in Windows Server 2003 allows for easier migration of objects from these other platforms.

- **Schema redefinitions permitted** Windows Server 2003 allows for the deactivations and redefinition of object attributes within the schema.

- **Domain renames permitted** Domains can be renamed within this functional level to accommodate major design changes on your network.

- **Cross-forest trusts permitted** This trust type is new to Windows Server 2003 and allows for resources to be shared between Active Directory forests.

The Windows Server 2003 forest functional level assumes that all domains have been raised to Windows Server 2003 prior to the forest being raised. All new features and enhancements become available; however, note that all new domain controllers introduced into the domain must be installed as a Windows Server 2003 product.

Requirements for Raising Forest Functional Levels
Raising the forest functional level has a number of important guidelines, as follows:

- To raise the functional level of a forest, you must be logged on as a member of the Enterprise Admins group.

- The functional level of a forest can be raised only on a server that holds the Flexible Single Master Operations Schema Master role. This server is the authority for all schema changes. The specific role will be discussed in Chapter 4, "Global Catalog and Flexible Single Master Operations (FSMO) Roles."

- All domain controllers in the entire forest must be running an operating system supported by the targeted forest functional level.

- Raising the forest functional level to the highest level, Windows Server 2003, requires all domains to be at the Windows 2000 native mode or Windows 2003 functional level.

- During a forest functional level advancement, all domains will automatically be raised to support the new forest functional level.

- Raising the forest functional level is an irreversible procedure.

Table 1-3 provides a summary of the forest functional levels and the included features.

Table 1-3 Summary of Forest Functional Levels

Forest Functional Level	Supported Operating Systems	Windows Server 2003 Features
Windows 2000	Windows NT 4.0 Windows 2000 Windows Server 2003	Install From Media Universal Group Caching Application Directory Partitions Enhanced User Interface
Windows 2003 interim	Windows NT 4.0 Windows Server 2003	All Windows 2000 forest features and the following: Link Value Replication (Group membership replication enhancement) Improved ISTG
Windows Server 2003	Windows Server 2003	All Windows 2003 interim functionality and the following: User objects can be converted to inetOrgPerson objects Schema modifications to attributes and classes Can create instances of Dynamic Auxiliary class objects called *dynamicObject* Domain renaming Cross-forest trusts

Understanding and Comparing Active Directory Trust Models

Do Exercise 1-2 now to practice choosing the appropriate functional levels.

Active Directory uses trust relationships to allow for access between domains and now, with Windows Server 2003, across forests. With regard to Windows 2000 and Windows Server 2003, interdomain and intraforest trust relationships are considered transitive. *Transitive* is defined by Merriam-Webster as "being or relating to a relation with the property such that, if the relation holds between a first element and a second, and between the second element and a third, it holds between the first and third elements." For example, you could say that if Sam trusts Henry and Henry trusts Susie, then Sam also trusts Susie. In Windows Server 2003, each child domain in a forest is automatically linked to its parent domain. This parent domain is linked to its parent domain, continuing the relationship up to the forest root. These trust relationships go both ways, in that each parent trusts the child and the child also trusts the parent.

Figure 1-11 shows the Microsoft Windows 2000 and Microsoft Windows 2003 trust relationships between domains in a forest. Note that each child domain is linked to its parent domain, continuing up to the forest root domain. If a user in Child

Domain B needs access to a resource in Child Domain D, the request is sent up through Child Domain A to the forest root domain. From there, it is sent to Child Domain C, and finally to its destination in Child Domain D. This process is called **tree-walking**. If the domains are divided by WAN links and this process takes exceedingly long, a **shortcut trust** can be created to form a direct path between Child Domain B and Child Domain D, as shown in Figure 1-12.

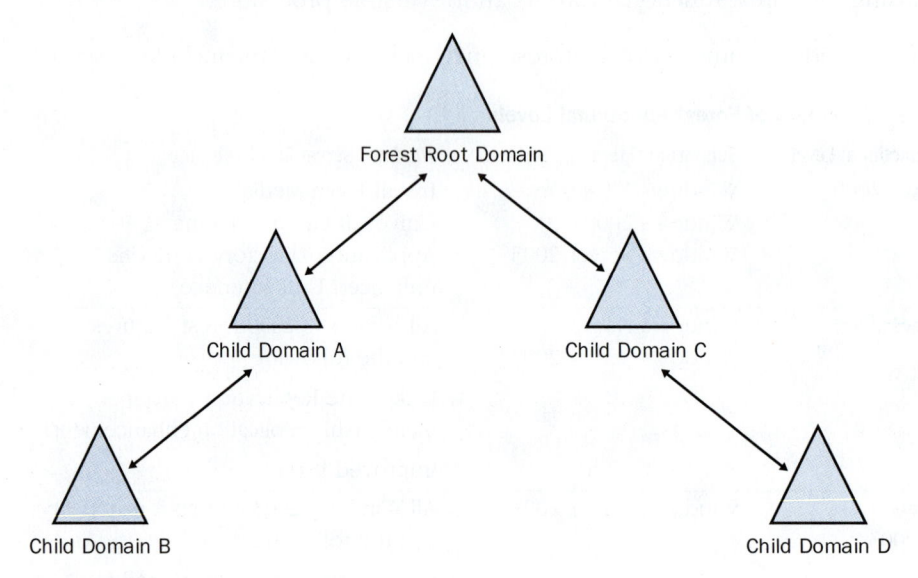

Figure 1-11 Domain trust model

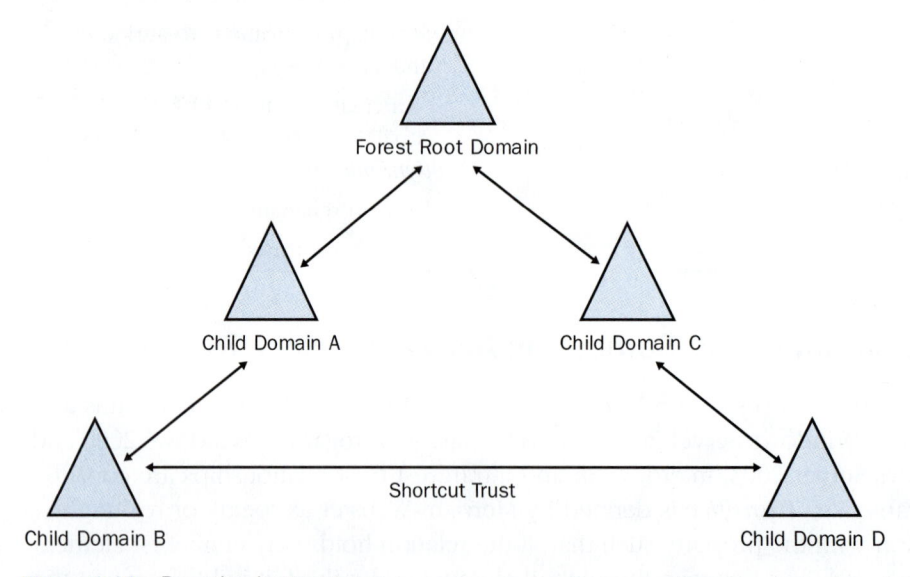

Figure 1-12 Domain shortcut trust

In Windows NT, specific trusts are created between domains to allow for access to resources. Additionally, all Windows NT trusts are one-way trusts only. To allow for two-way accessibility, two separate one-way trusts have to be created. Windows NT is not hierarchical, and therefore, there are no parent/child relationships among domains to facilitate resource access. Without explicit trusts, all domains are independent and resource sharing is not possible. Figure 1-13 depicts the Windows NT trust model.

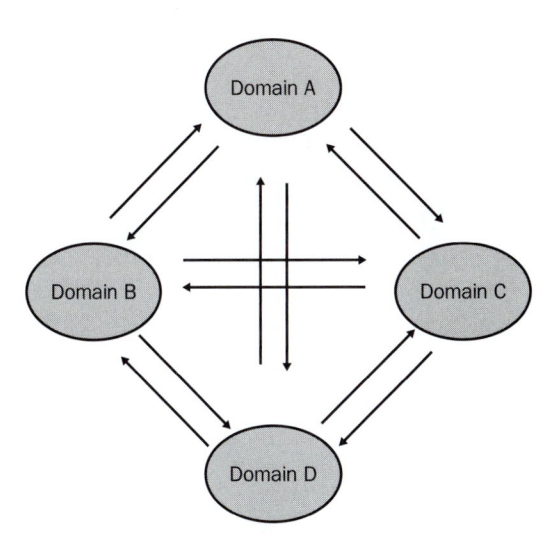

Figure 1-13   Windows NT trust model

Windows Server 2003 introduces a new type of trust called a **cross-forest trust**. Until now, it was not possible to create a trust path between forests; resource access from one forest to another was unsupported. Cross-forest trusts in Windows Server 2003 require the functional level to be set to Windows Server 2003. In addition, trusts must be created manually, and like shortcut trusts, must be done at both ends of the desired link for a two-way trust to exist. Once the trust is established, administrators can select users and groups from a trusted forest and include them on the ACL of an object. When a resource is accessed via the cross-forest trust, a secure link is established using the **Kerberos** authentication protocol. The user is not required to reenter any logon parameters since the single logon functionality is not compromised here. This new feature allows corporations to share resources with partners or new acquisitions without a complete design change or migration.

SUMMARY

- Active Directory is a database of objects that are used to organize resources according to a logical plan. These objects include containers such as domains and OUs in addition to resources such as users, computers, and printers.

- The Active Directory schema includes definitions of all objects and attributes within a single forest. Each forest maintains its own Active Directory schema.

- Active Directory requires DNS to support SRV records. In addition, Microsoft recommends that DNS support dynamic updates.

- Domain and forest functional levels are new features of Windows Server 2003. The levels defined for each of these are based on the type of server operating systems that are required by the Active Directory design. The Windows Server 2003 forest functional level is the highest functional level available and includes support for all Windows Server 2003 features.

- Two-way transitive trusts are automatically generated within the Active Directory domain structure. Parent and child domains form the trust path by which all domains in the forest can traverse to locate resources. The ISTG is responsible for this process.

- Cross-forest trusts are new to Windows Server 2003 and only available when the forest functionality is set to Windows Server 2003. They must be manually created and maintained.

EXERCISES

Exercise 1-1: Logical Versus Physical Structure

Use the following scenario to answer the questions below.

Southridge Video is about to set up a completely new network. The network will consist of approximately 10 servers and 500 client computers. The servers will run Windows Server 2003, and the clients will run Windows XP Professional. The plan is to connect the corporate headquarters to each of the company's five regional offices. Each regional office has several retail locations. Regional offices are connected to the corporate headquarters through leased fractional T-1 lines and routers that provide no less than 1 Mbps throughput. Retail locations are connected to regional offices through 56 Kbps dial-up connections. All client computers are expected to obtain resources and standard computer settings from the corporate headquarters and regional offices. Retail locations will have only two to five computers. All systems use TCP/IP for network communications.

1. What type of network administrative model (Workgroup or Domain) would work best for Southridge Video? Why?
2. Where would you expect domain controllers to be located?
3. If the company decided to configure sites, where would you expect them to be located?
4. What type of decisions would Southridge Video have to make about the logical structure of Active Directory?

Exercise 1-2: Functional-Level Decision Making

Use the following scenario to help answer the questions below.

A. Datum Corporation currently uses a Windows NT 4.0 domain model. There are five Windows NT Server 4.0 computers configured as domain controllers. A. Datum has decided to upgrade the Primary Domain Controller (PDC) to Windows Server 2003.

1. Which two types of forest functional levels will the company be able to select? Which functional level is the default?
2. If the company chooses the default forest functional level, which domain functional levels can the company use? Which domain functional level is the default?
3. If A. Datum decided to keep its Windows NT Server 4.0 backup domain controllers and didn't ever plan to have Windows 2000 domain controllers, what forest functional levels could it select to add functionality?

REVIEW QUESTIONS

1. What is the difference between a single-master and a multi-master domain replication model?
2. Which of the following are valid leaf objects in Active Directory?
    a. Domain
    b. User
    c. Printer
    d. OU
    e. Folder
    f. Site
3. Which of the following servers can be joined to a forest that is currently set at Windows 2003 interim mode?
    a. Windows 2000
    b. Windows Server 2003
    c. Windows NT 3.51
    d. Windows NT 4.0
4. You are planning an Active Directory implementation for a company that currently has sales, accounting, and marketing departments. Each department head wants to manage his or her own users and resources in Active Directory. What feature will permit you to set up Active Directory to allow each manager to manage his or her own container but not any other containers?
5. What is required by DNS for Active Directory to function?
    a. Dynamic update support
    b. DHCP forwarding support
    c. SRV records support
    d. Active Directory integration

6. Active Directory information is stored on each domain controller in a file called _____.

7. You are an administrator who manages a multiple-server environment. The shared folders that contain necessary files for user access are stored on different servers, making them difficult for users to find. What can you do to simplify the process of locating this data for the users?

8. If the user named Amy is located in the sales OU of the central.cohowinery.com domain, what is the correct syntax for referencing this user in a command line utility?

    a. amy.cohowinery.com

    b. cn=amy.ou=sales.dc=cohowinery.com

    c. cn=amy,ou=sales,dc=cohowinery,dc=com

    d. dc=com,dn=cohowinery,ou=sales,cn=amy

9. What is the default forest functionality set to when the first Windows Server 2003 domain controller is installed?

    a. Mixed mode

    b. Native mode

    c. Windows Server 2003

    d. Enterprise mode

10. Draw an Active Directory forest with multiple noncontiguous domains and at least one child domain for each parent domain. Using your domain model, add a shortcut trust and describe when this trust would be beneficial.

CASE SCENARIOS

Scenario 1-1: Rolling Out Windows Server 2003

You are the manager for the IT department of a large organization. Your company currently has a mixed environment of Novell, Microsoft Windows NT, and Windows 2000 servers. You are currently working with a network designer to assist in planning an upgrade of all servers to Windows Server 2003 over the next six months. Consider that the rollout will take place in phases and that the goal is for minimal downtime. Which new features in Windows Server 2003 will help you with this migration? Why will these new features assist you in your migration of the network?

Scenario 1-2: Accessing Resources in More than One Network

You are the network manager of a Windows Server 2003 network at a large organization. Your company recently acquired another company. The new acquisition company already has a Windows Server 2003 network in place that you want to maintain. However, you would like to be able to provide access to resources in both networks. What should you do to establish a path between the two networks? What do you need to check before doing so?

CHAPTER 2
IMPLEMENTING ACTIVE DIRECTORY

Upon completion of this chapter, you will be able to:

- Understand the requirements for installing an Active Directory directory service.
- Configure Domain Name System (DNS) for Active Directory.
- Create a forest and domain structure.
- Create and configure an application data partition.
- Modify the Active Directory schema.
- Raise the domain and forest functional levels.
- Establish and manage trust relationships.
- Create or delete a User Principle Name (UPN).

This chapter focuses on the process for installing and configuring Active Directory, including the important points you will need to understand in order to prepare for the installation and key post installation tasks. In particular, the chapter describes the key concepts involved in deploying the Microsoft Windows Server 2003 Active Directory forest.

REQUIREMENTS FOR ACTIVE DIRECTORY

When Active Directory is installed, the installed server is promoted to a domain controller. The domain controller participates in replication and provides Active Directory services such as a domain logon to network clients. Before deciding to install Active Directory on a server, you should first review and familiarize yourself with the network design to understand how the domain controller will fit into the network and/or existing domain structures. Generally, Active Directory can be installed on any server that has a Windows 2003–based operating system installed, relevant service packs and hotfixes, if any, and for which authentication, replication, and fault tolerance plans have been formulated. The **Active Directory Installation Wizard** (Dcpromo) guides you through the following processes: adding a domain controller to an existing environment, creating an entirely new forest structure, or demoting domain controllers and eventually removing a domain or forest.

Before installing Active Directory, consider these hardware, software, and administrative requirements:

- A server running Windows Server 2003 Standard Edition, Windows Server 2003 Enterprise Edition, or Windows Server 2003 Datacenter Edition.

    NOTE Windows Server 2003 Web Edition Active Directory cannot run on Windows Server 2003 Web Edition.

- An administrator account and password on the local machine.
- An NT file system (NTFS) partition for the Sysvol folder structure.
- 200 MB minimum free space on the previously mentioned partition for Active Directory database files.
- 50 MB minimum free space for the transaction log files. These files can be located on the same partition as the database files or elsewhere. However, to achieve optimal performance, these files should be located on a physical drive other than the one holding the operating system. Placing the database and log files on separate hard drives results in better performance, since they do not need to compete for the input/output (I/O) processes of a single drive.

    CAUTION Active Directory Fails When Out of Disk Space If you are planning to migrate users from another directory service, it is important to allocate enough free space to accommodate each user object. If Active Directory runs out of space, the directory service will not start.

- Transmission Control Protocol/Internet Protocol (TCP/IP) must be installed and configured to use DNS.
- An authoritative DNS server for the DNS domain must be installed to support service resource (SRV) records. In addition, Microsoft recommends that the server providing DNS for Active Directory support incremental zone transfers and dynamic updates. Zone transfer is the process of replicating DNS information from one DNS server to another. With an incremental zone transfer, bandwidth is conserved because the entire zone does not have to be transferred; only the changes are transferred. When the Internet Protocol (IP) address of a host changes, dynamic updates

allow the DNS database to be updated with the changed information. This allows for more efficiency in the maintenance of the database, resulting in fewer resolution problems for clients.

NOTE Integrating a DNS Server Running Berkeley Internet Name Domain (BIND) If you want to use a BIND DNS server to support Active Directory, it must be running version 8.1.2 or later of the BIND software. Previous versions of BIND do not support the requirements for Active Directory.

MORE INFO DNS For more information on DNS, see Appendix A, "DNS Overview."

CAUTION Risky Dynamic Updates Dynamic updates can offer a potential security risk in certain situations. Prior to deploying DNS, you should consult Chapter 3, "Deploying DNS," of the Windows Server 2003 Resource Kit. The entire resource kit is located at http://www.microsoft.com/windowsserver2003/techinfo/reskit/deploykit.mspx.

SIZING THE ACTIVE DIRECTORY DATABASE

Before you can install Active Directory, you will need to know the potential size of the Active Directory database. Active Directory space requirements are much smaller than you might think. The approximate sizes of objects and attributes in Active Directory are listed as follows:

- Security principle (User, Group, Computer) = 3600 bytes
- Organizational unit (OU) = 1100 bytes
- Security certificates mapped to a user = 1500 bytes
- Object attributes = ~100 bytes
- Access Control Entry (ACE) = 70 bytes per ACE

Taking these sizing requirements into consideration, a user account having 20 attributes and a certificate will take up approximately 7100 bytes of space. When planning space requirements, you will need to know the approximate number and types of objects you need to accommodate. After doing some simple math, you will find that the Active Directory database takes up relatively little space considering the amount of information it contains. Always be prepared to pad your final number to ensure you are not caught short in case you need to expand beyond your original projections.

PRE-INSTALLATION TASKS

Prior to running the Active Directory Installation Wizard, you should gather all of the information you will need during the installation process. This information can usually be obtained from the Active Directory design. However, you can create a checklist that will help you prepare for each page. This checklist should include the following:

- Local administrator password
- Domain controller type
- Domain name

- Desired location for database and log files if using other than the default locations
- Desired location for the Sysvol folder structure if using other than the default location
- DNS installation information such as whether or not DNS will reside on this server. If not, then an IP address and name of a preferred DNS server should be available.
- Permissions settings
- Desired Directory Services Restore Mode password
- The installation CD-ROM or the location of the installation files
- Any relevant service packs or hotfixes

After you have gathered the installation information, you can start the process as described in the following section.

THE ACTIVE DIRECTORY INSTALLATION PROCESS

You can launch the Active Directory Installation Wizard either from the Start/Run command line using dcpromo.exe or from the Manage Your Server Web page. The Manage Your Server Web page is launched automatically at system startup or it can be accessed through the shortcut provided in the Administrative Tools folder. The advantage of the Manage Your Server Web page method over using dcpromo.exe at the command line is that it will allow you to view other roles the server might be performing. Figure 2-1 shows the Configure Your Server Wizard page that was launched from the main page of the Manage Your Server Web page.

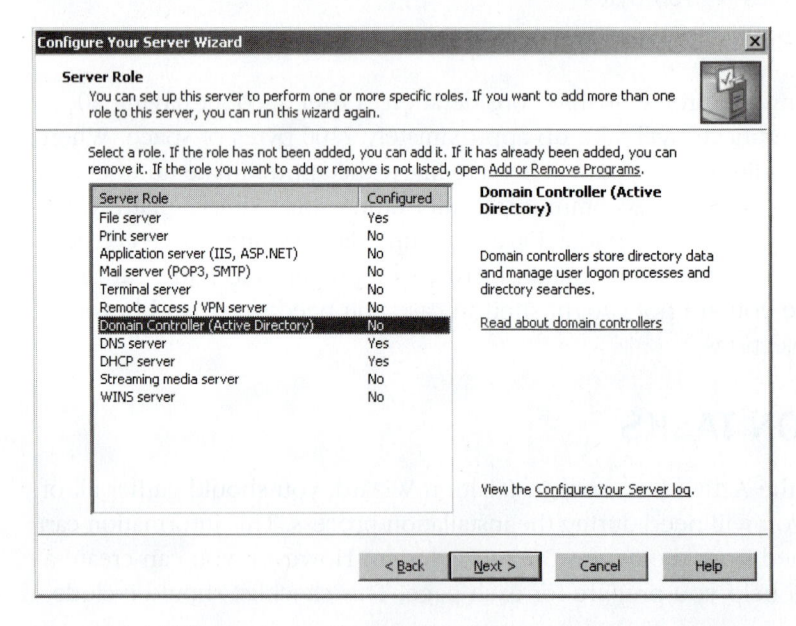

Figure 2-1 Adding a server role using the Configure Your Server Web page

Once the Active Directory Installation Wizard is launched, perform the steps described in the next section to continue the installation.

Creating a Forest Root Domain

The first Active Directory domain on the network is the **forest root domain**. The forest root domain is the parent domain to any child domains within the Active Directory infrastructure. The first server in this domain is named the forest root domain controller. This controller holds all of the **flexible single master operation roles** until replica domain controllers are added to the domain. Flexible single master operation roles are specific server roles that work together to enable the multi-master functionality of Active Directory.

Active Directory assigns per-forest and per-domain roles to specific domain controllers by default. Active Directory allows a domain administrator with the correct permissions to reassign these roles to other computers to optimize Active Directory performance after additional domain controllers have been created. For example, modifying the schema is a per-forest role since the Active Directory schema is shared among all domains in a forest. The server holding the schema master operations role needs to be accessible to all domains in the forest. After the initial domain controller creation, additional domain controllers can be installed and the roles can be transferred to the new domain controllers.

> **MORE INFO** Flexible Single Master Operation Roles Chapter 4, "Global Catalog and Flexible Single Master Operation (FSMO) Roles," discusses the management and placement of flexible single master operation roles.

What Type of Domain Controller?

To start the Active Directory Installation Wizard, select Start/Run and enter **dcpromo** in the prompt box. The first screen informs you that Windows Server 2003 has security settings that no longer support some versions of Microsoft Windows. These nonsupported versions include Microsoft Windows 95 and Microsoft Windows NT 4 SP3 or earlier. Any clients running these versions will not be able to log on or access resources in the Windows Server 2003 domain. Figure 2-2 shows the Compatibility page. This page offers explanations with regard to operating system compatibility, in addition to a link to the Help feature.

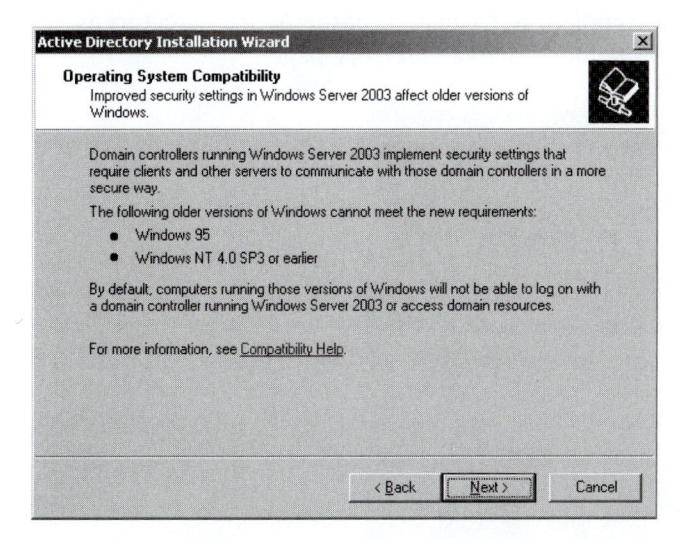

Figure 2-2 Operating System Compatibility page

Next the Active Directory Installation Wizard will attempt to detect another installation of Active Directory. If the wizard does not detect another installation of Active Directory, the Domain Controller Type page is displayed as shown in Figure 2-3. To create a new domain, select the first option, Domain Controller For A New Domain. To create a replica domain controller in an existing domain, select the second option, Additional Domain Controller For An Existing Domain. The Create New Domain page is displayed as shown below.

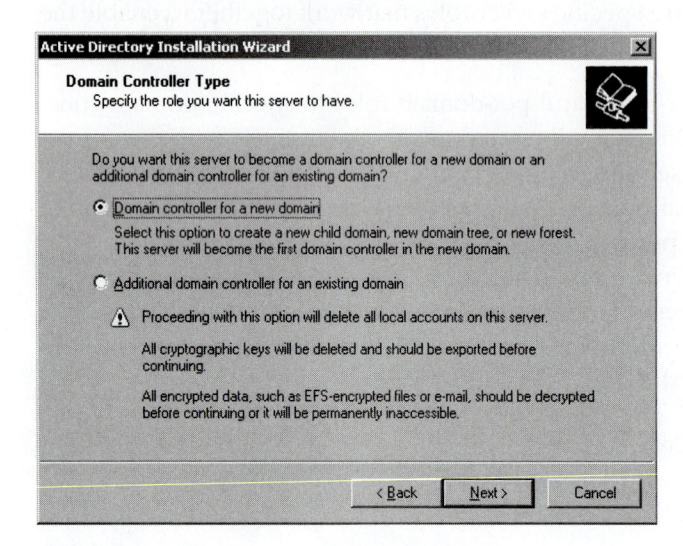

Figure 2-3   Domain Controller Type page

If the wizard detects another installation of Active Directory on the server, the wizard presents you with the option to remove Active Directory. Removing Active Directory demotes the domain controller to a member server within the domain. If the server is the last domain controller in a domain, demoting the server removes all Active Directory components and destroys any existing database files for that domain. If the server is the last server in the forest, the entire forest is removed when the domain controller is uninstalled. The outcome of this procedure is that all Active Directory services, including Netlogon, will not function. This procedure should be done only when a complete reinstallation of the Active Directory is required. Figure 2-4 shows the Remove Active Directory page.

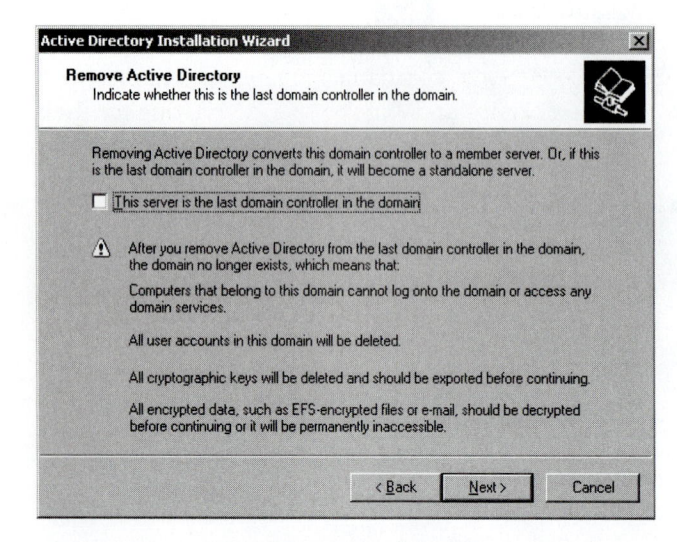

Figure 2-4   Remove Active Directory page

To Which Forest Should the Domain Controller Belong?

When the Domain Controller Type page is completed, the Create New Domain page is displayed to allow you to decide which role in the forest structure you want this server to assume, as shown in Figure 2-5. If this is the first domain in a new forest, select the first option, Domain In A New Forest. To create a child domain in an existing domain tree, select the second option, Child Domain In An Existing Domain Tree. Selecting this option allows your domain name to follow the contiguous naming within a tree as discussed in Chapter 1, "Overview of Active Directory Services." The third option, Domain Tree In An Existing Forest, allows you to create a new domain tree in an existing forest that will have a noncontiguous domain name.

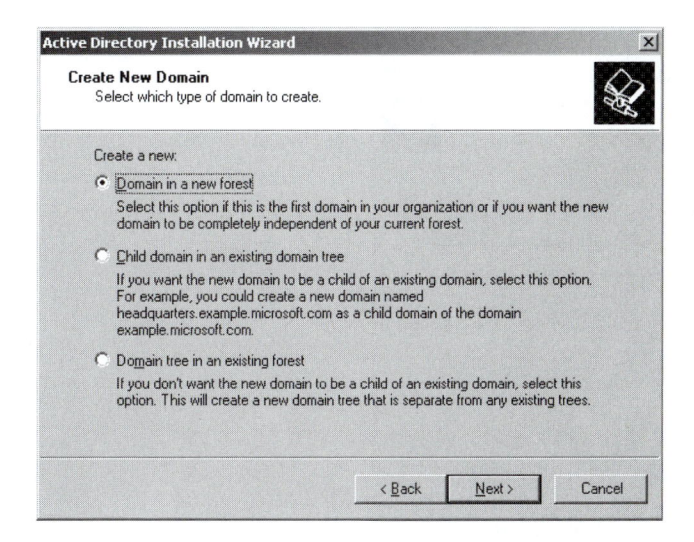

Figure 2-5 Create New Domain page

Entering the Domain and NetBIOS Names

After the Create New Domain page is completed, you will be prompted to enter the **Fully Qualified Domain Name (FQDN)** and confirm the **NetBIOS name**. The FQDN usually matches the DNS name registered by the company for use on the Internet. In some cases, the company may not have the intention to establish an Internet presence. If this is true, the domain name suffix can reflect *local* for the root. It is a good idea to register a name, even if you do not plan to have an Internet presence right away. With proper planning, it is possible for you to rename the entire forest with Windows Server 2003. Some companies register two names with the Internet Corporation for Assigned Names and Numbers (ICANN), one for their internal network and one for the external network. ICANN is a nonprofit organization that is responsible for coordinating the assignment of IP addresses, protocol parameters, and Internet domain names. Registering two names allows you to segregate your internal network from your external network and allows you to track potential intruders of your network. For example, you could register cohowinery.com as your external name and cohowinery.net as your internal name.

> **NOTE** *DNS Registration* ICANN's main Web site is located at: http://www.icann.org. If you are registering a domain name, you should contact one of ICANN's accredited registrars for this process. Domain name registrars can be located on the Internet at http://www.internic.net/origin.html.

The NetBIOS name reflects the domain name to use if prior versions of Microsoft operating systems, such as Microsoft Windows NT, Microsoft Windows 95, Microsoft Windows 98, and Microsoft Windows 3.*x*, need access to the domain. NetBIOS names consist of a 15-character name and a reserved sixteenth character that is used to reference NetBIOS-specified services. Entering a NetBIOS name is a required step, even if the company environment does not incorporate downlevel or earlier operating systems. Although the NetBIOS name does not need to be the same as the DNS name, it is much simpler and easier to troubleshoot if these names match. Figure 2-6 shows the New Domain Name page, while Figure 2-7 shows the NetBIOS Domain Name page. The two separate pages can be used to allow different domain and NetBIOS names, although the use of separate names is strongly discouraged.

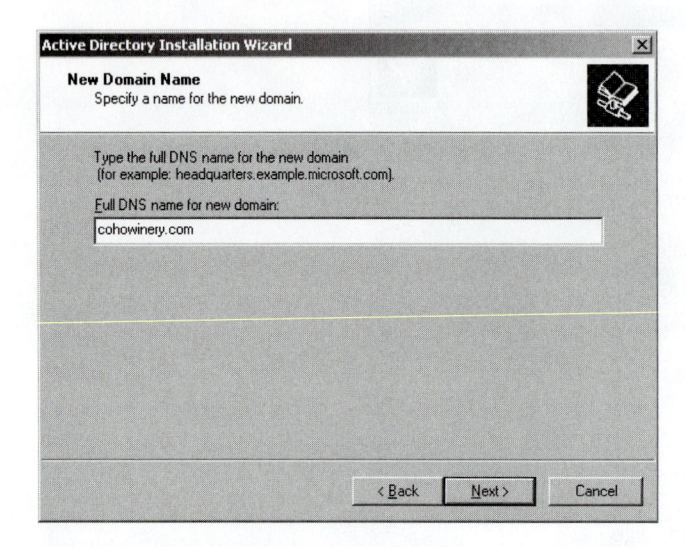

Figure 2-6 New Domain Name page

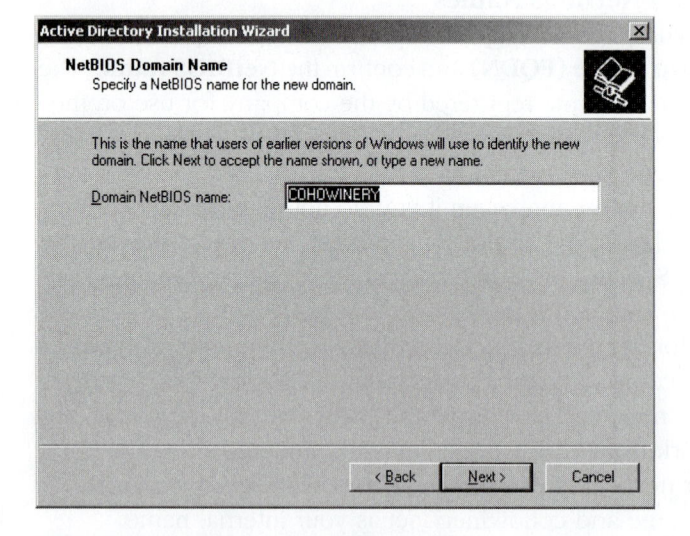

Figure 2-7 NetBIOS Domain Name page

Entering the Database, Log, and Sysvol Locations

Windows Server 2003 stores the database files for Active Directory by default in the *systemroot*\NTDS directory. The *systemroot* directory is located at C:\WINDOWS by default, unless the server was upgraded from Windows 2000 or Windows NT 4.0. These Windows operating systems both use C:\WINNT as their default location. It is also possible that another directory name may have been specified during the original installation. Figure 2-8 shows the Database And Log Folders page with the default locations pre-entered. This page also makes note of the performance benefit provided by placing the database and log files on different drives.

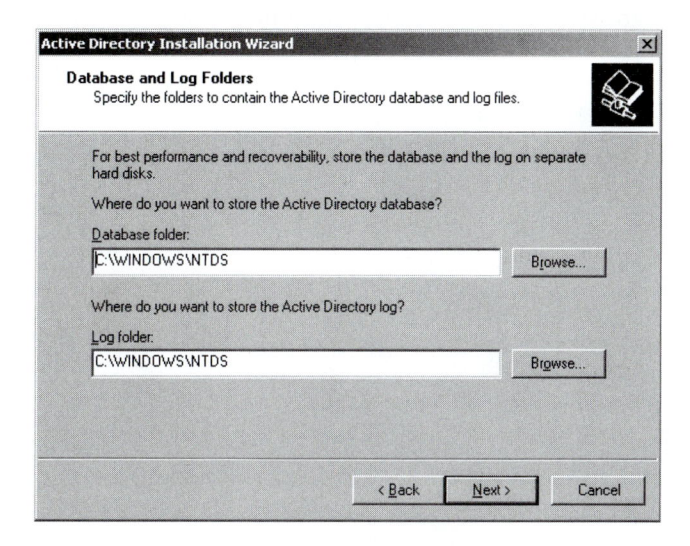

Figure 2-8   Database And Log Folders page

Figure 2-9 shows the Shared System Volume page. The **Sysvol folder** is a shared system folder that contains the domain's public files. The folder structure within the Sysvol share contains replicated data such as logon scripts and policies. The Sysvol folder must be stored on an NTFS partition. This page allows you to accept the default location of C:\WINDOWS\SYSVOL or select a different folder for these files.

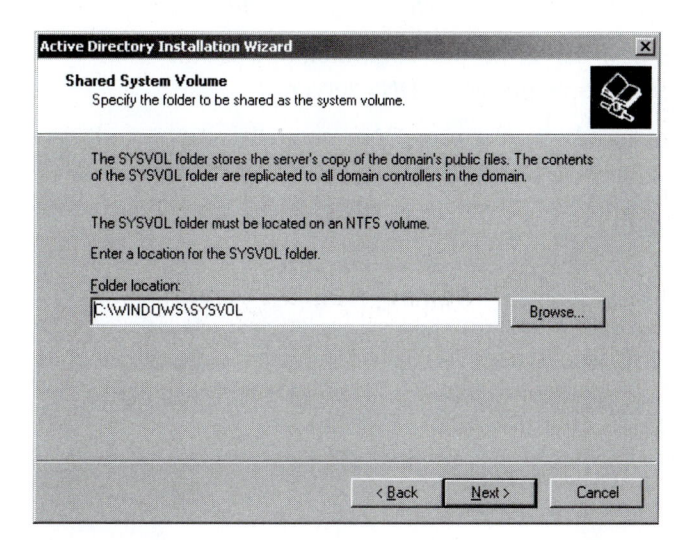

Figure 2-9   Shared System Volume page

DNS Detection and Installation

The DNS Registration Diagnostics page shows the results of a detection process that is performed based on the TCP/IP settings on the server. TCP/IP should be configured with an IP address that points to the server that will provide DNS resolution. If a DNS server already exists on the network, the Active Directory Installation Wizard will perform diagnostics to ensure this server is capable of supporting Active Directory. SRV records must be supported by the version of DNS that is used for Active Directory. If the wizard does not detect a valid DNS server, it returns an error message and you are prompted to decide how to proceed. Figure 2-10 shows the result of a DNS diagnostic on a server that could not contact a viable DNS server.

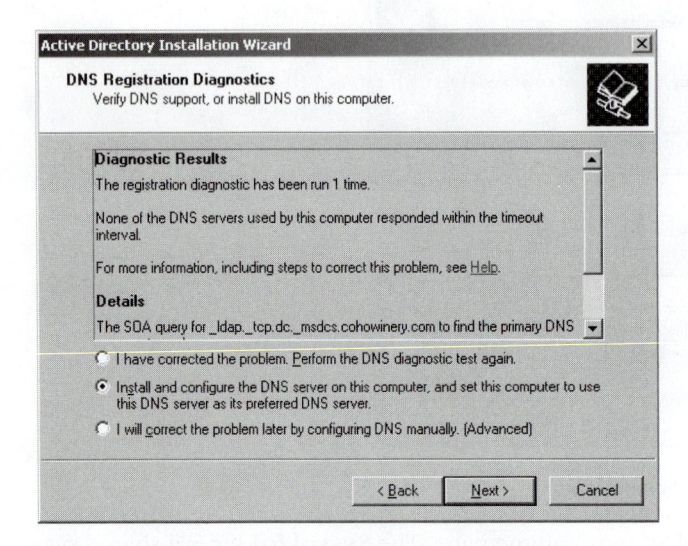

Figure 2-10 DNS Registration Diagnostics page

As shown in Figure 2-10, the DNS Registration Diagnostics page presents you with the following options:

- I have corrected the problem. Perform the DNS diagnostic test again.
- Install and configure the DNS server on this computer, and set this computer to use this DNS server as its preferred DNS server.
- I will correct the problem later by configuring DNS manually. (Advanced)

The first option assumes that you have modified the TCP/IP settings on the server to point to an existing DNS server.

> **MORE INFO** *Modifying TCP/IP Settings* *TCP/IP settings can be changed by accessing the appropriate Local Area Connection from the Network Connections option in Control Panel. For detailed instructions on changing TCP/IP settings, search for TCP/IP Configuration Methods in Windows Server 2003 Help.*

The second option begins the DNS installation on this server. When chosen, this option installs DNS on the server at the conclusion of the Active Directory installation.

The third option allows you to continue with the Active Directory installation without providing any DNS information. The DNS Registration Diagnostics page indicates that only advanced administrators should use this option. An advanced administrator is needed because all of the Active Directory related information will have to be manually added to the chosen DNS server at a later date. Without having a DNS server available, your Active Directory database will not be usable.

Default Permissions

As shown in Figure 2-11, the Permissions page requires you to set how you want permissions to be handled for users and groups on this domain. In Windows Server 2003, the pre–Windows 2000 compatible access group allows applications needing to access Active Directory, such as a pre–Windows 2000 remote access server (RAS), the ability to do so. A RAS allows users to dial in to the network. For example, if the RAS is running on a Windows NT 4.0 server that is a member of the Active Directory domain, you must ensure that the RAS is able to query the Active Directory domain controller for appropriate dial-in permissions. This is accomplished by using the pre–Windows 2000 compatible permissions. Although there is an elevated security risk with this level of permissions, they are required in circumstances of this type. The Permissions page has the capability to allow you to choose between pre–Windows 2000 and Windows Server 2003 permissions. The latter option is the more secure and recommended option. However, if the network still requires you to maintain servers on downlevel operating systems, this is something that can be changed post install, when all operating systems and application servers have been upgraded.

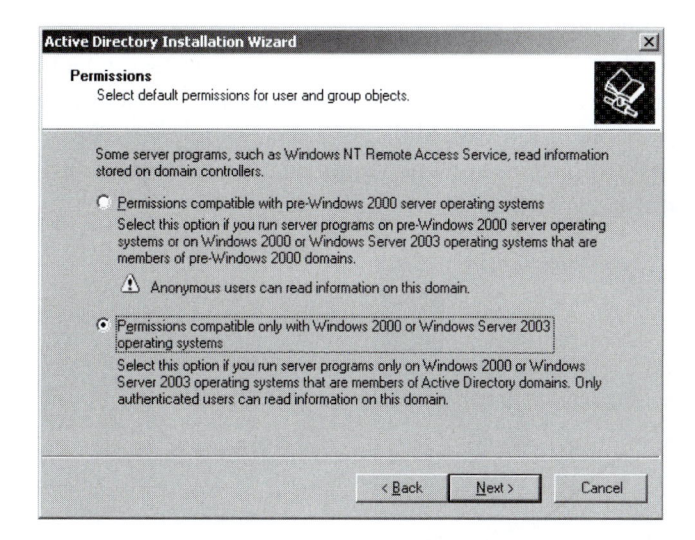

Figure 2-11   Permissions page

Directory Services Restore Mode Password

Directory Services Restore Mode is one of the methods used for disaster recovery. As shown in Figure 2-12, the Directory Services Restore Mode Administrator Password page allows you to set a password for the Directory Services Restore Mode administrator. This password allows the administrator to perform authoritative restores, or restores of Active Directory that will overwrite directory information during system recovery. This password should be different from the normal administrator account password. The Directory Services Restore Mode password should be carefully guarded since it may become your safety net in a restore situation. Chapter 11, "Active Directory Maintenance, Troubleshooting, and Disaster Recovery," will cover this tool in more detail.

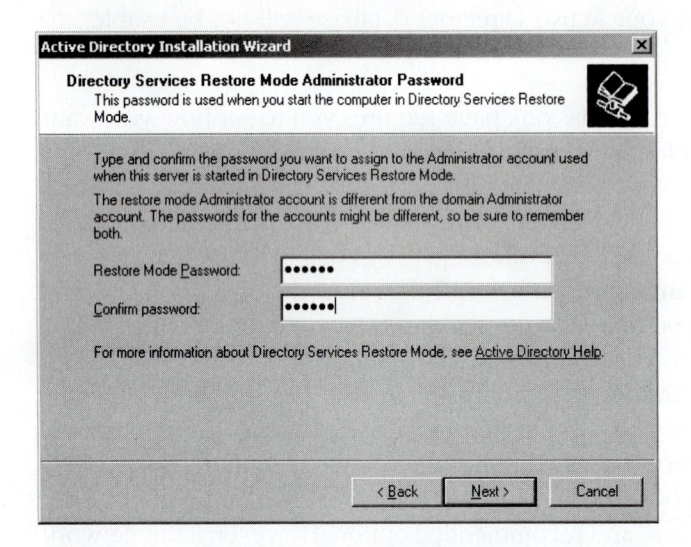

Figure 2-12 Directory Services Restore Mode Administrator Password page

Finalizing the Installation of Active Directory

To finalize the installation, the wizard displays the Summary page for your review as shown in Figure 2-13. Carefully review your choices and use the Back button to make changes if necessary. Click Finish to begin the completion process, which involves securing the disks, installing DNS if required, and finalizing the Active Directory installation. When complete, the wizard displays the Completing The Active Directory Installation Wizard page as shown in Figure 2-14. Click Finish and you will be prompted to perform a mandatory restart of your server.

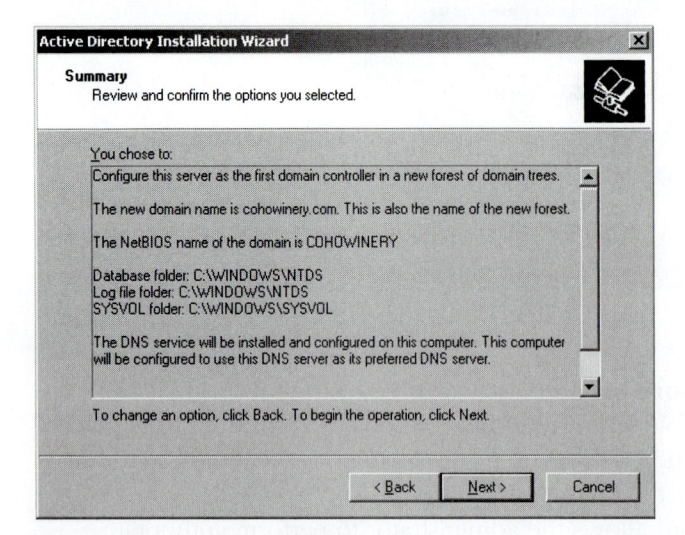

Figure 2-13 Summary page

CHAPTER 2: IMPLEMENTING ACTIVE DIRECTORY   39

To practice planning for an Active Directory installation, do Exercise 2-1 now.

Figure 2-14 Completing The Active Directory Installation Wizard page

POST-INSTALLATION TASKS

Upon completion of the Active Directory installation, you should verify a number of items before you consider it stable. The following sections discuss the basic items needed to create an Active Directory infrastructure that performs well and is mildly fault tolerant.

Verifying and Finalizing DNS Settings

Although DNS was installed as part of the Active Directory installation process, there are several items you should verify before considering that the installation is complete and operational. The items to finalize, verify, and configure are as follows:

- Application directory partition creation
- Aging and scavenging for zones
- Forward lookup zones and SRV records
- Reverse lookup zones

Verifying the Application Directory Partition Creation

Application directory partitions are used to separate forest-wide DNS information from domain DNS information. While DNS automatically sets the scope for each set of DNS data, the scope can be independently configured and added if necessary using either the DNS administration tool or tools from the Windows 2003 Server Resource Kit. Application partitions, new to Windows Server 2003, can store any hierarchy of objects, with the exception of security principal objects such as users or computers. The information in this partition can be configured to replicate to any domain controller in the forest, even if the chosen domain controllers are not all in the same domain. With regard to DNS, application directory partitions allow controlled replication of DNS information. This new type of partition can replace the need to create a copy of a read-only secondary DNS zone in a child domain for reduced traffic. Figure 2-15 shows the application directory partition for the cohowinery.com domain.

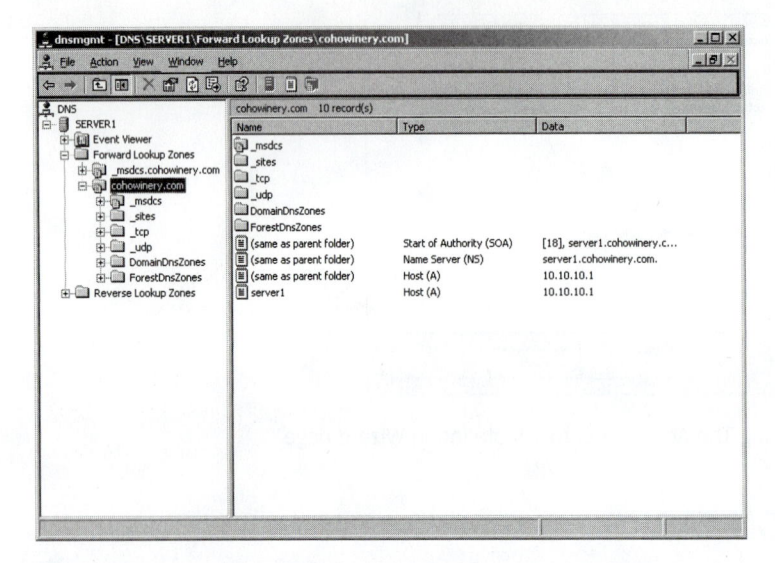

Figure 2-15 Application directory partition for cohowinery.com

There are two zones within the application directory partition that are shown in Figure 2-15. Using Figure 2-15 for reference, the zone type, its default zone name, and its purpose are explained in Table 2-1.

Table 2-1 Default Active Directory application partitions for cohowinery.com

Zone Type	Zone Name	Purpose
DomainDnsZones	DomainDnsZone.cohowinery.com	A single partition that allows DNS information to be replicated to all domain controllers running DNS within the domain.
ForestDnsZones	ForestDnsZones.cohowinery.com	A single partition that contains all DNS servers in the forest. Zones stored here are replicated to all DNS servers running on domain controllers in the entire forest.

The following are key points to understanding application directory partitions:

- Application directory partitions are automatically created when installing Active Directory Integrated DNS.

- You must be a member of the Enterprise Admins group to create or modify an application directory partition.

- If the DNS service was not able to create an application directory partition, the administrator can do so manually. If the partition already exists, the option to create an application directory partition will not exist.

▶ Creating an Application Directory Partition

To create an application directory partition that does not already exist, complete the following steps:

1. Open DNS from the Administrative Tools folder.
2. Right-click the desired DNS server, and choose Create Default Application Directory Partitions.
3. Follow the steps to finalize the procedure.

Aging and Scavenging

Although not enabled by default, **aging and scavenging** is a process that can be used by Windows Server 2003 DNS to clean up the DNS database when resource records are no longer required. Without this process, the DNS database would require manual maintenance to prevent server performance degradation and potential disk-space issues. The dynamic update feature of Windows Server 2003 DNS allows computers using Windows 2000, Windows XP, or Windows 2003 to add their IP address and name to the DNS database to permit them to be found on the network. When their IP address is added, a **timestamp** is placed on the record based on the current server time. Scavenging is the process of removing records that were not refreshed or updated within the specified time intervals. This will occur naturally with machines that are removed from the network. Since their records will not be updated or refreshed, all timers will expire. Aging and scavenging must be configured for both the DNS server and all desired zones. The following procedures will assist you in configuring aging and scavenging for DNS servers and zones. Figure 2-16 depicts the Zone Aging/Scavenging Properties dialog box.

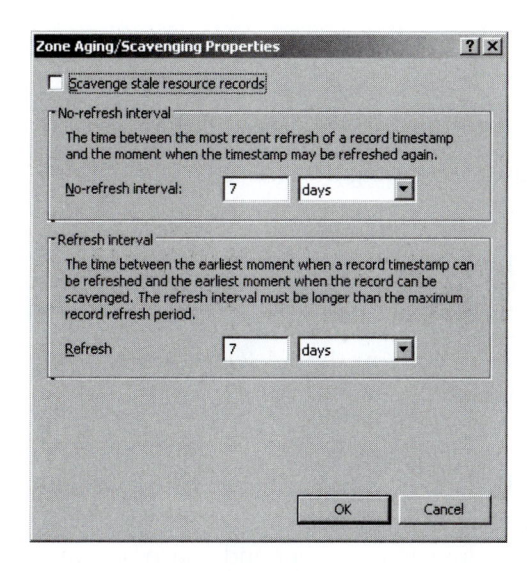

Figure 2-16 Zone Aging/Scavenging Properties dialog box

▶ Configuring a DNS Server for Aging and Scavenging

To configure the DNS server for aging and scavenging, complete the following steps:

1. Open DNS from the Administrative Tools folder.
2. Right-click the desired DNS server, and click Set Aging/Scavenging for all zones.

3. Select the Scavenge Stale Resource Records check box.

4. Modify any other desired properties, and click Apply to save any changes.

▶ **Configuring a DNS Zone for Aging and Scavenging**

To configure a DNS zone for aging and scavenging, complete the following steps:

1. Open DNS from the Administrative Tools folder.

2. Right-click the desired zone, and select Properties from the submenu.

3. Click the General tab, and click Aging.

4. Select the Scavenge Stale Resource Records check box.

5. Modify any other desired properties, and click Apply to save any changes.

> **NOTE** *DNS Aging and Scavenging Detailed information on the aging and scavenging process can be found at http://www.microsoft.com/technet/treeview/ default.asp?url=/technet/prodtechnol/windowsserver2003/proddocs/standard/ sag_DNS_imp_ManageAgingScavenging.asp.*

Verifying Forward Lookup Zones and SRV Records

Forward lookup zones are necessary for computer hostname–to–IP address mappings, which are used for name resolution by a variety of services. For example, when a user requests access to a server based on its hostname, the request is passed to a DNS server to resolve the hostname to an IP address. Most queries are based on forward lookups.

> **MORE INFO** *DNS Zones Appendix A, "DNS Overview" provides more detailed information on DNS zone types and their functions.*

▶ **Verifying Forward Lookup Zones**

To verify the creation of a forward lookup zone during the Active Directory installation, perform the following steps on a DNS server:

1. Open DNS from the Administrative Tools folder.

2. Under DNS, expand your server.

3. Expand the Forward Lookup Zones heading. You should see the currently configured forward lookup zones.

Support for SRV records is required by Active Directory in Windows 2000 and Windows Server 2003. SRV records are used by DNS to provide mappings of services to the computers that provide them. For example, when Active Directory is installed on a server, that server becomes a domain controller and it also becomes a Netlogon server. Clients attempting to authenticate to an Active Directory network need to be able to locate a Netlogon server. If a server named Server2 in the cohowinery.com domain is configured as a domain controller, it dynamically registers itself with DNS at startup. This registration includes both an A record for the server name and any appropriate SRV records for services running on the server. There will be one SRV record registered for each service the server is configured to provide. Clients attempting to authenticate to the network will use DNS to assist them in the process of finding an appropriate domain controller based on the requested service. SRV records can be found by default in the Forward Lookup zone of DNS.

When Active Directory is installed, a DNS subdomain named _msdcs.DnsDomainName is created. This subdomain contains records that reflect the specific services being provided and the servers to which these services are mapped. Each record follows a specific format beginning with the service being provided and includes information, such as protocol, domain name, time-to-live, class, priority, weight, and listening port. Much of this is useful for troubleshooting. Clients use the priority and weight fields to assist in determining which server is most appropriate to connect to requested services. There are two methods that can be used to verify the SRV records. The methods are:

- DNS Manager in the Administrative Tools folder
- Nslookup utility from the command line

▶ **Verifying SRV records with DNS Manager**

Using the DNS Manager tool, you can verify that the appropriate zone has been created, in addition to verifying the individual records themselves, by completing the following steps:

1. Open DNS from the Administrative Tools folder.
2. Expand the desired DNS server, and expand the DNS domain you wish to view.

   You should see the following entries:
   - _msdcs
   - _sites
   - _tcp
   - _udp

   In addition, you may see the following zones created for application directory partition information:
   - DomainDnsZones
   - ForestDnsZones

▶ **Verifying SRV Records with Nslookup**

Nslookup, which is a command line tool, is somewhat cumbersome at first use, but it is a powerful tool. To view the SRV records on a domain controller, complete the following steps:

1. From a command prompt, type **nslookup**, and press Enter.
2. Type **ls –t SRV** *domain* (replace the word *domain* with your domain name), and press Enter.

   SRV refers to the type of record you wish to query. It can be replaced with other record types to return additional information. For example, if you wish to view all A records stored in the domain, you would type **ls –t A** *domain*.

> **NOTE** **NSLookup Timeout** If the NSLookup Timeout command reports a timeout, you may need to configure a reverse lookup zone to receive the appropriate output. This is normal and is caused when DNS is servicing the same DNS domain as your Active Directory domain.
>
> **MORE INFO** **SRV Records** For more information on SRV records in DNS, see Appendix A, "Understanding DNS."

For domain controllers to be able to register with DNS at startup, dynamic updates must be turned on. By default, when a DNS zone is Active Directory integrated, dynamic updates are enabled and set to Secure. In this case, a client must be authenticated first before attempting to update or add information to the DNS database. This prevents unwanted or unnecessary records from being added to the database, ultimately creating performance, space, and potential security issues.

▶ Verifying Dynamic Updates

To verify that dynamic updates are turned on and secure, complete the following steps:

1. Right-click the desired zone, and click Properties.
2. View the selected type of updates for this zone. By default, if the zone is Active Directory integrated, it will be set to Secure only.

Reverse Lookup Zones

Reverse lookup zones answer a query where a client provides an IP address and DNS resolves the IP address to a hostname. This type of zone is not required or configured by default. However, it is good practice to add reverse lookup zones for troubleshooting, security checks, and reverse IP queries. A reverse lookup zone is called an in-addr.arpa domain and uses the reverse dotted decimal notation of a forward lookup zone. For example, if the forward lookup zone uses 192.168.1.200 for its IP address, the reverse lookup zone would appear as 200.1.168.192- in-addr.arpa. In addition to just the zone creation, a resource record called a **pointer (PTR) record** is necessary to map the address back to a host in the corresponding forward lookup zone.

▶ Creating Reverse Lookup Zones

To create a reverse lookup zone, complete the following steps:

1. Open DNS from the Administrative Tools folder.
2. Expand the desired server, and right-click Reverse Lookup Zone.
3. Click New Zone to begin the wizard.
4. Select the type of zone you wish to create. If this is the first reverse lookup zone, select Primary Zone. If this zone is to be stored on a domain controller running Active Directory integrated DNS, make sure the box at the bottom of this dialog box is selected. Click Next to continue.

5. Select the DNS server to which you want this zone replicated. The third option button, To All Domain Controllers In The Active Directory Domain *domainname,* is the default. Click Next to continue.

6. In the Reverse Lookup Zone Name dialog box, click the Network ID option, and complete the IP address. At completion of this step, the Reverse Lookup zone name should appear in the second option field. Click Next to continue.

7. Review the summary zone creation screen, and click Finish to complete the process.

8. Add any necessary resource records. This should include a PTR record that references the appropriate server in a forward lookup zone.

Adding a Second Domain Controller to the Forest Root Domain

During your planning of the Active Directory infrastructure, a second domain controller should be added to each domain for fault tolerance. This will provide some redundancy in case one of the domain controllers fails. In addition, since the first domain controller in the forest holds all single operations master roles, adding a second domain controller allows you to offload some of the work to another domain controller.

▶ **Adding a Second Domain Controller**

The basic steps for adding a second domain controller to the forest root domain are outlined in the following steps:

1. Install the server kernel operating system. When installing Windows Server 2003, a server is automatically a member server when it is installed in a domain until Active Directory is installed, making it a domain controller.

2. Install Active Directory, promoting this server to a domain controller by making it an additional server in an existing domain. This is the second option on the Domain Controller Type page in the Active Directory Installation Wizard.

3. Install DNS on this server manually. This will provide a second DNS server for added fault tolerance and performance in the forest. It is not necessary to configure any new zones since they already exist. The DNS Wizard prompts for zone creation by default. Select the option to create a forward and reverse lookup zone, and then select No from the confirmation page. After the installation of DNS, the Active Directory replication process automatically copies the necessary information from the existing domain controller. This can be verified by viewing the zone information after replication.

4. Transfer single operation master roles as necessary to this server. This process is discussed in detail in Chapter 4, "Global Catalog and Flexible Single Master Operations (FSMO) Roles."

MODIFYING THE ACTIVE DIRECTORY SCHEMA

The Active Directory schema will probably be modified at some time during the life of your implementation plan. Many applications used as common tools, such as e-mail, will require modification in order to add necessary objects to the database. For example, when Microsoft Exchange 2000 is installed, over 1,000 additional objects are added to the schema to support its operation. The schema content is held in the domain controller assigned the schema master role. By default, this is the first domain controller in the forest. The schema is replicated to all domain controllers in the forest during the Active Directory replication process. Planning for these changes involves an understanding of the following:

- Schema extensions are replicated to all domain controllers in the forest and have a global effect on the modified objects and attributes.

- Default system classes cannot be modified, but additional classes can be added and changed. The best example of this occurs when an application modifies the schema.

- Class and attribute additions to the schema cannot be removed. However, they can be deactivated. You can also deactivate definitions and reuse the object identifiers, which in effect allows you to change or reverse an added definition.

- When the schema is modified, it triggers replication within the forest. Planning for modification of the schema may require sensitivity to the time of day and the possible performance impact. If modifications are made during peak usage hours, users may experience some significant performance issues, in particular if Microsoft Exchange 2000 is being installed adding over 1,000 additional attributes to the schema.

- There is a certain amount of latency that can be expected before all domain controllers contain consistent schema information. This is due to the amount of time that it takes for changes and updates to make their way to all domain controllers in the forest.

As previously stated, some applications, such as Microsoft Exchange 2000, modify the schema and add new objects that contain attributes to the Active Directory database. You can also extend the schema manually using the Active Directory Schema snap-in. The following requirements must be met for the schema extension to be available:

- You must be a member of the Schema Admins group.

- The Active Directory Schema snap-in should be installed on the domain controller holding the Schema Operations master role.

- Ensure that you have Schema Administrator or equivalent permissions to modify the schema master information.

> **NOTE** **Modifying the Active Directory Schema** Many technical white papers and the Windows Server 2003 Resource Kit caution against modifying the schema unless it is absolutely necessary. Extending the schema can create problems that might be irreversible. Several of these concerns are documented at: http://www.microsoft.com/windows2000/en/advanced/help/default.asp?url=/windows2000/en/advanced/help/sag_ADschema_15.htm.

Installing the Schema Management Snap-in

The Schema Management snap-in is not installed by default in Windows Server 2003. To enable any type of editing of the Active Directory schema, it is necessary to have the snap-in available. Adding the Active Directory Schema snap-in to a **Microsoft Management Console (MMC)** window is the simplest way to modify the schema. MMC is a graphic tool similar to other tools included with Windows Server 2003. It allows you to customize a set of tools you wish to have available for easy management.

▶ **Adding the Active Directory Scheme Snap-in**

Complete the following steps to add the snap-in to the list of MMC choices:

1. From a command prompt, type **regsvr32 schmmgmt.dll**.
2. Close the Command Prompt window, click Start, and then select Run.
3. Type **mmc /a** in the dialog box, and click OK.
4. From the File menu, select Add/Remove Snap-in.
5. Click Add to see the list of available snap-ins.
6. Double-click Active Directory Schema in the list.
7. Click Close, and click OK.

If you want to save this console for future use, click File and then click Save. Then name your new console. MMC gives the console an .msc extension. By adding this step, you can simply open the console or create a shortcut on your desktop for easy accessibility.

> **CAUTION** **Performing Administrative Tasks Using Run As** *When performing administrative tasks, you should not be logged on as an administrator at a domain controller. Instead, it is recommended that administrative tasks be performed using a normal user account and the Run As program. Details on the Run As program and the security issues surrounding this warning are further explained in Chapter 6, "Security Planning and Administrative Delegation."*

> **NOTE** **Object Identifiers in the Schema** *Each object you add to the schema should have a valid Object Identifier (OID). As part of the X.500 structure, OIDs must be globally unique and are represented by a hierarchical dotted decimal notation string that is similar to an IP address. If you are familiar with the Simple Network Management Protocol (SNMP) namespace, you will recognize the OID structure. An example of a complete OID might be 1.55678.5.15. The International Organization for Standardization (ISO) has the number 1 and is responsible for generating OIDs for new public objects. The ISO is the root authority for all OIDs. The number 1 is used as a prefix for any other numbers assigned. Typically, each organization is assigned a number by the ISO. For example, if Coho Winery, Inc., is assigned the number 55678, all objects created for Coho Winery would have the prefix 1.55678. Internally, Coho Winery could then assign numbers to developers and applications that would be referenced in the X.500 structure as objects are created.*
>
> *OIDs can be obtained directly from the ISO at http://www.iso.org, from the American National Standards Institute (ANSI) at http://www.ansi.org, or by using the OSIGEN.EXE tool, another method for generating the OIDs, from the Windows 2000 Server Resource Kit.*

Modifications to the schema should be made only if required. There are many things in the schema that can go awry if changes are made incorrectly. To protect against possible midnight restores of a corrupted Active Directory, be sure you fully understand the ramifications of a change prior to making it. For example, if a change is made that renames an object attribute, it will be difficult to reverse the change after the fact. If the original attribute is called by another script or program, that script or program will not function properly until the issue is resolved. In addition, Microsoft recommends adding administrators who are to perform modifications to the schema to the Schema Admins group only for the duration of the task. Test any modifications in an isolated environment that closely matches your actual production environment before releasing the changes to the production network. Planning for modifications can sometimes delay the deployment of a desired application or feature, but is well worth the effort if something does not function as designed in the test environment. You may want to institute a Change Management Process (CMP) infrastructure prior to beginning modifications. The CMP will permit tracking of exactly what changes were made to the schema and who made those changes.

RAISING THE DOMAIN AND FOREST FUNCTIONAL LEVELS

Using the features of Windows Server 2003, you will need to raise domain functional levels. Upon raising all domains to the Windows Server 2003 functional level, you can proceed to the final phase of raising the forest functional level. Chapter 1, "Overview of Active Directory," mapped out the differences between each level in terms of supported operating systems and functionality. In this chapter, the focus is on the how-to steps for raising the functionality level and requirements for doing so.

Domain functional levels are available to provide backwards compatibility with previous Windows Server operating systems. Migrating your network to one consistent platform provides many administrative benefits and can lower your overall network cost of ownership. Prior to raising the domain functional levels, verify that there is not a need for any previous Microsoft Windows network operating systems in the domain. Careful planning will be required with regard to each company and their current network structure. If an organization is interested in any future acquisitions or mergers, raising the domain level could have an impact and this should be taken into careful consideration. Consider an enterprise organization that is growing rapidly by buying up the competition. It would be safe to assume that not all of the new acquisitions are running Windows Server 2003. Deciding how to best integrate network structures into your corporate enterprise will be a challenge. Many networks will have a mixed bag of operating systems. The Windows Server 2003 family brings with it several new enhancements to assist in making the transition easier. Some of the key facts and requirements for raising domain and forest functional levels are:

- A one-way operation: raised domain and forest functional levels cannot be reversed without a complete reinstallation of the domain.
- Each domain can be handled independently, thereby allowing a phased approach to increasing functionality. This allows corporations sufficient transition time to upgrade each location or domain. Some locations may need to purchase new hardware or upgrade existing infrastructure prior to a migration.

- The forest functional level cannot be raised until all domains in a forest have been raised to at least Windows 2000 native.

- You must be logged on as a member of the Domain Admins group to raise the domain functionality.

- You must be logged on as a member of the Enterprise Admins group to raise the forest functionality.

You can raise the domain or forest functionality by using Active Directory Domains And Trusts.

▶ Raising the Domain Functional Level

Complete the following steps to raise the domain functional level:

1. Open Active Directory Domains And Trusts from the Administrative Tools folder.

2. Right-click the domain you wish to raise, and select Raise Domain Functional Level.

3. Choose the level you wish to achieve from Select An Available Domain Functional Level, and then click Raise. You will be presented with a dialog box explaining the irreversible nature of this procedure. Click Raise to continue.

▶ Raising the Forest Functional Level

To raise the forest functional level, complete the following steps:

1. Open Active Directory Domains And Trusts from the Administrative Tools folder.

2. Right-click the Active Directory Domains And Trusts icon in the console tree, and select Raise Forest Functional Level.

3. If your domains have not all been raised to at least Windows 2000 native, you will receive an error indicating that raising the forest functional level cannot take place yet. If all domains have met the domain functionality criteria of Windows 2000 native or Windows Server 2003, you can click Raise to proceed.

ESTABLISHING AND MANAGING TRUST RELATIONSHIPS

Trust relationships exist to make resource accessibility easier between domains. Most trust relationships are established by default during the creation of the forest structure. However, there are four trust types that can be manually established in Windows Server 2003. They include:

- **Shortcut** A trust established to shorten the number of *hops* required to gain access to a domain. These are commonly used to link child domains in separate domain trees together. The source and target child domains do not need to be at the same level within the forest structure.

Example: Sam's user account resides in the south.cohowinery.com domain. Sam needs to gain access to a shared folder in the east.cohovineyard.com domain. Sam is able to do this, but he complains that it seems to take a very long time to establish the shared folder connection. Solution: As shown in Figure 2-17, you create a shortcut trust between the south.cohowinery.com domain and the east.cohovineyard.com domain. This creates a direct link from Sam's domain to his target shared folder and avoids the tree-walking process previously required through the forest root domain.

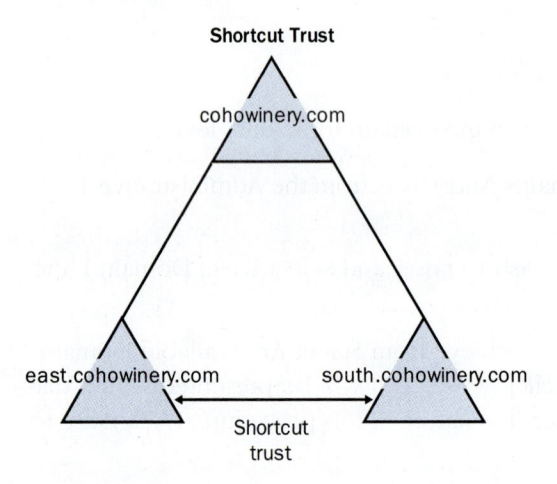

Figure 2-17 Shortcut trust

- **Cross-forest** A trust established to allow access to resources in separate forest structures. These are one-way by default. To share resources across both forests, two cross-forest trusts, from each forest mapped to its partner forest, needs to be manually established.

Example: Coho Winery, Inc., has just completed the acquisition of Coho Vineyard. Coho Vineyard has an established Windows Server 2003 forest that you wish to be able to access. For users in both forests to gain access to certain resources, you have decided to create a cross-forest trust. For users in both forests to be able to gain resource access, you must establish two one-way trusts. Once the trusts are established, it is possible to assign permissions to the appropriate resources. Figure 2-18 illustrates this example.

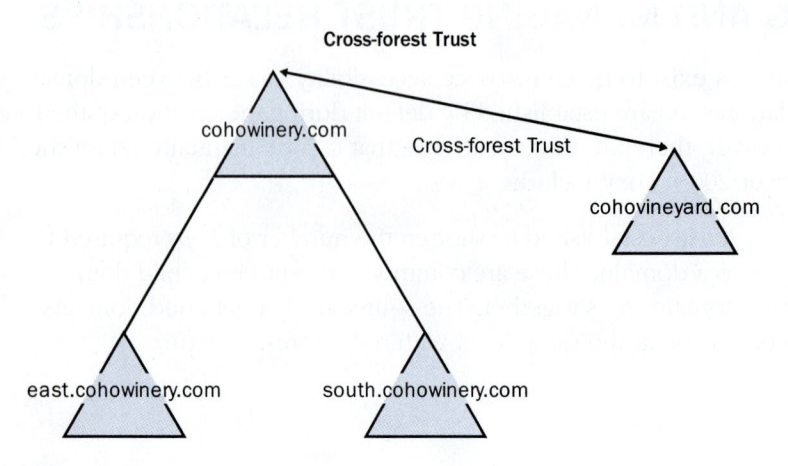

Figure 2-18 Cross-forest trust

- **External** A manual trust established between a domain in one forest and a domain in another forest. This is a more direct trust establishment than a cross-forest trust. An external trust allows a domain in one forest access to a domain in another forest, without going through the forest root domains. This provides faster accessibility between the child domains due to the direct connection.

    Example: Coho Winery, Inc., has just completed the acquisition of Coho Vineyard. Coho Vineyard has an established Windows Server 2003 domain that you wish to be able to access. Instead of creating a cross-forest trust, you have decided to simply create an external trust from one of your child domains to one of the child domains in the Coho Vineyard forest. You have made this decision for both performance and security reasons. Once the appropriate one-way trusts have been established, you can assign resource permissions as needed.

- **Realm** A trust established with a non-Windows platform that uses Kerberos as the authentication method. This is helpful to allow users from a non-Windows based network access to resources in a Windows Server 2003 domain.

    Example: Coho Winery, Inc., has acquired a company that is using a Linux computer for its network. You wish to be able to provide the Linux users with accessibility to the cohowinery.com domain. To do this, you establish a realm trust that will allow users in the Linux network to gain access to the Windows Server 2003 domain. Figure 2-19 illustrates this example.

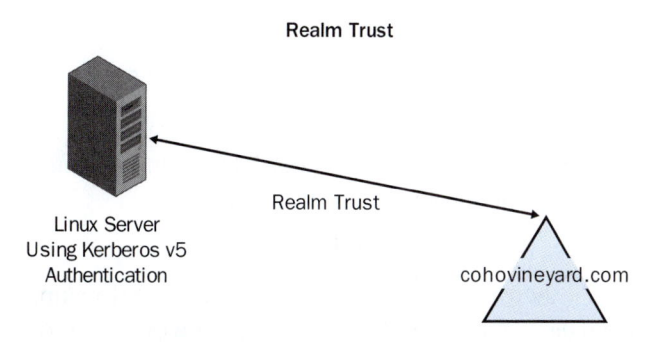

Figure 2-19 Realm trust

Active Directory Domains And Trusts can be used to establish trusts. When using the New Trust Wizard in this utility, you have the option of deciding if the trust will be one-way incoming, one-way outgoing, or two-way. A *one-way incoming trust* establishes that users from another domain, external trust source, or realm can gain access to resources in your domain. However, users in your source domain would not be able to gain access to resources in the trusted external domain. For example, suppose a company wishes to allow a vendor or other subsidiary to gain access to certain resources such as product lists or order information. Generally, the access would be limited, but would allow for the vendor or supplier to gain access to necessary business-related data. It may not be necessary or desirable for the vendor to allow the same permissions for your company to access their data.

A **one-way trust** allows this type of situation to take place securely. A *one-way outgoing trust* is the exact opposite of a one-way incoming trust. The vendor or supplier wishes to allow your organization accessibility, but you do not want them to gain access to your resources. If both organizations choose to allow access, a *two-way trust* is available and would achieve the same goal as establishing both a one-way incoming and a one-way outgoing trust. To establish domain-related trusts, you must be a member of the Domain Admins group. To establish cross-forest trusts, you must be a member of the Enterprise Admins group. If you have the appropriate administrative privileges in both the source and target forest or domain, you can create both sides of the trust relationship. To create a cross-forest trust, a secondary forward lookup zone needs to be created and pointed to the forest root of each side of the trust.

▶ **Creating Trust Relationships**

To create trust relationships, complete the following steps:

1. Open Active Directory Domains And Trusts from the Administrative Tools folder.

2. In the console tree on the left, right-click the domain for which you wish to establish a trust, and select Properties.

3. Click the Trusts tab, and click New Trust to begin the New Trust Wizard. Click Next to continue.

4. On the Trust Name page, type the DNS name of the domain, and click Next.

5. On the Trust page, select the desired trust type.

6. On the Direction Of Trust page, select the type and direction of the desired trust.

7. You may also wish to determine the desired permissions by modifying the trust properties. You have the choice of the following:

    a. Allow authentication for all resources in the local domain.

    b. Allow authentication only for selected resources in the local domain. Use this option when each domain belongs to a separate organization

Now that you understand how to create manual trusts, the next section discusses how to verify the functionality of these trusts.

Verifying Trusts

Once a manual trust has been established, you can verify the trust using either Active Directory Domains And Trusts or the Netdom tool at the command line. Because automatic trusts are part of the default functionality provided by Active Directory, only shortcut, external, and cross-forest trusts can be verified. Shortcut, external, and cross-forest trusts must be manually established and therefore manual verification is required.

▶ Verifying Trusts Using Active Directory Domains And Trusts

To verify trusts using Active Directory Domains And Trusts, complete the following steps:

1. In Active Directory Domains And Trusts, right-click the domain for which you want to verify trusts, and select Properties.

2. On the Trusts tab, select either Domains Trusted By This Domain (Outgoing), or Domains that Trust This Domain (Incoming). Select the appropriate trust, and click Properties.

3. Click Validate. At this point you will be prompted to answer Yes or No to validation of the trust. Choosing No requires the same procedure to be completed at the opposite end of the trust link to determine that both sides of the trust can be seen. Choosing Yes requires that you supply an administrative account and password for the reciprocal domain.

▶ Verifying Trusts Using Netdom

To verify trusts using Netdom, complete the following steps:

1. Open a command prompt, and type the following:

    netdom trust *TrustingDomainName* /d:*TrustedDomainName* /verify

    TrustingDomainName should be replaced with the domain that is allowing access to resources, while the *TrustedDomainName* is the domain that needs to gain access.

2. Press Enter.

    NOTE Using Netdom The use of Netdom requires the Windows Server 2003 Support tools to be available. For complete instructions on how to install the support tools, see http://www.microsoft.com/technet/treeview/default.asp?url=/technet/prodtechnol/windowsserver2003/proddocs/standard/tools_howto.asp.

Revoking a Trust

In some cases it may be necessary to remove an established trust. If a corporation relinquishes its business relationship with a supplier that was trusted, you will need to revoke the trust to renew the network security. Any type of access from the outside can be considered a breach in security. You can use Active Directory Domains And Trusts or Netdom to revoke a trust.

▶ Revoking a Trust Using Active Directory Domains And Trusts

To revoke a trust using Active Directory Domains And Trusts, complete the following steps:

1. In Active Directory Domains And Trusts, right-click the domain for which you want to verify trusts, and select Properties.

2. On the Trusts tab, select either Domains Trusted By This Domain (Outgoing), or Domains That Trust This Domain (Incoming). Select the appropriate trust, and click Properties.

3. Click Remove.

4. Complete the same procedure for the other end of the trust relationship.

▶ **Revoking a Trust Using Netdom**

To revoke a trust using Netdom, complete the following steps:

1. Open a command prompt and type:

   netdom trust *TrustingDomainName* **/d:***TrustedDomainName* **/remove**

2. Press Enter.

3. Complete the same procedure for the other end of the trust relationship.

CREATING AND DELETING USER PRINCIPAL NAMES

As your organization grows due to normal expansion, acquisitions, mergers, and new geographic locations, the Active Directory structure can become difficult to navigate. Users needing to gain access to more than one tree structure within the forest can find it cumbersome to recall what is contained in each domain. The distributed system can be cumbersome to navigate. To alleviate this confusion and provide a simple means for users to gain global access to the forest structure, Active Directory supports **User Principal Names (UPNs)**. UPNs are stored in the global catalog, which allows them to be available forest-wide. In addition, if a cross-forest trust exists, a UPN can be used to gain access to resources in a trusting forest. A UPN follows a naming convention that can reflect either the forest root domain or another alias configured by the administrator. The structure of a username follows this format: *username@domain_name*. One common practice is to configure the UPN to match the e-mail ID of the user. In the case of a company with different internal and external domain names, using the external name for the UPN is preferred. This is transparent to the user. When creating accounts, the default UPN suffix may need to be modified. To modify the default suffix for a UPN, you must have Enterprise Administrator credentials since this is a forest-wide operation.

▶ **Modifying the Default Suffix for a UPN**

Complete the following steps to change the default UPN suffix:

1. Open Active Directory Domains And Trusts from the Administrative Tools folder.

2. Right-click Active Directory Domains And Trusts, and choose Properties.

3. Click the UPN Suffix tab, type in the new suffix, and click Add. You can type in more than one suffix if your forest has more than one tree. Click OK when you are done.

When creating a new user account, the new suffixes will be available for you to assign to users as shown in Figure 2-20.

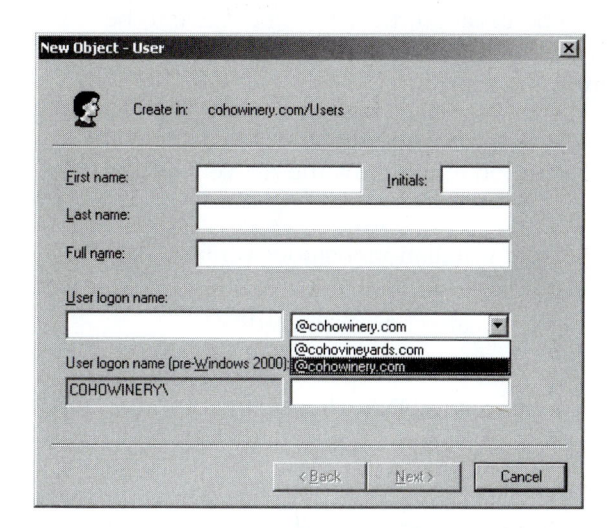

Figure 2-20 Selecting the UPN in Active Directory Users And Computers

CAUTION **UPN Removal** *Removing a UPN suffix that is in use will cause users to be unable to log on to the domain. You will receive a warning message stating this if you attempt to remove a UPN.*

SUMMARY

- Active Directory requires DNS to be installed. DNS does not have to be installed on a Windows Server 2003 machine, but the version of DNS used does need to support SRV records for Active Directory to function.

- Planning the forest and domain structure should include a checklist that can be referenced for dialog information required by the Active Directory Installation Wizard.

- Verification of a solid Active Directory installation includes verifying DNS zones and the creation of SRV records. Additional items, such as reverse lookups, aging, and scavenging, should also be configured.

- Application directory partitions are automatically created when Active Directory integrated zones are configured in DNS. These partitions allow for replica placement within the forest structure.

- System classes of the schema cannot be modified, but additional classes can be added. Classes and attributes cannot be deleted, but they can be deactivated.

- Planning forest and domain functionality is dependent on the need for downlevel operating system compatibility. Raising a forest or domain functional level is a procedure that cannot be reversed.

- Four types of manual trusts can be created: shortcut, external, cross-forest, and realm trusts. Manual trusts can be created by using either Active Directory Domains And Trusts or Netdom at a command line.

- UPNs provide a mechanism to make access to resources in multiple domains user-friendly. UPNs follow a naming format similar to e-mail addresses. You must be a member of the Enterprise Admins group in order to add additional suffixes that can be assigned at user object creation.

EXERCISE

Exercise 2-1: Planning for an Active Directory Installation

Margie's Travel has decided to install a Windows Server 2003 network. They plan to use the name margiestravel.com as their DNS name since it is already registered with the InterNic. Their headquarters is located in Detroit and they have additional branch locations in Chicago, Dallas, and Phoenix. They want to maintain a separate child domain in the forest representing each of the branches for ease of management. Create a pen and paper drawing of how you would design this forest structure. Be sure to include the recommended domain names within the forest.

REVIEW QUESTIONS

1. Which of the following are requirements for Active Directory installation?
   a. An IP address of a DNS server
   b. Any version of DNS
   c. Windows Server 2003 Web Edition
   d. An NTFS partition
   e. Dynamic Host Configuration Protocol (DHCP)

2. What two tools allow you to begin the Active Directory installation process?

3. What term refers to the first domain created on the network?

4. Which of the following are key points related to the Sysvol folder structure in Active Directory?
   a. It contains user data that should be backed up.
   b. It contains replicated data such as logon scripts.
   c. It contains the operating system boot files.
   d. It must be placed on a FAT32 partition.
   e. It must be placed on an NTFS partition.

5. Before you are able to create an application directory partition, you must be a member of which group?
   a. Domain Users
   b. Domain Admins
   c. Schema Admins
   d. Enterprise Admins

6. When trying to connect to a shared folder by typing \\SERVER1\DATA at a prompt, John receives an error that SERVER1 cannot be located. List three possible reasons why this could happen and the steps you would take to verify them.

7. You are the administrator for a large automotive parts company. Management has just released the names of several vendors that you will need to allow access to network resources. These vendors either have Microsoft Windows NT 4.0, Windows 2000, or Windows Server 2003 domains. You have established a domain that holds all the information that vendors will need to access within your forest. The vendors want to be able to gain access to these resources without permitting access for your company to their network. What do you need to do to make this happen?

8. What are the default names of the application directory partitions created by the DNS installation within the Active Directory Installation Wizard?

9. Using nslookup's /? switch, what would be the syntax needed to view all SRV records?

10. You have just installed a new application that has modified the schema by adding a new object. Another administrator at a different location does not have this object listed on his domain controller. What is the most likely reason for this? What should he do to resolve the problem?

CASE SCENARIOS

Scenario 2-1: Planning a Migration

You are an IT consultant working with a mid-sized corporation to improve its network. Currently the company is running six Windows NT 4 servers in three separate domains. The workstations run various versions of Microsoft Windows, including Windows 98, Windows 95, and Windows NT 4 Workstation. There are also several new Windows XP Professional machines being used by management. The company has decided to migrate to Windows Server 2003 using Active Directory in order to take advantage of centralized administration and better security. To assist you in consulting with your customer, answer the following questions.

1. What considerations should you make during the migration planning?
2. What recommendations will you make?
3. What functional level should be set initially?
4. Prepare an initial plan based on your answers and be prepared to share it with others.

Scenario 2-2: DNS Naming

The same client discussed in Scenario 2-1 already has a DNS name registered with the Internet. They use it for their Web site, which allows customers to access their product database and place orders online. They would like to use the same name for their internal network, but you have been advised that using the internal network may affect network security. What options would you suggest they explore to allow for some naming consistency while providing internal network security?

CHAPTER 3
WORKING WITH ACTIVE DIRECTORY SITES

Upon completion of this chapter, you will be able to:

- Define and manage sites and site links.
- Determine a site strategy based on the physical network infrastructure.
- Use Active Directory Sites And Services to configure replication.
- Understand the differences between intrasite and intersite replication.
- Explain the role of the Intersite Topology Generator (ISTG) and knowledge consistency checker (KCC) in site replication.
- Optimize replication by configuring bridgehead servers and site link bridging.
- Monitor replication using Replmon, Dcdiag, and Repadmin.

The multi-master replication model of Microsoft Windows Server 2003 requires that all domain controllers from each domain participate in the replication process for that domain. Replication is the process of duplicating information for purposes of fault tolerance and redundancy. As stated previously in this textbook, Active Directory is a replicated database containing user, group, printer, and computer accounts. Windows 2003 Active Directory domains do not replicate information with foreign domains, even though the other domain may be part of the same forest. This process of replicating the database and ensuring that updates to the database occur in a timely manner requires some definition of how this information is passed within a domain and throughout the forest. Active Directory sites are the means by which a **replica ring** is established and replication links are configured. All servers participating with each other in the replication of the Active Directory database form a replica ring. This chapter focuses on the details regarding the creation, configuration, replication, and monitoring of Active Directory sites.

OVERVIEW OF SITES AND SITE LINKS

Active Directory is made up of separate logical and physical structures. The logical structure defines the resource management structure of Active Directory consisting of forests, domains, trees, and organizational units (OUs). In contrast, the physical structure defines how information passes through the network and includes local area network (LAN) and wide area network (WAN) links, in addition to Active Directory sites and domain controllers. The logical structure can be viewed using Active Directory Users And Computers. The physical structure can be viewed and managed using Active Directory Sites And Services. As discussed in Chapter 1, "Overview of Active Directory," sites are based on IP subnets within the network. Subnets are created within Active Directory based on the physical network design. When logging on, network clients rely on the site topology to provide them with the closest available domain controller and other network resources. Domain controllers use the site topology to establish replica partners that will provide efficiency and keep the Active Directory database consistent. Upon the installation of the forest root domain controller in an Active Directory forest, a single site, the first subnet in the Active Directory forest, is established and named **Default-First-Site-Name**. This can be seen in the Active Directory Sites And Services tool as shown in Figure 3-1. The forest root domain controller *server object* is placed within the Servers folder of this site. As we will discuss later, the site can be renamed to more accurately reflect a physical location.

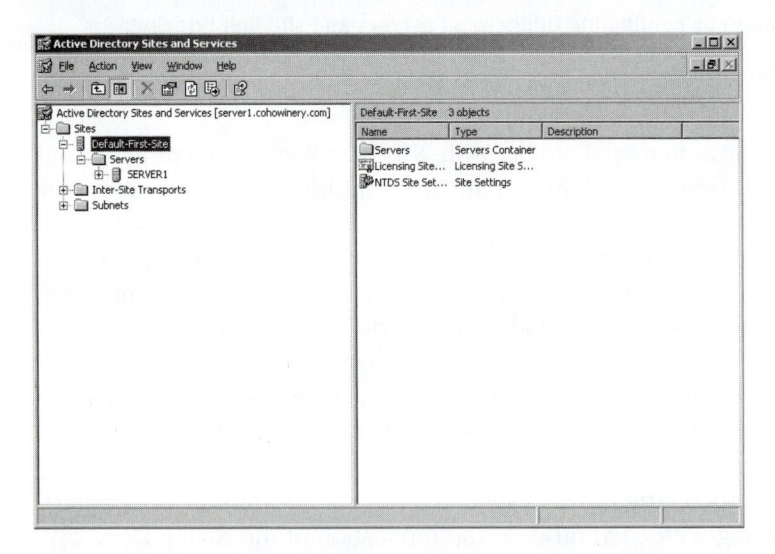

Figure 3-1 Default-First-Site-Name in Active Directory Sites And Services

After the first domain controller is installed and placed in the Default-First-Site-Name container, the domain administrator has the responsibility to further customize the sites to allow replication to take place between appropriate domain controllers. In general, all sites have the following characteristics:

- Sites are defined by IP subnets that are *well connected*. Well-connected is a generalization that simply means the network infrastructure in a site is fast and reliable, commonly understood to be a LAN.

- Sites organize the replication process by defining groups of servers that replicate with one another.

- During the logon process, the clients use sites to assist in determining appropriate domain controllers that will be used for Active Directory authentication.

- Sites are independent of the domain structure. Sites can contain multiple domains as shown in Figure 3-2, or a domain can contain multiple sites as shown in Figure 3-3.

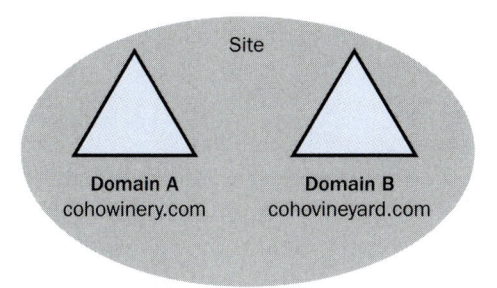

Figure 3-2 Site containing multiple domains

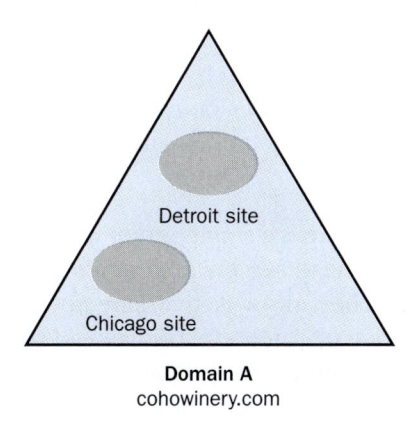

Figure 3-3 Domain containing multiple sites

Planning a site topology should be done as part of the Active Directory design process, which precedes the actual Active Directory deployment. Since sites are based on IP addresses, establishing a site topology prior to installing domain controllers allows you to take advantage of the automatic placement of a domain controller in its appropriate site. During the installation of a new domain controller, the domain controller is automatically placed in the site corresponding to the network address portion of the domain controller's IP address. However, if the sites are not created prior to adding a domain controller, the new domain controller will be placed in the Default-First-Site-Name container, requiring you to move it later. Creating sites according to your IP topology design before the Active Directory rollout saves you time and effort and delivers a more robust Active Directory implementation to the end users.

Sites and the Replication Process

The **replication topology** is created with the idea that all domain controllers in a domain should communicate Active Directory information to each other, in addition to communicating forest-wide information with other domains. The network topology defines the path used by replication traffic on the network and defines the basis for how Active Directory information is distributed. Replication is designed to efficiently track changes and provide fault tolerance to the Active Directory database. Replication occurs when one of the following conditions is met:

- An object is added or removed from Active Directory.
- The value of an attribute has changed.
- The name of an object has changed.

Tracking changes and determining which objects need to be replicated are done using a combination of several methods. First **Update Sequence Numbers** (USNs) are assigned by domain controllers when an object or attribute has changed. Consider a USN analogous to a software version number. The higher the number, the more recent the changes are with regard to the original version. If a property change occurs on a user account such as a password change, the USN number is incremented by one. Next a **timestamp** is placed on each change that occurs. If the same user changed his or her password several times, each change is stamped with the time that the change occurred. Active Directory uses both parts (USNs and timestamps) of the object's tracking method to determine which attribute value is the most recent.

When replicating between sites, a **bridgehead server** is a single server in each site selected to perform site-to-site replication. Bridgehead servers are the *gatekeepers* of Active Directory replication between sites. They allow Active Directory to update only one domain controller in a site. Once updated, the bridgehead server then proceeds to update the remainder of its domain controller partners with the newly replicated information. For example, suppose the WAN link is down for several hours between two locations of a corporate network. During this time, changes are made to objects and attributes. The USNs and timestamps of the changes are compared with those on the bridgehead server. If the same object is modified at both ends of the WAN when the link was down, the USN will be incremented to the same number. When this occurs, the timestamp is compared and the latest timestamp decides which object is the most recent. After determining what updated object is the authoritative object, the bridgehead server contacts its partner bridgehead servers located on the other side of its WAN connections and replicates the new Active Directory changes to the designated bridgehead servers, if necessary. Once the partner bridgehead servers are updated, they will in turn continue to replicate the newly obtained information with other partner domain controllers in the same site. When the complete propagation of a partition's objects and attributes has taken place at all domain controllers within a site, **convergence** has occurred.

To understand the details of how replication actually works, you need to understand the difference between **intrasite replication** and **intersite replication**.

The functional details and roles provided by these replication methods are described in the following sections.

Intrasite Replication

Intrasite replication takes place between domain controllers in the same domain and in the same site as shown in Figure 3-4. The knowledge consistency checker (KCC) uses an algorithmic process to map the logical, pre-existing network topology between the domain controllers, and determines when they should replicate and with whom they should replicate. The guiding principle involved is the *Rule of 3*, which states that no single domain controller should be more than three network hops away from an originating domain controller. This topology is fully automated and does not require administrator intervention, unless the administrator has a definite business reason for manually configuring the KCC topology. There is a significant disadvantage to the manual configuration of these links, which will be addressed in the next section. A site containing more than one subnet requires the KCC to determine which domain controllers belong in each site. The subnet mask identifies which domain controllers are located logically closest to each other, providing the KCC with the necessary information to determine replication partners. The KCC is a service that runs on domain controllers as part of the Local Security Authority (LSA) service. It cannot be deactivated or removed.

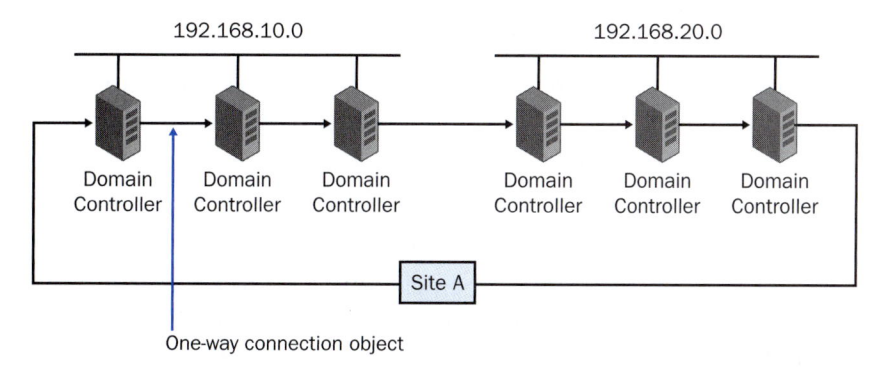

Figure 3-4 Intrasite replication

Since Active Directory has four different partitions—the domain, schema, configuration, and application partitions—the information within these partitions is replicated within a site. Domain partition information is replicated to all member domain controllers within a domain, while application partition information is replicated based on how this service has been administratively configured. Information that is forest-wide, such as the content of the schema and configuration partitions, is replicated to all domain controllers in all domains in the forest. Each partition can be referred to as a naming context and has a topology for replication based on its content. This topology defines which servers replicate their naming context information with each other.

As domain controllers are added to a site, they become part of the replica ring. Servers in the ring notify neighboring servers of changes that will be replicated at the next replication interval. The connections created between domain controllers by the KCC are named **connection objects**. The connection objects function as one-way paths within a site. Connection objects can be viewed under the NT Directory Service (NTDS) properties within Active Directory Sites And Services.

▶ **Viewing Connection Objects**

To view the connection objects, complete the following steps:

1. Open Active Directory Sites And Services.
2. Expand the Sites folder, the desired site, and then the Servers folder.
3. Expand the server name for which you wish to view connection objects, and right-click NTDS Settings. Select Properties.
4. Select the Connections tab, and note the replication partners.
5. Click Cancel to close the dialog box.

The KCC runs every 15 minutes and analyzes the best path and placement for connection objects. If a domain controller or a link between domain controllers has failed, the KCC automatically updates the topology, removing this connection from the list of possible replication paths. By default, intrasite replication is configured to minimize **latency** to allow changes to take place quickly. Latency is the amount of time or delay it takes for changes to be replicated to all participating domain controllers. Several means by which to minimize latency are as follows:

- The KCC creates a dual-counter rotating ring for the replication path. If one domain controller in the ring fails, traffic is routed in the opposite direction to allow replication to continue.

- As the site grows, additional connection objects are created to ensure that no more than three hops for replication exist between domain controllers.

- Intrasite replication traffic is not compressed, resulting in fewer CPU cycles at each domain controller during a replication event.

- Domain controllers notify each other when changes need to be replicated. Each domain controller will hold a change for five minutes before forwarding it. Since the maximum number of hops between domain controllers is three, the maximum replication latency for changes to reach their final destination is 15 minutes. When a change is marked as urgent, replication is triggered immediately, bypassing the 15-minute default. A security sensitive change such as an account lockout or password change is considered urgent and will trigger immediate replication.

NOTE Manual Replication Paths Although the KCC process of creating a replication path is fully automatic, it is possible to create manual connection objects between domain controllers within the same domain. Manual replication paths allow the administrator to override the replication topology created by the KCC. Once a manual connection object is created, all automatic connection objects are ignored.

To view the current connection objects, do Exercise 3-1 now.

Multiple Domain Intrasite Replication

When there are multiple domains in a site, each domain maintains its own independent replication topology. Schema and configuration naming context information from all domains replicates forest-wide. Consider the example in Figure 3-5.

Domain A and Domain B coexist within the same site. All domain information for Domain A replicates with Domain A servers only. The same is true of Domain B. However, the schema and configuration information replicates to all domain controllers in both domains due to the forest-wide nature of the information in both partitions.

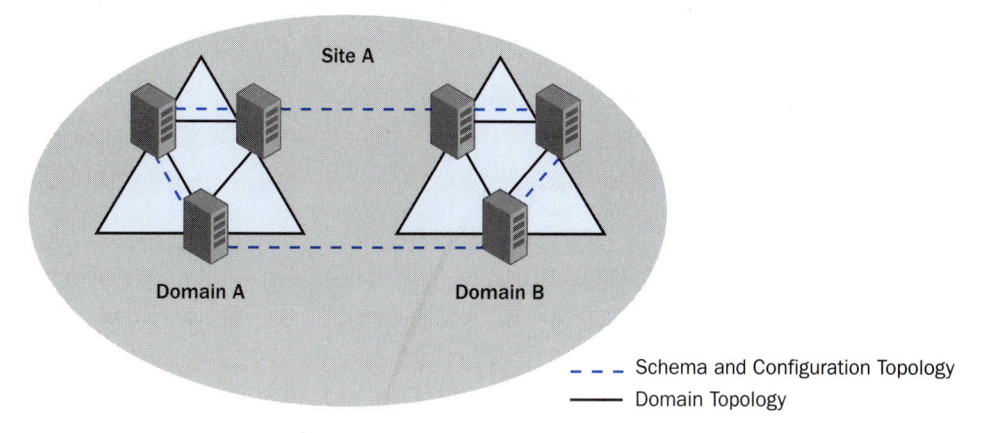

Figure 3-5 Multiple domain intrasite replication

Intersite Replication

If all Active Directory information was replicated only within a site, there would be no way to share object information in the global network. The enterprise network would be made up of many LANs that could not share resources. The idea of centralized administration and single sign-on from anywhere on the network would not be feasible. Recalling that each site consists of one or more IP subnets connected by fast and reliable links, we can now look at how these sites communicate with each other to form one enterprise network.

Figure 3-6 illustrates a multiple site network and will assist in understanding the concept of intersite replication. Site names generally reflect the name of a physical location and include domain controllers that participate in the domain replication process. The **subnet objects** reflect the physical network and, at a higher level, so do the sites. This is true because the sites are linked to the subnets that are physically supporting them. Consider a computer training company that has a network located in Chicago with four buildings connected by high-speed links; the subnets within these buildings could be part of the same site. If you add to this network a remote training site located in Minneapolis, you will need to create an additional site with subnets that reflect the location's IP address scheme. When a domain controller is installed at the Minneapolis location and configured for the same forest as the Chicago network, **site links** need to be created for replication to take place between Chicago and Minneapolis. A site link is a logical, transitive connection between two or more sites that mirrors the routed connections between networks and allows replication to occur. One domain controller within each site runs the Intersite Topology Generator (ISTG) process. ISTG is a derivative of the KCC and is responsible for selecting a bridgehead server and mapping the topology to be used for replication between sites.

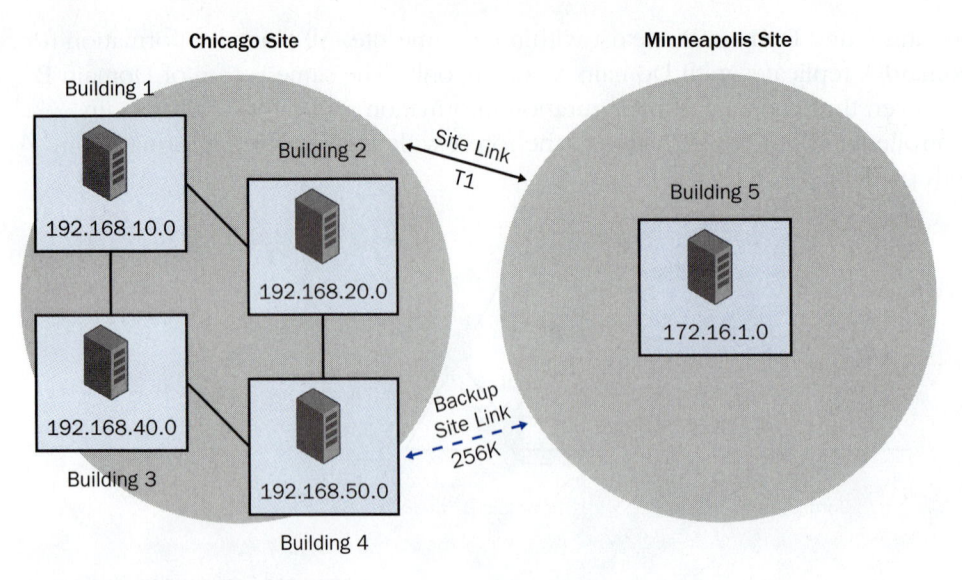

Figure 3-6 Intersite replication

Administratively created site links have the following characteristics:

- There must be two or more sites that need to communicate using the same protocol.
- The site link objects are manually defined.
- The site link objects correspond to the WAN links connecting the sites.
- The ISTG uses the site links to establish replication between locations.

Intersite replication should be configured to minimize bandwidth usage. Unlike intrasite replication, intersite replication can be configured to compress the replication information to assist in minimizing link utilization. When site link objects are created, they require three attributes to be configured to allow the administrator to control replication. These three attributes of site link objects are as follows:

- Cost
- Schedule
- Frequency

Cost Assigning cost to a link object allows the administrator to define the path that replication will take. If there is more than one path that can be used to replicate the directory, cost assignments will determine which path is chosen first. A lower-numbered cost value represents a preferred path over a higher-numbered cost value. Cost values can use a value of 1 to 99,999. There is no particular numbering scheme used here; instead, the values chosen are relational only to one another. The default cost value is 100.

Schedule The schedule of the site link object determines when the link can be used to replicate information. This is usually set to reflect off-peak business hours to ensure that WAN link bandwidth is not bogged down by replication traffic.

Frequency Frequency provides the *how often* information regarding the replication schedule. Replication will take place only during scheduled hours, but within that scheduled time, it can take place as often as the frequency attribute permits.

The default frequency is 180 minutes, but it can be configured for as little as every 15 minutes and as much as once per week.

Figure 3-7 illustrates the attributes described previously. Note the cost attributes and the WAN link speeds with which they are associated.

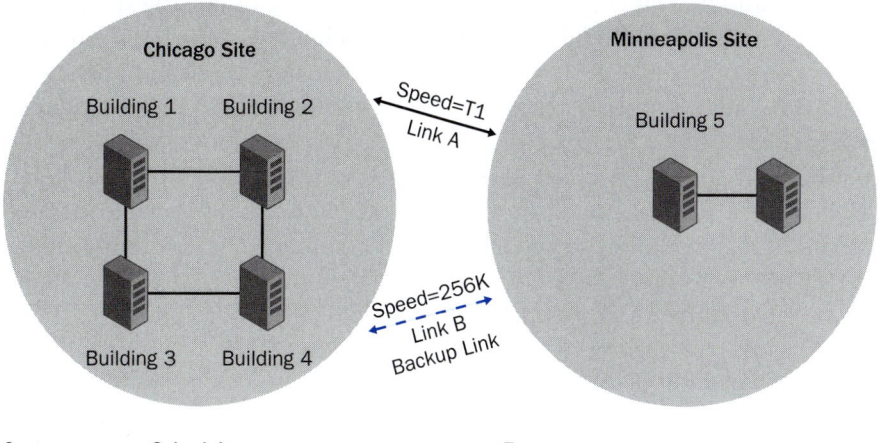

Cost
Link A = 100
Link B = 300

Schedule
Link A & B both set to replicate
Monday-Friday, 12 A.M. until 6 A.M.

Frequency
Link A & B left at 180-minute interval

Figure 3-7 Intersite replication attributes

These attributes need to be balanced carefully for maximum replication performance. Use the following guidelines when setting link properties:

- Cost attribute values should consider the speed and reliability of the links in use.

- Schedule attribute values should consider that there is a tradeoff between replicating during off-peak hours and having the most up-to-date information at all sites.

- Short frequency attribute values consume less bandwidth due to frequent small replication cycles, although they provide more up-to-date information. Longer replication intervals may require more bandwidth during replication and less up-to-date information between replication cycles.

Replication Protocols

When replicating between sites, two transport protocols are available to establish intersite communication as follows:

- RPC over IP
- SMTP

For intrasite and intersite replication, Active Directory uses **remote procedure calls (RPC) over Internet Protocol (IP)** for replication traffic by default. RPC is commonly used to call services on various computers throughout the network. IP is responsible for the addressing and routing of the data. RPC over IP replication keeps data secure while in transit by using both authentication and encryption.

Simple Mail Transport Protocol (SMTP) is an alternative solution for intersite replication when a direct or reliable IP connection is not available. SMTP, a member of the Transmission Control Protocol/Internet Protocol (TCP/IP) suite, is the standard protocol used for message transfer such as e-mail. SMTP site links communicate asynchronously, meaning each replication transaction does not need to complete before another can start because the transaction can be stored until the destination server is available. This protocol provides limited replication functionality because it can only replicate configuration, schema, and application directory partitions. SMTP cannot replicate domain directory partitions and it also requires an **enterprise certification authority (CA)** that is fully integrated with Active Directory. The CA signs SMTP messages exchanged between domain controllers, thereby ensuring the authenticity of directory updates. A CA is responsible for issuing digital certificates that allow two computers to communicate securely. Unlike RPC over IP, SMTP does not adhere to schedules and should be used only when replicating between different domains over an e-mail or Internet link.

> **MORE INFO** **Certification Authorities** For information on CAs and related concepts, see the Microsoft TechNet documentation provided at http://www.microsoft.com/technet/treeview/default.asp?url=/technet/prodtechnol/windowsserver2003/proddocs/entserver/sag_cs_topnode.asp.

Table 3-1 summarizes intrasite versus intersite replication.

Table 3-1 **Intrasite versus Intersite Replication**

Intrasite Replication	Intersite Replication
Replication within sites is not compressed and is optimized to reduce latency.	Replication between sites is compressed to optimize WAN bandwidth utilization.
Replication partners notify each other of the changes that need to be made.	Bridgehead servers are responsible for collecting replication data, compressing it, and sending it across site links.
Normal replication takes place at 15-minute intervals. Security-sensitive changes trigger immediate replication.	Site links must be configured for replication to take place between sites.
The KCC checks for site topology changes every 15 minutes.	The default replication schedule is set for every 180 minutes, seven days a week.
Replication uses the RPC over IP protocol within a site.	If two or more site links are configured for fault tolerance, the cost settings determine the preferred path.
	RPC over IP or SMTP can be used as the transport protocol. RPC over IP is the preferred choice for most situations.

Designating a Bridgehead Server

Although all domain controllers from the same domain *within* the same site participate in the replication process with each other, not all domain controllers from the same domain in the same site participate in the replication process with other sites simultaneously. Replicating from one site to another using all domain controllers is redundant and extremely bandwidth intensive. As discussed previously, to eliminate this potential traffic issue, a bridgehead server is assigned at each site. All traffic within a site is replicated to the bridgehead server. The bridgehead server is the domain controller that is responsible for then replicating all site changes for that domain to other sites.

The ISTG automatically assigns one server in each site as the bridgehead server, unless you override this by establishing a list of preferred bridgehead servers. The advantage of administratively assigning a preferred bridgehead server list is that you can determine which servers have the best processing power for the job of handling replication traffic. Remember that intersite replication traffic is compressed by default, and the bridgehead servers will be responsible for decompressing, compressing, sending, and receiving all replication traffic within the site and between sites. Configuring more than one preferred bridgehead server allows administrative control over the task of replicating between sites using the most efficient machines. When more than one preferred bridgehead server is configured and the preferred bridgehead server fails, the KCC will choose another server from the list.

When planning the use of bridgehead servers, consider the following guidelines:

- Configure a list of preferred bridgehead servers to assist in better performance from site to site. Servers should be chosen based on processing capabilities. Bridgehead servers need to efficiently perform compression and decompression of replication data. A server having the slowest processor on your network would not be the best choice for the role of bridgehead server.
- Configure multiple bridgehead servers for multiple partitions.
- If a server that has been designated by the ISTG as a preferred bridgehead server fails, the ISTG will assign a new bridgehead server from the configured list. This assumes that you have configured more than one server in the list.

   NOTE Sites Protected by Firewalls   Any site protected by a firewall must have the firewall proxy server designated as the preferred bridgehead server. If this is not the case, replication may fail between the protected site and other sites on your network. For more information on securing Active Directory replication using a firewall, see the TechNet article located at http://www.microsoft.com/technet/treeview/default.asp?url=/technet/ittasks/tasks/adrepfir.asp.

Site Link Bridges

Enabled by default, a **site link bridge** defines a chain of site links by which domain controllers from different sites can communicate. In the case where there is a centralized site that is connected to two subsites via site links, the site link bridge creates a direct link between the subsites using the total cost of both subsite links to the central site, as shown in Figure 3-8.

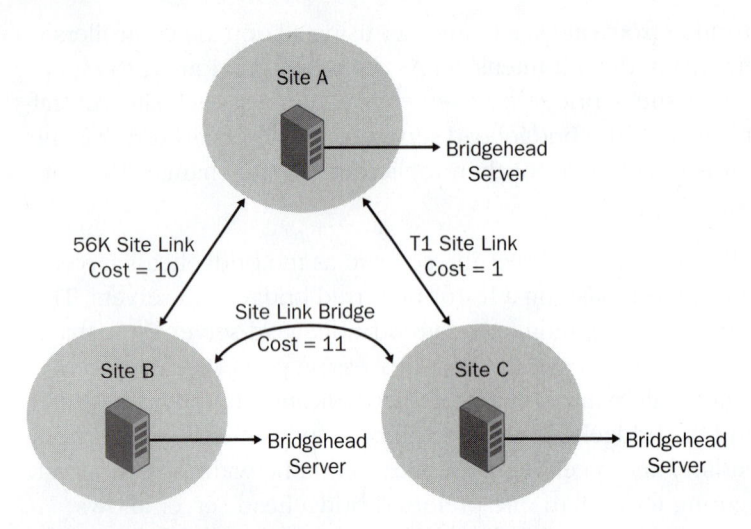

Figure 3-8 Site link bridge

All site links using the same transport protocol are considered to be *transitive*. Transitive means that you can connect any site to any other site through a combination of site links. In a fully routed IP network, this feature generally follows your routing topology and manual site link bridges do not need to be created. The ISTG uses this information when creating the replication topology, thereby allowing two or more sites to replicate in any direction using a two-way bridge. However, if your network is not fully routed, it is recommended that site link bridging be disabled and manual bridging defined according to the network infrastructure. This will allow the ISTG to create paths that are most appropriate for your topology and link speeds. The following situations warrant the creation of manual site link bridges:

- When your network is not fully routed, site link bridges allow better performance by creating a shortcut between sites that are not directly connected.
- There are many sites and the forest functional level has not yet been raised to Windows Server 2003 forest level.

Linked Multi-Valued Attribute Replication

Prior to Windows Server 2003, group membership changes needing to be replicated required that the entire group be replicated. The *member* list attribute was considered to be one attribute. A simultaneous change made by multiple administrators to the same group membership list caused some of the updates to be lost due to conflict resolution. The fact that the entire list had to be replicated also required more processing time and higher bandwidth utilization. With Windows Server 2003 set at the forest functional level, a single membership change to a group triggers the replication of only this change to each member in the list, rather than the entire membership list.

IMPLEMENTING AND MANAGING A SITE PLAN

Sites are created and managed using Active Directory Sites And Services. In addition to the automatic creation of the first site, additional sites can be created and managed. The following sections discuss the steps necessary to create, configure, and manage your site plan.

Creating the Site Structure

It is not uncommon to rename the Default-First-Site-Name to reflect your site strategy. The goal here is to name all elements intuitively, making it easy to understand how they correlate. When naming sites and other related objects, it is best to use only the following characters: A to Z, numbers from 0 to 9, and the hyphen character.

▶ Renaming the Default-First-Site-Name

To rename the Default-First-Site-Name, complete the following steps:

1. Open Active Directory Sites And Services, and expand the Sites folder.
2. Right-click the Default-First-Site-Name site object, and click Rename.
3. Type the name that reflects the site location on your site plan.

▶ Creating a New Site

To create a new site, complete the following steps:

1. In Active Directory Sites And Services, right-click the Sites folder, and select New Site.
2. In the New Object-Site dialog box, type the name for the site based on your plan.
3. Select the DefaultIPSiteLink from the link name list, and click OK to complete the site creation.

   NOTE *Selecting a Site Link* *After all sites and subnets are created, you associate the appropriate site link with the site. The procedure for this is outlined in the next section.*

Creating Subnets

Each subnet should correspond to a physical network segment. Once the subnets have been defined, you associate them with the appropriate sites. By default, there are no subnets created through the Active Directory installation process. All segments require manual definition. You should create subnets that reflect your physical infrastructure based on the TCP/IP scheme.

▶ Creating a Subnet

To create a subnet, complete the following steps:

1. In Active Directory Sites And Services, right-click the Subnets folder.
2. Select New Subnet from the menu.
3. In the New Object-Subnet dialog box, enter the IP address and subnet mask that corresponds to the segment in your design.

   As you enter the mask, it will be translated into Classless Inter-Domain Routing (CIDR) notation in the Name field. This form of notation shows the number of bits being used for the subnet mask. For example, if you are using an IP address of 192.168.64.0 with a mask of 255.255.255.0, the CIDR representation of this would be 192.168.64.0/24.

4. Select the site you wish to associate with this subnet, and click OK.

Creating Site Links

As discussed previously, site links define the paths that are used to replicate between sites. As part of the site link creation process, you define the cost, frequency, and schedule used by the replication process.

▶ **Creating a Site Link**

To create a site link, complete the following steps:

1. In Active Directory Sites And Services, expand the Inter-Site Transports folder.

2. Right-click the desired protocol, either IP or SMTP, and select New Site Link.

3. In the New Object-Site Link dialog box, type the name of the site link. This name should reflect the locations that will be connected using this link.

4. From the Sites Not In This Site Link list, select the sites you wish to associate with this link, and click Add. They will now appear on the right side of the dialog box under Sites In This Site Link. Click OK to complete the link creation.

▶ **Configuring a Site Link**

To configure the site link cost, frequency, and schedule, complete the following steps:

1. In Active Directory Sites And Services, expand the Inter-Site Transports folder, followed by the protocol folder containing the link you wish to configure.

2. Right-click the site link you wish to configure, and select Properties.

3. The cost is set to 100 by default; modify this number if necessary according to your site link plan. Remember that a lower number indicates a preferred path.

4. If you wish to change the replication frequency to something other than the default of 180, modify the Replicate Every *xx* Minutes field.

5. To modify the schedule to allow replication to take place only during non-peak business hours, click Change Schedule.

6. Select the days and hours you wish to disallow or allow replication, and adjust the option button at the right of the schedule chart to show the appropriate color. Days and hours highlighted in blue indicate replication is allowed. When finished, select OK to close the Schedule dialog box.

7. Upon completing all desired link configurations, click OK.

Creating a List of Preferred Bridgehead Servers

As discussed previously, you can add several servers for the ISTG to choose from when selecting a bridgehead server by designating these servers as preferred bridgehead servers.

▶ Creating a List of Preferred Bridgehead Servers

To create a list of preferred bridgehead servers, complete the following steps:

1. In Active Directory Sites And Services, expand the desired Sites folder, and then expand the Servers folder containing the server you wish to add to the bridgehead server list.

2. Right-click the domain controller you wish to configure, and select Properties.

3. From the list of transports on the left side, choose the appropriate protocol for replication, and then click Add. The protocol will appear on the right side, showing that this server will be added to the list of Preferred Bridgehead Servers for the chosen protocol.

Disabling Site Link Bridging

Site link bridging is enabled by default and works well in a fully routed network. However, as stated previously, disabling site link bridging in a network that is not fully connected will allow you to create the site links according to your network infrastructure or business guidelines.

▶ Disabling Site Link Bridging

To disable automatic site link bridging, complete the following steps:

1. In Active Directory Sites And Services, expand the Inter-Site Transports folder.

2. Right-click the protocol you wish to configure, and select Properties.

3. Clear the Bridge All Site Links check box.

Creating a Manual Site Link Bridge

To create a site link bridge, automatic site link bridging must be disabled. Be sure to complete the Disabling Site Link Bridging steps prior to beginning this procedure.

▶ Creating a Manual Site Link Bridge

To create a manual site link bridge, complete the following steps:

1. In Active Directory Sites And Services, expand the Inter-Site Transports folder.

2. Right-click the protocol you wish to bridge, and select New Site Link Bridge.

3. Select the site links you wish to bridge, and click Add. Type a description for the bridge, and click OK to finish.

Managing Replication

Replication errors and possible Active Directory inconsistencies are logged to the Event Viewer. For example, when simultaneous changes are made to an object's attributes from different domain controllers and the change cannot be updated due to a collision, the error is logged to the Event Viewer. Some of these errors may just be for informational purposes, while others may warrant some investigation and corrective action. This section describes some of the methods used to determine which domain controllers are contributors to the problems. In many cases, once the problem is isolated, it is necessary to initiate a forced replication to help get Active Directory up to date and consistent. The procedure to initiate a forced replication cycle is described in the following sections.

Refreshing the Replication Topology
Refreshing the replication topology is accomplished by forcing the KCC to run. Depending on whether you wish to refresh the intrasite topology or the intersite topology, the steps are slightly different. Refreshing the topology within a site requires the KCC to be triggered on one of the domain controllers within the site.

▶ **Forcing the KCC to Refresh Intrasite Topology**

To force the KCC to refresh the intrasite topology, complete the following steps:

1. In Active Directory Sites And Services, expand Sites, followed by the site you wish to run the KCC.
2. Expand Servers, and double-click one of the domain controllers.
3. In the details pane, right-click NTDS Settings, click All Tasks, and select Check Replication Topology.

   This will force the KCC to run within the site.

The ISTG role is held by one domain controller at each site. This role designation is fully automatic. The ISTG is responsible for the intersite topology and the designation of a bridgehead server, if they are not manually defined. Determining which server is running the ISTG service allows you to force the KCC to run and refresh the intersite replication topology.

▶ **Determining Which Server Holds the ISTG Role**

To determine which server holds the ISTG role, complete the following steps:

1. In Active Directory Sites And Services, expand the Sites folder, and then expand the appropriate site.
2. In the details pane, right-click NTDS Site Settings, and select Properties.

   The Properties page displays the server holding the ISTG role.

To force the KCC to regenerate the intersite topology, complete the steps outlined for refreshing the intrasite topology.

Forcing Replication
As noted previously, the Event Viewer logs events related to inconsistencies in Active Directory. When this happens, you can force replication in an attempt to correct the inconsistency. Replication can also be forced when you have changes, such as disabled user accounts, that you wish to replicate immediately, without waiting for the next replication interval.

▶ **Forcing Replication**

To force replication, complete the following steps:

1. In Active Directory Sites And Services, expand Sites, followed by the site that contains the connection for which you wish to force replication.

2. Locate the server in the Servers container that provides the connection object.

3. Click NTDS Settings in the console tree.

4. In the details pane, right-click the connection for which you want replication to occur, and select Replicate Now.

MONITORING REPLICATION

Monitoring replication is a vital part of managing your Active Directory network. Prevention of major problems can often be avoided by monitoring replication activity regularly. Windows Server 2003 provides tools that allow for problem discovery, diagnosis, and resolution. In addition to the directory service event log available in the Event Viewer, Windows Server 2003 provides several additional monitoring tools that must be installed from the Windows 2003 installation media. The tools discussed here are part of the Support Tools available on the Windows Server 2003 CD. They can be installed by running the package installer in the <cdroot>\Support\Tools folder.

▶ **Installing Windows Server 2003 Support Tools**

Complete the following steps to install the Windows Server 2003 Support Tools on your computer:

1. Log on as Administrator, as a member of the local Administrators group, or use the RUNAS command to launch the installation if logged on as a user.

2. Insert the Windows CD into your CD-ROM drive or connect to the installation source if hosted on the network.

3. Click No if you are prompted to reinstall Windows.

4. At the Welcome screen, click Perform Additional Tasks, and then click Browse This CD. (This will be seen only if you are using the CD-based installation.)

5. Navigate to the \Support\Tools folder, and double-click the Suptools.msi file or right-click this file, select the RUNAS command, and supply appropriate administrative credentials.

    The wizard will guide you through the remainder of the installation process.

The monitoring tools we will focus on here include:

- Dcdiag
- Repadmin
- Replmon

Dcdiag

Dcdiag is a command line tool used for monitoring Active Directory. When run from a command prompt, this tool can do the following:

- Perform connectivity and replication tests, reporting errors that occur.
- Report DNS registration problems.
- Analyze the permissions required for replication.
- Analyze the state of domain controllers within the forest.

To view all of the options and syntax for Dcdiag, use the /? option from a command prompt as follows:

```
Dcdiag /?
```

An example of the syntax required to check replication connections using Dcdiag is as follows:

```
Dcdiag /test:replications
```

Repadmin

Repadmin is a command line tool used for the following:

- To view the replication topology from the perspective of each domain controller. This aids in understanding how information is being transferred, ultimately assisting in the isolation of replication problems.
- To manually create a replication topology if site link bridging is disabled due to the network not being fully routed.
- To force replication between domain controllers when you need updates to occur immediately without waiting for the next replication cycle.
- To view the replication metadata, that is the combination of the actual data and the up-to-dateness vector or USN information. This is helpful in determining the most up-to-date information prior to seizing an operations master role.

As was true with the Dcdiag tool, you can view a complete list of syntax options for repadmin by using the /? switch. The following example illustrates this:

```
repadmin /?
```

An example of the syntax to show all replication partners for server1 in the cohowinery.com domain follows:

```
repadmin /showreps server1.cohowinery.com
```

Replmon

Replmon is a graphic utility executed from a command prompt or from the Support Tools program group that can be used to obtain extensive information.

Some of the main Active Directory–related benefits of this tool include the following abilities:

- View of current server status displaying errors.
- Replication topology check that shows a graphic view of replication partners.
- Synchronization of directory partitions by initiating replication across the domain.
- Status report generation that can be exported to a log file.
- View of all domain controllers in the domain.
- Replication topology output of all intersite paths within the forest.
- View of forest-wide bridgehead servers.

> **NOTE** **Running Replication Monitor** *Replication Monitor can be run on any domain controller, member server, or standalone server running Windows Server 2003.*

It is necessary to configure Replication Monitor before you can use the functionality it provides.

▶ **Configuring Replication Monitor**

The following steps are used to configure Replication Monitor and begin tracking replication changes:

1. Type **replmon** in the Start/Run dialog box, or double-click the executable in the Support Tools program group.
2. On the View menu, select Options.
3. In the Active Directory Replication Monitor Options dialog box, click the Status Logging tab.
4. Click Display Changed Attributes When Replication Occurs, and click OK.
5. On the left side, right-click Monitored Servers, and select Add Monitored Server.
6. In the Add Server To Monitor dialog box, click Add The Server Explicitly By Name, and click Next.
7. In the Enter The Name Of The Server To Monitor Explicitly dialog box, type the name of the server you wish to monitor. Click Finish.

> **MORE INFO** **Troubleshooting Replication Problems** *For more information on troubleshooting replication problems, see Chapter 11, "Active Directory Maintenance, Troubleshooting, and Disaster Recovery," in this textbook.*

SUMMARY

- Intrasite replication takes place between domain controllers within the same site. A site consists of one or more subnets connected by fast links.
- Intersite replication uses manually created site links that correspond to the physical WAN links.
- Site link objects define the path by which replication traffic travels between sites. When redundant connections exist, the preferred path is based on the cost attributes configured on the link object. The default cost for a site link is 100.
- The KCC is responsible for creating a replication topology. Within a site, it runs every 15 minutes to check for topology changes.
- Between sites, the ISTG is used to determine a bridgehead server for each site. The bridgehead server is responsible for sending and receiving all domain-specific replication traffic within a particular site.
- Any site protected by a firewall must have the firewall proxy server designated as the preferred bridgehead server.
- In addition to the directory service event log, Dcdiag, Repadmin, and Replmon are tools that can be used to monitor and manage Active Directory replication.
- Linked multi-valued attribute replication in Windows Server 2003 allows a single membership change in a group to trigger replication of only the change to each member in the list, rather than the entire membership. This new feature requires the functional level to be set at Windows 2003 forest functionality.
- Intrasite replication takes place on demand in that, when an object is added or changed, a change notification is immediately sent to all replication partners. Intersite replication is based on a schedule, which by default is set for seven days a week, every 180 minutes.

EXERCISES

Exercise 3-1: Viewing Connection Objects

Complete this exercise to guide you through the steps required to view replication connection objects.

1. Open Active Directory Sites And Services.
2. Expand the Sites folder, the Default-First-Site-Name site, and then the Servers folder.
3. Expand the server name for which you wish to view connection objects, and right-click NTDS Settings. Select Properties.
4. Select the Connections tab, and note the replication partners.
5. Click Cancel to close the dialog box.

REVIEW QUESTIONS

1. The KCC is responsible for calculating intrasite replication partners. During this process, what is the maximum number of hops that the KCC will allow between domain controllers?

    a. 2

    b. 3

    c. 4

    d. 5

2. Replication that occurs between sites is called _____ replication.

    a. Local

    b. Remote

    c. Intersite

    d. Intrasite

3. Company XYZ is a national company with locations in Detroit, Minneapolis, Phoenix, and Dallas. There are two connections between Detroit and Minneapolis. The first is a T-1 link and the second is a 128-Kbps link. When setting up the site links for replication, what should you do to ensure that the 128-Kbps link is used only if the T-1 is unavailable?

    a. Set a cost of 1 for the T-1 and a cost of 5 for the 128-Kbps link.

    b. Set a cost of 5 for the T-1 and 1 for the 128-Kbps link.

    c. Leave the costs at their default value of 100.

    d. Manually change the schedule to disallow replication on the 128-Kbps link until it is needed.

4. You are a consultant working on a site plan for a medium-sized organization. The organization consists of a main office and three branch offices. Two of the locations have standard IP links to the main office, while the third branch office is a separate domain and uses an Internet connection for e-mail. How should you configure the site links for the three branch offices to the main office?

5. Assuming the same scenario as in question 4, what information will be replicated between the third branch office and the main office?

6. You are the administrator for a network that has several sites. There is a site link from the main headquarters to each remote site for file transfer and replication purposes. You have been asked to create five new users on the network, and several of the users need immediate access to network applications. When asked by your manager how long replication of these new accounts will take, you answer with which of the following responses?

    a. Replication occurs every 180 minutes by default.

    b. Replication occurs at 15-minute intervals.

    c. Replication occurs as soon as the account is added.

    d. Replication occurs only between 12:00 A.M. and 6:00 A.M.

7. Modify the scenario in question 6 by placing all domain controllers in the same site. How would you answer your manager's question now?

    a. Replication occurs every 180 minutes by default.

    b. Replication occurs at 15-minute intervals.

    c. Replication occurs as soon as the account is added.

    d. Replication occurs only between 12:00 A.M. and 6:00 A.M.

8. What is the advantage of creating your sites and subnets prior to installing subsequent domain controllers?

CASE SCENARIOS

Scenario 3-1: Adding a New Facility to a Network

Your company is located in the United States and just added a location in Canada that will need to become part of your Active Directory network. Your network designer has provided you with the following configuration information regarding the new location servers and the connections that have been procured.

- There will be three new servers installed in the Canada facility with the following specifications:
    - Server 1: 2.4-GHz processor with 2 GB RAM will be installed as a domain controller.
    - Server 2: 2.0-GHz processor with 1 GB RAM will be installed as a domain controller.
    - Server 3: 2.0-GHz processor with 2 GB RAM will be installed as an application server.
- There are two links between the United States and Canada facilities that will be available. They are as follows:
    - A T-1 link for the primary connection
    - A 256-Kbps link for a backup connection
- Bandwidth should be used during the day mainly for file transfers and e-mail. Any network maintenance that requires bandwidth should be done only between 11:00 P.M. and 4:00 A.M. on weekdays. Weekends are available anytime for maintenance procedures.

Sketch a design that will meet the previous requirements and consider the following questions:

1. Should you configure a bridgehead server at the Canada facility? If so, which server would you recommend?

2. What will you configure the costs for on each link?

3. What should the replication schedule and interval be set for?

Scenario 3-2: Improving Replication Efficiency

You are the administrator for a mid-sized company network that consists of Windows 2000 and Windows Server 2003 domain controllers. Your plan is to eventually upgrade all domain controllers to Windows Server 2003. The five sites you have are not fully routed and therefore there have been some problems with regard to replicating Active Directory data. You know your budget will not allow you to add additional links or purchase additional equipment. What can you do to improve the efficiency of replication within your network?

CHAPTER 4
GLOBAL CATALOG AND FLEXIBLE SINGLE MASTER OPERATIONS (FSMO) ROLES

Upon completion of this chapter, you will be able to:

- Understand the global catalog and its role in Active Directory.
- Plan the placement of global catalog servers.
- Add and remove global catalog servers.
- Understand universal group caching.
- Enable universal group caching.
- Describe forest and domain FSMO roles.
- Plan FSMO role placement.
- Transfer and seize FSMO role assignments.

This chapter centers on a description of the five **flexible single master operations (FSMO)** roles and the global catalog. An FSMO role holder server is a domain controller that has been assigned a task that can occur from only one domain controller in the domain or forest. Each of the five roles plays a key part in the functionality of Active Directory. As you will learn, the placement of these roles within an Active Directory domain or forest can affect accessibility and performance. Planning, implementing, and managing the global catalog and FSMO roles is an important part of balancing network performance and accessibility. This chapter describes the guidelines for placement of these resources, in addition to discussing the advantages and disadvantages of different implementation plans.

UNDERSTANDING THE GLOBAL CATALOG

Although the **global catalog** is not one of the five FSMO roles, the services it provides are of major importance to the functionality of the Active Directory network. The global catalog holds a subset of forest-wide Active Directory objects. A global catalog server acts as a central repository by holding a complete copy of all objects from the host server's local domain, and a partial copy of all objects from other domains within the same forest. This partial copy of forest-wide data includes a subset of each object's attributes. The attributes included in this subset are necessary to provide functionality such as logon, object searches, and universal group memberships. By default, the first domain controller installed in the forest is designated as a global catalog server. However, any or potentially all domain controllers in a domain can be designated as global catalog servers. These assignments are made carefully to ensure that the benefits outweigh the costs. We will discuss these benefits and costs later in this chapter.

Understanding the Functions of the Global Catalog

The global catalog has three main functions:

- Facilitation of searches for objects in the forest
- Resolution of user principal names (UPNs)
- Provision of universal group membership information

The benefits of these functions are described in the next section.

Facilitation of Object Searches

When a user initiates a search for an object published in Active Directory, the request is automatically sent to TCP port 3268. Port 3268 is used by Active Directory to direct these requests to a global catalog server. You might wonder how this fits in to what we have already discussed. Chapter 2, "Implementing Active Directory," states that Active Directory requires support for SRV records in DNS. One of these records refers to the global catalog service or _gc service that uses port 3268 to respond to resolution requests.

Resolution of UPNs

UPNs allow users to log on to domains across the forest using a standardized naming format that matches the format used for e-mail addresses. When a local domain controller receives a request for logon via a UPN, it contacts a global catalog server to complete the logon process. For example, assume the user account for JSmith resides in the north.cohowinery.com domain, and JSmith is currently working from the east.cohowinery.com location. Since JSmith travels frequently between the various corporate locations, he uses the UPN, jsmith@cohowinery.com, to log on to both his network account and his e-mail account. Upon receiving a logon attempt from JSmith, a local domain controller searches for a global catalog server to resolve jsmith@cohowinery.com to a user name. When this process is complete, the global catalog server contains enough information about the user to either permit or deny the logon request. The success of the logon depends on

JSmith's permissions or restrictions associated with the domain. For example, if there is a time restriction that allows logons only during business hours and JSmith is attempting to log on after hours, the logon request will be denied. UPN logons are also possible between forests that have a cross-forest trust established.

Provision of Universal Group Membership Information
Users can be permitted or denied access to a resource based on their group memberships. This information is an important part of a user's access level. Global group memberships are stored at the domain level. Universal group memberships are stored in the global catalog. A **universal group** can contain users, groups, and computers from any domain in the forest. In addition, universal groups, through their membership in domain local groups, can receive permissions for any resource anywhere in the forest. For universal groups to be available, an Active Directory forest must be set to at least Windows 2000. A user who is a member of a universal group can be granted or denied permission to access resources throughout the domain.

When the forest is set to either Microsoft Windows 2000 or Windows Server 2003 functionality, a global catalog is required for a successful first-time logon. Without the global catalog available to query universal group memberships, a complete token cannot be created. However, if the user has successfully logged on in the past, the user will be able to log on using locally cached credentials stored on his or her computer. Allowing logon credentials to be cached on a local computer can pose a security threat for certain companies. For example, if you have a computer that is shared by multiple users with different access permissions, cached credentials could be used for an account to allow an unauthorized user to gain access to a resource. Group policies allow cached logons to be disabled on a local computer. We will discuss the use of group policies for security purposes at length in Chapters 7 through 10.

For sites that do not have a global catalog server available, Windows Server 2003 offers a new feature, **universal group membership caching**. This caching stores universal group memberships on the local domain controller to be used for logon to the domain, eliminating the need for frequent access to a global catalog server. This new feature is discussed below.

> **NOTE** *The Global Catalog on a Single-Domain Network* A global catalog is not required in a single-domain network for logon to be successful. However, Active Directory searches still require the use of a global catalog server. Recommendations for global catalog server placement will be discussed later in this chapter.

Universal Group Membership Caching

For domains set to Windows 2000 native or above, the universal group membership caching feature allows domain controllers to process a logon or resource request, without the presence of a global catalog server. Domains set to Windows 2000 mixed do not provide the ability to create universal groups; therefore, logons to Windows 2000 mixed domains do not require a global catalog server. In order for logon using universal group membership caching to work, a user must have had a successful logon when a global catalog server was available and, during that logon attempt, universal group membership caching was enabled. Universal membership caching records each user's information individually. For example, if universal group caching is not available to record the user's information into cache and the global catalog server goes offline, the logon attempt will fail. In addition, global catalog servers do not cache universal group memberships.

Universal group membership caching is enabled for an entire site. The information in the cache is refreshed every eight hours by default using a confirmation request sent by the domain controller to a global catalog server. The refresh schedule can be modified by the administrator within the replication schedule. Universal group caching has the following benefits:

- It eliminates the need to place a global catalog in a remote location where the link speed is typically slow or unreliable and updates are inconsistent.

- It provides better logon performance for users with cached information. If the global catalog is located across a WAN link, cached credentials can replace the need to have logon traffic sent across a slow or unreliable link.

- It minimizes WAN usage for replication traffic, since the domain controller does not have to hold information about forest-wide objects. In addition, these remote domain controllers are not listed in DNS as providers of global catalog services for the forest, further reducing bandwidth constraints.

Table 4-1 summarizes the logon process with regard to the global catalog and universal group membership caching.

Table 4-1 Logons, Global Catalog, and Universal Group Membership Caching

Logon Request Scenario	Response
The forest is set to Windows 2000 mixed.	Logon is processed based on the user's credentials. A global catalog server is not required, and universal groups are not available.
The forest mode is set to Windows 2000 or above. A global catalog server is available.	■ The domain controller receiving the authentication request attempts to locate a global catalog server. ■ A global catalog server is queried for the user's universal group memberships. ■ The user is either granted or denied access based on supplied credentials and the associated ACLs.
The forest mode is set to Windows 2000 or above. A global catalog server is not available. It is either not functioning or inaccessible due to a connectivity problem or a downed WAN link. Universal group membership caching is not enabled.	■ The domain controller receiving the authentication request attempts to locate a global catalog. ■ The user logon is denied because the global catalog server cannot be contacted.

(continued)

Table 4-1 **Logons, Global Catalog, and Universal Group Membership Caching**

Logon Request Scenario	Response
The forest mode is set to Windows 2000 or above. A global catalog server is not available. Universal group membership caching is enabled.	■ The domain controller receiving the authentication request attempts to locate a global catalog server. This query fails. ■ If the user has successfully logged on in the past when the global catalog server was online *and* universal group membership caching was enabled, the logon is processed and the user is either granted or denied access based on supplied credentials and ACLs. ■ If the user has not logged on in the past when a global catalog server was available and universal group membership caching was enabled, the logon will be denied.

> **NOTE** *Existence of Universal Groups* *Although universal groups are available in a domain set to Windows 2000 native mode or higher, universal group membership caching's functionality is not dependent on the existence of universal groups.*

Universal group membership caching must be enabled for an entire site. This means that once it is enabled for the site, all domain controllers, except a domain controller that is a global catalog server, can receive the cached information. You must be a member of the Domain Admins group in the forest root domain, Enterprise Admins group, or you must have received delegated permissions appropriate to this role to enable this feature.

▶ **Enabling Universal Group Membership Caching**

To enable universal group membership caching, complete the following steps:

1. Open Active Directory Sites And Services.
2. Select the site from the console tree for which you want to enable universal group membership caching.
3. In the details window, right-click NTDS Site Settings, and select Properties.
4. Select the Enable Universal Group Membership Caching check box.
5. In Refresh Cache From, select a site that you wish this site to receive updates from, or leave it at <Default> to refresh from the nearest global catalog server.

Planning Global Catalog Server Placement

By default, the first domain controller in a forest is a global catalog server. Therefore, your initial site will already contain a global catalog server. Placing additional global catalog servers as your forest grows should be considered. The following guidelines will help you to decide when you should add a global catalog server:

- Each site should contain a global catalog server to facilitate logons. If the site is located across an unreliable or slow WAN link, a locally placed global catalog server will allow logons and Active Directory searches to take place, regardless of the link state. If this is not possible and the forest functionality level is set to at least Windows 2000, universal group membership caching should be enabled.

- When placing a global catalog at a remote site, the amount of bandwidth that is necessary to replicate global catalog information should be considered. Responding to logon requests from other sites also provides bandwidth constraints.

- The domain controller on which you place the global catalog must have enough space on the hard drive to hold the global catalog.

- A site that contains an application using port 3268 for global catalog query resolutions should contain a global catalog server. As discussed previously, port 3268 is used for resolution of object searches.

Enabling a Global Catalog Server

When the Active Directory design warrants the addition of a global catalog server, actually adding this functionality to an existing server is a very simple process.

▶ **Enabling a Domain Controller to Be a Global Catalog Server**

To enable a domain controller to be a global catalog server, complete the following steps:

1. On the domain controller where you want the new global catalog, open Active Directory Sites And Services from the Administrative Tools folder.

2. In the console tree, double-click Sites, and then double-click the site name that contains the domain controller for which you wish to add the global catalog.

3. Double-click the Servers folder, and select your domain controller. Right-click NTDS Settings, and select Properties.

4. On the General tab, select the Global Catalog check box to assign the role of global catalog to this server. Click OK.

   NOTE *Completing the Addition of a Global Catalog Server* Allow sufficient time for the account and schema information to replicate to the new global catalog server. The length of time this process takes will vary depending on the number of objects to be replicated and the speed of the link they are transferred over. Event Viewer may show Event ID 1119 in the Directory Services log. The description for this event ID states that the computer is now advertising itself as a global catalog server. This is a normal occurrence.

UNDERSTANDING FSMO ROLES

Within an organization there are many people who play an important part in meeting the day-to-day company goals. Some perform routine daily tasks such as data entry, while others perform specialized duties such as management or sales. If more than one person performs the same function, it is important to keep track of who does what. For example, if one salesperson quotes a job to an individual and another salesperson quotes the same job for a lower price, there will be an internal conflict that arises as a result of the miscommunication. In addition, the customer may choose to do business elsewhere due to the conflict. A Windows Server 2003 network can be thought of in the same terms. Some domain controllers perform routine roles such as replication and logon services, while others provide specialized functions such as schema management and domain name tracking. These specialized roles are named FSMO roles; FSMO, operations master, and single-master operations server are all terms that are used interchangeably. Their purpose, beyond being a standard domain controller in the replica ring, is to provide services that are classified as **single-master operations**. This means only one domain controller in each domain or, in some cases, one domain controller in each forest can provide this particular service. By employing single-master operations servers, tasks that might cause problems in Active Directory if more than one domain controller can initiate them are assigned to only one domain controller.

As you have already learned, Active Directory domain controllers follow a multi-master replication model. This model ensures that there are multiple copies of all domain objects for ease of accessibility and fault tolerance. In addition, any domain controller can update the contents of the database when changes occur. This multi-master model provides a fast and efficient directory service when the implementation guidelines are followed.

Although Active Directory has mechanisms such as timestamps and update sequence numbers built in to assist in possible conflict resolution, there are more critical functions that need to have the assurance of little or no risk of errors. An example of a task that should not be subject to more than one simultaneous change is illustrated in the following scenario:

You are the network administrator for a mid-sized corporation. Your company has seven locations scattered throughout the world. As part of the application deployment team, you are assigned the job of installing a newly developed application on the network. Part of the instructions for the installation requires that you add a custom attribute to several objects in Active Directory. Unknown to you or your manager, another administrator at a different location has been assigned the same task. You both are working on the task at the same time.

Assuming the tasks you are each attempting to do simultaneously are being performed on a multi-master platform, you could end up with a corrupted database due to conflicting simultaneous changes. However, in Windows Server 2003, this type of situation will not occur. Microsoft has implemented FSMO roles to avoid this type of corruption. These roles are performed by only one specific server, which eliminates the risk associated with high-level tasks and corruption.

> **NOTE** **Failure of an FSMO** If a domain controller holding an FSMO role is removed from the network or experiences a failure, the role can be transferred to another domain controller. This will be discussed later in this chapter.

There are five FSMO roles in Active Directory. Their functionality is divided between domain-level tasks and forest-wide tasks. In a small-business scenario, where there may be only one domain and a single domain controller, all of the roles will exist on the same domain controller. As previously stated, a second domain controller is highly recommended for fault tolerance in any domain. When a second domain controller is implemented, several of the FSMO roles can be transferred to the new domain controller. This offers not only fault tolerance, but also performance improvements because the processing of tasks is balanced between more than one server.

In this section, we will discuss planning guidelines and assignment of the FSMO roles in a Windows Server 2003 network.

Domain-Specific Roles

There are three roles that are domain specific:

- **Relative Identifier (RID) Master** Responsible for assigning relative identifiers to domain controllers in the domain. Relative identifiers are variable-length numbers assigned by a domain controller when a new object is created.

- **Infrastructure Master** Responsible for reference updates from its domain objects to other domains. This assists in tracking which domains own which objects.

- **Primary Domain Controller (PDC) Emulator** Provides backward compatibility with Microsoft Windows NT 4.0 domains. For domains set to Windows 2000 or Windows Server 2003 native, it provides time synchronization within the domain, in addition to preferential account modification replication. Preferential account modification replication is defined as a security-critical change, such as a password change, taking place. The domain controller that initiates the change sends the change to the PDC emulator, which in turn updates the global catalog server and provides immediate replication to other domain controllers in the domain.

A detailed explanation of the domain roles is provided in the following sections.

The RID Master Role
A domain controller assigned the RID master role in a domain is responsible for generating a pool of identifiers that are used when new accounts, groups, and computers are created. These identifiers are named relative identifiers because they are *related* to the domain in which they are created. The RID is a variable-length number that is assigned to objects at creation and becomes part of the object's **security identifier** (**SID**). A SID is used to identify an object with its security level.

Part of the SID identifies the domain to which the object belongs, and the other part is the RID. This combination number uniquely identifies an object and where it lives in the domain. There can be only one RID master for each domain.

How the RID Works When there are two or more domain controllers in a domain, the RID master assigns a block of 500 identifiers to each domain controller. When an object is created, the domain controller where the object is created assigns a RID to it from the pool. When a domain controller has used 50 percent of the supply of RIDs that it originally received from the RID master, it must contact the RID master and request a new supply. Figure 4-1 depicts this process.

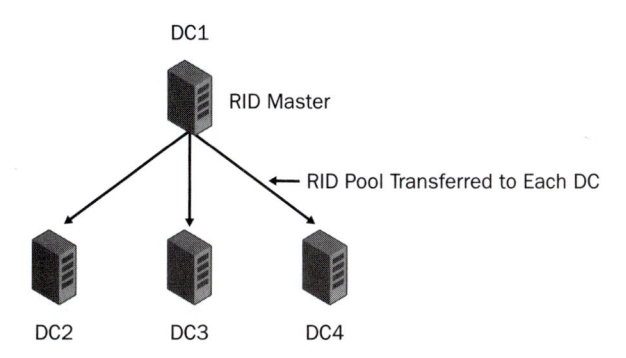

Figure 4-1 RID master role process

If the server functioning as the RID master goes down, another domain controller can be assigned this role. The absence of a RID master is transparent to users on the network. The adverse affects of not having an accessible RID master are:

- The possible inability to create new objects. This would be the case only if a domain controller did not have any remaining RIDs and attempted to contact an inaccessible RID master to obtain additional identifiers.

- The inability to move objects between domains, as explained in the next section.

When an object needs to be moved from one domain to another, you must be logged on to the RID master in the source domain, and the move operation must be performed against the RID master in the destination domain. To move an object to a different domain, the **Movetree.exe** command is required. The Movetree.exe command allows an object such as an organizational unit (OU) or user object to be moved to another domain within the same forest. Movetree.exe, like other previously discussed support tools, can be found on the Windows Server 2003 media in the \Support\Tools folder. The Movetree operation copies the source objects to the **Lost and Found container** on the source domain, and then they are moved to the destination domain. The Lost and Found container is a built-in container for orphaned objects whose parent container has been deleted. Movetree is a valuable tool that can be used for restructuring when companies move users and departments to new locations.

> **MORE INFO** *Movetree.exe* For additional information on the Movetree command, syntax, and examples, see Microsoft Knowledge Base article number 238394 located at http://support.microsoft.com/default.aspx?scid=kb%3ben-us%3b238394.

The Infrastructure Master Role

The domain controller functioning as the infrastructure master is responsible for replicating changes to an object's SID or distinguished name (DN). Recalling that the SID maintains the object's security identifier and the distinguished name reflects where the object is located in the forest, an object's SID and DN can change when the object is moved to another domain. However, the **globally unique identifier** (**GUID**) does not change. The GUID is a 128-bit hexadecimal number given at the time of object creation in the forest. This number is a combination of the date and time the object was created, a unique identifier, and a sequence number. This number never changes, even if the account is moved from one domain to another domain in the same forest.

How the Infrastructure Master Works If an object is moved or renamed, the infrastructure master replicates the change in name or location to all domains that have trust relationships with the source domain. This process ensures that the object maintains access to resources in other domains. The infrastructure master and the global catalog work closely together. The infrastructure master compares its objects to those in the global catalog. If it finds the global catalog has a newer copy of an object, it requests an update and then sends the updated information to other domain controllers in the domain. Since the global catalog and the infrastructure master work so closely with one another in a forest consisting of more than one domain and multiple domain controllers, these roles cannot be serviced by the same domain controller. When they are located on the same domain controller within a domain that is part of a multiple domain forest, they share the same database information, making it impossible for the infrastructure master to know what information has changed. In a large forest, this will cause the domain controllers to be out of synch with the global catalog contents. In a single-domain environment, or in a multi-domain environment with all domain controllers designated as global catalog servers, the infrastructure master placement would not matter. Event ID number 1419 will be logged in Event Viewer when the two roles exist on the same domain controller.

The PDC Emulator Role

The domain controller holding the PDC emulator role provides backward compatibility for computers that are considered to be downlevel clients, such as Windows 9x computers or Microsoft Windows NT 4.0 machines in a Windows 2000 mixed domain. As you learned in Chapter 3, Windows 2000 mixed domains can consist of Windows NT 4.0 **backup domain controllers** (**BDCs**), Windows 2000 Server domain controllers, and Windows Server 2003 domain controllers. A BDC is the second domain controller in a Windows NT environment. It acts as a backup to the PDC that is responsible for all major functions, such as logon and security changes in a Windows NT network. To support this backward compatibility, the PDC emulator is responsible for the following tasks:

- Copying Active Directory user and group account changes to the Windows NT 4.0 BDCs.

- Handling security-critical account changes for users and groups. Examples of this include password and account lockout changes.

In addition to providing backward compatibility for downlevel operating systems and clients, the PDC emulator is also responsible for the following:

- **Time synchronization** within the domain
- Preferential replication of password changes

As previously discussed, Active Directory updates are given a timestamp to help assist in conflict resolution. These timestamps are based on the time setting on the domain controller from which the change occurred. If all domain controllers do not agree on a time, it nullifies the importance of timestamps. Furthermore, by default there is only a five-minute clock skew allowed by Kerberos as part of the default maximum tolerance for the computer clock synchronization policy. If the clocks between a client and a server are off by more than five minutes, you might not be able to log on. The default maximum tolerance for computer clock synchronization can be changed through a group policy. Group policy implementation will be discussed in Chapters 7 through 10.

The PDC emulator in a domain sets its clock either to point to an arbitrary parent domain PDC emulator or, if it is the highest-level PDC emulator in the forest, it will be the primary time source. The highest-level PDC emulator in the forest should point to an external time source to get the correct time. External time sources include military time servers and external clocks. The following command shows the syntax that is used to point to an external time source:

```
net time \\ServerName /setsntp:TimeSource
```

The PDC emulator also receives preferential replication of password changes from other domain controllers. When a password change takes place, the change takes time to be replicated to all domain controllers. However, the password change is replicated to the PDC emulator immediately. If a logon request fails due to a bad password, the domain controller that receives the request will forward the request to the PDC emulator before returning an error message to the client.

As is true with the RID master and the infrastructure master, there can be only one PDC emulator in each domain.

Forest-Wide Roles

Forest-wide FSMO roles provide functionality that flows into all domains. Without these roles, an unwanted database problem, such as the duplication of a domain name or schema overwrites, could happen. The forest roles keep track of domain names and schema objects so that such corruption cannot take place. There can be only one of each of these role holders in a forest at any one time.

The two roles in Active Directory that have forest-wide implications include:

- **Domain Naming Master**   Has the authority to create and delete domains in the forest. When a new domain is created, the domain naming master ensures that the name being assigned is unique to the forest.
- **Schema Master**   Is responsible for making master changes to the Active Directory schema.

Each of these roles is detailed in the next section.

The Domain Naming Master Role

The domain naming master role is held on only one domain controller in the forest. When a new domain is created, the domain naming master is contacted to make sure the name being given is unique to the forest. To create a new domain, you must be a member of the Enterprise Admins group.

If your forest functional level is set to Windows 2000, the domain naming master role should reside on a global catalog server. When the forest functional level is set to Windows Server 2003, this is not necessary.

If the domain naming master server is down, new domains cannot be created and others cannot be deleted. This is the most significant problem that arises from this server's failure.

The Schema Master Role

The domain controller holding the schema master role is where all schema modifications must take place. When an object or attribute is modified, it is the responsibility of the schema master to make sure the change is replicated to all domains in the forest. Although it plays an important role in the maintenance of the Active Directory database, if the domain controller holding this role fails, it will not immediately affect users.

PLACING FSMO SERVERS

Although the default locations for FSMO role servers is sufficient for a single site design, a forest containing numerous domain controllers or sites requires that you transfer some of the roles to different domain controllers. Planning the locations for FSMO servers requires that you consider the following design aspects:

- The number of domains that are or will be part of the forest
- The physical structure of the network
- The number of domain controllers that will be available in each domain

Each of the above factors will assist you in deciding where to place FSMO roles that result in the best possible performance, accessibility, and fault tolerance. In addition, you will need to know which domain controllers might be able to take over a role for a server if the server is temporarily or permanently offline.

As previously stated, when you create the first domain in a new forest, all of the FSMO roles are automatically assigned to the first domain controller in that domain. Figure 4-2 shows a simple design and the default locations for the global catalog and all five FSMO roles.

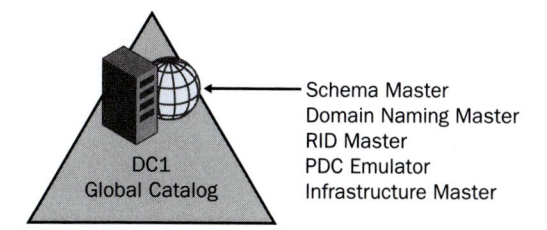

CHAPTER 4: GLOBAL CATALOG AND FLEXIBLE SINGLE MASTER OPERATIONS (FSMO) ROLES

Figure 4-2 Single domain and FSMO role placement

As shown in Figure 4-3, when you create a new child domain or the root domain of a new domain tree in an existing forest, the first domain controller in the new domain is automatically assigned the RID master, PDC emulator, and infrastructure master roles. Because there can be only one schema master and one domain naming master in the forest, by default these roles remain in the first domain on the first domain controller created in the forest.

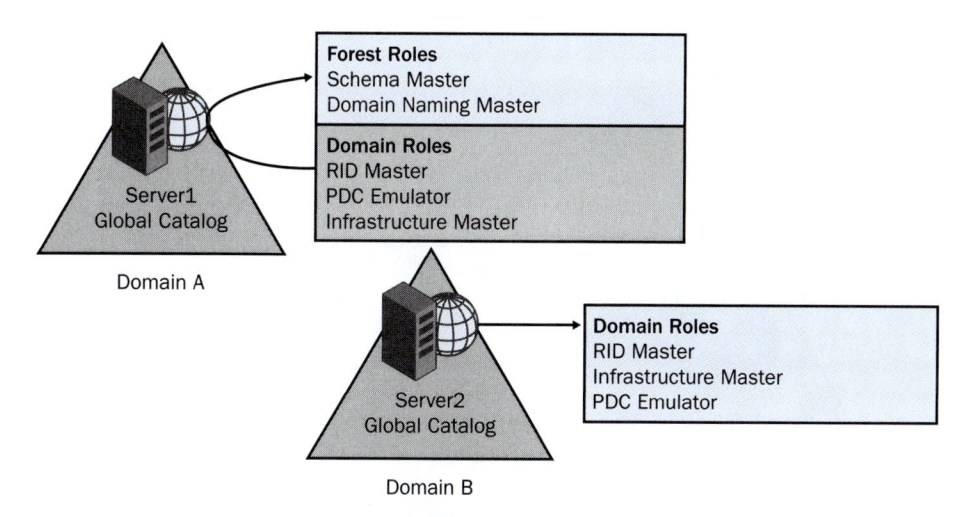

Figure 4-3 Simple multiple-domain forest and FSMO role placement

Expanding on the previous example, in Figure 4-4, a second domain controller, Server2, has been added to Domain A. The PDC emulator and the infrastructure master roles have been transferred to Server2, resulting in load balancing within the domain. Since the PDC emulator and the global catalog server usually experience heavier traffic volumes because of their roles in authentication, separating these roles can produce faster response times for users attempting logon. Moving the infrastructure master to Server2 allows the infrastructure master to keep track of object changes and properly replicate them to other domain controllers in the domain.

In Figure 4-5, another option for the previously mentioned second domain controller, Server2, is illustrated. In the figure, the first domain controller, Server1, continues to function as the primary FSMO server for this domain. Server2 is placed in the domain to function as a standby FSMO server, in case of a failure on Server1. As illustrated, the standby domain controller should have a manually created replication connection to the main FSMO domain controller.

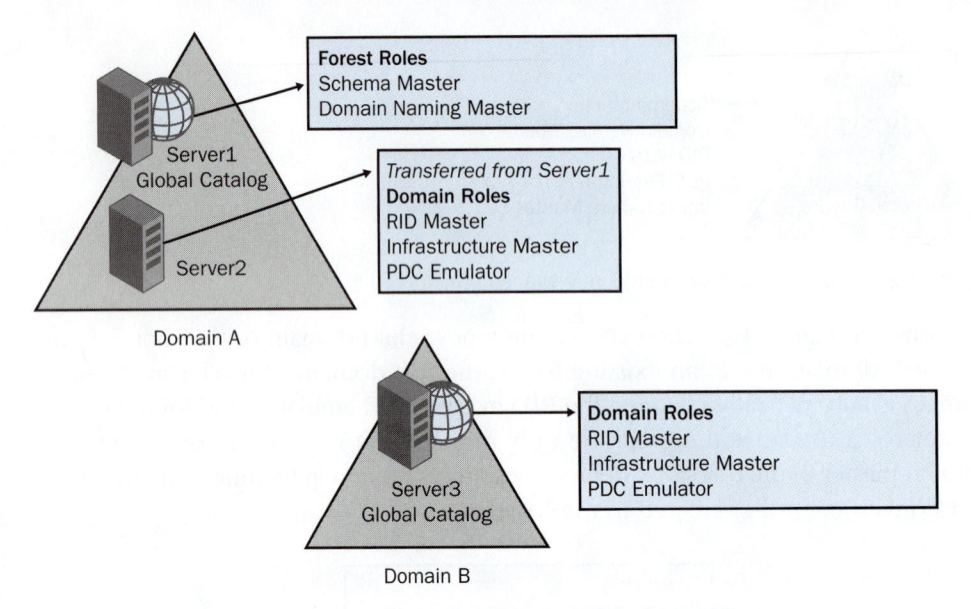

Figure 4-4 Adding a second domain controller to a domain

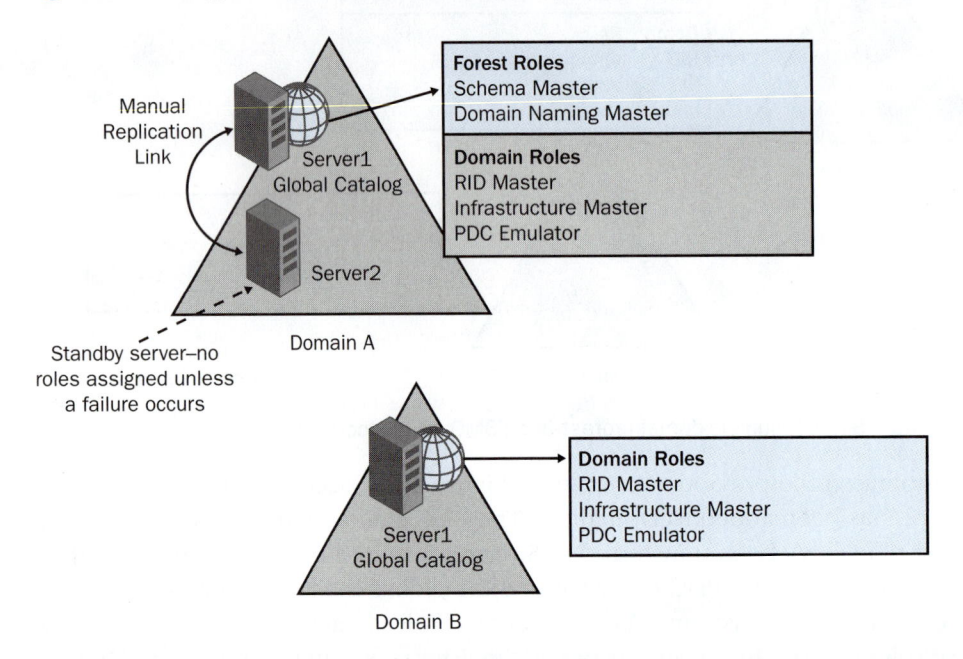

Figure 4-5 Second domain controller used as a standby server

As your company grows beyond a single site or physical location, you will need to consider placement of the FSMO roles that will accommodate growth, without compromising accessibility, fault tolerance, or performance. Table 4-2 shows a breakdown of each FSMO role and the recommended guidelines for placement. In this table, there are two attributes used to describe a domain controller: **highly available** and **high capacity**. As applied to domain controllers operating as FSMO servers, these terms are defined as follows:

- **Highly available** This domain controller is centrally located if possible and contains additional hardware such as a **redundant array of** independent disks (**RAID**) controller. RAID allows a server to keep functioning, even if one of the drives in the array experiences a failure.

- **High capacity** This domain controller has a greater processing ability relative to the other domain controllers available. A high-capacity server generally has a faster central processing unit (CPU), more memory, and faster network access.

Table 4-2 **FSMO Role Placement Planning Guidelines**

Role	Type	Guidelines
Schema Master	Forest	- One per forest. - Highly available since all schema changes take place from this domain controller.
Domain Naming Master	Forest	- One per forest. - Highly available since all domain creations and deletions must go through this domain controller. - If the functional level is set to Windows 2000, place this role on the same server as the global catalog. If the functional level is set to Windows Server 2003, this does not need to be the case.
PDC Emulator	Domain	- One per domain. - Highly available, since all domain controllers access this server for time synchronization, mismatched password logon attempts, and password changes. In addition, all BDCs and downlevel clients require this role to log on to the domain. - High capacity due to the increased load placed on this server for logon traffic and the aforementioned bulleted items. - Separate this domain controller from the global catalog server when possible to assist in providing higher capacity. - Consider lowering the SRV record's weight and priority to allow other domain controllers to have a higher priority to clients seeking authentication.
RID Master	Domain	- One per domain. - Highly available so that domain controllers needing to request identifiers for their pool have access. These RIDs are given in blocks of 500 at a time. - Place this role in a site from which most of the objects are created. This allows object creation to continue, even if a network link has failed. If all account administration does not take place from one location, place this role on a centrally located domain controller. - Configure a manual replication link between this domain controller and the one serving as a standby RID master. This minimizes the latency during replication if the role needs to be seized later. Role seizure will be discussed later in this chapter.

(continued)

Table 4-2 **FSMO Role Placement Planning Guidelines**

Role	Type	Guidelines
Infrastructure Master	Domain	■ Does not need to be placed on a high-capacity or highly available server. ■ Avoid locating this role on the same domain controller as the global catalog so that it can function properly in its role. ■ Place in the same site as the global catalog server so that they can communicate efficiently with regard to object updates.

Consider the following scenario and solutions as the corporate network described grows, using Table 4-2 as a technical reference.

Blue Yonder Airlines, a small private transportation company located in Seattle, is expanding beyond its single-location airport and office building. The current network is housed in a single building and has grown to include six domain controllers. The company's plan for growth includes the addition of several locations throughout the country. Some of these locations will be new locations, while others will be the result of planned acquisitions. Several of the planned acquisitions have Windows 2000 networks already in place. Due to this fact, the existing forest is set to Windows 2000. The first new airport and office are planned for Chicago. As shown in Figure 4-6, the initial link between the Seattle and Chicago airports will be a 256 K frame relay link. Each location will be in its own Active Directory site and configured as a child domain of blueyonderairlines.com. As locations are added, sufficient reliable links will be established to accommodate the necessary replication traffic between sites.

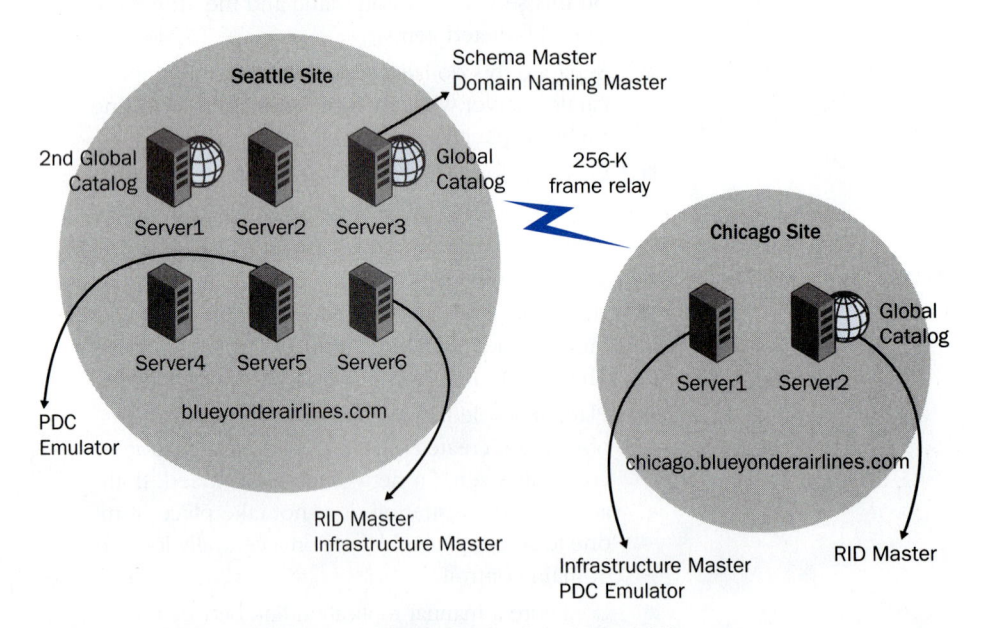

Figure 4-6 Blue Yonder Airlines FSMO plan for Seattle and Chicago

Since the Seattle location is the first domain in the forest, the schema master and domain naming master roles will reside here. In the Chicago location, the newly created child domain will have two domain controllers. These two domain controllers will provide local authentication for users in the Chicago site, while providing fault tolerance. Note the following guidelines that have been met in Figure 4-6.

CHAPTER 4: GLOBAL CATALOG AND FLEXIBLE SINGLE MASTER OPERATIONS (FSMO) ROLES

- The first domain is the forest root domain and contains the schema master and domain naming master roles.
- Each domain contains one and only one of the domain-specific roles.
- The PDC emulator and global catalog roles are on different domain controllers.
- The infrastructure master and the global catalog are separated.

Additional airport locations are planned for Atlanta and Dallas. Each of these locations will add complexity to the FSMO plan. Figure 4-7 illustrates the additional sites and a plan for FSMO placement based on the following guidelines:

- The first domain is the forest root domain and contains the schema master and domain naming master roles.
- Each domain contains one and only one of the domain-specific roles.
- The PDC emulator and global catalog roles are on different domain controllers. In addition, they are not located on domain controllers that serve any other FSMO roles. This allows faster access time for the clients.
- The infrastructure master and the global catalog are separated.

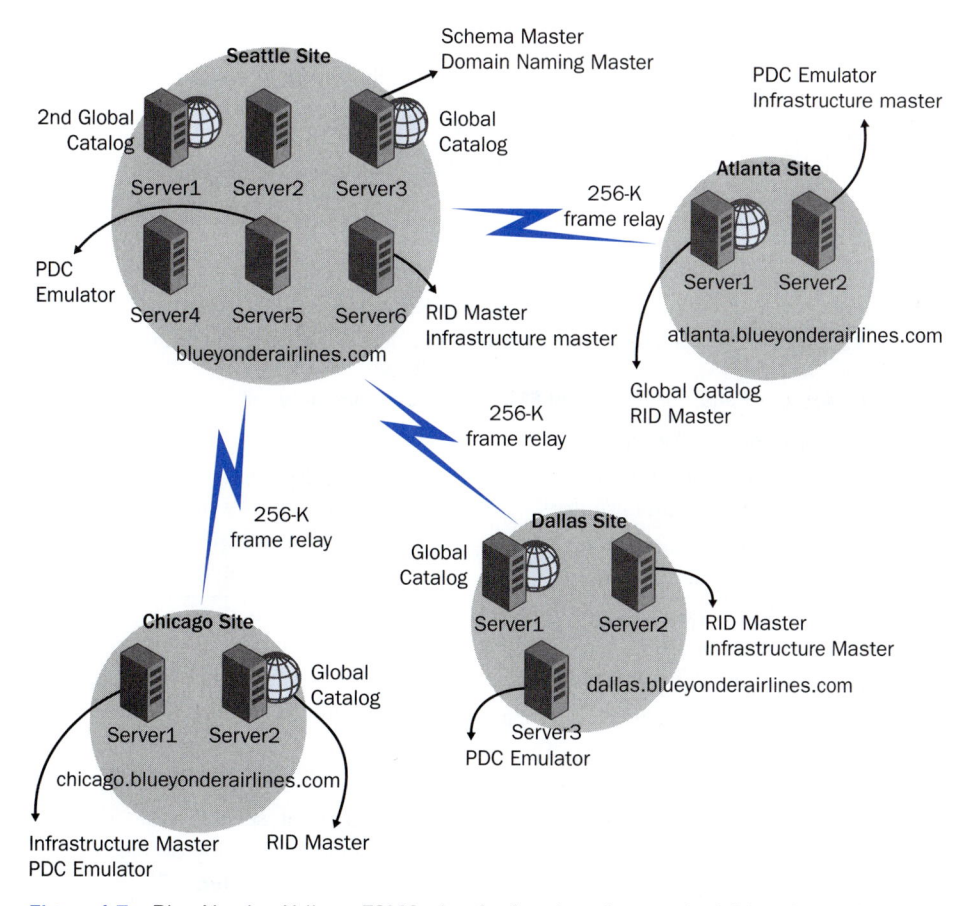

Figure 4-7 Blue Yonder Airlines FSMO plan for four locations and additional domain controllers

While reviewing this graphic, recall that if a child domain has a slow or unreliable link, a global catalog server could be replaced by enabling universal group caching.

MANAGING FSMO ROLES

Now that you have an understanding of each role and its functions and benefits, it is necessary to explain what to do when one of these roles is not accessible. In the descriptions of each role, the effects of a failure on the network are stated. Failures can be generally categorized into two areas: planned and unplanned. Planned failures are those that are based on regular maintenance, changes, or upgrades to the network. Unplanned failures are the ones that you do not expect to occur. Typically, these are the most stressful for administrators. However, the stress of an unplanned failure can be alleviated by gaining the necessary knowledge to deal with it before it happens. With regard to FSMO role management, there are two techniques that can be used to manage existing roles or recover from a failed role. These techniques are described here:

- **Role Transfer** A technique used when a role is moved gracefully from one domain controller to another. Transfers can be done as a management technique to provide improved performance or when a domain controller will be taken offline for maintenance.

- **Role Seizure** This technique is used only when there is a catastrophic failure of a domain controller holding a role. Seizing a role can be defined as a forced, permanent transfer. This procedure assumes that you cannot restore the domain controller that previously held the role.

Seizing a role is a drastic measure that should be done only if the original domain controller holding the role will not be brought back online. Prior to seizing a role, you will need to determine that this is true. If the cause for the role becoming inaccessible is a link failure, in most cases, you should wait for the role holder to become available again. The decision to seize a role also depends on the network impact of not having it available. Table 4-3 shows the impact of an unavailable FSMO role and several corrective actions that can be taken to resolve the problems created.

Table 4-3 Impact and Required Actions of FSMO Role Unavailability

Role	Impact of Unavailability	Action
Schema Master	■ Temporary loss not visible to users or administrators. ■ Visible when schema modification needs to take place.	■ If failure is deemed permanent, seize the role to a chosen standby schema master.
Domain Naming Master	■ Temporary loss not visible to users or administrators. ■ Visible when an attempt is made to create or delete a domain.	■ If failure is deemed permanent, seize the role to a chosen standby domain naming master.
RID Master	■ Temporary loss not visible to users or administrators. ■ Visible when attempt is made to create objects on a domain controller that has exhausted its relative identifiers.	■ If failure is deemed permanent, seize the role to a chosen standby domain naming master.

(continued)

Table 4-3 **Impact and Required Actions of FSMO Role Unavailability**

Role	Impact of Unavailability	Action
PDC Emulator	■ Affects network users who are attempting to log on from stations that do not have the Windows Server 2003 client installed. ■ Affects any BDCs on the network. ■ Can affect time synchronization.	■ Immediately seize the role to an alternate domain controller if users are being affected. ■ If the failure is not permanent, the role can be returned to the original domain controller when it comes back online.
Infrastructure Master	■ Temporary loss not visible to users or administrators. ■ Visible if a recent request is made to rename or move a large number of objects.	■ If failure is deemed permanent, seize the role to a chosen standby infrastructure master that is not a global catalog server in the same site. ■ If the failure is not permanent, the role may be seized and then returned to its original provider when it comes back online.

CAUTION *Bringing Failed FSMO Domain Controllers Back Online* *If the schema, domain naming, or RID master roles have been seized, the domain controllers they originated on should never be brought back online without first reformatting and reinstalling Windows Server 2003. Before performing a role seizure on any of these FSMO servers, be sure to physically disconnect the affected domain controller from the network.*

Knowing which domain controllers hold the current roles on your network is very important. This information should be included in the documentation of your network plan. However, should you need to obtain this information, the following procedures will assist you in doing so.

▶ **Viewing the Domain Roles of RID Master, PDC Emulator, or Infrastructure Master**

To view the domain roles of RID master, PDC emulator, or infrastructure master, complete the following procedure:

1. In Active Directory Users And Computers, right-click the Active Directory Users And Computers node, point to All Tasks, and select Operations Masters.

2. In the Operations Master dialog box, select the tab that represents the FSMO you wish to view. The name of the server holding your chosen role appears here.

3. Close the Operations Master dialog box.

▶ Viewing the Forest Role of Domain Naming Master

To view the forest role of domain naming master, complete the following procedure:

1. In Active Directory Domains And Trusts, right-click the Active Directory Domains And Trusts node, and select Change Operations Master. In the Change Operations Master dialog box, the name of the current domain naming master will be displayed.

2. Close the Change Operations Master dialog box.

▶ Viewing the Forest Role of Schema Master

To view the forest role of schema master, complete the following procedure:

1. Open the Active Directory Schema snap-in.

   NOTE **Accessing the Active Directory Schema Snap-in** For details on accessing the Active Directory schema snap-in, refer to Chapter 2, "Implementing Active Directory."

2. Right-click Active Directory Schema from the console tree and select Change Operations Master. The name of the current schema master role holder will appear in the Current Schema Master (Online) box.

3. Close the Change Schema Master dialog box.

Do Exercise 4-1 now to view your classroom network's current forest-wide FSMOs.

Transferring an FSMO Role

Transferring an FSMO role requires that both the source domain controller and the target domain controller are online. Table 4-4 lists the various roles to be transferred and the Active Directory console that is used for each. These are the same tools that were used to view the current role holders in the previously listed procedures.

Table 4-4 Active Directory Console Utilities for Transferring FSMO Roles

Role	Console Used
RID master, PDC emulator, and infrastructure master	Active Directory Users And Computers
Domain naming master	Active Directory Domains And Trusts
Schema master	Active Directory Schema snap-in

▶ Transferring a RID Master, PDC Emulator, or Infrastructure Master

To transfer a RID master, PDC emulator, or infrastructure master, complete the following procedure:

1. In Active Directory Users And Computers, right-click the Active Directory Users And Computers node, and select Connect To Domain.

2. In the Connect To Domain dialog box, type the domain name or click Browse to select the domain from the list, and then click OK.

3. In the console tree, right-click the Active Directory Users And Computers node, and select Connect To Domain Controller.

4. Complete this dialog box by selecting the name of the domain controller you wish to become the new role holder from the drop-down list. Click OK.

5. In the console tree, right-click the Active Directory Users And Computers node, point to All Tasks, and select Operations Masters.

6. Select the tab that reflects the role you are transferring, and click Change.

7. In the confirmation message box, click Yes to confirm the change in roles. In the next message box, click OK.

8. Close the Operations Master dialog box.

▶ **Transferring the Domain Naming Master Role Assignment**

To transfer the domain naming master role assignment, complete the following steps:

1. In Active Directory Domains And Trusts, right-click the Active Directory Domains And Trusts node, and select Connect To Domain Controller.

2. Complete this dialog box by selecting the name of the domain controller you wish to become the new domain naming master from the drop-down list. Click OK.

3. In the console tree, right-click the Active Directory Domains And Trusts node, and select Operations Master.

4. In the Change Operations Master dialog box, click Change.

5. Click Close to close the Change Operations Master dialog box.

▶ **Transferring the Schema Master Role Assignment**

To transfer the schema master role assignment, complete the following steps:

1. In the Active Directory Schema snap-in, right-click Active Directory Schema, and select Change Domain Controller.

2. In the Change Domain Controller dialog box, choose from the following:

    ❑ Any DC. This option allows Active Directory to select the new schema FSMO role holder.

    ❑ Specify Name. This option allows you to enter the name of the server to which you wish to assign the schema operations master.

3. Click OK.

4. In the console tree, right-click Active Directory Schema, and select Operations Master.

5. In the Change Schema Master dialog box, click Change.

6. Click OK to close the Change Schema Master dialog box.

Seizing an FSMO Role

Seizing an FSMO role is usually done because of an unrecoverable failure to the original FSMO server. If the original FSMO role server is still functioning, the role should be transferred, not seized. Seizing a role is a drastic measure that should be performed only in the event of a permanent role holder failure. The process requires two steps. In the first step, you must make sure that the domain controller that will hold the new role is up to date with regard to the updates performed on the failed role holder. This can be accomplished using the Repadmin command-line tool. The second step is the actual process of seizing the role using the Ntdsutil utility. Each of these steps is explained in the text that follows.

Determining the Status of the Target Domain Controller Using Repadmin.exe

Due to natural latency in the replication of Active Directory information in your domain, your target domain controller may not be perfectly in synch with the latest updates. To avoid losing data during a seizure operation, the target domain controller must have the latest information that was held by the previous role holder. The Repadmin.exe command line tool can be used to check the status of updates for a domain controller. This tool is included with the Windows Support Tools.

> **NOTE** **Windows Support Tools** Detailed instructions on how to install the support tools were provided in Chapter 3, "Working with Active Directory Sites."

To understand how you determine if the target domain controller is up to date, consider the following example.

You are the administrator for a domain that contains three domain controllers. ServerA is the RID master of the domain blueyonderairlines.com, ServerB is your planned new RID master if ServerA fails, and ServerC is the only other domain controller in the domain. You need to determine what the latest update to ServerA was before it stopped functioning. To do this, you would use the Repadmin tool with the /showutdvec switch to determine if ServerB has the most up-to-date information. For this example, you would type the following commands from a command line prompt:

```
C:\> repadmin /showutdvec serverB.blueyonderairlines.com dc=blueyonderairlines,dc=com
New-York\serverA        @ USN 2604      @ Time 2003-07-03 12:50:44
San-Francisco\serverC   @ USN 2706      @ Time 2003-07-03 12:53:36

C:\>repadmin /showutdvec serverC.blueyonderairlines.com dc=blueyonderairlines,dc=com
New-York\serverA        @ USN 2590      @ Time 2003-07-03 12:50:44
Chicago\serverB         @ USN 3110      @ Time 2003-07-03 12:57:55
```

The preceding commands reflect a query for replication information from the two domain controllers not affected by the failure. The output for ServerA is the most important information. On ServerB, the last update number received from ServerA was 2604, which is more recent than the update of 2590 shown on ServerC, in the results of the second command line. This output means that ServerB has more recent information than ServerC with regard to ServerA. If this information was reversed and you still wished to have the role seized by ServerB, you could wait until the next replication period or force an immediate synchronization. The key here is that you have made sure that the domain controller you wish to take over the RID master role in this domain has the most recent information.

To practice using Repadmin.exe, do Exercise 4-2 now.

Using Ntdsutil.exe to Seize an FSMO Role

The Ntdsutil tool allows you to transfer and seize FSMO roles. When you use the Ntdsutil command line tool to seize an FSMO role, the tool attempts a transfer from the current role owner first. Then, if the existing FSMO holder is unavailable, it performs the seizure.

▶ Seizing the FSMO Role Assignments

To seize the FSMO role assignments, complete the following steps:

1. Click Start, and then click Command Prompt.
2. At the command prompt, type **ntdsutil** and press Enter.
3. At the ntdsutil prompt, type **roles** and press Enter.
4. At the fsmo maintenance prompt, type **connections** and press Enter.
5. At the server connections prompt, type **connect to server**, followed by the fully qualified domain name, and press Enter.
6. At the server connections prompt, type **quit** and press Enter.
7. At the fsmo maintenance prompt, type one of the following:
   - **seize schema master** and press Enter
   - **seize domain naming master** and press Enter
   - **seize RID master** and press Enter
   - **seize PDC** and press Enter
   - **seize infrastructure master** and press Enter
8. At the fsmo maintenance prompt, type **quit** and press Enter.
9. At the ntdsutil prompt, type **quit** and press Enter.

SUMMARY

- The global catalog server acts as a central repository for Active Directory by holding a complete copy of all objects within its local domain and a partial copy of all objects from other domains within the same forest. The global catalog has three main functions: the facilitation of searches for objects in the forest, resolution of UPN names, and provision of universal group membership information.

- A global catalog should be placed in each site when possible. As an alternate solution when a site is across an unreliable WAN link, universal group membership caching can be enabled for the site to facilitate logon requests.

- Global catalog placement considerations include: the speed and reliability of the WAN link, the amount of traffic that will be generated by replication, the size of the global catalog database, and the applications that might require use of port 3268 for resolution.

- Operations master roles are assigned to domain controllers to perform single-master operations.

- The schema master and domain naming master roles are forest-wide. Every forest must have one and only one of each of these roles.

- The RID master, PDC emulator, and infrastructure master roles are domain-wide. Every domain must have one and only one of each of these roles.

- The default placement of FSMO roles is sufficient for a single-site environment. However, as your network expands, these roles should be divided to increase performance and reliability. Table 4-2 provides detailed guidelines.

- There are two ways to manage the FSMO roles: role transfer and role seizure. You transfer an FSMO role to other domain controllers in the domain or forest to balance the load among domain controllers, or accommodate domain controller maintenance and hardware upgrades. You seize an FSMO role assignment when a server holding the role fails and you do not intend to restore it. Seizing an FSMO role is a drastic step that should be considered only if the current FSMO role holder will never be available again.

- Repadmin is used to check the status of the update sequence numbers (USNs) when seizing the FSMO role from the current role holder. Ntdsutil is used to actually perform a seizure of the FSMO role.

EXERCISES

Exercise 4-1: Viewing Forest-Wide FSMOs

The domain naming master and schema master roles are forest-wide FSMO roles. The following exercise will show you how to view the holders of these roles.

To view the schema master FSMO holder, complete the following steps:

1. Add and open the Active Directory Active Directory Schema snap-in by completing the following substeps:

    a. From a command prompt, type **regsvr32 schmmgmt.dll**.

b. Close the command prompt window, click Start, and then select Run.

   c. Type **mmc /a** in the dialog box, and click OK.

   d. From the File menu, select Add/Remove Snap-in.

   e. Click Add to see the list of available snap-ins.

   f. Double-click Active Directory Schema from the list.

   g. Click Close, and then click OK.

2. Right-click Active Directory Schema from the console tree, and select Change Operations Master. The name of the current schema master role holder will appear in the Current Schema Master (Online) box.

3. Close the Change Schema Master dialog box.

To view the domain naming master FSMO holder, complete the following steps:

1. In Active Directory Domains And Trusts, right-click the Active Directory Domains And Trusts node, and select Change Operations Master. In the Change Operations Master dialog box, the name of the current domain naming master will be displayed.

2. Close the Change Operations Master dialog box.

Exercise 4-2: Using Repadmin

This exercise will assist you in learning about the functionality of the Repadmin.exe tool.

1. From a command prompt, type **repadmin /?**

2. Based on the help screen shown for the output, list three switches and describe their functions.

REVIEW QUESTIONS

1. What is the database that serves as a central repository for all Active Directory objects called?

   a. Main database

   b. Central catalog

   c. Global database

   d. Global catalog

   e. Enterprise catalog

2. Which of the following roles are forest-wide roles?

   a. PDC emulator

   b. Infrastructure master

   c. Domain naming master

   d. Schema master

   e. Global catalog

3. Your single-domain company is planning to add a second location that will access the domain via a frame relay connection. The frame relay service that has been used in the past in your area is unreliable, but it is the only choice you have for now. You have determined that the connection will not need to be used very frequently if you set things up properly. This location will have approximately 20 users. You plan to install a domain controller for these users to log on to and share data. What should you do at this site to allow users to log on to the network?

4. Use this scenario to answer the following questions.

   Contoso Pharmaceuticals has 500 employees in 14 locations. The company headquarters is in Hartford, CT. All locations are part of the contoso.com domain, contain at least two servers, and are connected by reliable links.

   a. Which FSMO roles are most likely held at the Hartford location?

   b. While trying to add new user accounts to the domain, you receive an error that the accounts cannot be created. You are logged on as a member of the Domain Admins group. What is most likely causing the problem?

   c. What should you consider placing at each location to facilitate logons?

5. Contoso Pharmaceuticals is expanding to include several newly acquired companies. Although they will each become part of the contoso.com forest, each of these companies wants to maintain their own decentralized management strategy. To accommodate this request, you have installed the subsidiaries as separate domain structures. One of them is named litwareinc.com.

   a. Which roles will this new domain need to accommodate?

   b. If litwareinc.com decides to have a small satellite office included in their domain for several users, without having logon traffic using their available bandwidth to the parent domain, what should they do?

   c. In contoso.com, your server functioning as the domain naming master has failed due to a power surge. You are unable to create a new child domain for a new location until this server is back online. Currently it is not expected that the domain naming master issue will be resolved in a reasonable amount of time. What steps should you take so that you can resolve this problem and create the necessary child domain?

   d. In one of the locations, you have Microsoft Windows 98 clients that cannot access resources in the domain. They have been functioning just fine until today. What might be causing them to not have the ability to access the domain?

CASE SCENARIOS

Scenario 4-1: Creating a Global Catalog and Assigning FSMO Roles

Create a plan for global catalog and FSMO role assignments using Figure 4-8. Figure 4-8 shows a network design for a mid-size organization. Complete Table 4-5 to document your plan.

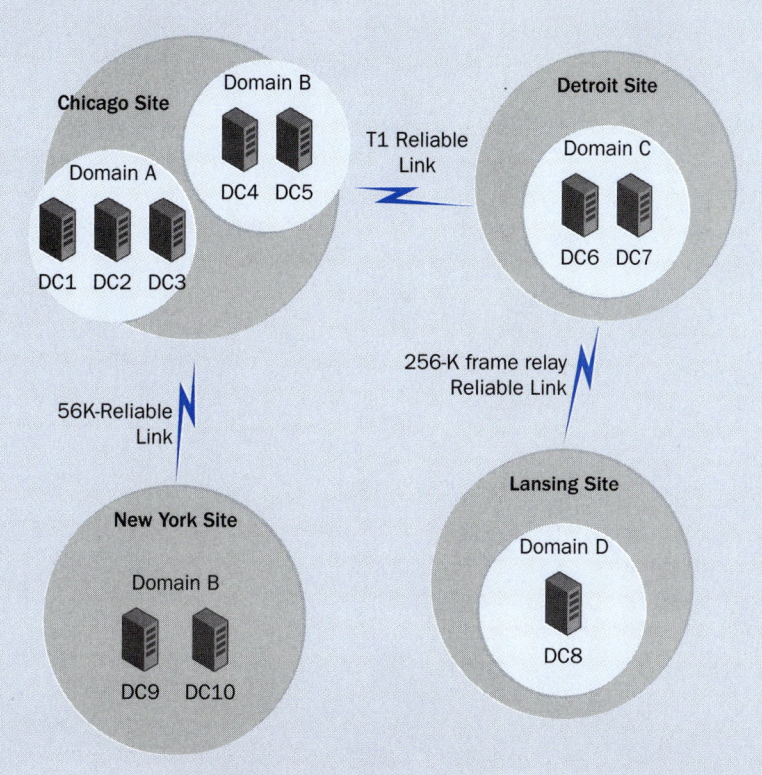

Figure 4-8 Network design for Scenario 4-1

Table 4-5 **FSMO Role Placement**

Server	Site	Domain	Global Catalog Yes or No	Roles Assigned
DC1	Chicago	A		
DC2	Chicago	A		
DC3	Chicago	A		
DC4	Chicago	B		
DC5	Chicago	B		
DC6	Detroit	C		
DC7	Detroit	C		
DC8	Lansing	D		
DC9	New York	B		
DC10	New York	B		

Scenario 4-2: Developing a Contingency Plan for a Failed FSMO

Develop a rules-based contingency plan for recovery from a failed FSMO role using your implementation plan from Scenario 4-1. You should include a plan for each server you assigned a role to in Scenario 4-1.

CHAPTER 5
ACTIVE DIRECTORY ADMINISTRATION

Upon completion of this chapter, you will be able to:

- Describe local, domain, and built-in user accounts.
- Understand security and distribution groups and their purpose in Active Directory.
- Understand, plan, and implement local, global, domain local, and universal groups.
- Understand, plan, and implement group nesting.
- Use scripting tools such as CSVDE, LDIFDE, and VBScript to modify, create, and delete multiple users and groups.

In this chapter, we will discuss Active Directory administration as it relates to user and group accounts. As you have already learned, users receive access to resources based on their permissions and the resource's access control list (ACL). The ACL associated with an object includes permissions granted to the individual user or computer account, and any groups to which either one belongs. This chapter focuses on planning and implementing appropriate user and group account types and the tools used to automate the creation of these accounts.

UNDERSTANDING USER ACCOUNTS

The user account is the center of security for resource access. All resource access takes place through user accounts. In order to gain access to the network, prospective network users must authenticate to a network using a specific user account for **authentication**. Authentication is the process of confirming that the user has the correct permissions to access the required network resources. This is done by validating the username and password supplied in the Logon dialog box with a username and password that are mapped against a matching account in the Active Directory database. Once this authentication process is complete, an access token is created for the user. The access token contains access permissions to resources for which the user has been granted access.

There are three types of user accounts that can be used in Windows Server 2003. They include **local user accounts**, **domain user accounts**, and **built-in user accounts**. Each of these account types is described here briefly.

- **Local user accounts**   These accounts are used for access to the local computer. Accounts are stored in the local security database, named the Security Accounts Manager (or the SAM database), on the computer in which these accounts were created. They are never replicated to other computers, nor do these accounts have access to the domain by default.

- **Domain user accounts**   These accounts are used for access to domain resources such as shared folders or printers. Account information for users and computers is stored in the Active Directory database and is replicated to all domain controllers within the same domain. A subset of the domain user account information is replicated to the global catalog, which is then replicated to other global catalog servers throughout the forest.

- **Built-in user accounts**   These accounts are automatically created when Microsoft Windows Server 2003 is installed. Built-in user accounts are created on a member server or a standalone server. However, when Windows Server 2003 is installed as a domain controller, the ability to manipulate these accounts is disabled. By default, there are two built-in user accounts created on a Windows Server 2003 computer: the Administrator account and the Guest account.

The Administrator Account

On a member server or standalone server, the built-in local Administrator account has full control of all files as well as complete management permissions for the local computer. This account is used to manage file access and computer settings such as Internet Protocol (IP) addresses. On a domain controller, the built-in Administrator account created in Active Directory has full control in the domain in which it was created. There is only one Administrator account per domain created by default automatically. This account is used to manage all aspects of the domain, including permission assignments, object creation and deletion, and security policy implementation and management. Neither the local Administrator account on a member server or standalone server nor a domain Administrator account can be deleted, but they can be renamed. Renaming an Administrator account prevents unauthorized users from having 50 percent of the information required to log on, namely the logon identity of *Administrator*.

The following list summarizes several security guidelines you should consider with regard to the Administrator account:

- **Rename the Administrator account.** As previously stated, this will frustrate intruders by removing from their scope of knowledge half of what is necessary to gain access to your domain.

- **Set a strong password.** The Guest account by default will allow a blank password. For security reasons, you should not allow blank passwords. Make sure that the password is at least seven characters in length and contains uppercase and lowercase letters, numbers, and alphanumeric characters. Microsoft refers to this technique as **strong passwords**. Details on this are covered in Chapter 6, "Security Planning and Administrative Delegation."

- **Limit knowledge of administrator passwords to only a few individuals.** Limiting the distribution of administrator passwords limits the risk of security breaches using this account.

- **Do not use the Administrator account for daily non-administrative tasks.** Microsoft recommends using a standard user account for normal work and using the Run As command either from a menu, a shortcut, or the command line when administrative tasks need to be performed. The Run As command is covered in Chapter 6, "Security Planning and Administrative Delegation."

The Guest Account

The built-in Guest account is used to provide temporary access to the network for a user such as a vendor representative or a temporary employee. Like the administrator account, this account cannot be deleted, but it can and should be renamed. In addition, the Guest account is disabled by default and is not assigned a password by default. In a high-security network, you might consider creating a different account for temporary user access. In this way, you can be sure the account follows corporate security guidelines defined for temporary users. However, should you decide to use the Guest account, review the following list of summarized guidelines:

- **Rename the Guest account after enabling it for use.** As discussed with regard to the Administrator account, this will deny intruders half of what is necessary to gain access to your domain.

- **Set a strong password.** The Guest account by default is configured with a blank password. For security reasons, you should not allow a blank password. Make sure that the password is at least seven characters in length and contains uppercase and lowercase letters, numbers, and alphanumeric characters. Microsoft refers to this technique as **strong passwords**. Details on this are covered in Chapter 6, "Security Planning and Administrative Delegation."

> **MORE INFO** **User Account Creation and Management** Additional information and steps for creating and managing user accounts can be found in the Microsoft Windows Server 2003 online product documentation located at: http://www.microsoft.com/technet/treeview/default.asp?url=/technet/prodtechnol/windowsserver2003/proddocs/entserver/ctasks005.asp.

GROUPS AND THEIR USES

When Microsoft Windows NT was released, groups were introduced to help make network permissions easier to administer. **Groups** are implemented to allow administrators to assign permissions to multiple users simultaneously. A group can be defined as a collection of user or computer accounts that is used to simplify the assignment of permissions to network resources. Group memberships act in a manner that is similar to memberships in a physical fitness center. Suppose the fitness center offers several different membership levels and associated privileges. For example, if you simply want to use the weight machines, treadmills, and stationary bicycles, you pay for a first-level membership. If you wish to use the swimming pool and spa privileges, you pay for the second level. You assume that when you purchase your membership level, you receive an access card that allows you to enter the parts of the building where these activities take place. This card contains a magnetic strip that is read at the door of the facility. If your card does not contain the appropriate permissions, access to that part of the building is denied. Similarly, all members who belong to a particular membership level receive the same benefits. The access card for your fitness center serves as proof that you have paid for certain usage privileges.

In Windows Server 2003, group membership functions in much the same way as any club membership. When a user logs on, an **access token** is created that identifies the user and all of his or her group memberships. This access token, like a club membership card, is used to verify permissions when a user attempts to use a resource. By using groups, multiple users can be given the same permission level for resources on the network. Suppose, for example, that you have 25 users in the graphics department of your company who all need access to print to a color printer. Either you can assign each user the appropriate printing permissions for the printer, or you can create a group containing the 25 users and assign the appropriate permissions to the group. By using a group object to access a resource, you have accomplished the following:

- Users who need access to the printer can simply be added to the group. Once added, the user receives all permissions assigned to this group. Similarly, you can remove users from the group when you no longer wish to allow them access to the printer.

- The users' level of access for the printer needs to be changed only once for all users. Changing the group's permissions changes the permission level for all group members. Without the group, all 25 user accounts would need to be modified individually.

Users can be members of more than one group. In addition, groups can contain other Active Directory objects such as computers, and other groups such as global groups, as members of domain local groups. In Windows 2000 native or higher domains, groups can also be added to other groups to further consolidate permission assignments. For example, consider a company that has two groups: marketing and graphic design. There is a group object created for both groups, and each one contains the users in their respective department. Graphic design group members have access to a high-resolution color laser printer that the marketing group personnel need to access. To simplify the assignment of permissions for the color laser printer to the marketing group, the marketing group object could simply be added as a member of the graphic design group. This would give the marketing group members the same permission to the color laser printer as the members of the graphic design group.

The following section describes the different group types and scopes that can be used in Windows Server 2003 to simplify administration.

GROUP TYPES

Group types define how a group is to be used. There are only two group categories that can be created and stored in the Active Directory database.

- **Distribution groups** Nonsecurity-related groups created for the distribution of information to one or more persons.
- **Security groups** Security-related groups created for purposes of granting resource access permissions to multiple users.

Distribution Groups

Applications use distribution groups as lists for nonsecurity-related functions. For example, a distribution group might be created to allow an e-mail application such as Microsoft Exchange to send messages to multiple users, or a software distribution program such as Microsoft Systems Management Server to update desktop applications. Only applications designed to work with Active Directory can use distribution groups.

Security Groups

Groups that can be assigned permissions to resources are named security groups. Multiple users that need access to a particular resource can be made members of a security group. The security group is then given permission to access the resource, as shown in Figure 5-1.

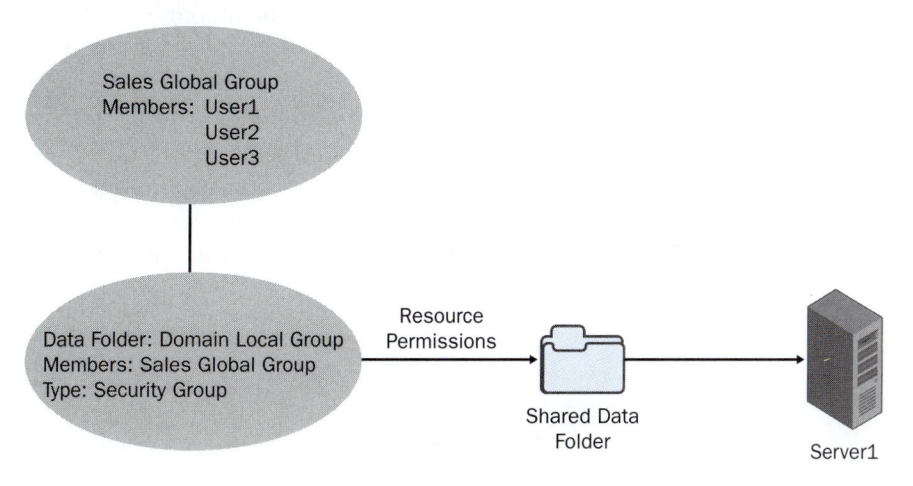

Figure 5-1 Security group membership and permissions

In addition to allowing permissions to be assigned, security groups can also function as distribution groups. For example, an e-mail message that is sent to a security group is received by all users that are members of that group. This scenario assumes that the group object's Contact List property is configured with valid e-mail addresses.

Converting Group Types

After a group is created, it can be converted from a security group to a distribution group, and vice versa, at any time, as long as the domain functional level is set to Windows 2000 native or higher. The Windows 2000 mixed domain functional level does not support the conversions of groups.

GROUP SCOPES

In addition to security and distribution group types, there are several **group scopes**. A group scope is defined by where it is located or stored. For example, if a group is located on a local computer, the permissions assigned to the group affect only the local computer, making its scope local. Similarly, if a group is located within the Active Directory domain, associated permissions affect either that specific domain or possibly the forest.

The domain and forest functional levels have an effect on the available group scopes in Windows Server 2003. The group scopes available in a domain with the functional level set to Windows 2000 native or higher include the **domain local**, **global**, and **universal** groups.

Domain Local Groups

- **Membership** Members can include user accounts, computer accounts, global groups, and universal groups from any domain, in addition to other domain local groups from the same domain.

- **Purpose** Domain local groups are used to assign permissions to resources. Resources for which you are assigning permissions must reside in the same domain as the domain local group.

Domain local groups can make permission assignment and maintenance easier to manage. For example, if you have 10 users that need access to a shared folder, you can create a domain local group that has the appropriate permissions to this shared folder. Next you would create a global or universal group and add the 10 user accounts as members of this group. Finally, you add the global group to the domain local group. The 10 users will then have access to the shared folder via their membership in the global group. Any additional users that need access to this shared folder can simply be added to the global group and they will automatically receive the necessary permissions.

> **NOTE** **Individual Accounts as Domain Local Group Members** Although individual accounts can be added to a domain local group, Microsoft recommends using global groups for user account organization and domain local groups for permission assignments.

Global Groups

- **Membership** Members can include user accounts, computer accounts, and/or other global groups from within the same domain as the global group when the domain functional level is set to Windows 2000 native or later.

- **Purpose** Global groups are used to organize users according to the needs of the organization. These needs may include access to resources. They can be used to facilitate permission assignments to any resource located in any domain in the forest. This is accomplished by placing the global group into a domain local group that has been given the desired permissions.

Global group memberships are stored at the domain level, which means that changes are replicated only to domain controllers within the same domain. Users with common resource needs should be placed in a global group to facilitate the assignment of permissions to resources. Changes to the group membership list can be as frequent as necessary to allow users the necessary resource permissions.

> **NOTE** **Global Groups Listed on the ACL of Resources** Although global groups can be added directly to the ACL of a resource, Microsoft recommends domain local groups for permission assignments. Global groups can be added as members of domain local groups that contain the desired resource permissions.

Universal Groups

- **Membership** Members can include user accounts, computer accounts, and/or other global or universal groups from anywhere in the forest. If a cross-forest trust exists, universal groups can contain similar accounts from a trusted forest.

- **Purpose** Universal groups, like global groups, are used to organize users according to their resource access needs. They can be used to organize users to facilitate access to any resource located in any domain in the forest through the use of domain local groups. To gain access to universal groups, the domain functional level must be set for Windows 2000 native or Windows Server 2003. Windows 2000 mixed does not support universal groups.

Universal groups are used to consolidate groups and accounts that either span multiple domains or span the entire forest. A key point in the application and utilization of universal groups is that group memberships in universal groups should not change frequently, due to the fact that these groups are stored in the global catalog. Changes to universal group membership lists are replicated to all global catalog servers throughout the domain. If these changes occur frequently, a significant amount of bandwidth could be used for replication traffic.

Universal groups are not available in a domain set to Windows 2000 mixed functionality.

The scope of previously described groups and their boundaries are shown in Figure 5-2.

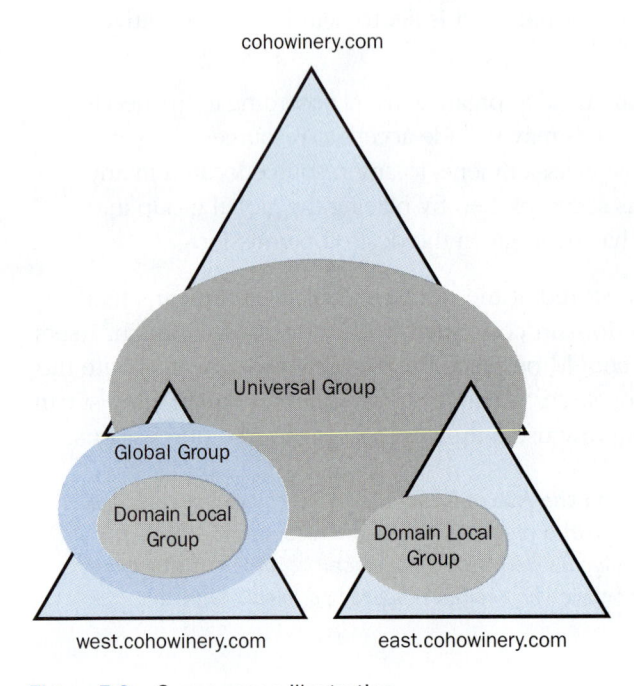

Figure 5-2 Group scope illustration

When you create a group, you must choose both the group type and the group scope. Figure 5-3 shows the New Object - Group dialog box in Active Directory Users And Computers. All options discussed thus far are available for selection in this dialog box.

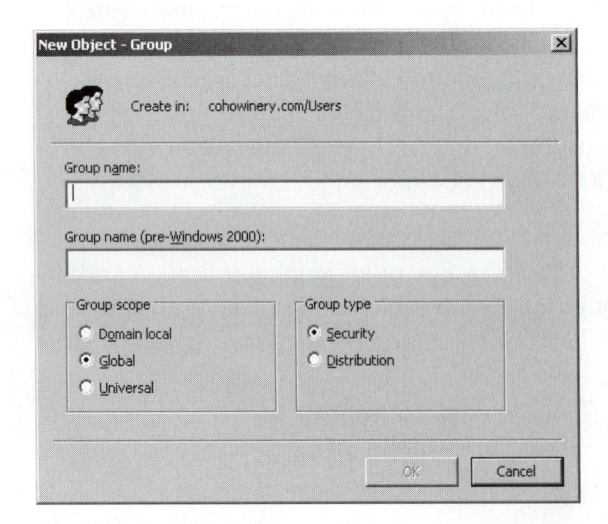

Figure 5-3 Dialog box for creating a group in Active Directory

Group Nesting

Nesting is the term used when groups are added as members of other groups. For example, when a global group is made a member of a universal group, it is said to be nested. Nesting helps to reduce the number of times permissions need to be assigned. For example, assume you have multiple locations in your company and the users in each location need to access an enterprise database application located in the parent domain. The simplest way to set up access to this application is as follows:

1. Create global groups in each location that contain all users needing access to the enterprise database.

2. Create a universal group in the parent domain. Include each location's global group as a member.

3. Associate the universal group with the required domain local group to assign the necessary permission to access and use the enterprise database.

Figure 5-4 illustrates the previously described process. Since the global groups are members of the requisite universal group, which has been mapped against the appropriate domain local group with the appropriate permissions, all users in the global group receive the permission to access the enterprise database. Although Windows Server 2003 operating systems set to either Windows 2000 native or Windows 2003 forest functional levels allow an increased number of groups over Windows 2000 to be nested, it is important to keep careful records of the hierarchy you create and the group memberships.

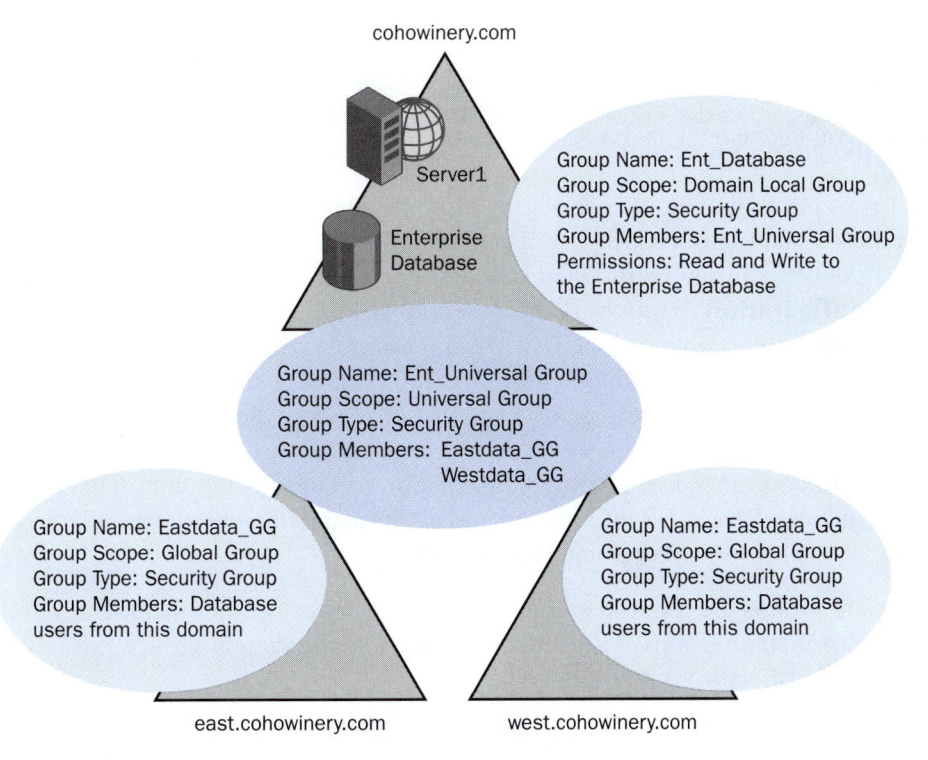

Figure 5-4 Group nesting used to simplify permissions

Functional Levels and Group Scopes

As mentioned earlier, the domain functional level has an effect on the available group scopes and their nesting abilities. Table 5-1 summarizes the information that was presented in regard to functional level settings and group options.

Table 5-1 Functional Levels and Group Scopes

Group Scope	In Domains with the Domain Functional Level Set to Windows 2000 Mixed, Scope Can Contain	In Domains with the Domain Functional Level Set to Windows 2000 Native or Windows Server 2003, Scope Can Contain
Global	User accounts and computer accounts from the same domain	User accounts, computer accounts, and global groups from the same domain
Domain local	User accounts, computer accounts, and global groups from any domain	User accounts, computer accounts, global groups, and universal groups from any domain; domain local groups from the same domain
Universal	Not available in domains with a domain functional level set to Windows 2000 mixed	User accounts, computer accounts, global groups, and other universal groups from any domain in the forest

Default Groups

Although there are many situations in which you create groups to organize users or computers and then assign permissions, there are several **built-in security groups** that are created when Windows Server 2003 Active Directory is installed. Many of the built-in groups are assigned a set of predefined rights that allow members to perform certain network-related tasks such as backup and restore. Accounts added to the membership of these default groups receive all of the rights to perform associated tasks, in addition to any resource access permissions to which the group is assigned.

The Users and Built-in container objects in Active Directory Users And Computers hold these default groups. The list of predefined groups you see in these containers vary depending on the installed services. For example, when the **Dynamic Host Configuration Protocol (DHCP)** service is installed, two new groups appear in the users container, the DHCP Administrators group and the DHCP Users group. The DHCP Administrators group has full control to manage the DHCP server, while the DHCP Users group can be used to view the DHCP server information. DHCP is the service used to deliver dynamic Transmission Control Protocol/Internet Protocol (TCP/IP) information to client computers. This information includes IP address information and additional parameters such as Domain Name System (DNS) server pointers and so on.

All default groups are security groups. Active Directory does not include any default distribution groups. Table 5-2 explains all of the default groups created when Active Directory is first installed.

Table 5-2 **Default Groups**

Group Name	Group Scope	Location in Active Directory	Default Members	Purpose	Special Notes
Account Operators	Domain local	Built-in container	None	Members can administer domain user and group accounts. Specifically, by default members can create, modify, and delete accounts for users, groups, and computers in all containers and organizational units (OUs) of Active Directory, except the Built-in folder and the Domain Controller's OU.	Members do not have permission to modify the Administrators, Domain Admins, and Enterprise Admins groups, nor do they have permission to modify the accounts for members of those groups.
Administrators	Domain local	Built-in container	Administrator account, Domain Admins global group from the specific domain, and the Enterprise Admins universal group.	Members have complete and unrestricted access to the computer or domain controller locally, including the right to change their own permissions.	None
Backup Operators	Domain local	Built-in container	None	Members can back up and restore all files on a computer, regardless of the permissions that protect those files. Members can also log on to the computer and shut it down.	None
Guests	Domain local	Built-in container	Domain Guests global group and the Guests user account.	Members have the same privileges as members of the Users group.	The Guest account is disabled by default.
Incoming Forest Trust Builders	Domain local	Built-in container	None	Members can create incoming, one-way trusts to this forest.	None
Network Configuration Operators	Domain local	Built-in container	None	Members have the same default rights as members of the Users group. Members can perform all tasks related to the client side of network configuration, except for installing and removing drivers and services.	Members cannot configure network server services such as the Domain Name System (DNS) and DHCP server services.

(continued)

Table 5-2 **Default Groups**

Group Name	Group Scope	Location in Active Directory	Default Members	Purpose	Special Notes
Performance Log Users	Domain local	Built-in container	None	Members have remote access to schedule logging of performance counters on this computer.	None
Performance Monitor Users	Domain local	Built-in container	Network Service from the NT Authority folder. This is a placeholder account that may or may not be used.	Members have remote access to monitor this computer.	None
Pre–Windows 2000 Compatible Access	Domain local	Built-in container	Authenticated Users from the NT Authority folder. This is a placeholder account that may or may not be used.	Members have read access on all users and groups in the domain. This group is provided for backward compatibility for computers running Microsoft Windows NT Server 4.0 and earlier.	None
Print Operators	Domain local	Built-in container	None	Members can manage printers and document queues.	This group exists only on domain controllers.
Remote Desktop Users	Domain local	Built-in container	None	Members can log on to a computer from a remote location.	None
Replicator	Domain local	Built-in container	None	This group supports directory replication functions and is used by the file replication service on domain controllers. The only member should be a domain user account that is used to log on to the replicator services of the domain controller.	Do not add users to this group. They are added automatically by the system.

(continued)

Table 5-2 **Default Groups**

Group Name	Group Scope	Location in Active Directory	Default Members	Purpose	Special Notes
Server Operators	Domain local	Built-in container	None	Members can do the following: ■ Log on to a server interactively. ■ Create and delete network shares. ■ Start and stop some services. ■ Back up and restore files. ■ Format the hard disk of the computer. ■ Shut down the computer. ■ Modify the system date and time.	This group exists only on domain controllers.
Users	Domain local	Built-in container	Domain Users global group, Authenticated Users Special Identity group, and Interactive Special Identity group.	Used to allow general access. Members can run applications, use printers, shut down and start the computer, and use network shares for which they are assigned permissions.	None
Cert Publishers	Domain local	Users container	None	Members of this group are permitted to publish certificates to Active Directory.	None
DnsAdmins (installed with DNS)	Domain local	Users container	None	Members of this group are permitted administrative access to the DNS server service.	None
HelpServices	Domain local	Users container	The account associated with Microsoft support applications such as Microsoft Remote Assistance.	This group allows administrators to set rights common to all support applications.	Do not add users to this group. It is managed automatically by the Help And Support service.

(continued)

Table 5-2 Default Groups

Group Name	Group Scope	Location in Active Directory	Default Members	Purpose	Special Notes
RAS and IAS Servers	Domain local	Users container	None	Servers in this group—for the Remote Access Service (RAS) and Internet Authentication Service (IAS)—are permitted access to the remote access properties of users.	None
TelnetClients	Domain local	Users container	None	Members of this group have access to Telnet Server on this system.	None
DnsUpdateProxy (installed with DNS)	Global	Users container	None	Members of this group are DNS clients who are permitted to perform dynamic updates on behalf of some other clients such as DHCP servers.	None
Domain Admins	Global	Users container	Administrator user account for the domain.	Members of this group can perform administrative tasks on any computer anywhere in the domain.	None
Domain Computers	Global	Users container	Members include all workstations and servers joined to the domain, in addition to any computer accounts manually created.	Any computer account created in a domain is automatically added to this group. The group can be used to make computer management easier through group policies, which are discussed in Chapters 7 through 10.	None
Domain Controllers	Global	Users container	Members include all domain controllers within the respective domain.	All computers installed in the domain as domain controllers are automatically added to this group.	None
Domain Guests	Global	Users container	Guest account.	Members include all domain guests.	None

(continued)

Table 5-2 **Default Groups**

Group Name	Group Scope	Location in Active Directory	Default Members	Purpose	Special Notes
Domain Users	Global	Users container	User account created in a domain is automatically added to this group.	Members include all domain users. This group can be used to assign permissions to all users in the domain. If, for example, you wish to allow all users in the domain permission to use an application, the Domain Users group can be added to the appropriate domain local group with the required access permissions.	None
Group Policy Creator Owners	Global	Users container	Administrator user account for the domain.	Members can modify group policy for the domain.	None
Enterprise Admins (appears only on forest root domain controllers)	Universal	Users container	Administrator user account for the forest root domain.	This group is added to the Administrators group on all domain controllers in the forest. This allows the global administrative privileges associated with this group, such as the ability to create and delete domains.	None
Schema Admins (appears only on forest root domain controllers)	Universal	Users container	Administrator user account for the forest root domain.	Members can manage and modify the Active Directory schema.	None

To practice viewing group object members and properties, do Exercise 5-1 now.

CAUTION Server Operators, Domain Admins, Enterprise Admins, and Schema Admins These groups have full control within their respective scopes. Add users with caution. Changes made using these accounts can cause irreversible damage to your network.

The groups described in the previous table are the groups that are visible by viewing their respective containers in the Active Directory Users And Computers snap-in. You may also encounter several additional groups when reviewing permission assignments. These are named **special identity groups**. You cannot manually modify the group membership of special identity groups, nor can you view their membership lists. Windows Server 2003 uses these groups to represent a class of users or the system itself. For example, the Everyone group is a special identity group that contains all authenticated users and domain guests. The Everyone group is explained in the next section.

Windows Server 2003 introduces several security enhancements, including the **Anonymous Logon group** modifications. Prior to Windows Server 2003, the special identity Anonymous Logon group was a member of the Everyone group. The Everyone group was by default granted full control to newly created network resources. Anonymous logon means the user does not have to supply a username or password to access the network. To disallow unauthorized access to resources intended for authenticated users, the administrator in a Windows NT or Windows 2000 network needs to remove the Everyone group from the ACL of resources. If this is inadvertently forgotten, it creates a security risk with regard to those resources.

The Anonymous Logon group is no longer a member of the Everyone group in Windows Server 2003. Resources for which you want to allow anonymous access must be specifically configured with the Anonymous Logon group as a member of the ACL for that resource.

Table 5-3 lists the special identity groups you will encounter in Windows Server 2003.

Table 5-3 **Special Identity Groups**

Group Name	Members	Purpose
Anonymous Logon	All users who log on without a username and password.	To allow anonymous users access to resources. Windows Server 2003 no longer places the Anonymous Logon group as a member of the Everyone group. This security enhancement prevents the potential for unauthorized access to resources that can occur if a Windows 2000 or earlier administrator inadvertently forgets to remove the Everyone group from a resource.
Authenticated Users	All users who log on with a valid username and password combination that is stored in the Active Directory database.	To allow controlled access to resources throughout the forest or domain.
Dialup	Includes users currently logged on using a dial-up connection.	To allow access to resources from a remote location.
Enterprise Domain Controllers	All domain controllers in the forest.	To facilitate access to forest-wide Active Directory services.
Everyone	On Windows Server 2003 computers: ■ Authenticated Users ■ Domain Guests On Windows NT Server 4.0 and Windows 2000 computers: ■ Authenticated Users ■ Domain Guests ■ Anonymous Logon	To provide access to resources for all users and guests. As a best practice, do not assign this group to resources. Instead, use groups that require authentication and have membership lists that can be administratively modified.

(continued)

Table 5-3 **Special Identity Groups**

Group Name	Members	Purpose
Interactive	Includes the user account that is currently logged on to the local computer either directly or through a Remote Desktop connection.	Provides access to physically local resources. Users logged on from across the network are not included in this group membership.
Network	Includes any user that currently has a connection from another computer to a network resource such as a shared folder on this computer.	Used to allow access to shared resources or services from across the network. Users logged on interactively are not included in this group membership.
Service	Includes all security principals: users, groups, or computers that are currently logged on as a service.	Used by the system to allow permission to protected system files in order for services to function properly.
Terminal Server User	When Terminal Services is installed in application serving mode, this group contains any users who are currently logged on to the system using a terminal server.	Used to allow access to applications via a terminal services connection.

Local Groups

A **local group** is an object that may contain a collection of user accounts on a computer. It is important to understand that local groups are very different from the previously described domain local groups. Local groups are created in the database of the local computer. They are used to assign permissions to resources that are found only on the computer in which they are created. They cannot be given access to resources within an Active Directory domain, nor can they become members of any other group. Local groups inhibit your ability to centralize administration of computer resources and therefore should be used only if there are no other options.

The next section discusses guidelines for developing an implementation plan using both default and administratively created groups.

Developing a Group Implementation Plan

Now that we have described the concepts behind group usage in Windows Server 2003, we will discuss the development of a plan for group implementation that considers the business goals of a company. A group implementation plan should serve current resource access needs and allow for easy revisions when changes arise. Today's corporate environments often impose frequent changes on network administrators due to acquisitions and changes of the organizational structure. When users move between departments and change responsibilities, generally resource access needs change as well. A user may need more or less access to a particular resource than in a previous job position. In addition, an entirely new set of resources may need to be used.

In a newly installed network, you have the opportunity to implement a plan that can be revised easily when changes such as user departmental moves occur. A plan that is created without goals and good practice guidelines in mind can cause problems in the future with regard to security access. For example, consider the following scenario:

A mid-sized accounting firm decided recently to upgrade from Windows 2000 to Windows Server 2003 as its network operating system. Over the last several months, the company has gone through a major restructuring of employees and their responsibilities. Each time a request is made to either remove a user's resource access permissions or add a user to a new resource, the change is at best difficult to implement without negative ramifications. Either the user loses privileges to a resource that was needed, or the groups that have privileges to the new resource have more permissions than is considered secure.

While looking into this situation further, you discover that user accounts are sometimes individually added to a resource's ACL, and the global groups that exist do not seem to have any relationship to the current organizational structure.

The previously described scenario can be all too common in some organizations. Generally, these types of situations arise when a solid plan that includes group and user implementation guidelines fails to be in place. When you develop a plan for implementing groups, you should include the following documented information:

- A plan that states who has the ability and responsibility of creating, deleting, and managing groups.
- A policy that states how domain local, global, and universal groups are to be used.
- A policy that states guidelines for new group creation and deletion of old groups.
- A naming standards document to keep group names consistent.
- A standard for group nesting.

After your plan is documented, it is important for you to take the time to periodically re-evaluate it to make sure there are no new surprises that might cause problems. Distributing copies of your implementation plan to all administrators that have responsibility for creating and managing groups helps to keep new group creations in line with your plan. It will be up to you to keep this system in check since there is no administrative tool available within the operating system to enforce specific guidelines.

CREATING USERS AND GROUPS

One of the most common tasks for administrators is the creation of Active Directory objects. Windows Server 2003 includes several tools you can use to create objects. The specific tool you use depends on how many objects you need to create, the time frame available for the creation of these groups, and any special circumstances that are encountered, such as importing users from an existing database. Generally, when creating a single user or group, most administrators use the

Active Directory Users And Computers tool. However, when you need to create many users in a short time frame or you have an existing database from which you wish to import users, you will want to choose a more efficient tool. Windows Server 2003 provides a number of tools you can choose according to what you want to accomplish. The following list describes the most commonly used methods for creating multiple users. Each method will be detailed in the next section.

- **Batch files** These files with either a .bat extension or a .cmd extension can be used to perform many routine tasks. To create or delete user and group objects, batch files are frequently used in conjunction with the NET command syntax in Windows Server 2003.

- **Comma-Separated Value Directory Exchange (CSVDE)** This command line utility is used to import or export Active Directory information from a comma-separated value (.csv) file. These files can be created in any text editor. This command line utility only imports or exports new objects; it cannot modify or delete existing objects.

- **LDAP Data Interchange Format Directory Exchange (LDIFDE)** Like CSVDE, this utility can be used to import or export Active Directory information. It can be used to add, delete, or modify objects in Active Directory, in addition to modifying the schema if necessary. It also can be used to import data from other directory services such as Novell NetWare.

- **Windows Script Host (WSH)** Script engines run script files created using either Microsoft Visual Basic Scripting Edition (VBScript) or JScript. WSH allows the scripts to be run from either a Windows desktop or a command prompt. The runtime programs provided to do this are WScript.exe and CScript.exe, respectively.

These tools all have their places in network administration and you need to find the best tool that fits the situation. For example, you might have two tools that can accomplish a job, but your first choice might be the tool that you are most familiar with or the one that can accomplish the task in a shorter amount of time. The next sections present scenarios and examples for using these tools.

Using Batch Files

Batch files are commonly used files that can be written using any text editor. You can write a batch file to create objects in Active Directory by following standard batch file rules and using the *Dsadd* command, which is specific to Windows Server 2003. Dsadd can be used to create, delete, view, and modify Active Directory objects including users, groups, and OUs.

To create a user using the Dsadd utility, you need to know the distinguished name for the user and the security account name (or SAM identity). The SAM identity is the same as the user's common name, while the distinguished name includes the common name, in addition to Active Directory location information. The syntax for creating a user account using Dsadd is as follows:

```
dsadd user userdn -samid sam_name
```

In this example, *userdn* and *sam_name* are replaced with the unique information necessary to create an account. The *userdn* parameter is replaced by the distinguished name of the object to be created. The *sam_name* parameter is replaced by the common name or pre–Windows 2000 account name.

Using the above syntax as a model, create a user account for Karen Archer in the Sales container of cohowinery.com by typing the following command at a command prompt:

```
dsadd user cn=karcher,ou=sales,dc=cohowinery,dc=com -samid karcher
```

To specify *MySecretC0de* as a password for Karen's account, type the following:

```
dsadd user cn=karcher,ou=sales,dc=cohowinery,dc=com -pwd MySecretC0de
```

To create a batch file using Notepad, use the syntax in these examples and place each command on a separate line. Once all commands have been entered, save the file and name it either using a .cmd or .bat extension. Files with either .cmd or .bat extensions are processed line by line when the filename is typed at a command prompt.

> **MORE INFO** Batch File Syntax and the Dsadd Utility For more information on using batch files for administrative tasks, access the following Microsoft web site: http://www.microsoft.com/windowsxp/home/using/productdoc/en/default.asp?url=/windowsxp/home/using/productdoc/en/batch.asp.
>
> For more information on using the Dsadd utility, access the following Microsoft Web site: http://support.microsoft.com/default.aspx?scid=kb;en-us;322684#3.

Using CSVDE

Microsoft Excel and Microsoft Exchange are two common applications where you might have a number of usernames, addresses, and contact information you wish to add to the Active Directory database. In this case you can import and export information from these applications by saving it to a file in CSV format. CSV format can also be used to import and export information from other third-party applications. For example, you may have the need to export user account information to a file for use in another third-party application such as a UNIX database. CSVDE can provide this capability as well.

CSVDE allows an administrator to import or export Active Directory objects. It uses a .csv file that is based on a **header record**, which describes each part of the data. A header record is simply the first line of the text file that uses proper attribute names. The attribute names must match the attributes allowed by the Active Directory schema. For example, if you have a list of people and telephone numbers you want to import as users into the Active Directory database, you will need to create a header record that accurately reflects the object names and attributes you want to create. Some common attributes used for creating a user account are as follows:

- **DN**   Refers to the distinguished name of the object so that the object can be properly placed in Active Directory.
- **saMAccountName**   Populates the SAM account field for the pre–Windows 2000 logon name.

- **objectClass**   Determines the type of object to be created, such as user, group, or OU.
- **telephoneNumber**   Populates the telephone number field.
- **userAccountControl**   Sets the account to enabled by using 514 in the data record or disabled by using 512 in the data record.
- **userPrincipalName**   Populates the User Principal Name field for the account.

As you create your database file, order the data to reflect the order of the attributes in the header record. If fields and data are out of order, either you will encounter an error when running the CSVDE utility, or you may not get accurate results in the created objects. The following is an example of a header record using the previously listed attributes to create a user object:

```
dn,sAMAccountName,userPrincipalName,telephoneNumber,userAccountControl,objectClass
```

A data record using this header record would appear as follows:

```
"cn=Scott Seely,ou=Sales,dc=cohowinery,dc=com",SSeely,SSeely@cohowinery.com,
    586-555-1234,512,user
```

After you have added a record for each account you wanted to create, save the file using .csv as the extension. Assuming that you create a file named Newusers.csv, type the following command to execute the creation of the user accounts:

```
csvde.exe -i -f newusers.csv
```

The -i switch tells CSVDE this operation will import users into the database. The -f switch is used prior to specification of the .csv file containing the database records.

> **MORE INFO**   **CSVDE Syntax**   *Microsoft Knowledge Base article number 237677 lists the parameters and syntax used with the CSVDE utility. You can access this article directly at http://www.microsoft.com/technet/treeview/default.asp?url= /technet/prodtechnol/windowsserver2003/proddocs/entserver/CSVDE.asp.*

Using LDIFDE

LDIFDE is a utility that has the same basic functionality as CSVDE and also provides the ability to modify existing records in Active Directory. For this reason, LDIFDE is a more flexible option.

Consider an example where you have to import 200 new users into your Active Directory structure. In this case you can use either CSVDE or LDIFDE to import the users. In addition, if LDIFDE is used for initial object creation, you can modify or delete these objects later simply by editing the original database.

Any text editor can be used to create your data file. The format for the data file containing the object records you wish to create is different from that of CSVDE. The main difference between CSVDE and LDIFDE is that LDIFDE uses a line-separated format, which means that each attribute is placed on its own line. The following example shows the syntax for a data file to create the same user account as was created using CSVDE:

```
Dn: cn=Scott Seely,ou=sales,dc=cohowinery,dc=com
ObjectClass: user
SAMAccountName: sseely
UserPrincipalName: sseely@cohowinery.com
TelephoneNumber: 586-555-1234
```

With LDIFDE, a data file that will add additional records, modify existing object attributes, or delete objects must contain a value that will specify the outcome of the record. The three main values include:

- **Add**   Used to specify that the record content contains a new object
- **Modify**   Used to specify that existing object attributes will be modified
- **Delete**   Used to specify that the record will delete the specified object

The next example illustrates the required syntax to modify the telephone number for the previously created user object. Note that the hyphen in the last line is required and a blank line needs to exist between two separate records.

```
Dn: cn=Scott Seely,ou=sales,dc=cohowinery,dc=com
changetype: modify
replace: telephoneNumber
telephoneNumber: 586-555-1111
-
```

After creating the data file, type the following syntax to read your script and modify Active Directory:

```
ldifde -i -f newusers.ldf
```

> **NOTE**   **LDIFDE Syntax**   Microsoft Knowledge Base article 237677 lists the parameters and syntax for using LDIFDE. This article can be accessed at http://support.microsoft.com/default.aspx?scid=http://support.microsoft.com:80/support/kb/articles/Q237/6/77.ASP&NoWebContent=1.

> **CAUTION**   **CSVDE and LDIFDE Default Account Settings**   CSVDE and LDIFDE both create accounts that are disabled by default and have blank passwords. Passwords cannot be included in the import file.

Using Windows Scripting Host

Windows Scripting Host (WSH) supports both Microsoft VBScript and JScript engines. It serves as an administration tool that has the flexibility of running scripts either from a Windows interface or from a command prompt. WSH is built into Windows 98, Windows 2000, Windows XP, and Windows Server 2003. It provides a robust scripting method that supports a multitude of administrative tasks such as creating Active Directory objects, mapping drives, connecting to printers, modifying environment variables, and modifying registry keys.

The following example is a VBScript that creates a user account for Scott Seely using WSH. You can use any text editor to write and edit the script. The script should be saved with a .vbs extension. Notice that the first few lines prepare the script to create a user object in the Sales OU of cohowinery.com. The fourth line of text begins the information that specifies Scott Seely and the Active Directory information for his account. Blank lines are used for visual purposes and are ignored during file processing.

```
Option Explicit
Dim ldapP, acctUser

Set ldapP = GetObject("LDAP://OU=sales,DC=cohowinery,DC=com")

Set acctUser = ldapP.Create("user", "CN=" & "Scott Seely")
Call acctUser.Put("sAMAccountName", "sseely")
Call acctUser.Put("userPrincipalName", "sseely" & "@cohowinery.com")
Call acctUser.Put("TelephoneNumber", "586-555-1234")
Call acctUser.Put("userAccountControl", &H200)

acctUser.SetInfo
acctUser.SetPassword ("MSpress#1")
Set acctUser = Nothing
```

Assuming the name of the previous script file is Newusers.vbs, type the following command from a command prompt to run it:

```
cscript c:\newusers.vbs
```

> **MORE INFO** **WSH, JScript, and VBScript Resources** More information on running WSH scripts can be found at http://www.microsoft.com/technet/treeview/default.asp?url=/technet/prodtechnol/windowsserver2003/proddocs/entserver/wsh_runfromcommandprompt.asp.
>
> Microsoft has an extensive online user's guide for JScript located at http://msdn.microsoft.com/library/default.asp?url=/library/en-us/script56/html/js56jsconjscriptusersguide.asp.
>
> The VBScript online user's guide is located at http://msdn.microsoft.com/library/default.asp?url=/library/en-us/script56/html/js56jsconjscriptusersguide.asp.

SUMMARY

- Three types of user accounts exist in Windows Server 2003: local user accounts, domain user accounts, and built-in user accounts. Local user accounts reside on a local computer and are not replicated to other computers by Active Directory. Domain user accounts are created and stored in Active Directory and are replicated to all domain controllers within a domain. Built-in user accounts are automatically created when the operating system is installed and when a member server is promoted to a domain controller.

- The Administrator account is a built-in domain account that serves as the primary supervisory account in Windows Server 2003. It can be renamed, but it cannot be deleted. The Guest account is a built-in account used to assign temporary access to resources. It can be renamed, but it cannot be deleted. This account is disabled by default and the password can be left blank.

- Windows Server 2003 group options include two types, security and distribution, and three scopes, domain local, global, and universal.

- Domain local groups are placed on the ACL of resources and assigned permissions. They typically contain global groups in their membership list.

- Global groups are used to organize domain users according to their resource access needs. Global groups are placed in the membership list of domain local groups, which are then assigned the desired permissions to resources.

- Universal groups are used to provide access to resources anywhere in the forest. Their membership lists can contain global groups and users from any domain. Changes to universal group membership lists are replicated to all global catalog servers throughout the forest. This group scope is available only in Active Directory forests set to Windows 2000 native or higher.

- The recommended permission assignment strategy places users needing access permissions in a global group, places the global group in a domain local group, and then assigns permissions to the domain local group.

- Group nesting is the process of placing group accounts in the membership of other group accounts for the purpose of simplifying permission assignments.

- Multiple users and groups can be created in Active Directory using several methods. Windows Server 2003 offers the ability to use batch files, CSVDE, LDIFDE, and WSH to accomplish your administrative goals.

EXERCISES

Exercise 5-1: Viewing Group Object Properties

To practice viewing group object properties and memberships, complete the following steps:

1. In Active Directory Users And Computers, open the Users container.

2. In the right window pane, locate the Domain Admins group and right-click it, and select Properties.

3. On the General tab, observe the group scope and group type.

   QUESTION *Can either of these be changed?*

4. Click the Members tab, and view and record the members of the Domain Admins group. Close the Properties window for the Domain Admins group.

Exercise 5-2: Exploring Special Identity Groups

Complete the following steps to view a special identity group:

1. Using Windows Explorer, create a folder called Test Share on your C: drive.

2. Right-click the new folder, and select Sharing And Security.

3. On the Sharing tab, select Share This Folder.

4. On the Security tab, click the Add button to add users to the permissions list.

5. In the Select Users, Computers, Or Groups dialog box, click Advanced.

6. In the expanded dialog box, click the Object Types button, and deselect the Users object. Click OK.

7. Click Find Now in the Select Users, Computers, Or Groups dialog box. You should see a complete list of all available groups that can be assigned to this folder. The special identity groups are shown using an icon with an arrow pointing up from the left side of the object. Note that although these objects are groups, their icon is different from that of non-special identity groups. Document several group names that you see here.

8. After observing several group names, click Cancel to close the advanced view of the Select Users, Computers, Or Groups dialog box. Click Cancel to close the main Select Users, Computer, Or Groups dialog box. Finally, click Cancel to close the shared folder Properties dialog box.

9. Delete the folder you created for this exercise.

REVIEW QUESTIONS

1. Which of the following two scripting languages are supported by WSH?
   a. WSH
   b. Java
   c. Basic
   d. JScript
   e. VBScript

2. Your company has just purchased a new printer that the owner wants all employees to be able to use. You currently have only one domain with two servers running Windows Server 2003. All users have accounts to authenticate daily to the network. As the administrator, what is the simplest and most secure way to assign permissions to all of the users in your domain?

   a. Create a domain local group with the proper permissions assigned to the printer and place all user accounts in the domain local group.

   b. Create a global group and place all of the user accounts on the membership list. Assign the global group permission to access the resource directly.

   c. Create a global group and place all of the user accounts on the membership list. Create a domain local group and add it to the ACL of the printer assigning the necessary permissions. Place the global group in the membership list of the domain local group.

   d. Create a domain local group and add it to the ACL of the printer assigning the necessary permissions. Place the built-in Domain Users account in the membership list of the domain local group.

   e. Create a domain local group and add it to the ACL of the printer assigning the necessary permissions. Place the Everyone special identities group account in the membership list of the domain local group.

3. You work for a local school district as the district-wide network administrator. Currently the district has a UNIX database that contains all student records. The district board of educators would like you to use the same usernames on the Windows Server 2003 network that currently are being used on the UNIX server. They have asked you how you intend to accomplish this task. What will you tell them?

4. Having just hired a new employee to help you with some administrative tasks, you would like this person to be responsible for network backups. Without giving more access than is necessary to perform this task, to which group should you add the new employee's user account?

   a. Server Operators

   b. Administrators

   c. Everyone

   d. Backup Operators

   e. Domain Admins

5. Your company network consists of four domains that include Windows NT Server 4.0, Windows 2000, and Windows Server 2003 servers. Each domain has a group of managers that need access to the same resource. You are trying to create a universal group to nest the managers' global groups, but the universal group option is dimmed out. What is most likely the cause for this condition?

6. What is the difference between a security group and a distribution group?

7. What is the difference between a domain local group and a local group?

8. You have just finished joining a newly installed Windows XP workstation into your domain. To which group will this computer be a member by default?

   a. Domain Controllers

   b. Local Computers

   c. Everyone

   d. Domain Computers

   e. Domain Workstations

CASE SCENARIOS

Scenario 5-1: Administering Groups for Humongous Insurance

You are a network administrator for Humongous Insurance. Humongous Insurance has a multi-domain forest. The forest root is humongousinsurance.com. There are also two child domains named west.humongousinsurance.com and east.humongousinsurance.com. The company has approximately 7,000 users, 7,000 client workstations, and 100 servers. The company's network configuration is shown in Figure 5-5.

```
                    ┌─────────────────────────┐
                    │ 10 Windows Server 2003  │
                    │ domain controllers      │
                    │ 5,000 users             │
                    │ 5,000 client computers  │
                    └─────────────────────────┘
                    humongousinsurance.com
                          /        \
                         /          \
          west.humongousinsurance.com   east.humongousinsurance.com
┌──────────────────────────┐           ┌───────────────────────────┐
│ 3 Windows Server 2003    │           │ 2 Windows Server 2003     │
│ domain controllers       │           │ domain controllers        │
│ 1,000 users              │           │ 3 Windows NT Server 4.0 BDCs│
│ 1,000 Windows XP computers│          │ 1,000 users               │
└──────────────────────────┘           │ 1,000 computers           │
                                       └───────────────────────────┘
```

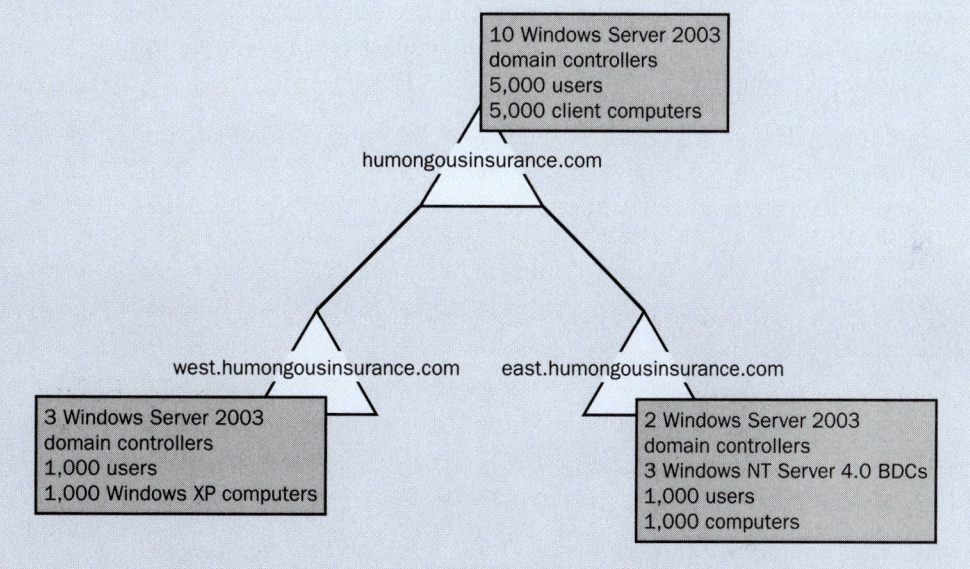

Figure 5-5 Humongous Insurance's forest structure

All domains are Windows Server 2003 domains. The forest root domain has 10 domain controllers. Five of those domain controllers are configured as DNS servers and two are configured as global catalog servers. The West domain has three domain controllers. Two of those domain controllers are configured as DNS servers. One of those domain controllers is configured as a global catalog server. The East domain has two Windows Server 2003 domain controllers and three Windows NT Server 4.0 Backup Domain Controllers (BDCs).

The forest root domain is located in College Station, Texas. The East domain is located in Gainesville, Florida. The West domain is located in San Diego, California. There is also an Active Directory site configured for each of these locations. The site for College Station is named Main_Site. The Gainesville site is named East_Site. The San Diego site is named West_Site.

You are one of several network administrators assigned to handle the forest root domain and College Station site. Your manager, Jean Trenary, has called a meeting of all network and desktop administrators. She wants to address several issues.

Given this information, answer the following questions:

1. Jean says there are four internal auditors in the forest root domain. There are two internal auditors in each of the child domains. Each set of internal auditors has been placed in a global group within each domain. These groups are named IA_Main, IA_East, and IA_West after their respective locations. Jean wants all of the members of these groups to be able to access the same resources in every domain. What is the recommended way to configure the groups to allow the desired functionality?

2. The network administrators from the East domain want to know why the option to create a universal group is not available in their domain. What can you tell them?

3. The network administrators from the West domain want to know why everyone always recommends placing global groups into universal groups, instead of just placing the users directly into the universal groups. What should you tell them?

4. Jean approves a plan to hire assistants for each domain to create and manage user accounts. How can you give the assistants the immediate ability to help in this way, without making them domain administrators?

5. Two employees have been hired to back up data, maintain the Windows Server 2003 domain controllers, and manage printers for the Main_Site. Which Built-in groups will give these users the permissions they require to manage the domain controllers? How should you set up their accounts and group memberships?

Scenario 5-2: Evaluating Scripts

This scenario will help you to find and evaluate one of the script types discussed in this chapter.

Part I. Describe each type of scripting that can be used to add users to Active Directory. List an example of when you might use each one.

Part II. Using the Internet as your resource, find an example of one of the script types and write a short description of the script and what it accomplishes.

CHAPTER 6
SECURITY PLANNING AND ADMINISTRATIVE DELEGATION

Upon completion of this chapter, you will be able to:

- Implement account security using strong passwords.
- Explain how smart cards are used to authenticate users.
- Explain the security risks associated with being logged on as a member of the Administrators group.
- Use the Run As program to perform administrative tasks.
- Plan an organizational unit (OU) strategy.
- Understand and describe the benefits of administrative delegation.
- Create an organizational unit structure.
- Delegate control of an organizational unit.
- Move objects between organizational units.

This chapter describes secure network access methods, including strong passwords, the Run As program for administrative tasks, and smart cards, and it describes the requirements for their implementation. Your decision to use either a centralized or decentralized management approach will play an important role in how you plan the organization's Microsoft Active Directory structure, because your Active Directory structure must facilitate this approach. This chapter discusses several planning strategies that will help you meet your administrative goals. You will learn how to create an organizational structure and delegate authority of Active Directory containers to other administrators or users in order to meet your design goals. In addition, you will learn how to move objects between OUs when necessary.

PLANNING AND IMPLEMENTING ACCOUNT SECURITY

The first and foremost consideration that should be taken into account when planning a secure network is user account security. Access to network resources begins with a user account and password for authentication purposes. Once this combination is established, users can gain access to the network resources for which they were granted permission. Compromising either part of the authentication combination poses a threat to network security.

The logon name typically follows a corporate naming standard set forth during the Active Directory planning stages. A **naming standards document** is usually created to outline standards for the naming of all Active Directory objects. This document specifies conventions such as the number and type of characters to use when creating a new object in Active Directory. Table 6-1 illustrates an example of a naming standard for user accounts.

Table 6-1 Naming Standards

Naming Standard	Example	Explanation
FLLLLLxx	JSmith01	First initial, followed by first five characters of the last name, appended with a number to ensure uniqueness when duplicate names may exist.
LLLLLFFM	SmithJoS or SmithJo1	First five characters of the last name, followed by the first two characters of the first name, appended with a middle initial. If a middle initial is not applicable, a unique number is used instead.

Since all user accounts typically follow the organization's corporate naming standard or an agreed-upon guideline, the logon name of a user can sometimes be guessed. The user account name is 50 percent of the combination required for a successful logon. By default, Microsoft Windows Server 2003 also requires a password for all user accounts. Most organizations implement passwords, but many fail to educate users on the security responsibilities associated with them. In this section we will discuss the following methods for securing user accounts:

- Education of users
- Usage of strong passwords
- Implementation of smart cards

Education of Users

Passwords and **personal identification numbers (PINs)** are becoming common in many areas of life, including banking, e-mail, voice mail, and keyless entry systems such as garage door openers. PINs typically consist of at least four characters or digits. For example, accessing your account at an automated teller machine (ATM) at a bank requires a PIN. The combination of the magnetic strip on the back of your ATM card and the PIN are matched against the credentials for your account. If you enter an incorrect PIN, you cannot gain access to your account. Your PIN serves as a password for your account.

All passwords protect information or resources from falling into the wrong hands. When a user account is given to an employee, the employee should be made aware of the security risks associated with sharing his or her logon information with others. The following is a list of password protection best practices to share with your users:

- When documenting passwords on paper, keep the document in a secure location such as a manager's safe. Do not leave the document out in the open where others can see it.

- Do not share your password with anyone. If you feel your password has been compromised for some reason, change it immediately.

- In higher security networks, do not save passwords to your computer such as for easy logon to Internet sites. Although many secure sites that require authentication offer an option to store the password on your computer, storing any passwords on your computer poses a potential security risk.

- When creating or changing your password, use **strong passwords**. Microsoft recommends the use of strong passwords for all accounts. Strong passwords are detailed in the next section.

Educating users can become part of your network security defense system. Distributing this information is easy when it is made part of new employee training programs or professional development sessions.

Strong Passwords

Windows Server 2003 has a new feature named *strong passwords*. A strong password can be simply defined as one that follows guidelines that make it difficult for a potential hacker to crack. Strong passwords are a combination of a minimum required password length, a password history, character types, and minimum password age. Password-cracking tools are improving daily. Password-cracking can be accomplished by intelligent guessing on the part of the hacker, dictionary attacks, and automation. Automation tools try every possible combination of characters until the correct sequence of characters is finally discovered. The goal of implementing a strong password is to deter these types of attacks by implementing passwords that require more time and processing abilities to crack.

Strong passwords can first be deployed during the installation of the operating system, when the administrator account is created. If the password is blank or does not meet the default complexity requirements, a dialog box appears warning you of the risks of not using a strong password for the Administrator account. Furthermore, the default policy for new user accounts in Windows Server 2003 produces a similar warning as the one shown in Figure 6-1.

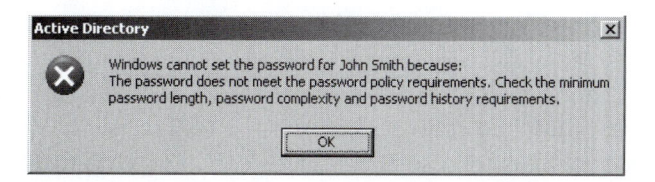

Figure 6-1 User account setup Strong Password Warning dialog box

The Administrator account should not be the only account where a strong password is implemented. All user accounts should also implement strong passwords. A password policy can be defined to force users to use strong passwords when they create or change their passwords. You will learn how to implement password policies in Chapter 8, "Configuring the User and Computer Environment Using Group Policy." For now, it is necessary to understand what constitutes a strong password.

A strong password contains the following characteristics:

- A combination of at least eight characters in length and contains upper and lowercase letters, numbers, and non-alphabetic characters
- At least one character from each of the previous character types
- It should be different from other previously used passwords by more than one character

A strong password should not contain the following:

- Your user name, real name, or company name
- A complete dictionary word
- Do not leave it blank

Windows passwords for Windows Server 2003 and Microsoft Windows XP clients can be up to 127 characters in length. However, Microsoft Windows 95 and Microsoft Windows 98 support passwords only up to 14 characters long. Be sure to consider this limitation when planning for user authentication from different versions of Windows.

Using the criteria for creating strong passwords will help in developing a more secure network environment. The following is an example of a strong password based on these criteria:

MspR3s5#1

To practice planning a username standard and password strategy, do Exercise 6-1 now.

This example is based on the term "MSPress." It uses upper and lowercase letters, and uses the number 3 to replace the "e" and the number 5 to replace the last "s," and ends using the pound symbol (#), followed by the number 1. It is also more than seven characters in length.

Using Smart Cards for Authentication

The password implementation plans discussed thus far work well when followed. However, it is difficult to deter such matters as users writing down their passwords, storing them in insecure locations, or forgetting them altogether. Windows 2000 and Windows Server 2003 both provide **smart cards**, offering administrators a solution to these problems, and providing an even higher level of security than most complex password policies. Many high-security organizations have implemented smart cards for authentication and access to company resources. A smart card is a credit card–sized device, or a token-style device such as a USB device, that is used with a PIN to enable logon to the enterprise. Smart cards contain a chip that stores user information such as the user's private key for certificate-related services, and user credentials such as the username and a public key certificate. This requires the implementation of a **public key infrastructure (PKI)**. PKI is a system of digital certificates, certification authorities (CAs), and other registration authorities (RAs) that verify and authenticate the validity of each party involved in an electronic transaction, through the use of public key cryptography. Using a credit card type smart card, the user inserts the card into a card reader attached to the computer. With a USB device, the user inserts the USB device into a USB port and is prompted to enter a PIN. Once the PIN is verified, the card is read and access is granted to the network.

Smart Card Benefits and Considerations

Implementation of smart cards in your Windows Server 2003 environment provides the following benefits:

- Users no longer have to remember complex passwords.
- All information is stored on the smart card, making it difficult for anyone, except the intended user, to use or access.
- Security operations such as cryptographic functions are performed on the smart card, rather than on the network server or local computer. This provides a higher level of security for sensitive transactions.
- Smart cards can be used from remote locations such as a home office to provide authentication services.
- The risk of remote attacks using a username and password combination is significantly reduced by smart cards.

Along with the benefits of implementing smart cards in your environment, there are also costs and considerations. You need to consider the following infrastructure needs prior to deploying smart cards:

- As stated previously, you must have a PKI in place. This requires you to install Certificate Services in your Windows Server 2003 environment. When configuring Certificate Services, you must install your CAs as **enterprise CAs**. An enterprise CA can issue certificates only to users and computers in its own forest.
- Windows Server 2003 supports industry standard **Personal Computer/ Smart Card (PC/SC)**–compliant smart cards and readers. PC/SC was developed by the PC/SC Workgroup. The PC/SC Workgroup's mission is to promote standardization and application development for the smart card industry. Although some manufacturers may provide drivers for non-Plug-and-Play smart card readers, it is recommended that you purchase only those that are PC/SC compliant.
- All users who will be using smart cards for authentication must have smart card readers installed at their workstations or they must have an available USB port for a **token-style card**. A token-style card is one that is the approximate size of a key and uses a USB port for access to the system.

- You must set up at least one computer as a smart card enrollment station and authorize at least one user to enroll other users. This authorized user is issued a special enrollment card that contains an **enrollment agent certificate**. Enrollment agent certificates are generated by the enterprise CA and are used to generate a smart card logon certificate for users in the organization. Since these enrollment agent certificates can generate smart cards with authentication credentials for anyone in the organization, you should make sure there are strong security policies in place for issuing enrollment agent certificates. A smart card can be generated for the purpose of impersonating a user on the network. One method of protecting your network from this type of misuse is to disable the CA from being able to create enrollment agent certificates, until they are required, and limit the number of enrollment agent certificates that are distributed for smart card creation.

MORE INFO *PC/SC Workgroup* For more information on the PC/SC Workgroup and their efforts, visit the following Web site: http://www.pcscworkgroup.com/.

After determining the cost of implementation, you need to also define a support process. You should establish a plan that outlines procedures for PIN management and for forgotten cards. Users who have forgotten either their PINs or their smart cards cannot gain access to the network. In these situations, you may create a temporary smart card containing a certificate with a limited lifespan and limited access. You might also consider allowing a user to authenticate using a username and password temporarily. In addition, for security reasons, you may consider placing users in a group with limited resource access so that they can perform their job with some limitations. All of these considerations are important to balancing resource access with network security.

Enabling a User Account for Smart Card Authentication

You must enable the user account in Active Directory for smart card authentication. Figure 6-2 illustrates the dialog box for enabling smart card authentication.

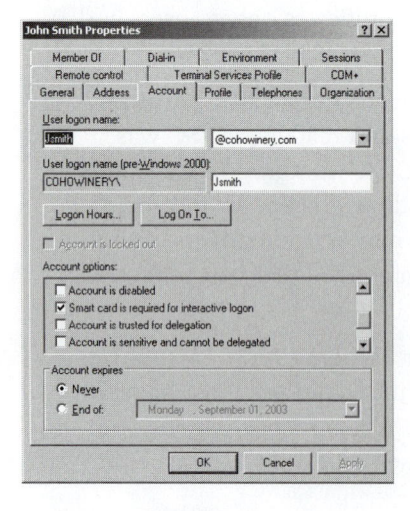

Figure 6-2 Enabling smart card logon for a user account

▶ **Enabling a User Account for Smart Card Authentication**

To enable the user account in Active Directory for smart card authentication, complete the following steps:

1. Open Active Directory Users And Computers.

2. Navigate to the container holding the user you wish to modify. Right-click the user account, and select Properties.

3. In the Properties dialog box, select the Account tab. In the Account Options list, click Smart Card Is Required For Interactive Logon, and then click OK.

MORE INFO *Smart Card Deployment Checklist* *Microsoft offers a checklist you can use when deploying smart cards into your enterprise. This checklist is located in the online product documentation for Windows Server 2003 at http://www.microsoft.com/technet/treeview/default.asp?url=/technet/prodtechnol/windowsserver2003/proddocs/entserver/sag_SC_Checklist.asp.*

Administrator Account Security

Setting user account guidelines is an important part of securing your network. However, a hacker who has access to a standard user account cannot damage your network nearly as much as a hacker with administrative permissions. Therefore, securing the Administrator account is a critical security task. Chapter 5, "Active Directory Administration," discussed several guidelines for securing the Administrator account, including renaming the account, using a strong password, and limiting the distribution of the Administrator account password. The Administrator account should not be used for daily work. It should be reserved for tasks that require administrator privileges. Using the Administrator account or an account that is a member of Domain Admins, Enterprise Admins, or Schema Admins for daily tasks offers an opportunity for hackers to attack your network and potentially cause severe and irreversible damage. For example, accessing an Internet site or opening a virus-infected e-mail message can lead to accounts or files being deleted, the formatting of drives, or the creation of phantom Administrator accounts for future use. Limiting the use of the Administrator account for daily tasks, such as e-mail, application use, and access to the Internet, reduces the risk of this type of damage.

The recommended solution for reducing the risks associated with the Administrator account is to use a standard user account and use the Run As program when it is necessary to perform an administrative task. The following is a list of characteristics of the Run As program:

- The Run As program allows you to maintain your primary logon as a standard user and creates a secondary session for access to an administrative tool.

- During the use of a program or tool opened using Run As, your administrative credentials are valid only until you close that program or tool.

- Run As can be used either from the command line or from the graphical user interface.

- Some tasks, such as upgrading the operating system and configuring system parameters, do not support the use of Run As. You must be logged on interactively to perform such tasks.

- Run As requires the **Secondary Logon service** to be running. The Secondary Logon service provides the ability to log on with an alternate set of credentials to that of the primary logon.

- Run As can be used to start two separate instances of an administrative application, such as Active Directory Domains And Trusts or Active Directory Users And Computers. Each instance can be directed at a different domain or forest. This allows you to perform interdomain or interforest administration tasks efficiently.

- Run As is not limited to administrator accounts. You can use Run As to log on with separate credentials from any account. This can be a valuable tool in testing resource access permissions.

▶ **Using Run As within the User Interface**

To run a program with secondary credentials from your Windows desktop, complete the following steps:

1. From the Start button, navigate to the application you wish to run. Hold down the Shift key and then right-click the desired application, and select the Run As option.

2. In the Run As dialog box, enter the username and password for the secondary account, and then click OK.

▶ **Using Run As from the Command Line**

Running a program based on secondary credentials using the command line utility works in much the same way as using the graphical user interface. For example, to run the DNS Management snap-in using a domain administrator account named domainadmin in the cohowinery.com domain, complete the following steps:

1. Open a command prompt window.

2. At the command prompt, type:

   ```
   runas /user:cohowinery.com\domainadmin "mmc %windir%\system32\dnsmgmt.msc"
   ```

   NOTE *Run As Syntax* Complete syntax information can be found for the Run As command line utility in the Windows Server 2003 online product documentation at: http://www.microsoft.com/technet/treeview/default.asp?url=/technet/prodtechnol/windowsserver2003/proddocs/standard/runas.asp.

PLANNING AN ORGANIZATIONAL UNIT STRATEGY

Chapter 1, "Overview of Active Directory," discussed the concept of OUs, including the objects they can contain and how they can be created to represent your company's functional or geographical model as a foundation. This section expands on that foundation to include additional benefits for planning an OU structure. The main reasons to create OUs in your Active Directory structure are as follows:

- To represent the functional or geographical model of your company so that resources can be placed according to the users who need them
- To allow sub-administrative control over a container's resources by delegating administrative responsibility for certain tasks to container administrators
- To impose control over client computers or users through the use of Group Policy objects
- To hide objects within your domain structure

Representing the Company Model

OUs can be created to represent geographic locations or functional needs of a company. For example, if you have a company that has three locations in a single domain, you may choose to represent these locations by creating an OU for each location. To organize your structure even further, you may wish to nest OUs for each department beneath their respective locations.

Delegating Administrative Responsibility

When creating OUs that represent locations and departments, you may find that administrative tasks would be easier to accomplish if an administrator from that location was designated to perform them. For example, if you have a department that tends to have a high turnover in employees and job responsibilities, it might be easier to allow the manager of that department to create and delete user accounts as necessary. In addition, a local administrator could add and remove his or her users from the groups that give them resource access. Some administrators create OUs specifically for the delegation of administrative tasks. This allows some of the daily tasks, such as account creation and password resets, to be offloaded to lower-level administrators.

Implementing Group Policies

When group policies are created for an OU, the policies are applied to that OU and all child OUs within the hierarchy, by default. Designing an OU structure with this in mind will assist in simplifying such things as application deployments and account logon policies. Since there are multiple ways to manage group policies but only one way to manage OU delegation, plan your OU structure with administrative delegation as your first priority, above Group Policy implementation. The specifics of Group Policy creation and management will be discussed in Chapters 7 through 10.

Hiding Objects

You may have a need to create an OU to hide objects within the Active Directory structure. For example, you may want to create a container for help desk or administrative personnel. By creating the OU and allowing only the users in the OU to see it, you limit the number of people who know the logon identity for administrative accounts. You can accomplish this goal by modifying the access control list (ACL) of the OU and restricting the users who have List Contents permission to the OU. The List Contents permission allows objects to be seen in the Active Directory structure using either a command line tool or the Active Directory Users And Computers snap-in.

> **NOTE** **Finding Active Directory Objects** *Generally, users do not use the Active Directory OU structure to locate resources. The most efficient way for users to find resources is to query the global catalog. As discussed in Chapter 1, "Overview of Active Directory," published resources are easy to locate in Active Directory.*

CREATING AN OU STRUCTURE

OUs can be nested to allow for a hybrid design. This allows administrators to take advantage of the benefits of the solid OU design listed previously. As with groups, you will want to limit the number of OUs that are nested. Nesting too many levels of OUs slows the response time to resource requests and complicates the application of Group Policy settings.

As shown in Figure 6-3, when Active Directory is installed, there is only one OU created by default: the Domain Controllers OU. An OU is represented in Active Directory Users And Computers by a folder with an icon of an open book on it. The other containers that are created during the installation, such as the Users container, appear as folders with no icons on them. All other OUs must be created by a domain administrator.

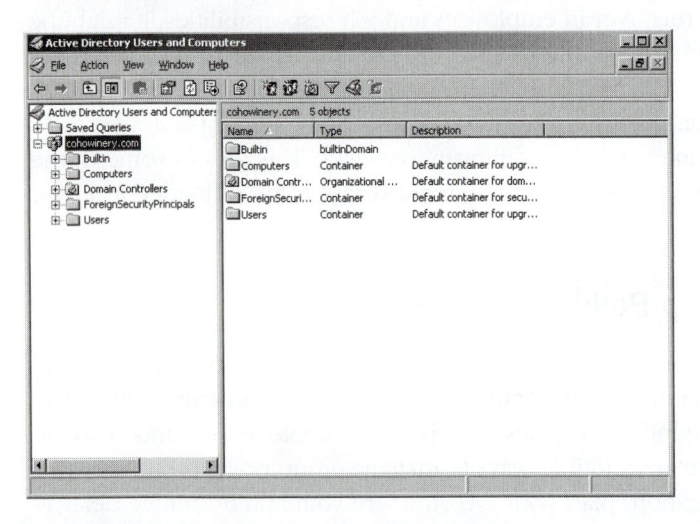

Figure 6-3 Default container and OU structure

As previously discussed, when implementing an OU structure, all delegated administrative permissions or policies assigned to a parent OU are inherited by each child OU by default. When planning your OU hierarchy, you will want the plan to be pyramid shaped, with first-level OUs at the top, and sub-OUs nested beneath them. For example, in Figure 6-4, you can see that the domain OU structure employs first-level OUs for specific locations. Departments at each location are nested within these OUs to represent users and their resource needs. This plan allows you to use the top-level OUs for delegated authority and Group Policy assignments to all departments, and also assign departmental authority for each sub-OU that does not affect the entire location or other departments.

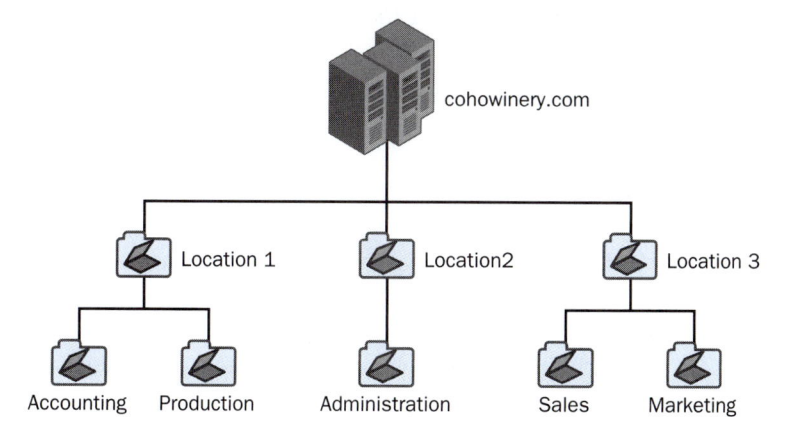

Figure 6-4 Pyramid OU structure

NOTE *Security Principals and OUs* *OUs are not considered security principals. This means that you cannot assign access permissions to a resource based on membership to an OU. Herein lies the difference between OUs and global, domain local, and universal groups. Groups are used for assigning access permissions.*

Creating a completely flat structure such as the one shown in Figure 6-5 defeats the purpose of using OUs for effective authority delegation and Group Policy assignments. For example, assuming that you wish to assign a Group Policy to all users in location 1, it is difficult to assess which departments are included in location 1. Once you determine this, you need to assign the policy to both the Sales and the Production containers. However, if you implement the pyramid structure shown in Figure 6-4, you assign the policy to the Location 1 OU, which inherits down to all departments. Simplification of resource access and management of policies and permissions should be one of your primary goals when you create an OU structure.

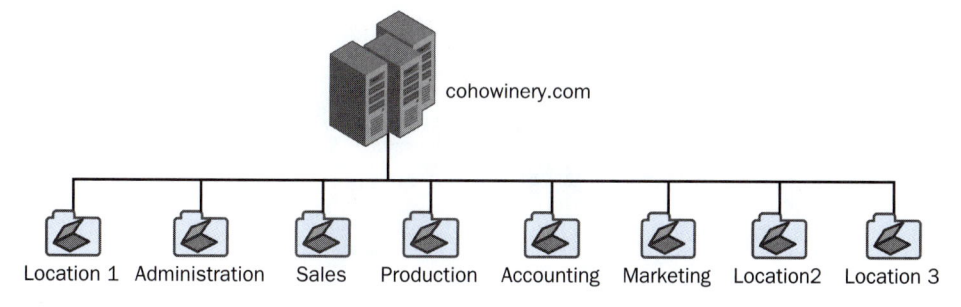

Figure 6-5 Flat OU structure

Using OUs to Delegate Active Directory Management Tasks

Creating OUs to support a decentralized administration model provides you with the ability to allow others to manage portions of your Active Directory structure, without affecting the rest of the structure. Delegating authority at a site level affects all domains and users within the site. Delegating authority at a domain affects the entire domain. However, delegating authority at the OU level affects only that OU and its hierarchy. By allowing administrative authority over an OU structure, as opposed to an entire domain or site, you gain the following advantages:

- Minimize the number of administrators with global privileges. By creating a hierarchy of administrative levels, you limit the number of people that require global access.

- Limit the scope of errors. Administrative mistakes such as a container deletion or group object deletion affect only the respective OU structure.

Using Delegation Of Control Wizard

Using the **Delegation Of Control Wizard**, you have the ability to delegate permissions for domains, OUs, or containers, using a simple interface. The interface allows you to specify to which users or groups you want to delegate management permissions, and the specific tasks you wish them to be able to perform. You can delegate pre-defined tasks or you can create custom tasks that allow you to be more specific.

▶ **Delegating Administrative Control of a Domain, OU, or Container**

To delegate administrative control of a domain, OU, or container, complete the following steps:

1. Open Active Directory Users And Computers, right-click the object to which you wish to delegate control, and click Delegate Control.

2. Click Next on the Welcome To The Delegation Of Control Wizard page.

3. As shown in Figure 6-6, click Add on the Users Or Groups page.

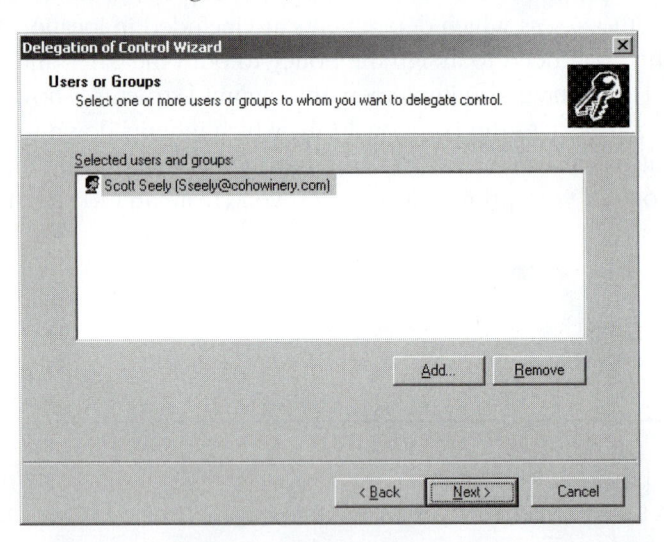

Figure 6-6   Delegation Of Control Wizard, Users Or Groups page

4. In the Select Users, Computers, Or Groups dialog box, type the user or group to which you want to delegate administration in the Enter The Object Names To Select box, and click OK. Click Next to proceed.

5. As shown in Figure 6-7 on the Tasks To Delegate page, choose from one of the following options:

   If you choose this option, proceed to Step 8.

   ❑ **Delegate The Following Common Tasks**   This option allows you to choose from a list of pre-defined tasks. Click Next to proceed.

CHAPTER 6: SECURITY PLANNING AND ADMINISTRATIVE DELEGATION 151

- **Create A Custom Task To Delegate** This option allows you to be more specific about the task delegation.

After choosing one of these, click Next to proceed.

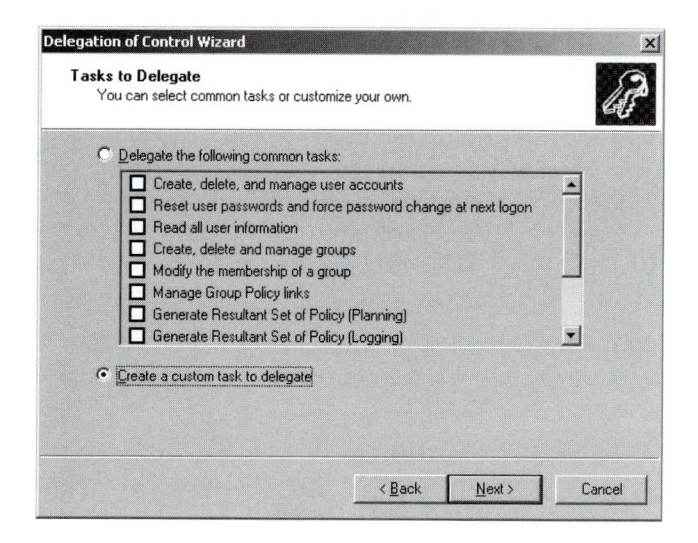

Figure 6-7 Delegation Of Control Wizard, Tasks To Delegate page

6. As shown in Figure 6-8 on the Active Directory Object Type page, choose one of the following options:

    - **This Folder, Existing Objects In This Folder, And Creation Of New Objects In This Folder** This option delegates control of the container, including all of its current and future objects.

    - **Only The Following Objects In The Folder** This option allows you to select specific objects to be controlled. You can select Create Selected Objects In This Folder to allow selected object types to be created, or select Delete Selected Objects In This Folder to allow selected object types to be deleted.

After choosing one of the previous options, click Next to proceed.

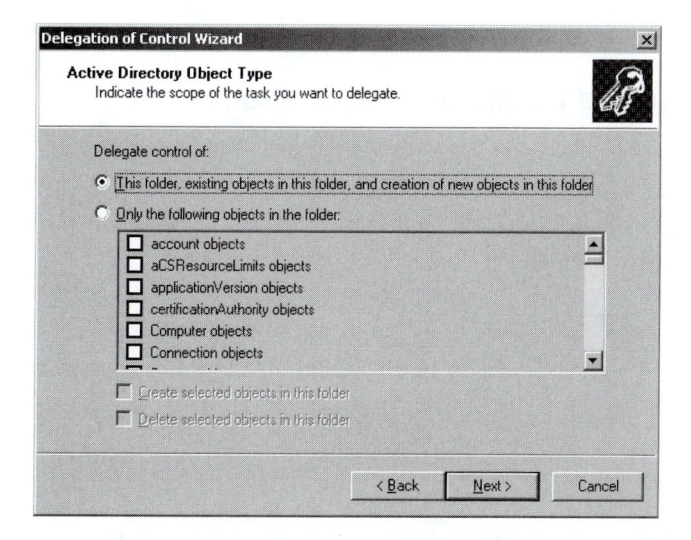

Figure 6-8 Delegation Of Control Wizard, Active Directory Object Type page

7. As shown in Figure 6-9, on the Permissions page, set the delegated permissions according to your needs for the user or group that has delegated control:

    - **General** Displays general permissions, which are equal to those displayed on the Security tab in an object's properties. For example, selecting Full Control For General Permissions is inclusive of all property rights as well.

    - **Property-Specific** Displays permissions that apply to specific attributes or properties of an object. If you select the Read permission using the General option, all read-specific properties are selected.

    - **Creation/Deletion Of Specific Child Objects** Displays permissions that apply to creation and deletion permissions for specified object types.

    After selecting the appropriate permissions, click Next to proceed. The Completing The Delegation Of Control Wizard page appears.

    You can combine permissions from all three of the bulleted options.

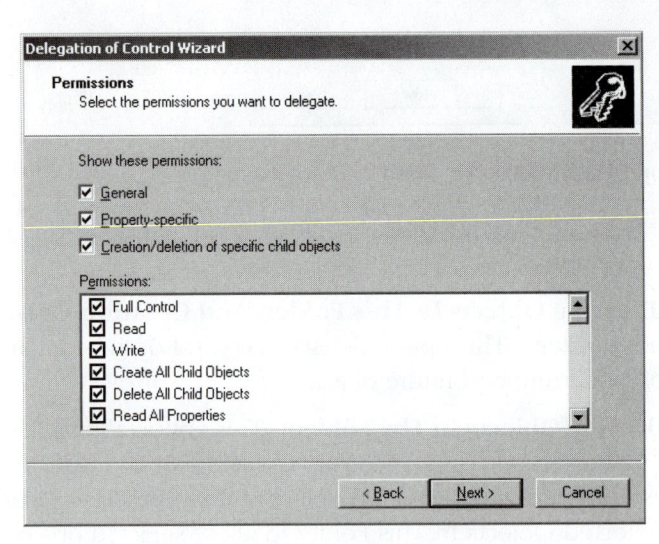

    Figure 6-9 Delegation Of Control Wizard, Permissions page

8. Review your choices carefully on the Completing The Delegation Of Control Wizard page, and click Finish.

Verifying and Removing Delegated Permissions

Although the Delegation of Control Wizard can be used to give permissions to users or groups, it cannot be used to verify or remove permissions. To verify or remove permissions that were delegated, you must use the Security tab in the Properties dialog box of the delegated object.

▶ Verifying Delegated Permissions

To verify delegated permissions, complete the following steps:

1. In Active Directory Users And Computers, on the View menu, click Advanced Features. This allows you to see the Security tab as required in step 3.

2. Navigate in the left pane to the object for which you wish to verify delegated permissions, right-click, and select Properties.

3. On the Security tab, click Advanced.

4. On the Permissions tab, under Permissions entries, view the assigned permissions.

To remove delegated permissions, continue to step 5.

5. Select the user or group for which you wish to remove delegated control privileges, and click Remove. Click OK twice to exit the Properties window.

MOVING OBJECTS BETWEEN OUs

You can move objects from one OU to another for administrative or business purposes. For example, consider a scenario where you are a consultant who has been called in to analyze and recommend changes to make network administration simpler and more effective. If all users are created in the Users container, it probably would be best to restructure these users according to resource needs and administrative goals. Windows Server 2003 allows you to restructure your Active Directory database by moving leaf objects such as users, computers, and printers between OUs, in addition to moving OUs into other OUs to create a nested structure. When you move objects between OUs in a domain, permissions that are assigned directly to objects remain the same and the objects inherit permissions from the new OU. All permissions that were inherited previously from the old OU no longer affect the objects. Windows Server 2003 provides the following methods for moving objects between OUs in the same domain:

- Drag and drop within Active Directory Users And Computers.
- Use the Move menu option within Active Directory Users And Computers.

NOTE *Moving Objects Between Domains* *If you wish to move objects between domains, use the MoveTree command supplied by the Windows Server 2003 Support Tools. The steps to install the Windows Server 2003 Support Tools are described in Chapter 3, "Working with Active Directory Sites."*

Using Drag and Drop

The drag-and-drop feature is new in Windows Server 2003. This ability is welcomed by administrators of the previous version of Active Directory, which did not support it. The drag-and-drop feature functions the same way as it does in Windows Explorer, the main file management system within all Windows-based operating systems.

▶ **Moving an Object Between OUs By Dragging and Dropping**

To move an object between OUs using the drag-and-drop feature, complete the following steps:

1. In Active Directory Users And Computers, select the object you wish to move. If you wish to move multiple objects, hold down the Ctrl key while selecting the objects you wish to move.

   All objects selected will be ready for step 2.

2. While holding down the left mouse button, drag the object to the desired destination OU and release the mouse.

   The object will appear in its new location.

Using the Move Option

Using the drag-and-drop feature can be cumbersome and sometimes produces undesired results if you are not accurate with the mouse. The Move option in Active Directory Users And Computers offers a safer method than the drag-and-drop feature, but has the same results.

▶ **Using the Move Option to Restructure Active Directory**

To use the Move option to restructure Active Directory, complete the following steps:

1. In Active Directory Users And Computers, select the object you wish to move. If you wish to move multiple objects, hold down the Ctrl key while selecting the objects you wish to move. All objects that are selected will be ready for step 2.

2. Right-click the selected object(s), and select Move from the shortcut menu.

3. In the Move dialog box, select the container object you wish to be the destination for the selected objects, and click OK. Active Directory will refresh and the objects will appear in their new location.

To practice moving objects in Active Directory, do Exercise 6-2 now.

NOTE *Using Dsmove Dsmove offers a command line method for moving and renaming objects in an Active Directory domain. For more information on the syntax and usage of dsmove, consult the Windows Server 2003 online documentation at http://www.microsoft.com/technet/treeview/default.asp?url=/technet/prodtechnol/windowsserver2003/proddocs/entserver/dsmove.asp.*

SUMMARY

- Creating a naming standards document will assist in planning a consistent Active Directory environment, which results in one that is easier to manage.
- Securing user accounts includes educating users to the risks of attacks, implementing a strong password policy, and possibly introducing a smart card infrastructure into your environment.
- Smart cards require a PKI to be in place. This can be accomplished through the installation of Certificate Services. In addition, your CA must be installed as an enterprise CA in the Windows Server 2003 environment.
- Windows Server 2003 only supports PC/SC–compliant smart cards by default. Although some manufacturers may claim to produce drivers that work, Microsoft recommends implementing only PC/SC–compliant cards.
- You must have a workstation that is set up as your enrollment station, and also a user that is given an enrollment certificate to create smart cards on behalf of the users.
- Contingency plans that include temporary user identities or temporary access cards should be developed for situations where smart card access is not possible.
- As part of creating a secure environment, you should create standard user accounts for administrators and direct them to use Run As when performing administrative tasks.
- When planning your OU structure, consider the business function, organizational structure, and administrative goals for your network. Delegation of administrative tasks should be a consideration in your plan.
- Administrative tasks can be delegated for a domain, OU, or container to assist in achieving a decentralized management structure. Permissions can be delegated using the Delegation Of Control Wizard. Verification or removal of these permissions must be achieved through the Security tab in the Properties dialog box of the affected container.
- Moving objects between containers and OUs within a domain can be achieved using the Move menu command, the drag-and-drop feature in Active Directory Users And Computers, or the dsmove utility from a command line.

EXERCISES

Exercise 6-1: Planning a Naming Standard and Password Strategy

Create a naming standard and password strategy based on the fact that your network consists of Windows XP, Windows 98, and several Windows 95 workstations. Using your own name as an example, complete the standards chart in Table 6-2 according to your strategy.

Table 6-2 **Username and Password Plan**

Your Name	
Naming Standard	
Example	
Password Strategy	
Example	

Exercise 6-2: Moving Objects in Active Directory

Complete the following steps to practice moving an OU and its contents in Active Directory.

1. In Active Directory Users And Computers, create an OU using your last name and your computer number (for example, Smith01).

2. In your newly created OU, create a user object using the first five characters of your last name, followed by your first initial (for example, smithj).

3. Create an additional OU using your first name and first initial of your last name (for example, JohnS).

4. Select the OU you created in step 1 that contains your user object.

5. Using either the drag-and-drop method or the Move menu option, relocate this OU to the OU you created in step 3 using your first name and first initial of your last name.

6. Verify that your container and user account were moved successfully into the target OU.

REVIEW QUESTIONS

1. You are preparing to implement smart cards into your organization for all users. Which Windows Server 2003 service must you install in order to support smart card authentication?
    a. Secondary Logon Service
    b. Certificate Service
    c. Domain Name Service
    d. PKI Service

2. Based on strong password characteristics, what is wrong with the password TiGer01? What would you recommend changing to make this password stronger?

3. One of your employees is unable to gain access to the network because she left her smart card at home. Keeping in mind that your network has fairly high security guidelines, which of the following choices is the most secure solution for this situation?
    a. In Active Directory Users And Computers, reset her account to not require the use of a smart card and assign her a password that does not expire.

b. In Active Directory Users And Computers, reset her account so that it does not require the use of a smart card, and assign her a password that expires at the end of the business day.

c. Create a temporary user account and password for this user and assign all necessary permissions for her to access her resources.

d. Create a temporary smart card for her with a certificate that expires at the close of the business day.

4. You are the main administrator for an enterprise environment consisting of four domains in separate locations. Your network is becoming increasingly difficult to manage due to the number of users in separate geographic locations. Each location has people who are willing to learn to maintain their part of the network. In addition, as departments grow, you want each department to have control over their user accounts and resources. The CEO has asked you to come up with a plan to set up decentralized administration. What will you include in your plan?

5. Which tool must you use to move a user object from one domain to another domain?

    a. Active Directory Users And Computers

    b. The drag-and-drop feature

    c. Movetree

    d. Dsmove

6. You are attempting to use the Run As program to open Active Directory Users And Computers, but you receive an error message and are unable to do this. What should you check?

    a. Check to make sure you are logged on locally.

    b. Check to make sure Certificate Services is functioning properly.

    c. Check to make sure that the Log On Locally policy has not been changed.

    d. Check to make sure the Secondary Logon service is running.

7. What must you have in order to be able to create a smart card on behalf of a user in your organization?

    a. An enrollment certificate

    b. A token-style card

    c. An administrator user account

    d. Full control in the Active Directory domain

8. List the hardware requirement for each workstation from which you wish to gain smart card access to your network.

9. List an administrative benefit of being able to move objects from one OU to another within your domain.

10. Which of the following statements should be considered most important when planning your OU structure?

    a. Delegation of administrative tasks

    b. Group Policy implementation

    c. User access to resources

    d. Ease of user navigation

CASE SCENARIOS

Scenario 6-1: Planning Active Directory for Contoso Pharmaceuticals

You are a consultant working with Contoso Pharmaceuticals to assist them in planning their Active Directory infrastructure. Contoso Pharmaceuticals is a medical research and experimental drug company that participates in government projects. The information on the company's network is very sensitive and therefore security is the CEO's primary concern. The plan that is implemented should have the strongest precautions against attacks from the outside.

The company currently is using a Microsoft Windows NT Server 4.0 domain and will be transitioning to Active Directory with the migration of their network to Windows Server 2003. The company currently has a single domain and will be expanding to include a single forest and one domain for each of their five locations when the new network is installed. An administrator has been designated for each location. In addition, the accounting and human resource departments, which are located at the main site, want to be able to manage their own containers.

1. Based on this scenario, should administration be centralized or decentralized?

2. How will you achieve the goal set forth by the accounting and human resource departments?

3. What will you propose for a secure logon method?

Scenario 6-2: Smart Card Implementation Proposal

You are the main administrator for a large enterprise organization that has recently experienced several network intrusions via user accounts and passwords. Although you have implemented strong passwords and educated your users on the importance of following company policy, you feel that you need to convince upper management that smart cards will alleviate your problems. In order to do this, you will need to come up with the following information:

- A list of benefits to a smart card program
- A list of items to be added to the budget for implementation and support of this new program
- A rough implementation plan that lists the basic steps required to implement this new technology

Address each one of these points in a plan for this new program.

CHAPTER 7
INTRODUCTION TO GROUP POLICY

Upon completion of this chapter, you will be able to:

- Explain Group Policy.
- Describe the benefits of Group Policy to users and administrators.
- Understand Group Policy Objects (GPOs).
- Describe local and nonlocal group policies.
- Describe the Default Domain Policy and the Default Domain Controllers Policy.
- Use Group Policy Object Editor to view Group Policy settings.
- Explain how group policies are processed during computer startup and user logon.
- Understand the exceptions to Group Policy processing default behavior.
- Describe the techniques that can be used to alter the inheritance of group policies.
- Describe the Computer Loopback setting.
- Analyze a set of policies to determine the effective policies that apply to an object.

As computer network dependency grows within organizations, the need to find more efficient methods to manage users, computers, and software becomes more important. Organizations, faced with the need to maintain upgraded applications and software, seek network management tools to help them accomplish their goals. Organizations must offer this support in addition to providing tighter network security and consistency in the computing environment. In this chapter and the next three chapters, we will discuss **Group Policy** and the associated management tools available within a Microsoft Windows Server 2003 network to help organizations achieve their goals. This chapter will emphasize the concepts associated with Group Policy, including the terminology, available tools, and administrative strategies. In addition, we will discuss the benefits of group policies to users, administrators, and the corporate accounting bottom line.

WHAT IS GROUP POLICY?

Group Policy is a method of controlling settings across your network. Group Policy consists of user and computer settings on the Windows Server 2003 family, Microsoft Windows 2000 family, and Microsoft Windows XP Professional platforms that can be implemented during computer startup and user logons. Managed settings that can be defined or changed through group policies include the following:

- Registry-based policies such as user desktop settings and environment variables to provide a consistent, secure, manageable environment that addresses the users' needs and the administrative goals of the organization.

- Software installations and repairs so that users always have the latest version of applications. If application files are inadvertently deleted, repairs are made without user intervention.

- Folder redirection that allows files to be redirected to a network drive for backup and accessibility from anywhere on the network.

- Offline file storage, which works with folder redirection to provide the ability to cache files locally. This allows files to be available even when the network is inaccessible.

- Disk quotas that can be used to track each user's redirected folders and space usage on a server.

- Scripts including logon, logoff, startup, and shutdown commands that can assist in configuring the user environment.

- Remote Installation Services (RIS) to assist in rebuilding or deploying workstations quickly and efficiently in your enterprise environment.

- Microsoft Internet Explorer settings and maintenance functionality. These settings provide quick links and bookmarks for user accessibility, in addition to browser setting options such as proxy use, acceptance of cookies, and caching options.

- Security settings to protect resources on computers in your enterprise.

Depending on the needs of your organization, you can choose which features and settings you wish to implement. For example, you may need to create a policy for a public access computer in a library that configures the desktop environment with a proprietary library access system. In addition, you may wish to disable the ability to write to the computer's hard drive. As you determine the needs of different users and address those needs within corporate security and computing policies, you can plan the best methods to implement Group Policy.

Although the name Group Policy implies that policies are applied directly to groups, this is not the case. Group policies can be assigned to sites, domains, or organizational units (OUs) and are applied to users and computers within these Active Directory containers. In fact, the term Group Policy refers to a group of settings or policies applied to Active Directory objects. In this chapter you will learn how security for the application or denial of policy processing can be assigned to specific users and groups.

In the next section you will learn some of the benefits of Group Policy to users, administrators, and budget-minded corporations.

GROUP POLICY BENEFITS

For the most part, corporations no longer use the pen-and-paper method of recording their accounting activities. Conversely, they also do not want to spend money needlessly in the implementation and management of their corporate computing systems. Rather, corporations always consider two criteria when evaluating networks: **Return on Investment (ROI)** and **Total Cost of Ownership (TCO)**. ROI can be measured by tangible benefits such as implementation costs and ongoing support. In addition, ROI can be measured by intangible benefits such as increased user productivity and other factors that are difficult to measure from a financial standpoint. TCO can be calculated based on how much ownership costs over the lifetime of a business resource. For example, the TCO of a network includes costs, such as original purchases of equipment, upgrades, implementation costs, and management costs, spread out over the life of the network. The goal of implementing group policies is to both increase a company's ROI and decrease the company's TCO. These two benefits can be achieved by carefully planning your group policies to align with company policies and administrative goals.

User Benefits

Users may initially view group policies as being a heavy-handed management tactic to keep them from using certain computer functions. However, if presented appropriately, users will understand that they also benefit from group policies. Some of the Group Policy benefits to users include:

- Users can have access to their files, even when network connectivity is intermittent. This is accomplished by using folder redirection and offline files.
- The user environment can be set up to be consistent, regardless of the user's logon location or workstation access point.
- User files can be redirected to server locations that allow them to be backed up regularly, saving the user from the headaches of lost data due to the failure of their workstation.
- Applications that become damaged or need to be updated can be maintained automatically.

Although it is possible to lock down a workstation tightly and allow minimal user freedom, in most cases, that is not the goal. Instead, the goal is to provide a consistent, user-friendly environment in which the user can be confident. If you provide users with clear understanding of the benefits Group Policy implementation achieves, you will make your job as an administrator easier.

Administrator Benefits

Group policies probably have their largest impact on reducing TCO due to the benefits they provide in administration. Administrators find that Group Policy implementation helps them to achieve centralized management. The following is a list of administrative benefits to Group Policy implementation:

- Administrators have control over centralized configuration of user settings, application installations, and desktop configurations.
- Problems due to missing application files and other minor application errors can often be alleviated by the automation of application repairs.
- Centralized backup of user files eliminates the need and cost of trying to recover files from a damaged drive.
- The need to manually make security changes is reduced by the rapid deployment of new settings through Group Policy.

Understanding how to put these benefits into practice will be covered in this chapter and the next three chapters. You may find that some of the benefits will be seen immediately upon implementation of a Group Policy plan, while others are seen over time as your network complexity grows.

UNDERSTANDING GROUP POLICY OBJECTS

Group Policy Objects (GPOs) contain all of the Group Policy settings that you wish to implement to user and computer objects within a site, domain, or OU. The GPO must be associated with the container to which it is applied. This association occurs by linking the policy to the desired Active Directory object. We will learn how to link GPOs to containers after we define GPOs and where they are stored.

There are two types of GPOs: **local Group Policy Objects** and **nonlocal Group Policy Objects**. They are defined in the next sections.

Local Group Policy Objects

Each computer running Windows Server 2003, Windows XP Professional, or Windows 2000 has only one local GPO. The GPO settings are stored on the local computer in the *Systemroot/System32/GroupPolicy* folder. A local GPO has the following characteristics:

- Local GPOs contain fewer options. They do not support folder redirection or Group Policy software installation. There are fewer available security settings.
- When a local and a nonlocal (Active Directory–based) GPO have conflicting settings, the local GPO is overwritten by the nonlocal GPO.

In a networked environment, local GPOs are not typically used since their settings are often overwritten by nonlocal GPOs.

Nonlocal Group Policy Objects

As part of a domain, nonlocal GPOs are created in Active Directory and are linked to sites, domains, or OUs. Once linked to a container, by default, the GPO is applied to all users and computers within that container. The content of a nonlocal

GPO is actually stored in two locations. These locations are as follows:

- **Group Policy container (GPC)**—an Active Directory object that stores the properties of the GPO.
- **Group Policy template (GPT)**—located in the Policies subfolder of the Sysvol volume, the GPT is a folder that stores policy settings such as security settings and script files.

Each of these locations is further explained in the next sections.

Group Policy Container Object

This directory service object includes subcontainers that hold GPO policy information. By default, when Active Directory is first installed, two policies are placed in this container. These default policies are discussed later in this chapter in the section "Default Group Policy Objects." Each Active Directory GPC is named according to the globally unique identifier (GUID) that is assigned to it when it is created. The default GPC containers are created when Active Directory is installed. A new GPC is created to store policy information and settings. The GPC contains two subcontainers, one for Computer configuration information and another for User configuration information. The more specific information included in each GPC is described as follows:

- Status information that indicates whether the related GPO is enabled or disabled
- Version information to ensure that the GPC is synchronized and up-to-date with the most current information
- A list of components that have settings in this GPO

Computers access the GPC to locate Group Policy templates via a link or connection reference to the GPT. Domain controllers access the GPC to get version information. If the version information for a GPO is not current, replication occurs to update the GPO with the latest version. The Group Policy container can be found in Active Directory Users And Computers using Advanced View. Figure 7-1 shows the Group Policy container discussed in this section.

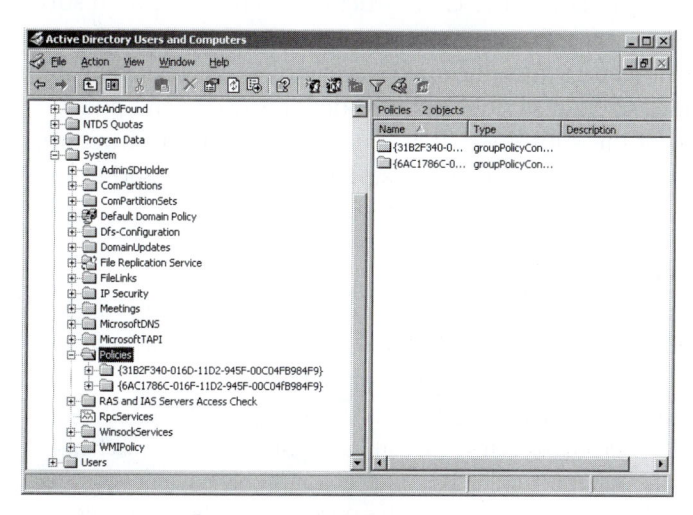

Figure 7-1 Viewing the Group Policy container

▶ **Viewing the GPC**

To view the GPC, complete the following steps:

1. In Active Directory Users And Computers, on the View menu, select Advanced Features.

   This allows you to see additional objects in Active Directory.

   NOTE **Advanced Features** *If Advanced Features already has a check mark next to it, clicking it again hides the Advanced Features view options. Make sure there is a check mark next to Advanced Features before proceeding to step 2.*

2. In the left console pane, expand the System folder.

3. In the System folder, locate the Policies folder and expand it by clicking the plus sign (+).

   This opens the folder and you should now see the two default policies, with each named using its GUID. GUIDs were discussed in Chapter 1, "Overview of Active Directory."

Group Policy Template

The GPT folder structure is located in the shared Sysvol folder on a domain controller. By default, two folders that refer to the default domain policies are named when they are created by Active Directory. These GUIDs should be the same as those described for the GPCs. When additional GPOs are created, a corresponding GPT folder structure is created that contains all of the policy's settings and information. As with the GPC, computers connect to the GPT folder structure to read these settings.

The path to the default GPT structure for the cohowinery.com domain is as follows:

systemroot\sysvol\sysvol\cohowinery.com\Policies\

Systemroot should be replaced with the folder location for the operating system files. In a clean Windows Server 2003 installation, this is the Windows folder location. Notice that the namespace for the cohowinery.com domain is included as part of the path.

For each GUID that refers to a policy in the GPT structure, there are several subfolders and a gpt.ini file. The gpt.ini file exists for every Group Policy that is created. It contains the version and status information regarding this specific GPO. The subfolders contain more specific settings that are defined within the policy. Table 7-1 explains several of the subfolders that are part of the GPT structure, and their contents. This table is not all-inclusive since some folders and their contents are created when policy settings are defined.

Table 7-1 GPT Folder Structure

Folder	Content
\Adm	Administrative template files for this specific GPT. Administrative templates are discussed later in this chapter.
\Machine	This folder contains a Registry.pol file that makes changes to the HKEY_LOCAL_MACHINE hive in the registry based on machine-specific settings. This file is created automatically when a policy has used the Administrative Templates option within the Computer Configuration node. For example, enabling Disk Quotas for a machine creates a Registry.pol file. Disk Quotas are discussed in Chapter 8, "Configuring the User and Computer Environment Using Group Policy."

(continued)

Table 7-1 **GPT Folder Structure**

Folder	Content
\Machine\Applications	**Application advertisement script (AAS)** files that include instructions for assigned or published application packages. This folder does not exist until package files used to deploy software applications are assigned to the Computer Configuration node of the GPO.
\Machine\Microsoft \WindowsNT\SecEdit	This folder is created when security settings such as account lockout specifications are defined in the policy. A file is created in this folder named GptTmpl.inf. It contains the specific settings to be applied with the GPO.
\Machine\Scripts	Contains settings for any startup or shutdown scripts that are in effect when the computer affected by this GPO is started or shut down.
\User	This folder contains a Registry.pol file that makes changes to the HKEY_CURRENT_USER hive in the registry based on user-specific settings. This file is created automatically when a policy has used the Administrative Templates option under the User Configuration node. For example, setting a user's account to autoenroll for a certificate creates a Registry.pol file. Autoenrolling for a certificate is discussed in Chapter 8, "Configuring the User and Computer Environment Using Group Policy."
\User\Applications	AAS files that include instructions for assigned or published application packages. This folder does not exist until package files used to deploy software applications have been assigned to the User Configuration node of the GPO.
\User\Scripts	Contains settings for logon and logoff scripts that are applied when a user affected by this GPO logs on or off the network.

Default Group Policy Objects

When Active Directory is first installed, there are two nonlocal Group Policy objects that are created by default. These two GPOs are named by their GUID and can be found both in the Active Directory Users And Computers and in the Sysvol folder structure as demonstrated earlier. These GUIDs represent the following default policies:

- **Default Domain Policy**   This policy is linked to the domain and its settings affect all users and computers in the domain.

- **Default Domain Controllers Policy**   This policy is linked to the Domain Controllers OU and it affects all domain controllers within this object. As domain controllers are added to the domain, they are automatically placed in this OU and are affected by any settings applied with this policy.

To view the GPC and the GPT structures, complete Exercise 7-1 now.

These two policies are very important in your domain. Settings in these policies can affect security and your administrative abilities throughout the domain. We will be discussing these two policies and several of the main settings that are important in subsequent chapters. For now, you need to understand what they are and the extent of their effects.

Using Group Policy Object Editor

Group Policy Object Editor is the Microsoft Management Console (MMC) snap-in used to create and modify group policies and their settings. Group Policy Object Editor can be opened several different ways, depending on what you wish to accomplish. For example, if you wish to create a GPO for an OU and automatically link it to the OU, you must edit the properties of the OU. The following steps guide you through creating and linking a GPO to an OU.

▶ **Creating and Linking a GPO to an OU**

1. In Active Directory Users And Computers, navigate through your structure to find the OU for which you wish to create a GPO. Right-click this OU, and select Properties.

2. On the Group Policy tab, click New, and type a name for your GPO.

3. With the newly named GPO selected, click Edit. Group Policy Object Editor opens and you can proceed with defining your policy settings.

Figure 7-2 shows Group Policy Object Editor open for a GPO being created in the cohowinery.com domain. Notice that the parent node of the GPO shows the domain name in which this GPO resides.

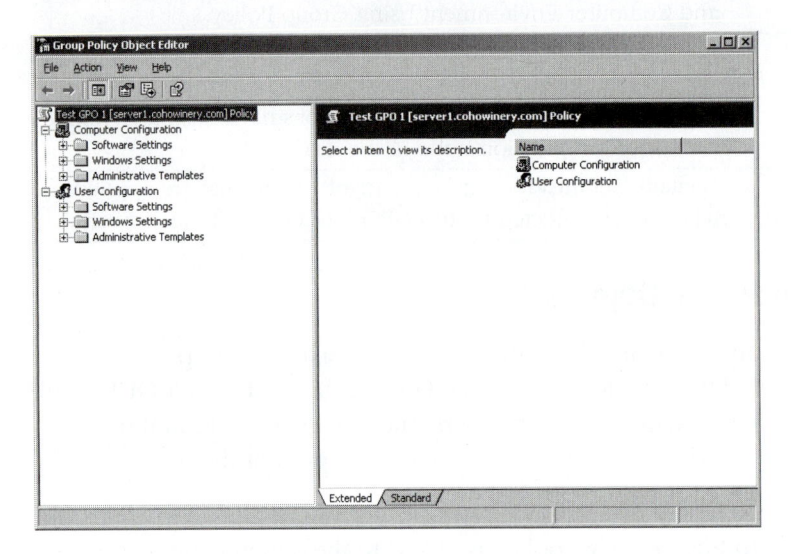

Figure 7-2 Group Policy Object Editor

When you create a group policy directly from a domain, site, or OU object, the group policy is automatically linked to that object. This means that the settings apply to all child objects within the object. For example, if you create a GPO from the domain object in Active Directory Users And Computers, it applies to all users and computers in the domain. On a larger scale, if a GPO is created for a site that contains multiple domains, the group policy is applied to all domains and the child objects contained within them, which is also named *inheritance*.

Group Policy Object Editor can also be opened using the MMC. Using MMC to open Group Policy Object Editor allows you to browse Active Directory and choose the GPO you wish to edit.

▶ **Opening Group Policy Using MMC**

To open Group Policy using MMC, complete the following steps:

1. From the Start/Run text box, type **mmc**, and click OK.
2. On the MMC menu bar, click File, and then click Add/Remove Snap-In.
3. In the Add/Remove Snap-In dialog box, on the Standalone tab, click Add.
4. In the Add Standalone Snap-In dialog box, click Group Policy Object Editor, and then click Add.
5. On the Select Group Policy Object dialog box, choose from the following options:
    - Accept Local Computer, which is the default, to view or modify the local computer policy, and then click Finish.
    - Choose Browse to find a GPO that is associated with an Active Directory container. In the Browse For A Group Policy Object window, you can use the tabs to assist you in finding the policy you wish to view or edit. Select the policy you want, and click OK. After confirming your choice, click Finish.
6. Click Close in the Add Standalone Snap-In dialog box.
7. In the Add/Remove Snap-In dialog box, click OK.

Group Policy Object Editor shows that your selected GPO is now available for editing.

Group Policy Settings

Group Policy settings allow you to customize the configuration of a user's desktop, environment, and security settings. The actual settings are divided into two subcategories: Computer Configuration and User Configuration. The subcategories are referred to as **nodes**. A node is simply a parent structure that holds all related settings. In this case, the node is specific to computer configurations and user configurations. Nodes provide a way to organize the settings according to where they are applied. Defined settings can be applied to client computers, users, or member servers and domain controllers. The application of settings depends on the container to which the GPO is linked. By default, all objects within the container with which the GPO is associated are affected by the GPO's settings.

Both the Computer Configuration and the User Configuration nodes contain three subnodes or extensions that further organize the available Group Policy settings within them. Within the Computer Configuration and User Configuration nodes, the subnodes are as follows:

- Software Settings
- Windows Settings
- Administrative Templates

Each of these is explained in the following sections.

Software Settings

The Software Settings folder located under the Computer Configuration node in Group Policy Object Editor contains settings that apply to all users who log on from that specific computer. Settings modified here are computer-specific, meaning that no matter who logs on to the computer, these settings are applied before the user is allowed to log on to the desktop.

Contrary to being computer-specific, the Software Settings folder located under the User Configuration node contains settings that are applied to users designated by the Group Policy, regardless of the computer from which they log on to Active Directory.

Windows Settings

The Windows Settings folder located under the Computer Configuration node in Group Policy Object Editor contains security settings and scripts that apply to all users who log on to Active Directory from that specific computer. This means that the settings are computer-specific.

The Windows Settings folder located under the User Configuration node contains settings related to folder redirection, security settings, and scripts that are applied to associated users. The computer from which a user logs on does not affect these policy settings. Rather, the policies are applied, regardless of the logon location.

Administrative Templates

Windows Server 2003 includes more than 220 new **administrative template** policies, bringing the total number of available policy settings to over a thousand. Administrative templates contain all registry-based policy settings. Administrative templates are actually text files with the .adm extension. They are used to generate the user interface for the Group Policy settings that you can set using Group Policy Object Editor. By default, there are five .adm files included with Windows Server 2003, and others can be written if necessary. The Windows Server 2003 .adm files are Unicode-based text files, unlike the Windows 2000 .adm files, which are American National Standards Institute (ANSI) text files. The five administrative template files included with Windows Server 2003 are:

- **System.adm**   Contains over 550 system settings that pertain to the user and computer system options.
- **Intres.adm**   Contains over 90 Internet Explorer settings that are used to set security and usability options.
- **Wuau.adm**   Contains settings for the functionality of Windows Update.
- **Wmplayer.adm**   Contains settings for the functionality of Windows Media Player.
- **Conf.adm**   Contains settings for the functionality of NetMeeting.

Settings in Wmplayer.adm and Conf.adm are not available on the 64-bit versions of Microsoft Windows XP Professional or Windows Server 2003. Template settings in these templates generally can be applied to Windows 2000 and Windows

Server 2003 clients and servers. You will learn later in this chapter how to determine which operating system platforms support which settings.

> **MORE INFO** **Administrative Templates Information** Microsoft has published an Excel spreadsheet that lists all administrative templates, their contents, and the default registry setting. This resource can be found in the download center at: http://www.microsoft.com/downloads/details.aspx?displaylang=en&familyid=7821c32f-da15-438d-8e48-45915cd2bc14.

The settings in the Administrative Templates folder of the User Configuration node write changes to the HKEY_CURRENT_USER registry key, while settings in the Computer Configuration node write changes to the HKEY_LOCAL_MACHINE registry key. Administrative templates are the only area of Group Policy, with the other areas being software settings and Windows settings, that allows you to make modifications by adding new administrative templates. There are three types of administrative templates that can be used in Windows Server 2003. They include the following:

- **Default** These are provided with the Windows Server 2003 operating system and were listed previously.

- **Vendor-Supplied** These are not part of the operating system. You may need to install them separately before they can be used with Group Policy. The settings provided generally include product-specific items. For example, you can download templates specific to Microsoft Office 2000 that can be used to customize your applications.

- **Custom** These templates can be created using the .adm language with specific security or application needs in mind. Developers generally write custom administrative templates. One could be written to serve as a policy for a proprietary application.

> **MORE INFO** **.adm Files** For more information on .adm files and for an example of a template file, visit the Microsoft Developer Network link at http://msdn.microsoft.com/library/default.asp?url=/library/en-us/policy/policy/administrative_template_file_format.asp.

Administrative Template Setting Options

Since administrative templates are an area of Group Policy where many commonly used administrative settings reside, it is important to be familiar with how you can determine what each setting does. In Group Policy Object Editor, you can view descriptions of policy settings using three methods. These methods are:

- The Explain tab in the setting's Properties dialog box, as shown in Figure 7-3.

- Administrative Templates Help, which is a new feature in Windows Server 2003, as shown in Figure 7-4. This comprehensive help feature describes policy options, the operating systems that support the policy, and the template in which the option is stored.

- The Extended tab in Group Policy Object Editor, which is a new feature in Windows Server 2003, as shown in Figure 7-5.

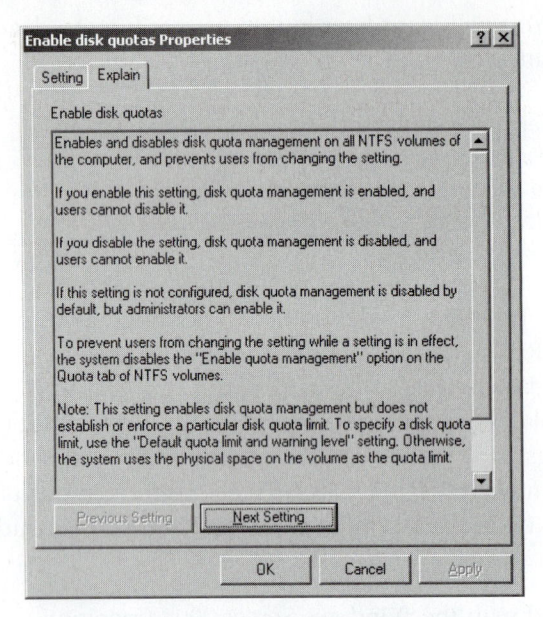

Figure 7-3 The Explain tab of a GPO setting

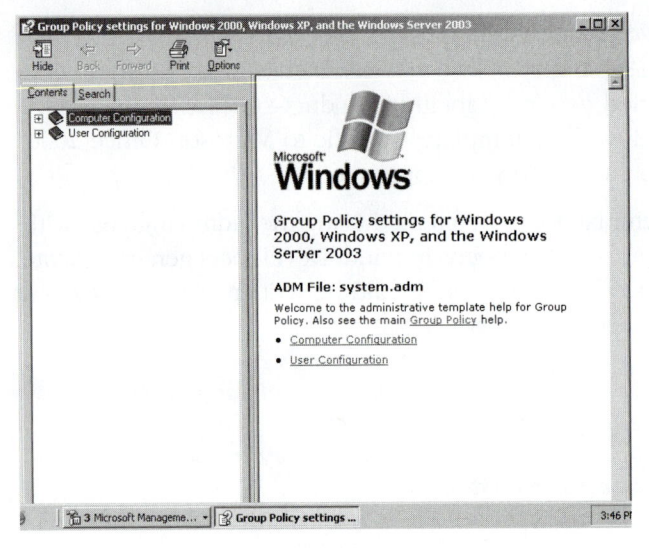

Figure 7-4 Administrative Template Help

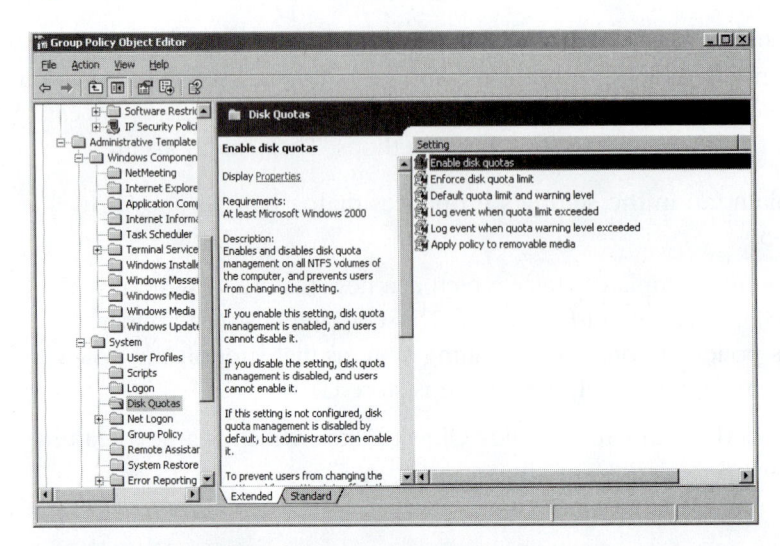

Figure 7-5 Group Policy Object Editor's Extended tab

To work with administrative template settings, you need to understand the three different states of each setting. Figure 7-6 shows the available options. First, a setting can be set to *Not Configured*, which means that no modification to the registry from its default state occurs. Not Configured is the default setting for the majority of GPO settings. When a GPO with a Not Configured setting is processed, the registry key affected by the setting is not modified or overwritten. Next, a setting can be set to *Enabled*, which means the registry key is modified by this setting. Last, a setting can be set to *Disabled*, which means the policy setting is not selected. A Disabled setting will *undo* a change made by a prior Enabled setting.

> To practice viewing explanations of administrative template settings, do Exercise 7-2 now.

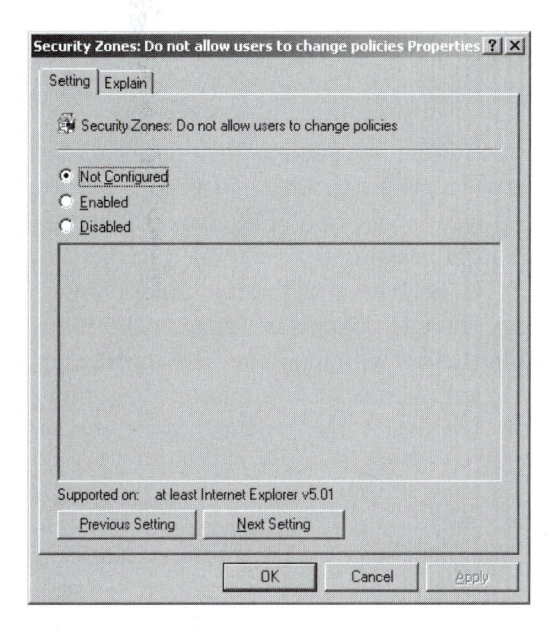

Figure 7-6 Administrative Template setting options

Group Policies and the Active Directory Structure

As we have discussed, nonlocal GPOs are created in Active Directory and linked to container objects. Nonlocal GPOs can be linked to Active Directory sites, domains, or OUs. They cannot be linked to built-in containers such as the default Users, Builtin, or Computers container. These containers can receive policies only through domain or site-linked policies that flow down to all objects within them. Policies affect the containers to which they are linked in the following ways:

- Site-linked policies affect all domains within the site.
- Domain-linked policies affect all users and computers within the domain and within any containers in the domain. This includes objects in built-in containers, as well as objects within OUs of the domain.
- OU-linked policies affect all objects within the OU and any other OU structures nested within them.

How Group Policies Are Processed

As previously discussed, you can have local policies, site policies, domain policies, and OU policies within your domain structure. In order to learn how to best implement group policies to serve the organization, you need to understand the order in which the policies are applied. To begin, policies are processed in the following order:

1. Local policies
2. Site policies
3. Domain policies
4. OU policies

Following the order of processing from steps 1 to 4, the settings in the policies that are processed last, that is, the policies that are assigned to an OU in step 4, override any conflicting settings in the policies that were processed in the preceding steps 1 to 3. For example, suppose you have a policy setting that is applied to the site and affects all domains and their contents. If you have modified the same setting to produce a different result in an OU policy, the OU policy settings prevail. This behavior is intentional and provides administrators with flexibility in Group Policy application. In addition, as policies are applied, each container inherits the settings of the parent container policies by default. To further illustrate this point, consider the following example:

Figure 7-7 shows the Active Directory domain structure for The School of Fine Art. The school has registered the domain name fineartschool.net. It has one location and plans to add a second one within a year. Within the first location, there are several departments represented by OUs. Since there is only one site, there are no policies applied to the site. At the domain level, the default domain policy has not been modified. The *Current Location* OU has a GPO with several settings. As shown, these settings are inherited to the *Administration* and *Education* OUs. The Education OU has an additional GPO with several additional settings. Note that the background graphic file that is applied to the user's desktop if the user resides in the Education OU is a different graphic file than that of its parent container. Furthermore, Figure 7-7 clearly shows that policy settings from a parent container are inherited by the child containers by default. As shown, since the Education department's OU policy is the last to be processed, the settings in this policy are inherited by users in the Education OU and the Music and Dance child OUs. It should be noted also that if settings in the User Configuration node and the Computer Configuration node are in conflict, the computer settings always take precedence. In addition, the default **inheritance** settings can be changed.

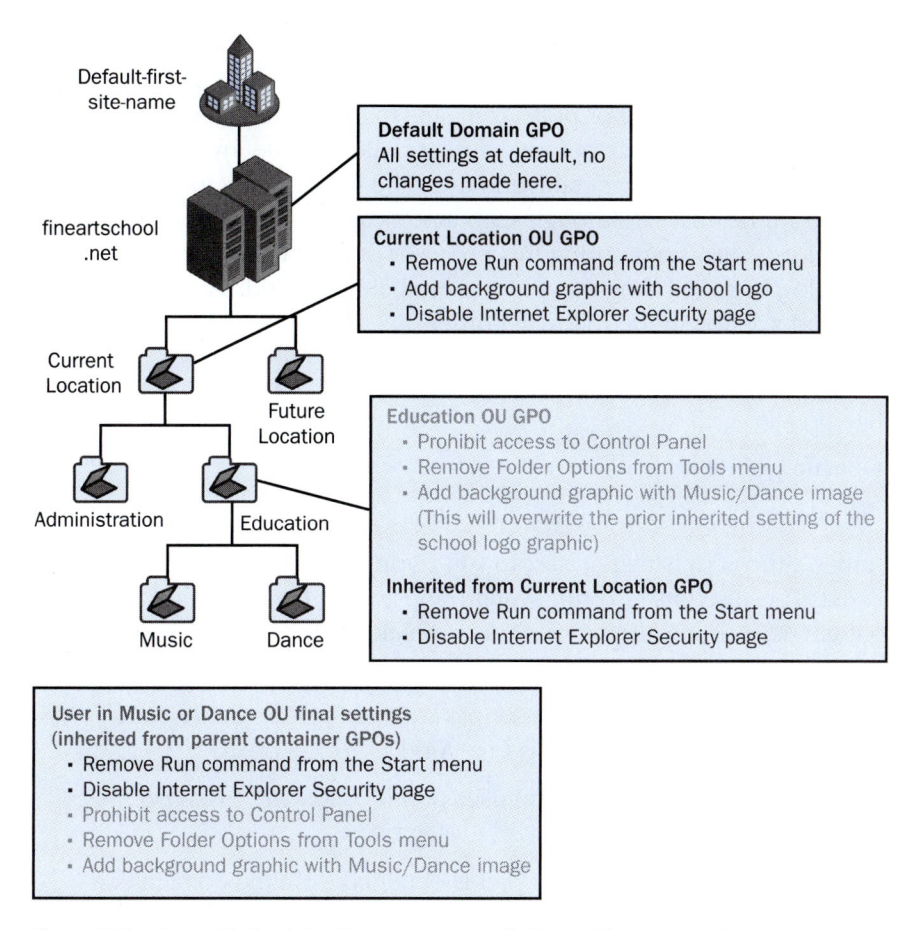

Figure 7-7 Group Policy inheritance and cumulative settings example

Multiple Policies Linked to a Container

Domains, sites, and OUs can have multiple group policies linked to them. Expanding on the previous example, you might have more than one policy linked to the Education department's OU. In this situation, the top GPO in the list is processed last. When there are multiple GPOs linked to a container, the first GPO in the list has the highest priority. In other words, by default the list of linked GPOs is processed from the bottom to the top.

Policy Processing and Startup, Logon, Logoff, and Shutdown

As previously discussed, policies can be applied to containers and the user and computer objects that reside in them. Computer Configuration settings are processed when a computer first starts, followed by User Configuration settings, which are processed during user logon. There are also two types of scripts that can run during startup: computer startup scripts and user logon scripts. In addition, there are two scripts that can run during shutdown: user logoff scripts and computer shutdown scripts.

The following steps describe the process that is taken to implement the settings of the assigned GPOs for a computer and user.:

1. The computer starts up, and as it initializes, a list of GPOs to be applied is obtained. This list is obtained after a secure link between the computer and a domain controller is established.

2. Computer configuration settings are applied synchronously during computer startup before the Logon dialog box is presented to the user. **Synchronous processing** of policies means that each policy must be read and applied completely before the next policy can be invoked. The synchronous behavior is by default and it can be modified by the system administrator if necessary, although such modification is discouraged. No user interface is displayed during this process with the exception of a Startup dialog box indicating that policies are being applied. The policies are read and applied in the following order:
   - Local policies
   - Site policies
   - Domain policies
   - OU policies

3. Next any startup scripts that are set to run during computer startup are processed. These scripts also run synchronously and have a default timeout of 600 seconds (10 minutes) to complete. This process is hidden from the user.

4. When the Computer Configuration scripts and startup scripts are complete, the user is prompted to press Ctrl+Alt+Del to log on.

5. Upon successful user validation, the user profile is loaded based on the Group Policy settings in effect.

6. Next, a list of GPOs specific for the user is obtained from the domain controller. User Configuration settings are processed in the same order as those of the Computer Configuration settings: local, site, domain, and OUs. The processing of the GPOs is again transparent to the user and the policies are processed synchronously.

7. After the user policies have run, any logon scripts run. These scripts, unlike the startup scripts, run asynchronously by default. **Asynchronous processing** allows processing to occur for multiple scripts, without waiting for the outcome of a previously launched script to occur. However, the user object script runs last.

8. The user's desktop appears after all policies and scripts have been processed.

> **NOTE** *Exceptions to the Default Policy Processing* *The previously outlined process demonstrates the default processing of policies. There are several exceptions that can be made to improve performance and alter the policy outcomes.*

Exceptions in Processing Group Policies As with most rules, there are usually exceptions and this is true of Group Policy processing and inheritance. The purpose of having exceptions, to the default processing of Group Policy options is to allow greater control and flexibility over the final settings that are applied. In this section, we will discuss several options that provide exceptions to the Group Policy processing rules. These exceptions include the following features:

- **No Override** Set on a policy to force the settings to flow down through the Active Directory, without being blocked by child OUs.

- **Block Policy Inheritance** Set on a site, domain, or OU to block all policies from parent containers from flowing to this container. It is not policy-specific, but rather, it applies to any and all policies that are applied at parent levels. GPO links that are set to No Override are not affected by this setting; they are still applied.

- **Loopback** A setting that provides an alternative method of obtaining the ordered list of GPOs to be processed for the user. When set to Enabled, this setting has two options, Merge and Replace. These options are explained in detail in the next sections.

No Override As we discussed earlier, if you assign a GPO policy at a site level, it is inherited by all domains within that site. The inheritance process takes place in the same order as group policies are applied. Specifically, this process results in site policies inheriting to domains, domain policies inheriting to OUs, parent OU policies inheriting to child OUs, and then in turn to all objects within the OU. Since child container settings can overwrite the settings that were invoked at a parent container, you can assign the No Override attribute to a GPO to force a parent setting to keep it from being overwritten by a child setting with which it conflicts. The No Override option denies the ability of child objects to apply the Block Policy Inheritance setting, as we will discuss next. Figure 7-8 shows the No Override option for a Group Policy.

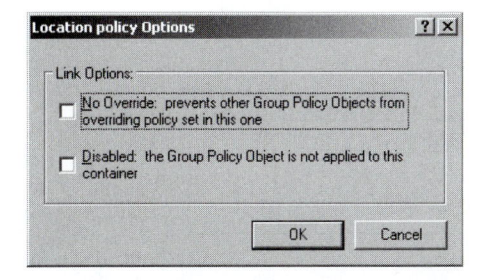

Figure 7-8   Group Policy No Override option

Block Policy Inheritance The second setting that can affect policy processing is the Block Policy Inheritance setting. As shown in Figure 7-9, this setting is applied to an entire container, instead of to a single policy. This setting is useful when you wish to start a new level of policy inheritance, or when you do not want to have objects in a particular container affected by a parent policy. This can be useful; however, when a parent policy is set to No Override, the Block Policy Inheritance feature does not block settings from this particular parent policy. As a further illustration, consider the following example.

Figure 7-10 shows The Fine Arts School Active Directory structure and the GPOs applied at each OU. At the domain level, the default Domain Policy has been modified to include several User Configuration settings that you wish to be invoked by all users in the domain. This policy is set to No Override so that all containers have these settings, regardless of their individual settings.

The administrator of the Current Location OU has implemented a policy that prevents users from using the Run command from the Start menu. In addition, the group policy is being used to push an application to all users in this location.

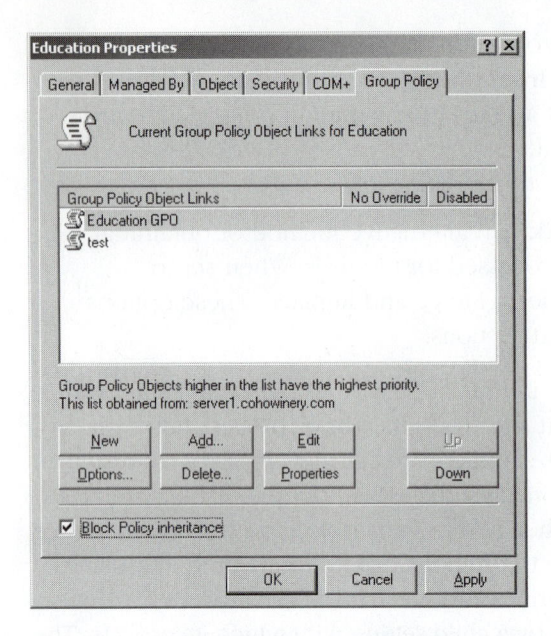

Figure 7-9 Block Policy Inheritance option set on a container object

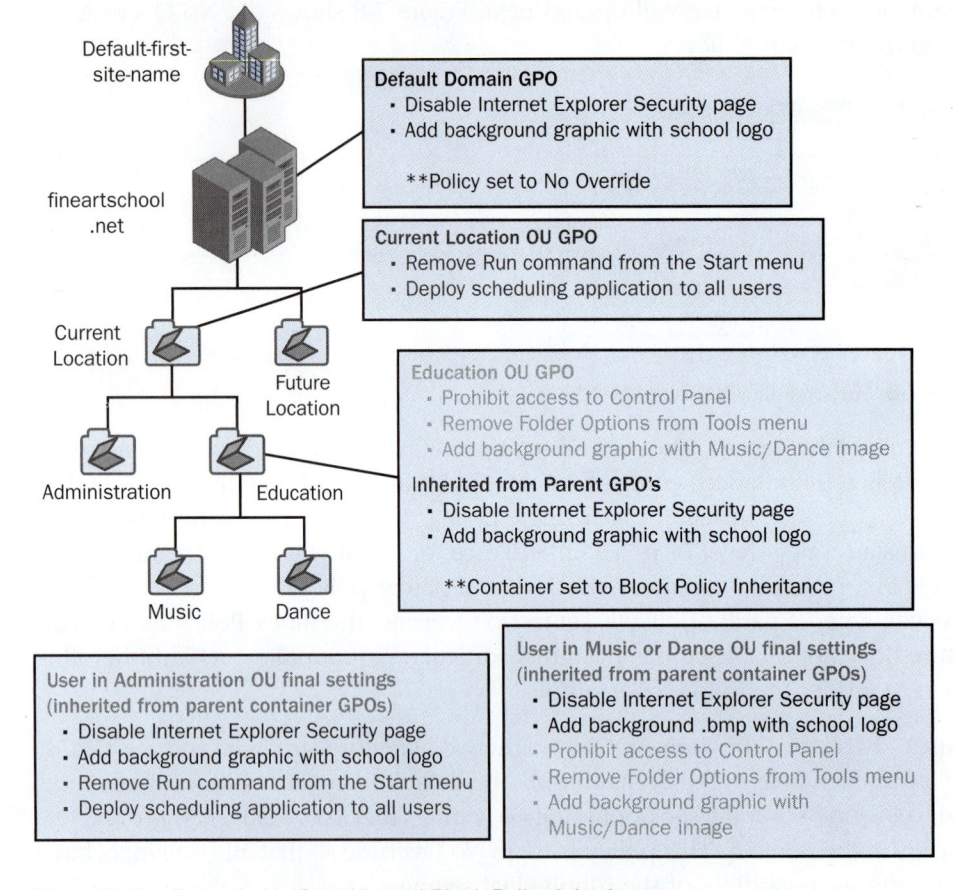

Figure 7-10 Example No Override and Block Policy Inheritance

In the Education OU, several additional settings have been defined to further customize the users in these areas. The education manager has asked that the desktop wallpaper be changed for the Music and Dance departments to reflect a different graphic. Although this container's properties reflect the Block Policy Inheritance setting, when the user interface is presented for users in the Education OU and the Music and Dance child OUs, they receive the logo graphic from the

Default Domain Policy. This is because the Default Domain Policy is set to No Override, which supercedes the Block Policy Inheritance setting. Note also that the Run command is available to these users, and the application set to be deployed based on the Current Location container does not appear. This is due to the Block Policy Inheritance setting on the Education OU.

Finally, note the difference between the effective policies for the Administration OU and the Music and Dance OUs. As you can see, the No Override and Block Policy Inheritance settings can make policy application tricky to follow and at times the results may not be desirable. Understanding how these settings work and using them sparingly helps when you need to troubleshoot the effects of policy settings and their point of origin.

Loopback setting When a computer starts up and its Active Directory container object is located, a list of GPOs that apply to the computer is generated and processed. Similarly, when a user logs on, a list of GPOs based on the user object's Active Directory location is processed. In certain situations, you might not want to have user-specific settings applied to certain computers. For example, when you log on to a domain controller or member server computer, you probably do not want a software application that is associated with your user object to be installed on that computer. Since user policies are applied after computer policies, you might want to alter this situation. This is where the Loopback setting is an asset. As the name implies, Loopback allows the Group Policy processing order to circle back around and reapply the computer policies after all user policies and logon scripts have run. When it is enabled, you can choose from either the Merge option or the Replace option.

When the Merge option is selected, after all user policies have run, the computer policy settings are reapplied, which allows all current GPO settings to merge with the computer policy settings being reapplied. In instances where conflicts arise between computer and user settings, the computer policy supercedes the user policy. This all takes place before the user is presented with a desktop. The settings here are simply appended to what was already processed. Merging may not overwrite all of the settings implemented by the User Configuration settings.

The Replace option overwrites the GPO list for a user object with the GPO list for the computer from which the user is logging on. This means that the computer policy settings entirely remove any user policy settings that conflict with the computer settings component of the GPO.

In addition to the previous example of logging on to a domain controller or server, the Loopback setting is a very valuable tool for managing computers shared by more than one user, as in a kiosk, classroom, or public library. Using the Replace option can greatly reduce the need for you to undo actions such as application installs and desktop changes that are made based on the settings associated with a user object. For example, consider an academic environment in which administrative accounts such as teachers and staff are placed in an Admin OU and student user accounts are placed in student OUs named for the students' graduation year. All computers are located in a Lab OU. In the computer labs, anyone can log on to the network. However, when users in the Admin OU log on, they are configured to print on printers located in their offices, and applications that are assigned to them are installed on the lab computers. Teachers complain that they have to walk back to their offices to pick up print jobs that should be printing on the printers located in the lab. In addition, applications that should not reside on the lab computers have been installed and now need to be removed. One solution to the problem outlined here is to use Loopback's Replace option. When the Replace option is set, only the user settings from the Lab OU will be applied. This resolves the issue of applying unwanted settings on shared computers from other locations in the Active Directory hierarchy.

SUMMARY

- Group Policy consists of user and computer settings that can be implemented during computer startup and user logon. These settings can be used to customize the user environment, to implement security guidelines, and to assist in simplifying user and desktop administration. Group policies can be beneficial to users and administrators. They can be used to help to increase a company network's ROI and to decrease the overall TCO for the network.

- In Active Directory, group policies can be assigned to sites, domains, and OUs. There is one local policy per computer by default. Local policy settings are overwritten by Active Directory policy settings.

- Group Policy content is stored in an Active Directory GPC and in a GPT. While the GPC can be seen using the Advanced Features view in Active Directory Users And Computers, the GPT is a GUID-named folder located in the systemroot\sysvol\SYSVOL*domain_name*\Policies folder.

- The Default Domain Policy and the Default Domain Controller Policy are the two policies that are created by default when Active Directory is first installed.

- Group Policy Object Editor is the tool used to create and modify group policies and their settings.

- GPO nodes contain three subnodes, including Software Settings, Windows Settings, and Administrative Templates. Administrative templates are Unicode text files with the .adm file extension. There are five .adm files included with Windows Server 2003.

- Local policies are processed first, followed by site, domain, and finally OU policies. This order is an important part of understanding how to implement effective policy settings for an object.

- Policies applied to parent containers are inherited by all child containers and objects. Inheritance can be altered by using the No Override, Block Policy Inheritance, or Loopback setting.

EXERCISES

Exercise 7-1: Viewing and Comparing the GPC and GPT Folders

To view and compare the GPC and GPT structures for your domain, complete the following steps:

1. In Active Directory Users And Computers, on the View menu, select Advanced Features. This allows you to see additional containers in Active Directory.

   NOTE Advanced Features *If Advanced Features already has a check mark next to it, clicking it again hides the Advanced Features view options. Make sure there is a check mark next to Advanced Features before proceeding to step 2.*

2. In the left console pane, expand the System folder.

3. In the System folder of the left console pane, locate the Policies folder, and expand it by clicking the plus sign (+). This opens the folder and you should now see the two default policies.

4. Copy the names of the two GUIDs that you see here.

5. Locate and open the Sysvol share for your domain from your computer. (Hint: You can do this from the Run dialog box using a UNC name.)

6. Open the folder that represents your domain name.

7. Open the Policies folder. You should now see at least two folders with GUID names. Copy the GUID folder names you see.

8. Compare these names with the names you copied in step 4.

   QUESTION   *What do you conclude? Why do you think this is true?*

Exercise 7-2: Finding Explanations for Administrative Template Settings

To view the Explain tab or the Extended tab on an administrative template setting, complete the following steps:

1. In Active Directory Users And Computers, locate an OU you created in a prior lab or exercise. Because you cannot save any changes to this OU, it should not matter which one you select.

2. Right-click your chosen OU, and select Properties.

3. In the Properties dialog box, select the Group Policy tab.

4. Click New, type Test GPO to name your new GPO, and press Enter.

5. Click Edit to open Group Policy Object Editor.

6. Under the Computer Configuration node, expand the Administrative Templates folder, followed by the System folder.

7. In the left console pane, click the Disk Quotas folder.

8. In the right details pane, click Enable Disk Quotas. At the bottom left side of the right details pane, make sure that the Extended tab is active. You should now be able to read the description on the left side of the right details pane.

9. To see the Explain tab instead, in the right details pane, right-click Enable Disk Quotas, and select Properties.

10. Click the Explain tab to read the description. After reading the description, click Cancel.

11. Close Group Policy Object Editor.

12. With your newly created GPO selected, click Delete.

13. In the Delete dialog box, select the Remove The Link And Delete The Group Policy Object Permanently, and click OK. Click Yes to confirm your deletion.

14. Click Close to close the Properties of your selected OU.

REVIEW QUESTIONS

1. You are a new administrator taking over for an employee who has just retired. You have recently created several policies that are being used to configure workstations throughout the network. Several users complain that their desktop wallpaper seems to be correct only when they log on locally. What do you suspect is the problem?

2. What is the default order in which policies are processed?

    a. site, domain, OU, local

    b. domain, site, OU, local

    c. local, domain, site, OU

    d. local, site, domain, OU

3. You have just completed the installation of Active Directory on the first domain controller in a new forest. How can you confirm that the two default policies have been created?

4. While studying the Group Policy folder structure, you notice that there is a Registry.pol file in one of the policies' \Machine subfolder, but not in another policy's \Machine subfolder. What is the difference between these two policies?

5. List in order the necessary steps to create a GPO on an OU in Active Directory.

6. You are the administrator for an Active Directory network with several policies that are being applied at each OU. You have just implemented several workstations that can be used by any user who needs access to the network from one of the conference rooms. During your testing of these stations, you notice that when you log on as the different users, the workstation is modified based on the user's policy settings. This creates a problem since you do not want individual user settings to affect these workstations. What should you do to stop this from happening, but still allow multiple users to use their normal logon names for these computers?

7. Since you implemented group policies throughout your organization, some users have complained that it takes a long time to log on to the network. When your manager comes to you and asks for an explanation for the performance degradation, what will you tell him?

8. You have created a policy for your organization at the site level that includes several security settings that no other policies within your Active Directory structure should override. What can you do to ensure this will happen?

    a. Set the container to Block Policy Inheritance.

    b. Set the policy to No Override.

    c. Set the Loopback policy setting to Enabled.

    d. Set the Policy to Block Policy Inheritance and also No Override.

9. You have created a container that holds all of the administrator user accounts. This container should not have any of the group policies applied to it from any of the parent containers. How do you accomplish this?

10. You are fairly new to using group policies and administrative templates. What features are available to help you understand what each setting in Administrative Templates will do?

CASE SCENARIOS

Scenario 7-1: Determining Group Policy Placement

You are the main administrator for Contoso Pharmaceuticals. The Active Directory structure is as shown in Figure 7-11. You are beginning to plan for Group Policy implementation and your boss has several key policies that you need to decide where to place. Using Figure 7-11, complete Table 7-2 documenting how you can accommodate the following goals.

- You need to have an e-mail application installed and configured on all desktops company wide.
- You need to implement account security for all accounts, but the West location password guidelines will be slightly different from the East location guidelines.
- All locations in the West OU should have several options in Internet Explorer modified.
- The Detroit departments should both have NetMeeting configured.

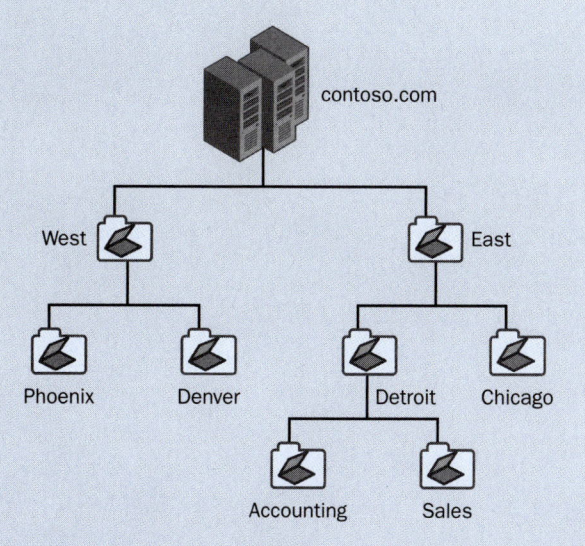

Figure 7-11 Contoso Pharmaceuticals Active Directory structure

Table 7-2 Scenario 1 Group Policy Plan

Location	Policy Goals and Special Settings

Scenario 7-2: Understanding Group Policy Planning

You are the administrator for Coho Winery, Inc., a large wine distribution company that has locations in the United States and Canada. In the last six months, Coho Winery, Inc., has purchased several smaller distribution companies. As you integrate them into your forest, you want to allow them to remain autonomous in their management of desktops and security. In the process of making their domains part of your corporate network, you have some policies that you want to become part of their environment, and others that you do not want to implement at this time. As you discuss this with your IT team, your manager asks you to explain which features in Windows Server 2003 allow you to provide the Group Policy flexibility needed by the new Active Directory structure. List several of the features in Windows Server 2003 Group Policy that will allow Coho Winery, Inc. to achieve their post-acquisition goals. Be prepared to discuss your answers in class.

CHAPTER 8
CONFIGURING THE USER AND COMPUTER ENVIRONMENT USING GROUP POLICY

Upon completion of this chapter, you will be able to:

- Understand and apply security settings to users and computers using Group Policy.
- Use Group Policy to create a request for a computer or user certificate.
- Implement the autoenrollment of certificates for smart cards.
- Understand and explain the benefits of folder redirection and offline files.
- Implement folder redirection and offline files.
- Understand and implement **disk quotas** using Group Policy.
- Understand the policy refresh process.
- Use Gpupdate to force the refresh of a policy.

Chapter 7, "Introduction to Group Policy," focused on familiarizing you with Group Policy concepts, terminology, features, and benefits. In this chapter, you will take a closer look at account security policies, folder redirection, offline file abilities, and disk quotas that can be implemented using Group Policy. It will be important for you to know the difference between user and computer settings. In addition to learning about these settings and categorizing them based on where they are applied, you also look at the default policy refresh process. Specifically, the chapter discusses how the policy refresh process works, and how to invoke a manual refresh of group policies when necessary.

SECURITY POLICIES

Centralized management of security settings for both users and computers can be accomplished using Group Policy. Most of the settings that pertain to security are found in the Windows Settings folder within the Computer Configuration node of a Group Policy Object (GPO). Security settings can be used to govern how users are authenticated to the network, what resources they are permitted to use, group membership policies, and events related to user and group actions that are recorded in the event logs. Table 8-1 briefly describes the security settings that can be configured within the Computer Configuration node.

Table 8-1 **Computer Configuration Node Security Settings**

Setting	Description
Account Policies	Includes settings for Password Policy and Account Lockout Policy. A domain-wide policy such as the Default Domain Policy GPO includes Kerberos Policy settings.
Local Policies	Contains three subcategories that pertain to the local computer policies. These subcategories include Audit Policy, User Rights Assignment, and Security Options.
Event Log Policy	These settings pertain to Event Viewer logs, their maximum size, retention settings, and accessibility.
Restricted Groups Policy	This setting allows administrators to have control over the Members property and Members Of property within a security group.
System Services Policy	These settings can be used to define the startup mode and access permissions for all system services. Each service can be configured as disabled, start automatically, or start manually. In addition, the access permissions can be set to Start, Stop, or Pause.
Registry and File System Policies	These settings can be used to set access permissions and audit settings for specific registry keys or file system objects.
Wireless Network (IEEE 802.11) Policies	Allows definition of a policy for an IEEE 802.11 wireless network. Settings include preferred networks and authentication types, in addition to several other security-related options.
Public Key Policies	This node includes options to create an Encrypted File System (EFS), automatic certificate request, trusted root certificates, and an enterprise trust list.
Software Restriction Policies	This policy can be used to specify software that you wish to run on computers. It can be used to disallow applications to run that might pose a security risk to the computer or organization.
IPSec Policy on Active Directory	Includes policy settings that allow an administrator to define mandatory rules applicable to computers on an IP-based network.

In Chapter 7, you also learned that policy settings created within the Computer Configuration node apply to a computer, regardless of who is logging on. More security settings can be applied to a specific computer than can be applied to a specific user. Table 8-2 describes the security settings that can be applied within the User Configuration node of Group Policy.

Table 8-2 **User Configuration Node Security Settings**

Setting	Description
Public Key Policies	Includes the Enterprise Trust policy that allows an administrator to list the trusted sources for certificates. In addition, autoenrollment settings can be specified for the user within this node.
Software Restriction Policies	This policy can be used to specify software that you wish to run for the user. Specifically, it can be used to disallow applications that might pose a security risk if run.

The next several sections discuss many of these settings in detail. In addition, examples will be presented to help you understand when and how to implement these policy settings.

Account Policies

Account policies influence how a user interacts with a computer or a domain. They are specified within the Computer Configuration node of Group Policy. The Account Policy for a domain account is specified in the Default Domain Policy GPO. This Account Policy is applied to all accounts throughout the domain. Within the Account Policies category of the security settings, there are three subcategories, which include Password Policies, Account Lockout Policies, and Kerberos Policies.

Password Policy

Figure 8-1 shows the expanded Password Policy category within the security settings of the Default Domain Policy GPO for cohowinery.com. Note that the figure shows default settings for this policy. Settings in this category focus on enforcing password lengths, password history, and so on. Password policies can be used for domain and local user accounts.

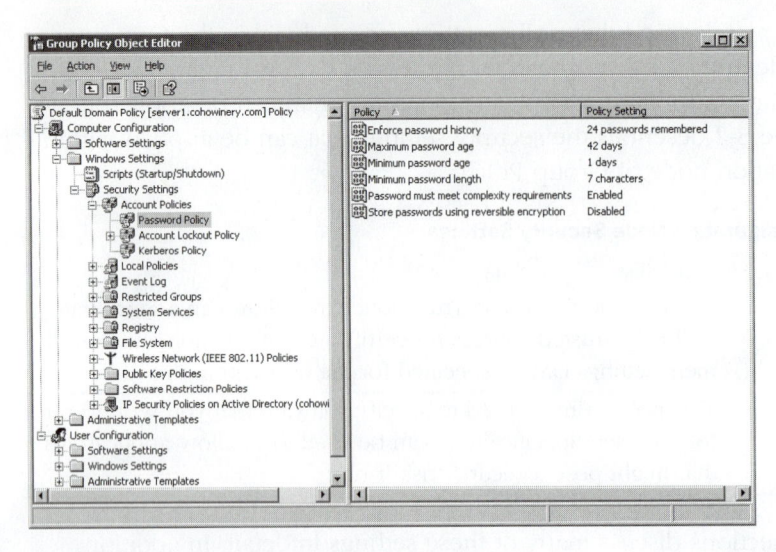

Figure 8-1 Computer Configurations/Windows Settings/Security Settings/Account Policies/Password Policy GPO Extension

▶ **Configuring a Password Policy**

To define a password policy, complete the following steps:

1. In Active Directory Users And Computers (MMC snap-in), right-click your domain name in the left window pane, and select Properties.

2. On the Group Policy tab of the domain's Properties dialog box, select the Default Domain Policy and click Edit. This opens a Group Policy Object Editor window for this policy.

3. In the left window pane, expand the Computer Configuration node and expand the Windows Settings folder. Then, expand the Security Settings node. In the Security Settings node, expand Account Policies, and select Password Policy. This displays the available settings for this category of the GPO.

4. All settings reflect the implemented defaults when the domain was created. To modify a setting, double-click the setting in the right window pane to open the Properties dialog box for the setting. Then make the desired value changes.

5. Click OK to close the setting's Properties dialog box.

6. Close the Group Policy Object Editor window for this policy.

7. Click OK to close the Properties dialog box for the domain object in Active Directory Users And Computers (MMC snap-in).

Account Lockout Policy

Figure 8-2 illustrates the expanded Account Lockout Policy category within the security settings of the Default Domain Policy GPO for cohowinery.com. Account Lockout Policies can be used for both domain and local user accounts. An Account Lockout Policy specifies the number of unsuccessful logon attempts that, if made within a contiguous time frame, may constitute a potential security threat from an intruder. An Account Lockout Policy can be set to lock the account in question after a specified number of invalid attempts. Additionally, the policy specifies the duration that the account remains locked.

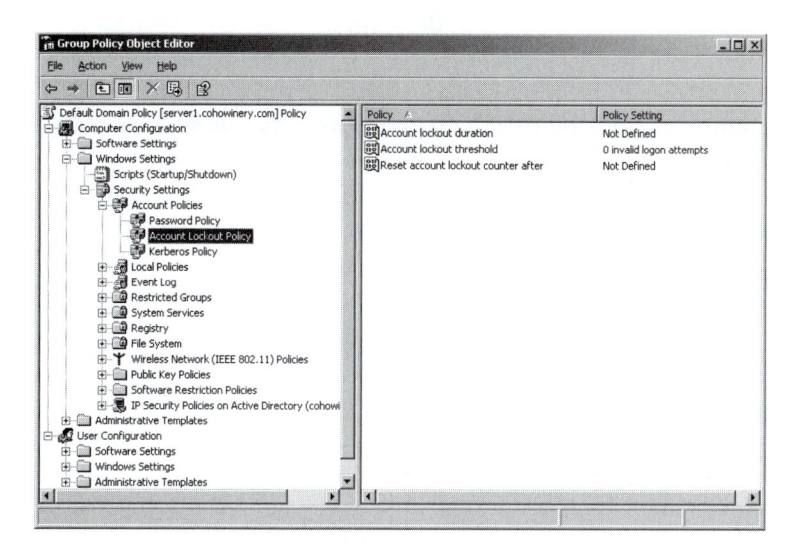

Figure 8-2 Computer Configurations/Windows Settings/Security Settings/Account Policies/ Account Lockout Policy GPO Extension

▶ **Configuring an Account Lockout Policy**

To define this setting in the Default Domain Policy GPO, complete the following steps:

1. In Active Directory Users And Computers (MMC snap-in), right-click your domain name in the left window pane, and select Properties.

2. On the Group Policy tab of the domain's Properties dialog box, select the Default Domain Policy, and click Edit. This opens a Group Policy Object Editor window for this policy.

3. In the left window pane, expand the Windows Settings folder, and then expand the Security Settings node. In the Security Settings node, expand Account Policies, and select Account Lockout Policy. This displays the available settings for this category of the GPO.

4. In the right window pane, double-click the Account Lockout Duration policy setting to view the Properties dialog box.

5. Select the Define This Policy Setting check box. Note the default setting of 30 minutes for Account Lockout Duration. If you want to change the account lockout duration, you may do so here.

6. Click OK to accept the specified lockout duration. You are presented with the Suggested Value Changes dialog box that indicates other related settings and their defaults. Click OK to automatically enable these other settings. Click Cancel to go back to the Account Lockout Duration Properties dialog box.

7. Click OK to accept the additional setting defaults.

8. Make any additional changes as necessary to the other individual Account Lockout Policy settings.

9. Close the Group Policy Object Editor window for this policy.

10. Click OK to close the Properties dialog box for the domain object in Active Directory Users And Computers (MMC snap-in).

Kerberos Policy

For domain user accounts only, Kerberos Policy allows you to configure several settings that govern authentication functionality. Figure 8-3 shows the settings available within this security setting on a domain GPO. Kerberos is the default mechanism for authenticating domain users in Microsoft Windows Server 2003 and Microsoft Windows 2000. Kerberos is a ticket-based system that allows domain access by using a Key Distribution Center (KDC) to issue session tickets to users. These tickets have a finite lifetime and are based in part on system time clocks. In Chapter 4, "Global Catalog and Flexible Single Master Operations (FSMO) Roles," we discussed the importance of time synchronization in Active Directory and client clock synchronization. It was also noted that Kerberos has a five-minute clock skew tolerance between the client and the domain controller. If the clocks are off by more than five minutes, the client will not be able to log on. Although you can modify the Maximum Tolerance value for Computer Clock Synchronization setting beyond the five-minute default, the setting is not persistent. If the computer restarts after configuring this setting, it reverts to the default setting of five minutes. Another main setting, Enforce User Logon Restrictions, is enabled by default. This setting tells Windows Server 2003 to validate each request for a session ticket against the rights associated with the user account. Although this process can slow down the response time for user access to resources, it is an important security feature that should not be overlooked.

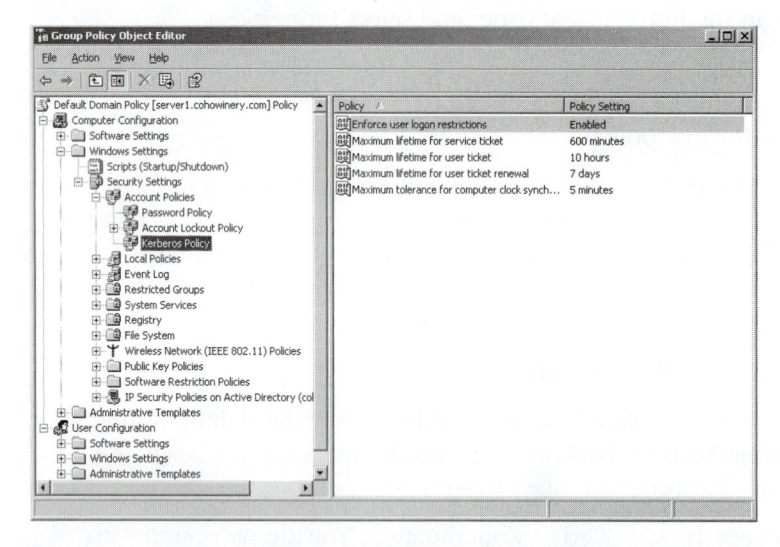

Figure 8-3 Computer Configurations/Windows Settings/Security Settings/Account Policies/Kerberos Policy GPO Extension

▶ **Configuring the Kerberos Policy**

To modify the default settings for the Kerberos Policy, complete the following steps:

1. In Active Directory Users And Computers (MMC snap-in), right-click your domain name in the left window pane and select Properties.

2. On the Group Policy tab of the domain's Properties dialog box, select the Default Domain Policy and click Edit. This opens a Group Policy Object Editor window for this policy.

3. In the left window pane, expand the Windows Settings folder, and then expand the Security Settings node. In the Security Settings node, expand Account Policies, and select the Kerberos Policy. This displays the available settings for this category of the GPO.

4. All settings reflect the defaults that were implemented when the domain was created. To modify a setting, double-click the setting in the right window pane to open the Properties dialog box for the setting. Make the desired value changes.

5. Click OK to close the setting's Properties dialog box.

6. Close the Group Policy Object Editor window for this policy.

7. Click OK to close the Properties dialog box for the domain object in Active Directory Users And Computers (MMC snap-in).

MORE INFO **Additional Account Policy Information** *The Windows Server 2003 product documentation provides additional details on account policies, their uses, and best practices. Information specific to Account Policy security settings is located at http://www.microsoft.com/technet/treeview /default.asp?url=/technet/prodtechnol/windowsserver2003/proddocs/entserver /AccountPoliciestopnode.asp.*

Local Policies

Local policies allow administrators to set user privileges, on the local computer, that govern what users can do on the computer, and if these actions are tracked within an event log. Tracking events, also referred to as *auditing*, is an important part of monitoring and managing network activity. This policy setting area has three subcategories that include Audit Policy, User Rights Assignment, and Security Options. As discussed in each of the next sections, keep in mind that local policies are local to a computer. When they are part of a GPO in Active Directory, they affect the local security settings of computer accounts to which the GPO is applied.

Audit Policy

The **Audit Policy** allows administrators to log successful and failed security events such as logon, account access, and object access. Figure 8-4 illustrates the policy settings available for auditing. Auditing can be used to track user activities and system activities. Planning to audit requires that you determine the computers for which you want to audit events, in conjunction with the types of events you wish to track. When you specify an event to audit, such as account logon events, you determine whether you wish to audit successful logon attempts, failed logon attempts, or both successful and failed attempts. Tracking successful events allows you to find out how often resources are accessed. This information can be valuable in helping you plan your resource usage and budget for new resources when necessary. Tracking failed events can help you determine when there are security breaches that you should resolve. For example, if you notice frequent failed logon attempts using a specific user account, you may want to investigate further.

> **CAUTION** **Auditing Event Failures** Although auditing failed events can help you to know when your network is potentially being hacked, your logging of failed events may also increase the potential for an intruder to launch a successful **Denial-of-service attack (DoS)** on your network. For example, if you have the Audit: Shut Down System Immediately If Unable To Log Security Audits policy setting enabled, and an intruder starts a DoS attack that fills up the log with failed events, you will experience a system shutdown. In this case, the only remedy is for an administrator to reset the CrashOnAuditFail value in the registry to continue normal operation. To modify this registry setting, see Microsoft Knowledge Base Article 140058, "How To Prevent Auditable Activities When Security Log Is Full."

When an audited event occurs, Windows Server 2003 writes an event to the security log on the domain controller or computer where the event took place. If it is a logon attempt or other Active Directory–related event, the event is written to the domain controller. If it is a computer event, such as access of a floppy drive, the event is written to the local computer's event log. Security logs are viewed using Event Viewer.

Figure 8-4 is based on the Default Domain Policy GPO. Note that none of the settings are defined by default. In contrast, Figure 8-5 illustrates the Default Domain Controllers GPO. In the Default Domain Controllers GPO, all options are set to be audited based on successful events, with the exception of Audit Object Access, Audit Privilege Use, and Audit Process Tracking. These three settings are intentionally disabled by default. The latter two are used rarely, while the Audit Object Access setting needs to be modified if you want to audit file or folder access for a file or folder that is stored on a domain controller. Simply creating this policy in the domain controller's local computer policy allows it to be overwritten by the Default Domain Controllers GPO that is processed after the local GPO settings. This example of a local policy being overwritten by a Group Policy reiterates the Group Policy processing concepts that were discussed in Chapter 7, "Introduction to Group Policy."

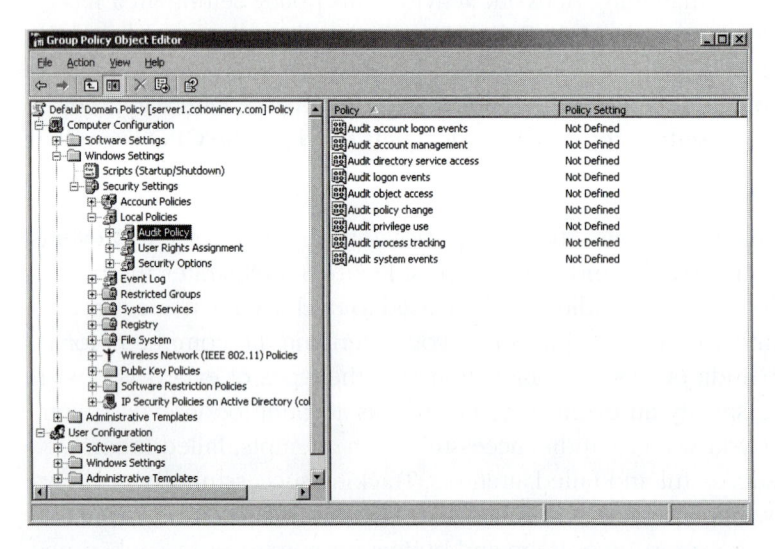

Figure 8-4 Computer Configurations/Windows Settings/Security Settings/Local Policy/Audit Policy GPO extension on the Default Domain Policy GPO

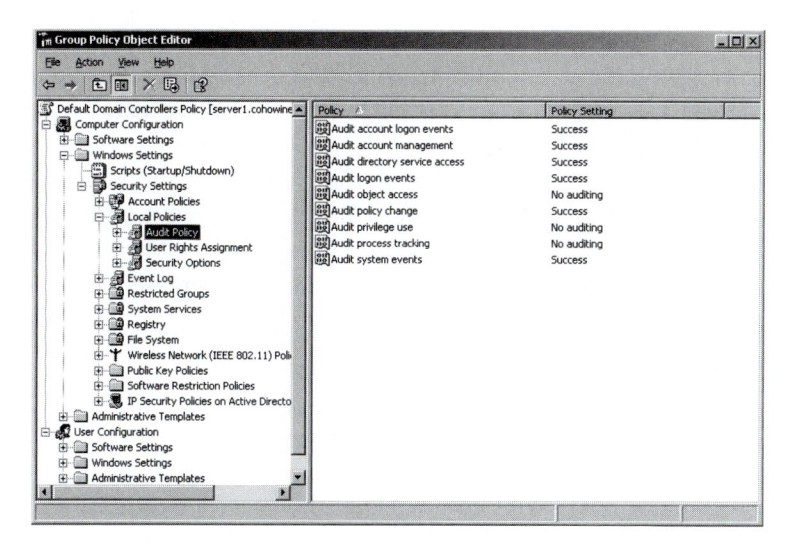

CHAPTER 8: CONFIGURING THE USER AND COMPUTER ENVIRONMENT USING GROUP POLICY

Figure 8-5 Computer Configurations/Windows Settings/Security Settings/Local Policy/ Audit Policy GPO extension on the Default Domain Controllers GPO

▶ **Using Audit Policy settings to specify events**

To specify events to be audited using the Audit Policy settings, complete the following steps:

1. In Active Directory Users And Computers (MMC snap-in), right-click your domain name in the left window pane and select Properties.

2. On the Group Policy tab of the domain's Properties dialog box, select the Default Domain Policy, and click Edit. This opens a Group Policy Object Editor window for this policy.

3. In the left window pane, expand the Windows Settings folder, and then expand the Security Settings node. In the Security Settings node, expand Local Policies, and select Audit Policy. This displays the available settings for this category of the GPO.

4. In the right window pane, double-click the Audit Policy setting you want to modify. This opens the Properties dialog box for the chosen setting. Select the Define This Policy Setting check box.

5. Select the appropriate check boxes to audit Success, Failure, or both under Audit These Attempts.

6. Click OK to close the setting's Properties dialog box.

7. Close the Group Policy Object Editor window for this policy.

8. Click OK to close the Properties dialog box for the domain object in Active Directory Users And Computers (MMC snap-in).

Planning an Audit Policy Auditing is turned off by default and, as a result, you need to decide which computers, resources, and events you want to audit. The following guidelines will help you plan your Audit Policy.

- **Audit only pertinent items.** Determine the events you want to audit and consider whether it is more important to track successes or failures of these events. You should only plan to audit events that will aid gathering network information. When auditing object access, be specific about the type of access you want to track. For example, if you want to audit read access to a file or folder, only audit the read events, not Full Control. Auditing of Full Control would trigger writes to the log for every action on the file or folder. Auditing does take system resources in order to process and store events. Therefore, auditing unnecessary events will create overhead on your server and make it more difficult to monitor for administrators.

- **Archive security logs to provide a documented history.** Keeping a history of event occurrences can provide you with supporting documentation. Such documentation can be used to support the need for additional resources based on the usage of a particular resource. In addition, it also provides a history of events that may indicate past security breach attempts. If intruders have administrative privileges, they can clear the log, leaving you without a history of events that document the breach.

- **System events category.** Events that trigger a log entry in this category include system startups and shutdowns, changes of system time, exhaustion of system event resources, such as when an event log is filled and can no longer append entries, the clearing of the security log, or any event that affects system security or the security log. In the Default Domain Controllers GPO, this setting is set to log successes by default.

- **Policy change category.** By default, this policy is set to audit successes in the Default Domain Controllers GPO. Policy change audit log entries are triggered by events such as user rights assignment changes, establishment or removal of trust relationships, IPSec policy agent changes, and grants or removals of system access privileges.

- **Account management category.** This policy setting is set to audit successes in the Default Domain Controllers GPO. This setting triggers an event that is written based on changes to account properties and group properties. Log entries written due to this policy setting reflect events that occur related to user or group account creation, deletion, renaming, and the enabling or disabling of an account.

- **Logon event category.** This setting logs events related to successful user logons on a computer. The event is logged to the Event Viewer Security Log on the computer that processes the request. The default setting is to log successes in the Default Domain Controllers GPO.

- **Account logon event category.** This setting logs events related to successful user logons to a domain. The event is logged to the domain controller that processes the request. The default setting is to log successes in the Default Domain Controllers GPO.

- **Configure the size of your security logs carefully.** You need to plan the size of your security logs based on the number of events that you anticipate logging. Event Log Policy settings can be configured under the Computer Configuration\Windows Settings\Security Settings\Event Log node of a GPO.

Once you have established a plan for auditing significant events on your network, you will need to begin its implementation. The next section discusses several key tasks of which you will need to be aware in order to implement your plan.

Implementing Your Audit Policy Plan Implementation of your plan requires awareness of several factors that can affect the success of your audit policy plan. You must be aware of the administrative requirements in order to create and administer a policy plan. There are two main requirements necessary to set up and administer an audit policy. First, you must have the Manage Auditing And Security Log user right for the computer on which you want to configure a policy or review a log. This right is granted by default to the Administrators group. However, if you wish to delegate this task to a subadministrator, such as a container administrator, he or she must possess the specific right. Second, any files or folders to be audited must be located on NTFS volumes. This is a requirement that carries over from prior Windows operating system versions, such as Windows 2000.

Actual implementation of your plan requires that you specify the categories to be audited and, if necessary, configure objects for auditing. Configuring objects for auditing is necessary when you have configured either of the two following event categories:

- **Audit Directory Service Access** This event logs user access to Active Directory objects such as other user objects or organizational units (OUs).

- **Audit Object Access** This event logs user access to files, folders, registry keys, and printers.

Each of these event categories requires additional set up that is outlined next.

▶ **To configure an Active Directory object for auditing:**

1. In Active Directory Users And Computers (MMC snap-in), using the View menu, make sure the view is set to Advanced Features.

2. Navigate to the object that you wish to audit. Right-click the object and select Properties.

3. On the Security tab, click Advanced.

4. In the Advanced Security Settings dialog box for the object, on the Auditing tab, click Add.

5. Select the users or groups for whom you want to audit Active Directory object access, and click OK.

6. In the Auditing Entry dialog box for the object, select the events you want to audit on this object. There are two tabs in this dialog box, one for object access and one for property access. Select the Successful check box, the Failed check box, or both, depending on what you want to track.

7. In the Apply Onto list, specify where objects are audited. This box is set to This Object And All Child Objects by default.

8. Click OK to return to the Advanced Security Settings dialog box for the object.

9. Choose whether you wish auditing entries from parent objects to be inherited to this object, by either selecting or clearing the Allow Inheritable

Auditing Entries From Parent To Propagate To This Object check box. If the check boxes in the Access box are shaded in the Auditing Entry dialog box for the object, or if Remove is unavailable in the Advanced Security Settings dialog box for the object, auditing has been inherited from the parent object.

10. Click OK to complete this process.

▶ **To configure files or folders for auditing:**

1. In Windows Explorer, right-click the file or folder you want to audit, and select Properties.

2. On the Security tab in the Properties dialog box for the selected file or folder, click Advanced.

3. In the Advanced Security Settings dialog box for the file or folder, select the Auditing tab, and click Add. Select the users and groups for whom you want to audit file or folder access and then click OK.

4. In the Auditing Entry dialog box for the file or folder, select Successful, Failed, or both check boxes for the events you wish to audit.

5. In the Apply Onto list, specify where objects are audited. This box is set to This Folder, Subfolder And Files by default. This means that changes you make are inherited to lower levels in the file system directory.

6. Click OK to return to the Advanced Security Settings dialog box for the object.

7. Choose whether you wish auditing entries from parent objects to be inherited to this object, by either selecting or deselecting the Allow Inheritable Auditing Entries From Parent To Propagate To This Object And All Child Objects check box. If the check boxes in the Access box are shaded in the Auditing Entry dialog box for the object, or if Remove is unavailable in the Advanced Security Settings dialog box for the object, auditing has been inherited from the parent object.

8. Click OK to complete this process.

User Rights Assignment

As shown in Figure 8-6, the user rights assignment settings are extensive, and include settings for items that pertain to rights needed by users to perform system-related tasks. For example, logging on locally to a domain controller requires that a user either has the Log On Locally right assigned to his or her account, or be a member of the Account Operators, Administrators, Backup Operators, Print Operators, or Server Operators group on the domain controller. Other similar settings included in this collection are related to user rights associated with system shutdown, taking ownership privileges of files or objects, restoring files and directories, and synchronizing directory service data.

> **MORE INFO** *Details on User Rights Assignment* Information on each of the available settings in this policy area can be found in the Windows Server 2003 product documentation. User rights assignment specifics are found at http://www.microsoft.com/technet/treeview/default.asp?url=/technet/prodtechnol/windowsserver2003/proddocs/entserver/URAtopnode.asp.

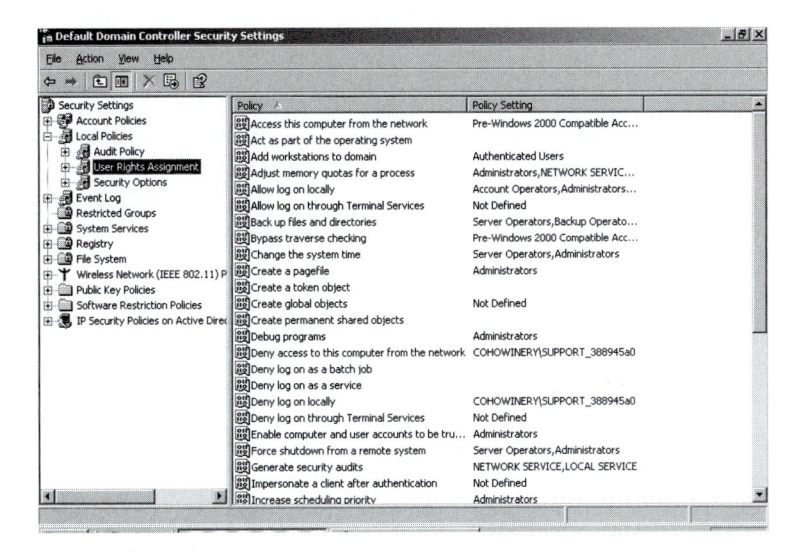

Figure 8-6 User Rights Assignment policy settings

Security Options

The security options category includes security settings related to interactive logons, digital signing of data, restrictions for access to floppy and CD-ROM drives, unsigned driver installation behavior, and logon dialog box behavior.

> **MORE INFO** **Details on Security Options** Information on each of the available settings in the Security Options policy area can be found in the Windows Server 2003 product documentation located at http://www.microsoft.com/technet /treeview/default.asp?url=/technet/prodtechnol/windowsserver2003/proddocs /entserver/50topnode.asp.

Event Log Policy

The Event Log Policy settings area allows administrators to configure settings that control the maximum log size, retention of logs, and access rights for each log. Depending on the services you install, the number of logs you have can vary on Windows Server 2003. For example, if your server is configured as a domain controller, you will have a Directory Service log that contains Active Directory–related entries. In addition, if your server is configured as a Domain Name System (DNS) server, you will have a DNS log that contains entries specifically related to DNS. The Event Log Policy settings area covers only settings for the three primary log files, which include the Application, Security, and System logs. In addition to using Event Log Policy settings to modify the default log sizes, you can also manually configure the log sizes and actions to be taken when the log reaches its maximum size.

▶ **Altering Log File Settings**

To manually alter the log file settings, complete the following steps:

1. From the Administrative Tools menu, open Event Viewer.
2. Right-click the log for which you want to view or modify the settings, and select Properties.
3. Modify the desired settings and click OK.

To practice viewing the current event log sizes, do Exercise 8-1 now.

> **NOTE** **Manual Settings versus Group Policy Settings** When the maximum log file size has been increased manually and there is a Group Policy setting that is of a lower value, the log file size retains the manual log size until the log file is cleared and the computer is restarted. This behavior is by design, because anytime a log file is decreased in size, the decreased setting does not take effect until the log is cleared.

Restricted Groups Policy

The Restricted Groups Policy allows an administrator to specify group membership lists. Using this policy setting, you can control membership in important groups such as the local Administrators and Backup Operators groups. This policy setting allows you to configure both who is a member of the group and in which groups the specified group is nested. Consider that you wish to allow the default administrator account, in addition to Scott Seely and John Smith, as members of the built-in Administrators group. As shown in Figure 8-7, you would add these users to the Members Of section of this group list for the restricted Administrators group. If another user is added to the Administrators group using Active Directory Users And Computers (MMC snap-in), for malicious or other reasons, the manually added users are removed when the Group Policy is reapplied during the refresh cycle. The refresh process will be discussed later in this chapter. Only those users who are part of the restricted group membership list within the policy setting will be applied.

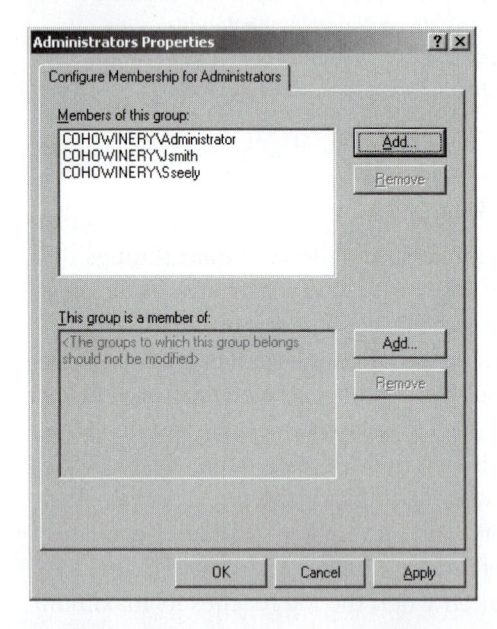

Figure 8-7 Restricted Groups membership lists

In addition, the Restricted Groups setting can be used to populate a local group's membership list with a domain group such as Domain Administrators. This allows administrative privileges to be transferred to the local workstations, making management and access to resources easier.

System Services Policy

The System Services Policy settings category is used to configure the startup and security settings for services running on a computer. Figure 8-8 shows this policy area within the Default Domain Controllers Policy GPO. The service startup options available include automatic, manual, and disabled. Each functions as follows:

- **Automatic** Starts a service automatically during system startup.
- **Manual** Starts a service only by user intervention.
- **Disabled** The service cannot start.

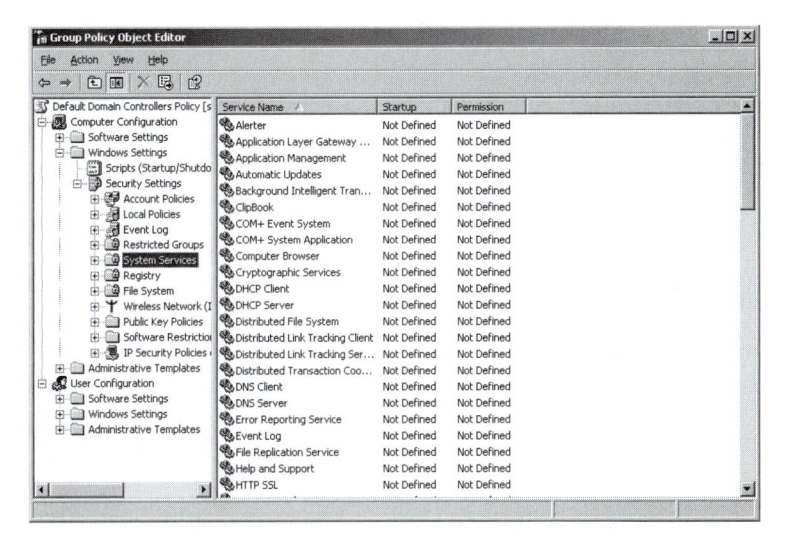

Figure 8-8 Computer Configurations/Windows Settings/Security Settings/System Services GPO extension on the Default Domain Controllers GPO

> **NOTE** *Policy Processing Performance* To optimize performance when using the policy category, set unused services to Manual. This speeds the processing of the policy settings, resulting in quicker configuration of the computer environment at startup and logon.

When using the Automatic setting, you should test the setting to make sure that the service starts automatically as expected. If certain services do not start as expected, users may not have the desired network functionality, and this may result in unnecessary downtime for users.

In addition to startup settings, the System Services Policy area also allows administrators to determine who has permissions on the service. For example, you may need to give certain users the ability to stop and restart a service that is malfunctioning, which includes start, stop, and pause permissions to the service. Permissions are defined by clicking Edit Security after defining the policy. Figure 8-9 shows the Security page for a System Services Policy setting.

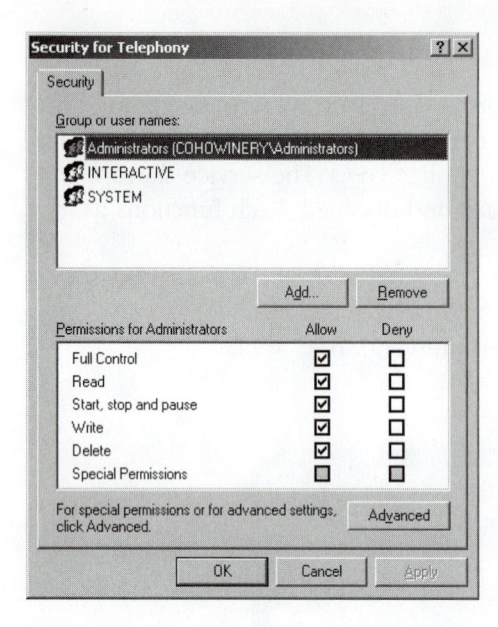

Figure 8-9 Permissions for a system service

Registry and File System Policies

These two registry and file system areas are discussed together because they are similar in function. The Registry security area is used to configure security on registry keys. The File System security area is used to configure security for file system objects. Both of these areas allow administrators to set user permissions that reflect certain registry keys or files, and the permissions users have to view and modify them. In addition, you can also set auditing on both of these items so that changes can be tracked for reference later.

Wireless Network (IEEE 802.11) Policies

Institute of Electrical and Electronics Engineers (IEEE) 802.11 wireless networking is supported in all versions of the Windows Server 2003 family. Wireless networking is becoming more prominent in the business community. Among the many benefits that can be seen by implementation of a wireless network is the reduction in the cost of physical wiring. Although there are costs associated with the initial installment of a wireless network, the long-term benefits can quickly outweigh the costs. Many companies are extending their networks by including wireless access points, instead of physical cable.

Windows Server 2003 includes the ability to create a wireless network policy to address the security aspects of implementing wireless clients on your network. The Wireless Network Policy Wizard is provided to enable administrators to specify appropriate settings for the corporate environment.

> **MORE INFO** *Wireless Network Policy Resources* Planning a wireless network is an important task that involves much research, planning, and testing. Microsoft has downloadable documentation in the Deploying Network Services book within the Windows Server 2003 Deployment Kit. This book can be downloaded at http://www.microsoft.com/downloads/details.aspx?familyid=D91065EE-E618-4810-A036-DE633F79872E&displaylang=en.

Public Key Policies

The settings available in the Public Key Policies area of Group Policy allow greater administrative control in establishing rules and governing the issuance, maintenance, and guidelines within a public key infrastructure (PKI). Group Policy is not required to create a PKI, but as is true with other Group Policy settings, the benefit lies in the ability to automate processes, provide consistency, and ease management across your network. Settings that are available in the Public Key Policies category are described in the following sections.

Encrypting File System

When users are allowed to encrypt files in an effort to secure them, there must be a mechanism in place in order to recover these files should the user lose the private key due to a computer failure, or a user with ownership of encrypted files no longer works for the organization. When computers are part of a domain, a recovery policy can be established to add users to the list of those who can recover encrypted files. By default, in a Windows Server 2003 domain, the Administrator account is issued a recovery certificate that can be used for all encrypted files. Therefore, the administrator can recover files when one of the previously mentioned situations occurs. An organization may wish to delegate recovery of files to a subadministrator or to the user who needs to access and use the encrypted files. In response, the encrypting file system (EFS) policy allows an administrator to modify the list of recovery agents by adding other accounts as recovery agents. This setting is only available in the Computer Configuration node.

Automatic Certificate Request

This setting allows computers to automatically submit a request for a certificate from an Enterprise Certification Authority (CA) and install that certificate. A CA serves as the digital world's passport to accessing computer resources that require verification of validity to use them. Without a CA to verify the validity of a user or computer, processing of a related request such as file or resource access is denied. In order for computers to participate in any type of cryptographic operations, they must have a certificate installed. This setting is only available in the Computer Configuration node.

Trusted Root Certification Authorities

Trusted root certification authorities determine whether or not users can choose to trust root CAs and the criteria that must be met by the CA to fulfill user requests. For example, when a user or computer presents a certificate, there must be a way to verify that the certificate comes from a valid entity. If your organization has its own Windows 2000 or Windows Server 2003 CAs in place, you do not need this policy setting. However, if you are using root CAs that are not running Windows 2000 or Windows Server 2003, you should implement this setting to distribute your organization's root certificates.

Enterprise Trust

Enterprise Trust allows an administrator to define and distribute a certificate trust list (CTL) for external root CAs. A CTL is a list of root CAs deemed reputable sources by the administrator. Many applications such as e-mail and Web browsers have certificates embedded in their applications in order to allow digitally signed communications over the Internet. In an organization that does not have internal CAs used for certificate services, you need to implement a CTL to establish a list of trusted external CAs based upon the needs of your organization.

Certificate Autoenrollment

Certificate Autoenrollment allows an administrator to enable or disable the automatic enrollment of computer and user certificates, in addition to renewing and requesting certificates based on certificate templates. This setting is particularly useful when dealing with smart cards. Consider a large organization that is planning to deploy smart cards to all users for authentication and ease of password management. You might recall that as password requirements become more complex, smart cards can ease user frustration. Users insert the smart card into a card reader, and when prompted, they enter a personal identification number (PIN) that allows the card parameters to be read and transferred to the network for authentication purposes. A PIN that has access to all pertinent logon parameters replaces the need for the complexity of strong passwords that are long and possibly difficult to remember. Although this may be a convenience for the user and a better method of ensuring network security integrity, smart cards can be very costly to implement and manage. Instead of manually having to set up each smart card with a certificate, autoenrollment can be used to write certificate information to the smart card. This can be done through the Group Policy settings defined for a domain.

The process for autoenrollment requires several infrastructure components. These components include the following:

- Clients must be running Microsoft Windows XP or Windows Server 2003. Autoenrollment settings that are configured within a GPO can be applied only to Windows XP and Windows Server 2003 clients.

- An Enterprise CA running on a Windows Server 2003 server.

- At least one version 2 certificate template is required for the Windows Server 2003 family, but autoenrollment manages certificate requests for other versions as well.

Figure 8-10 shows the Autoenrollment Settings Properties dialog box. This dialog box allows the administrator to determine whether to allow or disallow autoenrollment of certificates. If autoenrollment is enabled, the dialog box also allows administrative control over whether or not to allow certificate renewal, updates of pending certificates, removal of revoked certificates, and updates to certificates based on certificate template settings changes.

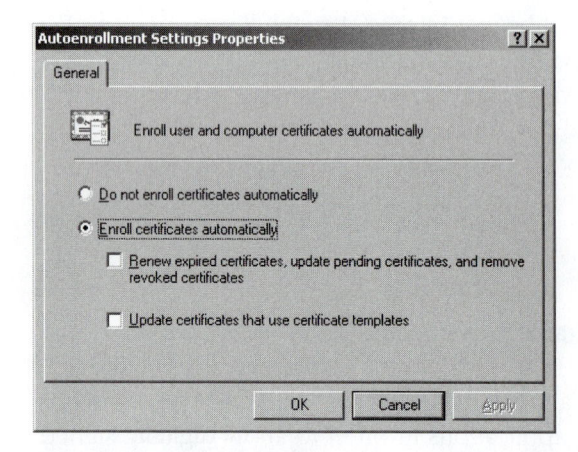

Figure 8-10 Computer Configurations/Windows Settings/Security Settings/Public Key Policies/Autoenrollment Settings

Although autoenrollment may be enabled, the policy setting cannot be applied without the supporting infrastructure components and user permissions. The high-level tasks that need to be completed in order to configure autoenrollment for smart card logon are as follows:

- Install and configure an Enterprise CA.
- Define an autoenrollment certificate template.
- Assign the appropriate user permissions to the certificate template.
- Add the autoenrollment certificate template to the Enterprise CA.
- Modify the Default Domain Policy GPO security settings to allow autoenrollment of certificates.

▶ **Configuring Certificate Autoenrollment**

The following steps detail the high-level tasks listed previously, and are based on the need to configure the Domain Users group for autoenrollment of certificates.

1. Install and configure an Enterprise CA from which the certificates are issued.

2. Define an autoenrollment certificate template. To do this, complete the following steps:

    a. Open an MMC window by typing **mmc** from the Start/Run command-line window. From the File menu, select Add/Remove Snap-In. Click Add, and select the Certificate Templates snap-in from the Add Stand-Alone Snap-In dialog box. Click Add, and then click Close.

    b. Click OK to open the MMC windows for the Certificate Templates snap-in.

    c. Expand the Certificate Templates node in the left window pane. You should now see all of the available templates in the right window pane. Your console should appear as shown in Figure 8-11.

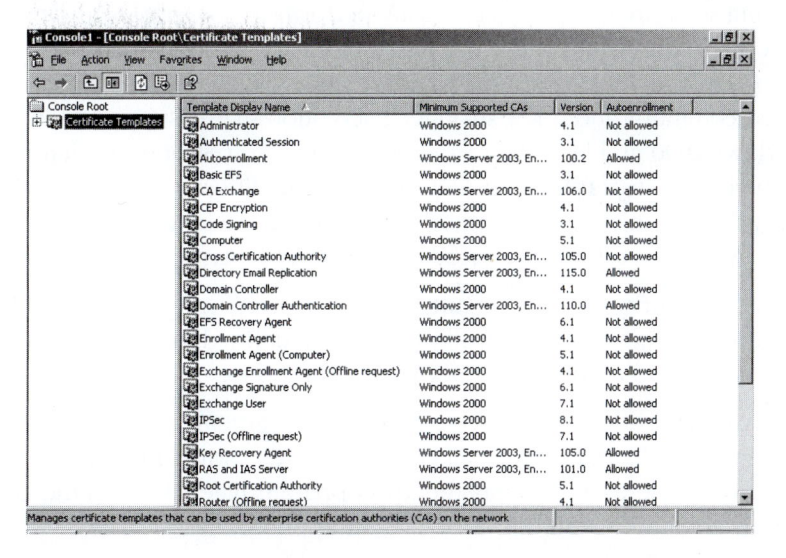

Figure 8-11 Certificate Template MMC window

d. In the right window pane, right-click the Smartcard Logon template and select Duplicate Template. In the Properties Of New Template window, type a name for your new certificate template.

e. Select the Publish Certificate In Active Directory check box. Also note the validity period and the renewal period in this dialog box. Make any necessary adjustments according to your plan for certificates. Click Apply to save your settings and proceed in your configuration.

3. On the Request Handling tab of the newly created autoenrollment certificate, choose Signature And Smartcard Logon from the Purpose drop-down list. Figure 8-12 shows the available settings on the Request Handling tab of the certificate.

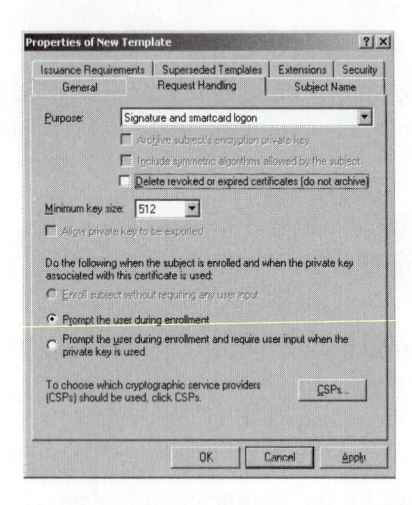

Figure 8-12 Autoenrollment certificate Request Handling tab

4. Click CSPs, and select the appropriate **cryptographic service provider (CSP)**. In some cases, the hardware manufacturer of your smart card may define a CSP that is compatible with your smart card. A CSP is an independent software module that actually performs cryptography algorithms for authentication, encoding, and encryption. You can generally select the Microsoft Base Cryptographic Provider (v1.0) for international, digitally signed communication. For stronger encryption that is supported in Windows 2000 and later, you can choose Microsoft Strong or Microsoft Enhanced Cryptographic Provider options. The difference between CSPs rests primarily in the type of algorithm used and the length of the encryption key. Once you have selected the desired CSP type, click OK.

5. Select the Security tab on your autoenrollment certificate template. This is where you assign the autoenroll permissions defined in this template to users. Click Add to locate the Domain Users group.

6. For the newly added Domain Users group, select the Apply check box for the Read, Enroll, and Autoenroll permissions, as shown in Figure 8-13. This gives these user accounts the appropriate privileges when the GPO settings associated with this template are applied.

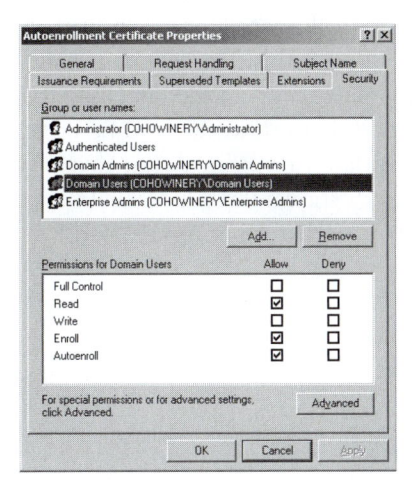

CHAPTER 8: CONFIGURING THE USER AND COMPUTER ENVIRONMENT USING GROUP POLICY   203

Figure 8-13 Security settings for Autoenrollment Certificate Properties

7. On your Enterprise CA, open the Certification Authority snap-in from either an MMC window or from the Administrative Tools folder. Figure 8-14 shows the Certification Authority snap-in.

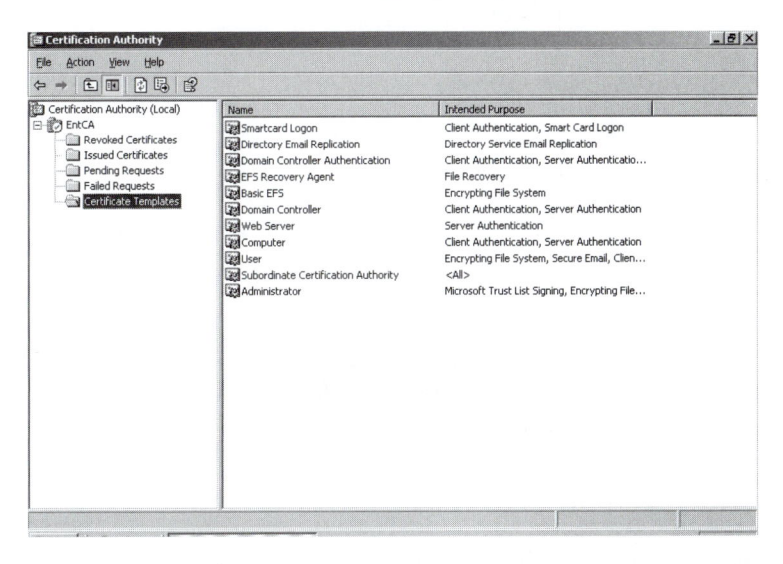

Figure 8-14 Certification Authority snap-in

8. Right-click Certificate Templates and select New, then click Certificate Template To Issue. Select the newly created autoenrollment certificate and click OK. You can close the Certification Authority snap-in.

9. In Active Directory Users And Computers (MMC snap-in), right-click on your domain name node, and select Properties.

10. On the Group Policy tab, select the Default Domain Policy and click Edit.

11. Open the User Configuration node, followed by the Windows Settings extension, the Security Settings extension, and the Public Key Policy extension.

12. In the right window pane, right-click Autoenrollment Settings, and select Properties. In the Autoenrollment Settings Properties dialog box, select Enroll Certificates Automatically. You also need to select the check boxes for Renew Expired Certificates, Update Pending Certificates, and Remove Revoked Certificates, in addition to the Update Certificates That Use Certificate Templates check box. Figure 8-15 shows the Autoenrollment Settings Properties dialog box with the appropriate options selected.

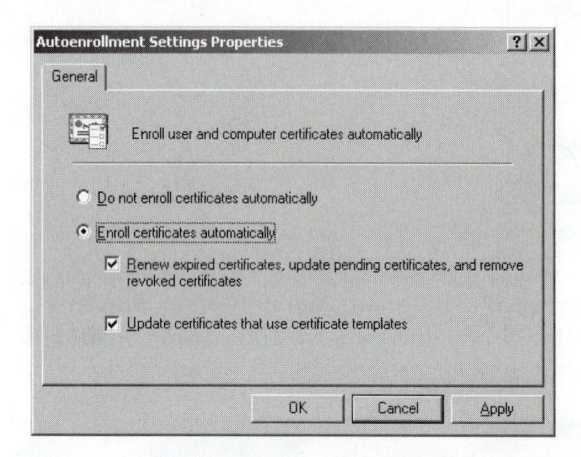

Figure 8-15 Autoenrollment Settings Properties dialog box

13. Close Group Policy Object Editor, Active Directory Users And Computers (MMC snap-in), and any other open snap-ins.

Although the steps demonstrated previously are based on autoenrollment settings for a user account, autoenrollment settings are available for both Computer Configuration and User Configuration nodes.

> **MORE INFO** *Cryptographic Service Providers (CSPs)* The Microsoft Developer Network (MSDN) Web site has plenty of additional information on PKI, smart cards, and CSPs. Information on CSPs currently supported in Microsoft operating systems can be found at http://msdn.microsoft.com/library/default.asp?url= /library/en-us/security/security/microsoft_cryptographic_service_providers.asp.

Software Restriction Policies

Access to software from multiple sources can be problematic in a network environment. The Internet opens up many opportunities for virus-infected applications to be installed. In addition, e-mail messages have become a delivery tool for malicious code and executables. These types of circumstances pose a significant threat to the integrity and security of your network. In Windows Server 2003 and Windows XP, a new feature, Software Restriction Policy, allows administrators to control the execution of applications and apply rules that govern which applications and files can be executed. Software Restriction Policy is discussed in further detail in Chapter 9, "Managing Software."

> **CAUTION** *Misinterpretation of Software Restriction Policy Use* Software restriction policy settings should never be used as a replacement for anti-virus software. All networks should have an aggressive plan in place to prevent possible security breaches. This includes the use of anti-virus software, firewalls, and frequent updates to the virus definition files. Software Restriction Policy adds an additional level to your plan, but should not be used to replace any portion of a disaster prevention plan.

FOLDER REDIRECTION

Folder redirection is a Group Policy folder that is located within the User Configuration node of a Group Policy linked to an Active Directory container object. Folder redirection provides administrators with the ability to redirect the contents of certain folders to a network location or to another location on the user's local computer. Folders on a local computer located in the Documents And Settings folder, including the My Documents folder, the My Pictures subfolder of My Documents, and the Application Data, Desktop, and Start Menu folders, can have their contents redirected. Depending on the folder being redirected, user data can be redirected to either a dynamically created folder, a specified folder that is created by the administrator, the user's home directory, or the local user profile location. Redirection of the data from a user's local computer to a network location provides the following benefits:

- Files can be backed up during the normal network server backup process. It is important to remember that typical users do not back up their own data. Folder redirection eliminates the problems that arise when a local computer has failed and a user has stored all documents on the local hard drive. When the data is redirected to a server hard drive, the data is backed up and therefore is not lost due to hardware failure.

- When users log on to the network from a workstation other than their own, they have access to their files since files are stored on a network server, as opposed to the local computer.

- Performance is enhanced when roaming user profiles are used. Only necessary information is transferred to the user's desktop. User data is not copied from the server during logon.

Redirecting a folder and files to a separate drive on the local computer can allow administrators to automatically redirect data files to a location separate from the operating system files. In this case, if the operating system needed to be reinstalled, the data files would not need to be deleted, nor would they be automatically overwritten by anything else.

Figure 8-16 shows the Folder Redirection Policy setting within the User Configuration node of a GPO.

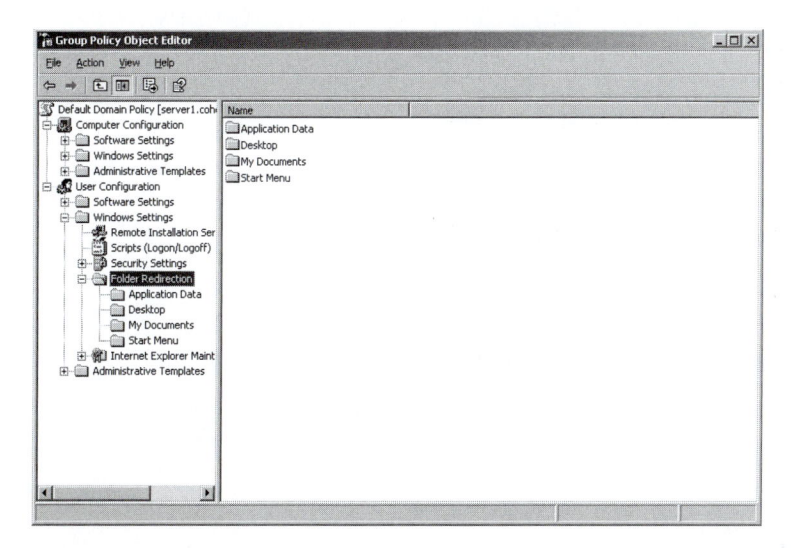

Figure 8-16 User Configuration/Windows Settings/Folder Redirection Group Policy extension

▶ **Configuring Folder Redirection**

Several tasks must be properly configured before you can achieve folder redirection functionality.

To configure folder redirection for the My Documents folder:

1. Create a GPO or modify an existing GPO with the necessary Folder Redirection Policy setting. Using Group Policy Object Editor for the desired GPO, locate the Folder Redirection policy extension in the User Configuration/Windows Settings/node.

2. Right-click the My Documents folder in the left window pane and select Properties.

3. As shown in Figure 8-17, using the Setting drop-down box of the Target tab, select one of the following options in the My Documents Properties dialog box:

   - **Basic – Redirect Everyone's Folder To The Same Location** Selecting this option requires that you create a shared folder to which all subfolders are appended. This will be discussed in further detail later in this section. If this setting is chosen, proceed to step 4 now.

   - **Advanced – Specify Locations For Various User Groups** Selecting this option allows you to redirect folders to specified locations based on security group membership. For example, if you wish to redirect the Application Data folder for users in the accounting group to one location and the Application Data folder for users in the engineering group to another location, this setting allows you to do so. If you select this setting, you can proceed to step 5 now.

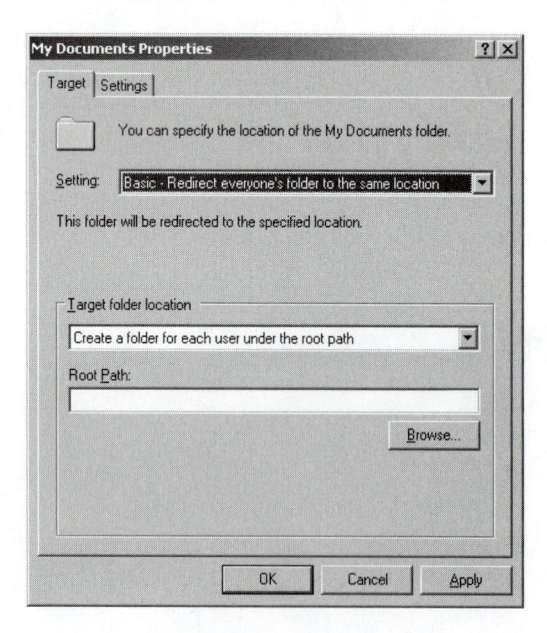

Figure 8-17 My Documents Properties dialog box

4. If you chose Basic – Redirect Everyone's Folder To The Same Location, you must specify the Target folder location in the Settings dialog box. Choose from the following options:

- **Create A Folder For Each User Under The Root Path**   This option is the default. When a user's folders are redirected using this setting, a subfolder is created automatically using the username based on the %username% variable and the folder name of the redirected folder. Allowing the system to create the subfolder structure automatically ensures that the appropriate user permissions are implemented. However, in order for the subfolder structure creation to work, each user must have appropriate permissions on the shared folder to create a folder. For the root path, it is recommended to use a Universal Naming Convention (UNC) name, rather than a drive letter–referenced path that may change.

- **Redirect To The Following Location**   This option allows you to specify the path to which you want the My Documents folder redirected. This option can be used to redirect the folder to a server share or to another valid local path. When specifying a path, it is recommended to use a UNC name, rather than a drive letter–referenced path that may change.

- **Redirect To The User's Home Directory**   This option redirects the My Documents folder to a preconfigured home directory for the user. This setting is not recommended unless you have already deployed home directories in your organization and wish to maintain them. Security is not checked automatically using this option and the assumption is made that the administrator has placed appropriate permissions on the folders. Administrators have full control over the users' My Documents folder when they are redirected to the user's home directory, even if the Grant The User Exclusive Rights To My Documents check box is selected.

- **Redirect To The Local User Profile Location**   This option allows you to return redirected folders to their original default locations. This setting copies the contents of the redirected folder back to the user profile location. The redirected folder contents are not deleted. However, the user continues to have access to the content of the redirected folder, but from the local computer, instead of the redirected location.

5. If you chose Advanced – Specify Locations For Various User Groups in step 3, you must specify the target folder location for each group that you add in the Settings dialog box. The choices are the same as those outlined in step 4; however, you need to associate each group selected with a specific target location. Click Add to select the groups and choose the target folder location for redirected files.

6. The Settings tab for the My Documents Properties dialog box provides several additional selections. You should ensure that the check boxes for Grant The User Exclusive Rights To My Documents and Move The Contents Of My Documents To The New Location are both checked.

7. Select from the following options in the Policy Removal box of the Settings tab:

    ❑ **Leave The Folder In The New Location When Policy Is Removed** This option keeps the redirected folder in its redirected location, without doing anything to the data. If the policy is removed, the user continues to have access to the contents at the redirected folder.

    ❑ **Redirect The Folder Back To The User Profile Location When Policy Is Removed** With this option enabled, the folder and its contents are copied back to their user profile location. The user can continue to access the contents on the local computer. With this option disabled, the folder returns to its user profile location, but the contents are not copied or moved back with the redirection process. The user can no longer see or access the files.

    NOTE *Policy Removal* If the policy is changed to Not Configured, it will have no bearing on the redirection of user data. Data continues to be redirected until the policy removal setting is changed to redirect the folder to the user profile location. This is an example of tattooing with Group Policy. The term "tattooing" means that the setting continues to apply until it is reversed using a policy that overwrites the setting.

8. Since My Pictures is a subfolder of My Documents, you will need to decide if you want to redirect My Pictures as a subfolder of My Documents, or set My Pictures to not be administratively defined by the policy. Select the bullet that indicates your preference from the My Pictures Preferences area of the Settings tab.

9. Upon completion of all pertinent settings listed here, click OK. Close the Group Policy Object Editor window.

    CAUTION *Redirecting the Start Menu Folder* Although the Start Menu folder is an option in the Folder Redirection policy extension, the contents of each user's Start Menu folder on Windows XP computers is not copied to the redirected location. To configure Start Menu options, it is recommended to use alternate Group Policy settings to control the Start Menu content. This can be accomplished by using the Administrative Templates\Start Menu and Taskbar extension.

    MORE INFO *Additional Folder Redirection Recommendations* More information on recommendations for folder redirection, including integration with EFS, can be found at http://www.microsoft.com/technet/treeview/default.asp?url=/technet/prodtechnol/windowsserver2003/proddocs/deployguide/dmebc_dsm_hyio.asp.

OFFLINE FILES

Offline Files is a separate policy that can be used to allow files to be available to users, even when they are disconnected from the network. The Offline Files feature works well with Folder Redirection. When Offline Files is enabled, users can access necessary files as if they were connected to the network. When the network connection is restored, changes made to any documents are updated to the server. Folders can be configured so that either all files within the folder are available for offline use or just selected files. When combined with Folder Redirection, users have the benefits of being able to redirect files to a network location, and still have access to the files when the network connection is not present.

Offline Files is configured on the Sharing tab of a folder. As shown in Figure 8-18, on a Windows XP or Windows 2000 Professional workstation, shared folders can be set for Manual Caching Of Documents, Automatic Caching Of Documents, or Automatic Caching Of Programs And Documents. In contrast, as shown in Figure 8-19, on a Windows Server 2003 family computer, the following options are available:

- **Only The Files That Users Specify Will Be Available Offline** This option is equivalent to the previously mentioned Manual Caching feature. As the default selection, it provides offline caching of only those files that have been selected. Users can choose the files they wish to have available when they are disconnected from the network.

- **All Files And Programs That Users Open From The Share Will Be Automatically Available Offline** This option replaces the previously mentioned Automatic Caching Of Programs And Documents and the Automatic Caching Of Documents options. All files that have been previously opened in the shared folder are available for offline use.

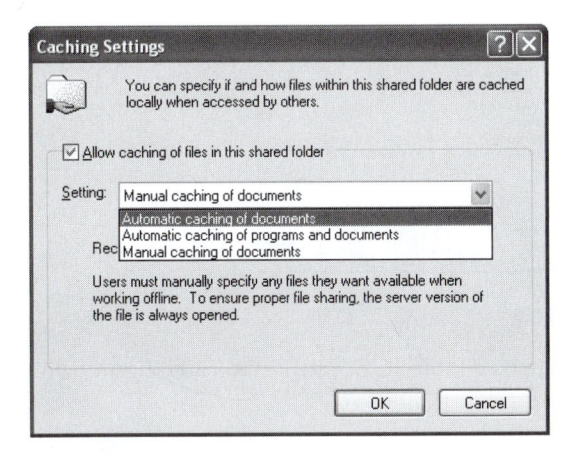

Figure 8-18 Caching Settings on a Windows XP or Windows 2000 Professional workstation

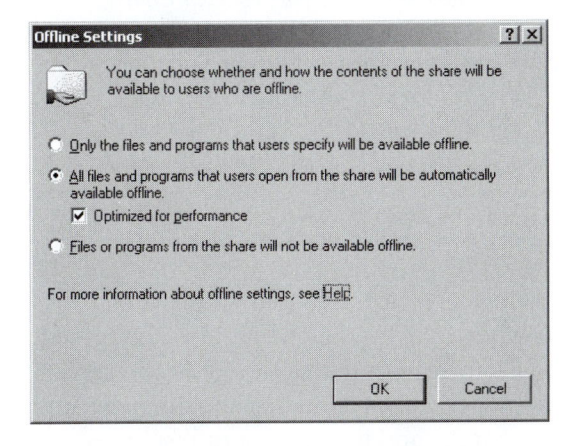

Figure 8-19 Offline Settings on a Windows Server 2003 computer

- **Files Or Programs From The Share Will Not Be Available Offline** This option stops any files in a shared folder from being available offline. This setting is particularly useful in preventing users from storing files for offline use.

Group Policy allows administrators to define the behavior of offline files for users in an Active Directory domain. For example, in Windows XP and Windows Server 2003, all redirected folders are cached automatically by default. This default behavior can be changed by enabling the Do Not Automatically Make Redirected Folders Available Offline policy setting in the User Configuration\Administrative Templates\Network\Offline Files extension. When this policy setting is enabled, users must manually choose which files to cache for offline use. Figure 8-20 shows the available User Configuration node Group Policy settings for Offline Files.

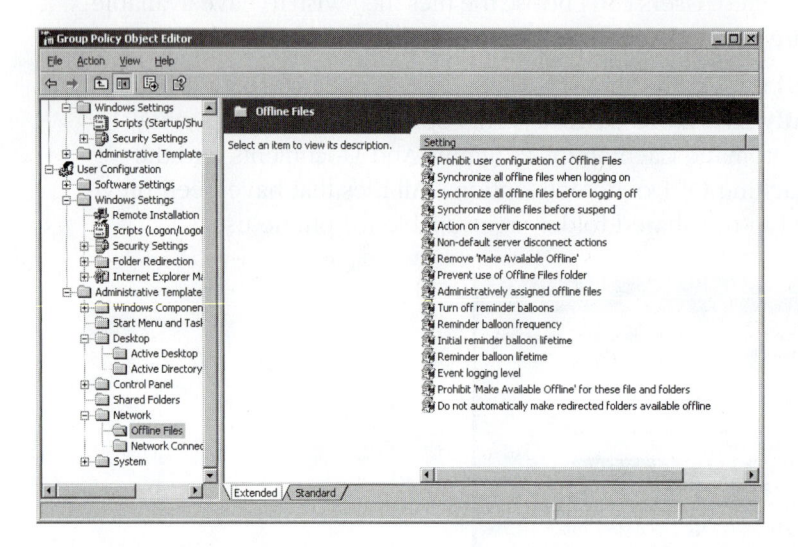

Figure 8-20 Offline Files Group Policy settings

Note that most of the policy settings are available in both the User Configuration and Computer Configuration nodes of Group Policy.

> **CAUTION** **Offline File Caching and Security** Allowing users to choose the files they want to cache locally can be a security concern. In high-security networks, offline file caching is disabled to prevent the possibility of sensitive data from leaving the corporate environment. Consider exploring policy settings such as At Logoff, Delete Local Copy Of Users Offline Files, and Prohibit User Configuration Of Offline Files. More information on configuring offline files with Group Policy are located at http://www.microsoft.com/technet/treeview/default.asp?url=/technet/prodtechnol/windowsserver2003/proddocs/deployguide/dmebc_dsm_atgi.asp.

DISK QUOTAS

Disk quotas can be used to limit the amount of space available on the server for user data. By implementing disk quotas when folder redirection is also configured, administrators can control the amount of information that is stored on the server. This is important for a couple of reasons. When information that should be backed up is stored on the server, your backup strategy and the amount of resources that it takes to implement can be directly impacted by the amount of data to be backed up. Backup resources include the hardware involved, such as a tape backup

CHAPTER 8: CONFIGURING THE USER AND COMPUTER ENVIRONMENT USING GROUP POLICY 211

device, and tapes or media to store the data. A network backup strategy usually takes into consideration the time that it takes to back up information, the amount of media that is used, and the time it takes to restore the information if necessary. Considering all of this, disk quotas allow administrators to have control over the amount of information that is backed up for each user. When a disk quota limit is reached, the users cannot store additional data until either their limit is increased, or they can clean up allocated space by deleting unnecessary files or archiving old files to make room for new data.

Disk quotas can be implemented manually through the Properties dialog box of a drive volume, as shown in Figure 8-21. This requires individual configuration of quotas for each volume that you wish to limit. The disk quota feature is only available on volumes formatted with the NTFS file system.

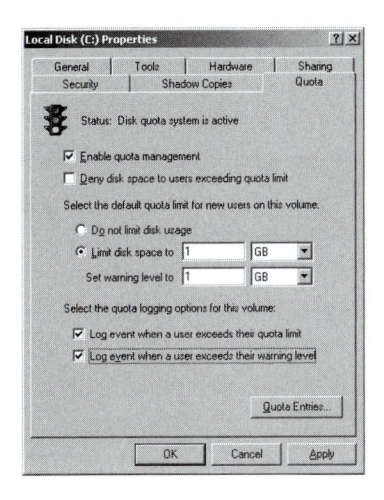

Figure 8-21   Disk quota manual settings

Using Group Policy to configure disk quotas enables all NTFS volumes on all computers running Windows 2000, Windows XP, and Windows Server 2003 affected by the GPO to be configured with consistent disk quota settings. This policy setting is located in the Computer Configuration\Administrative Templates\System\Disk Quotas extension of a GPO. Figure 8-22 shows the available settings within this GPO extension.

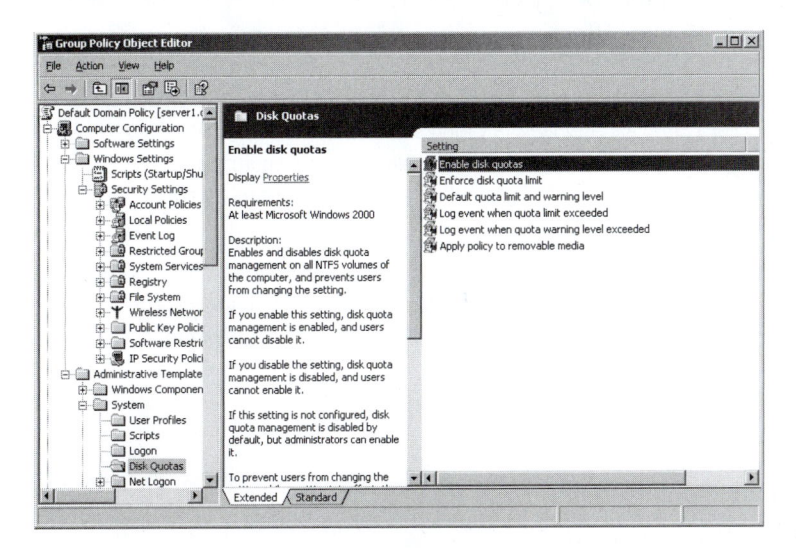

Figure 8-22   Computer Configuration\Administrative Templates\System\Disk Quotas GPO settings

The following list describes each policy setting within this GPO area:

- **Enable Disk Quotas**   This setting enables or disables disk quota management on all NTFS volumes of computers affected by the GPO.

- **Enforce Disk Quota Limit**   Enabling this setting enforces the space limitations designated by the Default Quota Limit And Warning Level setting for all users on the volume from that point forward. Existing files on the volume owned by the user are not counted against his or her quota limit. When a limit is set, the same limit applies to all users on all volumes. If this setting is not configured and disk quotas are enabled, users are able to write as much data to the volume as is physically available. Allowing this to occur defeats the purpose of enabling disk quotas.

- **Default Quota Limit And Warning Level**   This setting requires that the previous setting of Enforce disk quota limit is enabled. This setting allows administrators to determine the space limitation and warning settings when the limit is reached.

- **Log Event When Quota Limit Exceeded**   When enabled, this setting allows quota limit events to be logged to the Application log in Event Viewer. This setting requires that the Default Quota Limit And Warning Level setting is configured.

- **Log Event When Quota Warning Level Exceeded**   When enabled, this setting writes an event to the Application log that indicates when a user is approaching his or her disk quota limits.

- **Apply Policy To Removable Media**   This setting allows the policy settings to be applied to NTFS volumes located on removable media such as external drives.

When applying disk quotas to your network, careful planning of the necessary amount of disk space required by each user is very important. Realistic expectations of drive usage should be calculated. Since the Group Policy settings for disk quotas enforce the same limits to all users, it is best to plan for a larger space limit than to inconvenience users that need more space with error messages stating that the drive is full. When disk quota policy changes are made, you need to restart the server in order for them to take effect.

> **MORE INFO**   **Disk Quotas Details**   Microsoft Knowledge Base Article 326212, "HOW TO: Manage Disk Capacity and Usage Using Disk Quotas in Windows Server 2003," outlines the procedures and outcomes of manually implementing disk quotas on NTFS volumes. This article is located at http://support.microsoft.com /default.aspx?scid=kb;en-us;326212.
>
> The Windows Server 2003 online product documentation provides additional details on disk quotas at https://www.microsoft.com/technet/treeview/default.asp?url= /technet/prodtechnol/windowsserver2003/proddocs/datacenter/nt_diskquota _overview.asp.

The final sections of this chapter will discuss the Group Policy refresh process, manual policy refresh procedures, and recommendations for policy settings to increase performance.

REFRESHING GROUP POLICY

Computer Configuration and Domain Controller policies are refreshed by default when a computer starts up. User Configuration policies are refreshed during user logon. When a policy is refreshed, all settings are reprocessed, enforcing all of their policy settings. For example, settings that were previously enabled and are set to disabled are overwritten by the new setting and vice versa. In addition, settings that were previously enabled and set to Not Configured are simply ignored, leaving the setting in the registry unchanged. Each policy type has a default refresh cycle that takes place in the background to ensure that the most recent policy changes are applied, even if the system is not restarted or the user does not log off and back on. Although this is generally true, some policy settings will only process on initial startup or during user logon. For example, a policy that is used to install an application may interfere with another application's files for a program that is currently running on the user's computer. This could cause the installation to be incomplete or to fail. For this reason, software installation policies are only processed during computer startup. In addition, Folder Redirection policies are only processed during user logon. In the next sections, you will look at each policy type, the default refresh period, and where administrators can change the default refresh period.

- **Computer Configuration Group Policy Refresh Interval**   The setting for the refresh interval for computers is located in the Computer Configuration\Administrative Templates\System\Group Policy node in the Group Policy Object Editor window for a GPO. By default, computer policies are updated in the background every 90 minutes with a random offset of 0 to 30 minutes.

- **Domain Controllers Group Policy Refresh Interval**   The setting for the refresh interval for domain controllers is located in the Computer Configuration\Administrative Templates\System\Group Policy node in Group Policy Object Editor. By default, domain controller group policies are updated in the background every five minutes.

- **User Configuration Group Policy Refresh Interval**   The setting for the refresh interval for user policy settings is located in the User Configuration\Administrative Templates\System\Group Policy node in Group Policy Object Editor for a GPO.

The available period that each background refresh process can be set to ranges from 0 to 64,800 minutes (45 days). If you set the refresh interval to zero, the system attempts to update the policy every seven seconds. This can cause a significant amount of traffic and overhead on a production network and should be avoided except in a lab or test environment. On the other hand, setting a policy refresh interval to 45 days is also extreme for domain controllers and servers that are shut down infrequently. It is also possible to turn off the background refresh of a Group Policy entirely. This setting is available in the Computer Configuration \Administrative Templates\System\Group Policy node. This setting prevents any policy refreshes, except when a computer is restarted.

Manually Refreshing a Group Policy

When settings are modified that you wish to be immediately invoked without requiring a restart, a new logon session, or waiting for the next refresh period, you have the option of forcing a manual refresh. This process uses the Gpupdate.exe tool. This command line tool is new to Windows Server 2003 and replaces the previously used secedit /refreshpolicy command. Windows 2000 platforms still require the secedit command utility. An example of the syntax necessary for Gpupdate.exe to refresh all the user settings affected by the User Configuration node of the Default Domain GPO is as follows:

```
Gpupdate /target:user
```

To refresh the Computer Configuration node policy settings, the syntax would be as follows:

```
Gpupdate /target:computer
```

Without the /target switch, both the user and computer configuration policy settings are refreshed.

To look up additional information on the Gpupdate command, do Exercise 8-2 now.

Policy Processing Optimization

When processing a policy that uses computer or user settings, but not both, the setting area that is not configured should be disabled for faster processing. For example, if you wish to configure a computer policy that applies to all computers within an OU, you should disable the User Configuration node settings so that the policy processing is faster. When one part of the policy is disabled, that section is ignored and the settings are disregarded. This speeds up the completion of the policy processing, since each setting does not need to be read for changes.

▶ **Disabling User or Configuration Node Settings**

To disable user or configuration node settings of a Group Policy:

1. In Active Directory Users And Computers (MMC snap-in), right-click on the domain node in the left window pane, and select Properties.
2. On the Group Policy tab, select the Default Domain Policy, and click Edit.
3. Right-click the Default Domain Policy node at the top of the left window pane, and select Properties.

CHAPTER 8: CONFIGURING THE USER AND COMPUTER ENVIRONMENT USING GROUP POLICY

4. As shown in Figure 8-23, on the General tab, select the appropriate check box to disable the policy setting area that is not needed, and then click OK.

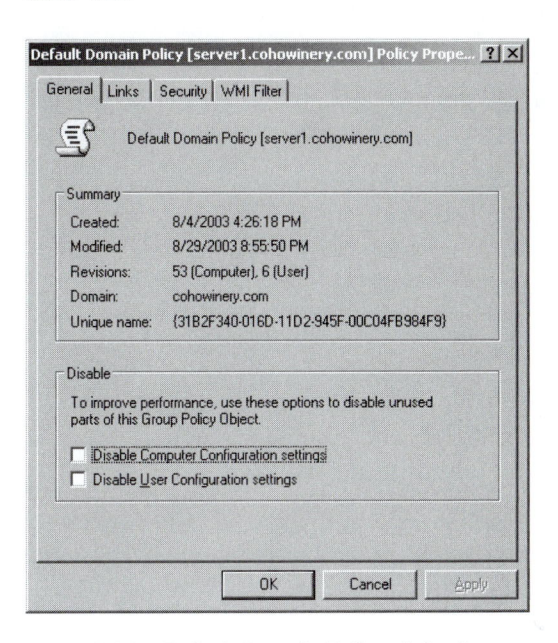

Figure 8-23 Default Domain Policy dialog box

5. Close Group Policy Object Editor. Click OK on the Domain Properties dialog box.

SUMMARY

- Most security-related settings are found within the Windows Settings node of the Computer Configuration node of a GPO.

- Policy settings that you wish to apply to all computers or users within a domain should be made within the Default Domain Policy GPO. Generally, domain-wide account policies such as password policies, account lockout, and Kerberos settings are modified here.

- Local policy settings govern what users can do on a specific computer and if the actions are logged in an event log. This is where audit policies are created.

- Auditing can be configured to audit successes, failures, or both. Careful planning of auditing should be completed prior to implementation. Events that are not important to your documentation and information needs can cause unnecessary overhead when audited. Auditing can be a very important security tool when used prudently.

- Because events that are audited are logged in the appropriate event log, it is necessary to understand the Event Log Policy setting area. This area allows control over maximum log sizes, retention of logs, and access rights to each log.

- Restrictions on group memberships can be accomplished using the Group Restriction policy setting. Implementing this policy removes group members that are not part of the configured group membership list.

- The Public Key Policies area allows definition of settings for EFS, in addition to many aspects of implementing a PKI, including automatic certificate requests, certificate trust lists (CTLs), and certificate autoenrollment settings for smart cards.

- Autoenrollment within a GPO can only be applied to Windows XP and Windows Server 2003 clients. Autoenrollment requires the installation and configuration of an Enterprise CA, an autoenrollment certificate template, appropriate user permissions to the template, and modification of the Default Domain GPO to allow autoenrollment to occur.

- Folder Redirection can be configured for folders located on a local computer within the Documents And Settings folder. The Offline Files settings allow redirected folders to be available when a network connection is not present. These two setting areas complement each other.

- Disk quotas can be used to control storage space on a network drive. Implementing disk quotas allows administrators to have tighter control over drive usage, which can affect tape backup and restore functionality.

- Computer configuration group policies are refreshed every 90 minutes by default. Domain controller group policies are refreshed every five minutes. These settings can be altered based on the frequency in which policy changes occur.

- Disabling unused portions of a Group Policy object increases the time it takes to complete the processing of a policy.

EXERCISES

Exercise 8-1: Documenting Log File Settings

To view the current log file settings:

1. From the Administrative Tools menu, open Event Viewer.
2. Right-click the Application log and select Properties.

   QUESTION What are the current and maximum sizes of your Application log and what action takes place when the log is filled?

3. Click Cancel to close the Application Log Properties dialog box.
4. Right-click the Security log, and select Properties.

   QUESTION What is the current size of your Security log and what action will take place when the log is filled?

5. Click Cancel to close the Security Log Properties dialog box.
6. Right-click the System log and select Properties.

   QUESTION What is the current size of your System log and what action occurs when the log is filled?

7. Click Cancel to close the System Log Properties dialog box.

   QUESTION Are there any other logs located in Event Viewer on your computer? If so, what are they and what type of events are most likely logged here?

Exercise 8-2: Finding Out More About Gpupdate

Research is a large part of being a network administrator, engineer, or technical consultant. Microsoft has provided a broad library of articles and documentation that can be used to deepen your knowledge in many areas. In this exercise, you will search for information about Gpupdate using the Internet.

1. In your browser window, type **http://www.microsoft.com/technet**, and press Enter.
2. In the Search window at the left side, type **gpupdate**, description and press Enter.
3. Look in the search results window for a document that describes the Gpupdate tool. What is the article number?
4. Click on the article title to open it. In this article, find the description of the /force switch and briefly describe it here.
5. Close your browser window.

REVIEW QUESTIONS

1. Which of the following event categories should you audit if you want to find out if an unauthorized person is trying to access a user account by entering random passwords or by using password-cracking software? Choose all that apply.

    a. Logon Events – success events

    b. Logon Events – failure events

    c. Account Logon – success events

    d. Account Logon – failure events

2. Since you have expanded your organization and are now following a decentralized approach to network management, you want to make sure that you track when Active Directory objects are created or removed, in addition to when changes to certificate services take place such as denial of certificate requests and so on. How can you do this?

3. Due to new corporate policies that have stronger security guidelines for your network, you decide to increase the minimum password length, enforce strong passwords, and make sure user accounts are locked after three invalid logon attempts within a 15-minute time frame. These settings should apply to all domain users on your network. Where do you configure these settings?

4. What is stored in the Security log?

5. You are the administrator for a mid-sized accounting firm with approximately 50–100 users and three servers in a single domain environment. Over the past few months, you have been monitoring the amount of available drive space weekly and have noticed that users seem to be using more and more space. You want to somehow control the amount of space each user has access to on the servers, so that you do not run into trouble later. You want users to each have a limit of 500 MB and receive notification when they have only 50 MB left. Some users only use minimal space, while others, such as the marketing department, use quite a bit of space. What should you do?

6. Based on your answer to question 5, list the steps you will take to accomplish this.

7. Consider that you have enabled the Autoenrollment settings on the Default Domain Policy GPO so users begin using their smart cards immediately. To test your configuration, you immediately attempt to use your smart card from your workstation by inserting it into the reader. When you try to log on, your attempt fails. What could be causing this to occur?

8. The CEO of your company has been speaking with a friend who informed him that he can have his files from his laptop redirected to the server. He has created a file system structure on his local hard drive that is stored in C:\Data\Workfiles. He would like you to redirect them to the server and have them available for offline use. What is your response to this request?

CASE SCENARIOS

Scenario 8-1: Lucerne Publishing and Offline Files

You are a computer consultant. Linda Randall, Chief Information Officer of Lucerne Publishing, asks for your help. The Lucerne Publishing network consists of a single Active Directory domain with four domain controllers running Windows Server 2003, three file servers, and 300 clients that are evenly divided between Windows 2000 Professional and Windows XP Professional.

Recently, several publishing projects stored in electronic format were lost when an employee's laptop was stolen from a publishing convention. Previously, another employee lost important publishing project files during a fire sprinkler system incident in which the employee's computer was destroyed.

Employees typically store documents in the My Documents folder on their local systems. Linda wants all employees to store their data on the network servers. The data on the network servers is backed up regularly. Linda tells you that her editors tend to work on sensitive data that requires special handling. She is especially worried about that data being backed up and secured.

All client computers have P drive mappings that are supposed to be used for storing files. However, many employees do not understand drive mappings. They often store files in their My Documents folder and then copy them over to the P drive. This is also an issue because many employees forget to copy their files to the server until something occurs, such as a data loss.

Given the concerns of Lucerne Publishing as outlined above, answer the following questions:

1. How would you address Linda's concern that some employees do not understand drive mappings and others forget to store their data on the server?
2. How can you address the situation concerning the sensitive data editors use?
3. How would you address the users with mobile computers so that they could work on their files while traveling?
4. Linda warns that some users may have huge amounts of data already stored in the My Documents folder on their local computer. How might this affect your recommendations?

Scenario 8-2: Smart Card Setup and Enrollment

As part of your company's secure computing efforts, you are implementing smart card readers for all users. You want to automate the process of implementing this new technology to help ease the administrative burden and lower the Total Cost of Ownership (TCO). Your network consists of 50 Windows 98 computers, 100 Windows XP Professional computers, and three Windows Server 2003 computers. Your CEO has requested that you answer the following questions so that a plan can be created that lists any necessary hardware or software upgrades in addition to the required procedures for implementing this new technology.

1. What feature in Windows Server 2003 do you need to implement in order to allow users to participate in the initial setup of the smart card program?

2. Do the Windows 98 computers support this new technology? Why or why not?

3. What technology needs to be implemented as infrastructure support for this new program?

CHAPTER 9
MANAGING SOFTWARE

Upon completion of this chapter, you will be able to:

- Understand the phases in the life cycle of software installations.
- Define the **Windows Installer Service**.
- Use Group Policy to install, manage, and maintain software applications.
- Understand the difference between assigning and publishing software applications.
- Create **software categories** within a Group Policy object.
- Define and configure **software restriction policies**.

Group Policy can be used to install, upgrade, patch, or remove software applications when a computer is started, when a user logs on to the network, or when a user accesses a file associated with a program that is not currently on his or her computer. In addition, Group Policy can be used to fix problems associated with applications. For example, if a user inadvertently deletes a file from an application, Group Policy can be used to launch a repair process that will fix the application. To understand how Group Policy can be used to perform all of these tasks, we will discuss the Windows Installer Service and its purpose. We will also discuss Software Restriction Policies, their benefits, and how you configure them to meet the needs of your organization.

THE SOFTWARE LIFE CYCLE

The process that takes place from the time an application is first evaluated for deployment in an organization until the time when it is deemed old or not suitable for use is referred to as a software life cycle. The software life cycle is a derivative of the **System Development Life Cycle (SDLC)**. The SDLC is used to develop information systems software, projects, or components through a structured process that includes analysis, design, implementation, and maintenance. The software life cycle consists of four phases that are derived from the SDLC model as follows:

- **Planning** This phase defines all planning activities, including the analysis of the software to be installed, verification of its compatibility, supported methods of installation, and the identification of any risks associated with the software and the desired deployment method.

- **Implementation** This phase is used to prepare for deployment. Using Group Policy as a tool, the implementation phase includes a set of steps for a deployment, such as creating a shared access location for files and creating or using the appropriate package files. Once all of the deployment steps have been achieved, the actual deployment takes place in this phase.

- **Maintenance** The maintenance phase includes the elements that are required to keep the software running smoothly. Examples of this include upgrading software to the latest version, installing patches when necessary, and self-healing functions that allow the software to detect and correct problems such as missing or deleted files.

- **Removal** The removal phase is the final phase before the software life cycle begins again with a new software deployment plan. When software is scheduled to be retired due to obsolescence or software requirement changes, this phase requires a clean removal of the software to be performed.

This chapter describes how Group Policy can be used to accomplish the latter three phases. Understanding how to use Group Policy to install, manage, maintain, and remove software is extremely helpful in streamlining the management of software across your enterprise.

WINDOWS INSTALLER

Microsoft Windows Server 2003 uses **Windows Installer** in conjunction with Group Policy to install and manage software that is packaged into an .msi file. Windows Installer consists of two components, one for the client-side component and another for the server-side component. The client-side component is named the Windows Installer Service. This client-side component is responsible for automating the installation and configuration of the designated software. The Windows Installer Service requires a package file that contains all of the pertinent information about the software. This package file consists of the following information:

- An .msi file. This file is a relational database file that is copied to the target computer system, along with the program files it deploys. In addition to providing installation information, this database file is used to assist in the self-healing process for damaged applications and the clean removal of applications.

- External source files that may be required for the installation or removal of software.
- Summary information about the software and the package.
- A reference point to the path where the installation files are located.

In order for software to be installed through Group Policy, Windows Installer–enabled applications must be used. An application that has an approval stamp from Microsoft on its packaging, including the Designed for Windows Server 2003, Designed for Windows XP, or Designed for Windows 2000 logos, is Windows Installer–enabled by default. This means the application provides support for Group Policy deployments using an .msi file.

Using Transform Files

There are times when you may need to modify Windows Installer files to better suit the needs of your corporate network. Modifications to .msi files require **transform files**, which have an **.mst** extension. Consider an example where you are the administrator of a corporate network in which you use .msi files to deploy your desktop applications. All of the Microsoft Office XP applications, except for Microsoft Access, are required by the users at each location. Office XP contains an .msi file that installs all of the Office XP applications. However, since you do not wish to install Access, you will need to create an .mst file to modify the .msi file. This is accomplished by using the Custom Installation Wizard included with Office XP. When the .mst file is placed in the same directory as the original .msi file, it customizes the installation by installing all of the Office XP applications, with the exception of Access. In addition, transform files can be created to add new features to the package, such as document templates for Microsoft Word, that are specific to your organization.

Windows Installer files with the **.msp** extension serve as patch files. Patch files are used to apply service packs and hotfixes to installed software. Unlike an .msi file, a patch package does not include a complete database. Instead it contains at minimum a database transform procedure that adds patching information to the database of its target installation package. For this reason, .msp files should be located in the same folder as the original .msi file when you want the patch to be applied as part of the Group Policy software installation. This allows the patch file to be applied to the original package or .msi file.

To learn how to deploy software and patches from the command line, do Exercise 9-1 now.

Repackaging Software

Not all software on the market provides .msi support. This being true, you may not be able to take advantage of Windows Installer with all of your enterprise applications. You may want to consider repackaging some software packages to take advantage of the Windows Installer technology. There are several third-party package-creation applications on the market that allow you to repackage software.

Repackaged software does not support some of the features of an original .msi such as self-healing. For this reason, a careful analysis that considers the cost of implementation and long-term benefits might be advisable.

> **MORE INFO** *Package Creation Applications* Microsoft references several products to assist in package creation and modification. The Web resources link located at http://www.microsoft.com/windows/reskits/Webresources includes third-party resources for many aspects of the Windows Server 2003 operating system family. As noted here, the home page for Wise Solutions, Inc., is listed as a resource for Windows Installer. Wise Solutions is located at http://www.wise.com.

In the simplest case, the process of repackaging software for .msi distribution includes taking a snapshot of a clean computer system before the application is installed, installing the application as desired, and taking a snapshot of the computer after the application is installed. A clean computer system is defined as a system with no other applications installed and only those service packs, hotfixes, and operating system patches that are required for functionality of the operating system. The repackaged application takes into account the changes to the registry, system settings, and file system caused by the installation itself. When you repackage an application, you are creating a relational database that tracks the installation parameters associated with the application.

The Windows Installer uses the database to find these items at installation time. Windows Installer does not create the repackaged file; this must be done by using a third-party application. Generally, application manufacturers do not support the re-engineering of their own .msi packages. However, you can use the .mst process to modify manufacturer-supplied .msi packages to reflect the needs of your organization. Once the process is understood, it provides a well-documented and reliable method of software deployment.

When repackaging an application is not an option and a Windows Installer file is not available, you can use a **.zap** file to publish an application. A .zap file is a non-Windows Installer package that can be created in a text editor. A .zap file looks and functions very similar to an .ini file. The disadvantages of creating .zap files are as follows:

- They can be published, but not assigned. These two options will be discussed in detail later in this chapter.
- Deployments require user intervention, instead of being fully unattended.
- Local administrator permissions may be required to perform the installation.
- They do not support custom installations or automatic repair.
- They do not support the removal of applications that are no longer needed or applications that failed to install properly.

Determining which applications you wish to deploy and assessing the type of files that are necessary to provide functionality with Windows Installer should be included as part of the planning phase of your deployment plan. Once these needs have been researched, analyzed, and documented, you can move into the implementation phase of your plan.

MORE INFO .zap Files For more information on creating .zap files, see Microsoft Knowledge Base article 231747, titled "HOW TO: Publish non-MSI Programs with .zap Files."

IMPLEMENTING SOFTWARE USING GROUP POLICY

Group Policy allows administrators to deploy required user software either when the computer starts, when the user logs on, or on demand based on file associations. From the user's perspective, applications are available and functional when they need them. From the administrator's perspective, the applications for each user do not have to be installed manually. Once again, note that there is a reduction in the Total Cost of Ownership (TCO) for applications when the time to install each application for each user is eliminated or is at least significantly reduced. The Software Installation extension in Group Policy can be used to deploy software to computers running any version of the Microsoft Windows 2000, Microsoft Windows XP, or Windows Server 2003 operating systems.

The next section describes each task that is used to set up software deployment using Group Policy.

Creating a Distribution Share

This shared folder, also named the **software distribution point**, is a network location from which users can download the software that they need. In Windows Server 2003, the network location can include software distribution points located in other forests when two-way forests trusts have been established on your network. This shared folder contains any related package files and all of the application files that are required for installation. Each application that you wish to install should have a separate subfolder in the parent shared folder. For example, if you wish to create a distribution point called SharedApps and include a word processing program, a spreadsheet program, and a graphics program as shown in Figure 9-1, you should create a subfolder for each of these applications. Windows Installer uses this directory to locate and copy files to the workstation. Users who are affected by the Group Policy assignment should be assigned NTFS Read permission to the folder containing the application and package files.

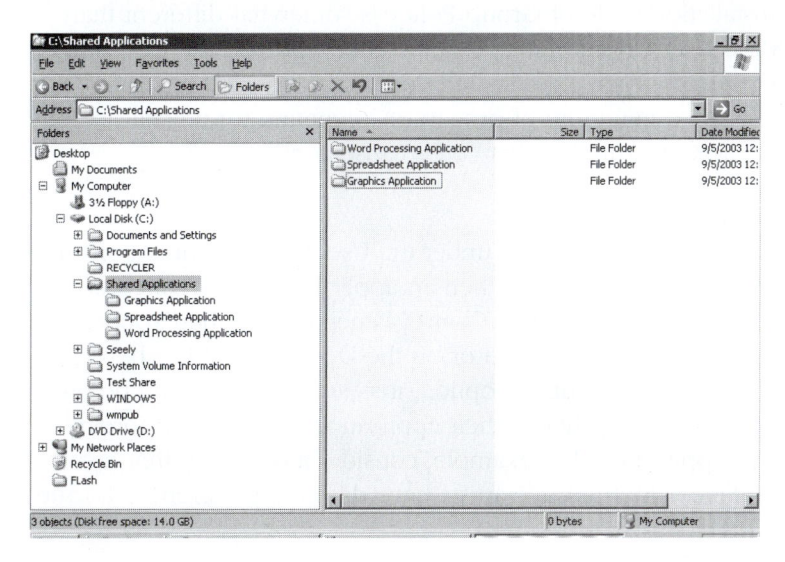

Figure 9-1 Shared distribution point recommended folder structure

CAUTION *Creating a Shared Distribution Folder Structure* *Folder structures that have too many levels can create an impact on performance when applications are being installed from across the network.*

Creating or Modifying a Group Policy Object

After a software distribution point is created, you must either create a Group Policy Object (GPO) or modify an existing GPO to include the software installation settings. As part of configuring a GPO for software installation, you have to decide whether you are going to *assign* or *publish* the application. The Assign option is helpful when you are deploying required applications to pertinent users and computers. The Publish option allows users to install the applications that they consider useful to them. These two deployment types are an important part of configuring your GPO settings to meet your business needs and are discussed in the next sections.

Using the User Configuration Node to Assign an Application

When an application is assigned to a user, the application is advertised on the Start menu of the user's workstation. The actual installation of the application is triggered when the user attempts to access it through the Start menu. This allows the software to be installed on demand. For example, suppose the Sales department needs to have all users running Microsoft Excel in order to complete their daily sales report. Using a Group Policy on the Sales organizational unit (OU), you can modify the settings to include the assignment of the Excel package file. When a member of the Sales OU logs on, Windows Installer adds Excel as a selection on the Start menu and changes the registry to associate .xls files with Excel. When the user attempts to access the program for the first time using the Start menu selection, the installation process begins. Additionally, if the user attempts to open a file named with an .xls extension, and Excel is not already installed, Windows Installer automatically begins the installation, and the file that was originally accessed will be opened upon completion. As we will discuss later in this chapter, installations can be configured to be totally automated or they can require some user input.

Using the Computer Configuration Node to Assign an Application

The behavior of assigning an application using the Computer Configuration +\Software Settings\Software Installation node of Group Policy is somewhat different than assigning it within the User Configuration node. When you use the Computer Configuration node, the application is installed during startup. This is a safe method because there are a minimum of processes competing for utilization and few, if any, other applications running that could cause conflicts.

Publishing an Application

Publishing an application is only available under the User Configuration\Software Settings\Software Installation extension. When an application is published, it is advertised in Add Or Remove Programs in Control Panel. A published application is not listed as an option on the Start Menu or on the Desktop as it is when an application is assigned. Using the Publish option, instead of Assign, may be preferred when users are allowed to choose their applications, rather than forcing them to use a specific application. For example, consider a company that has many graphic artists. Since all of graphic artists have different preferences for the software they prefer to use, it has been determined that three applications will be available and each user can install the application they prefer to use. Publishing a list of available applications allows users to install their preferred application or they can install all of them if desired.

> **NOTE** **Add Or Remove Programs in Control Panel** If you have blocked the availability of the Add Or Remove Programs application in Control Panel, published applications will not be accessible by users. Prior to publishing applications, be sure to check that accessibility to Control Panel or Add Or Remove Programs has not been blocked.

Using the Publish method of distributing applications also allows a file-activated installation to take place. This functionality is identical to what was discussed earlier for assigned applications. When a user opens a file associated with an application that does not currently exist on their workstation, the application is then installed.

> **CAUTION** **Testing Applications** As a precautionary step, you should test the available applications to ensure that they can all function together if the user opts to install them all. With certain application types such as multimedia applications, there can be conflicts in the required versions of supporting files and this may cause a malfunction. It is always prudent to test each application and its compatibility before it is distributed to the user population. In addition, testing the deployment to be sure that applications are distributed only to the intended recipients is equally important.

Using Software Categories

Allowing users to choose the applications they prefer provides them with some level of control over their working environment. It is possible to publish all of the available applications to give the users complete control over their environment. However, when a larger number of applications are published, the users may get confused and have difficulty understanding the purpose of each application. In addition, they may have difficulty locating the programs they need from a long list of selections. Situations such as these can be resolved by creating software categories.

Software categories allow published applications to be organized within specific groupings for easy navigation. For example, an administrator may create categories for each type of application such as word processing applications, spreadsheet applications, database applications, graphics applications, and so on. Alternatively, the administrator could create categories that are used within different departments in an organization. These categories would contain the appropriate applications on a per-department basis. When publishing many different applications, software categories facilitate user navigation and help the user to select the applications that are appropriate for their needs.

When you create or add software categories, they apply to the entire domain and are not GPO-specific. You will learn how to create software categories in the next section.

Configuring a Policy to Deploy Applications

This section lists the required steps to configure a GPO to deploy applications using the Assign or Publish options.

▶ Configuring a GPO to assign or publish an application

To configure a GPO to assign or publish an application, complete the following steps:

1. As shown in Figure 9-2, open the Group Policy Object Editor window for either a new or existing GPO object, and expand either the User Configuration or the Computer Configuration node, followed by Software Settings.

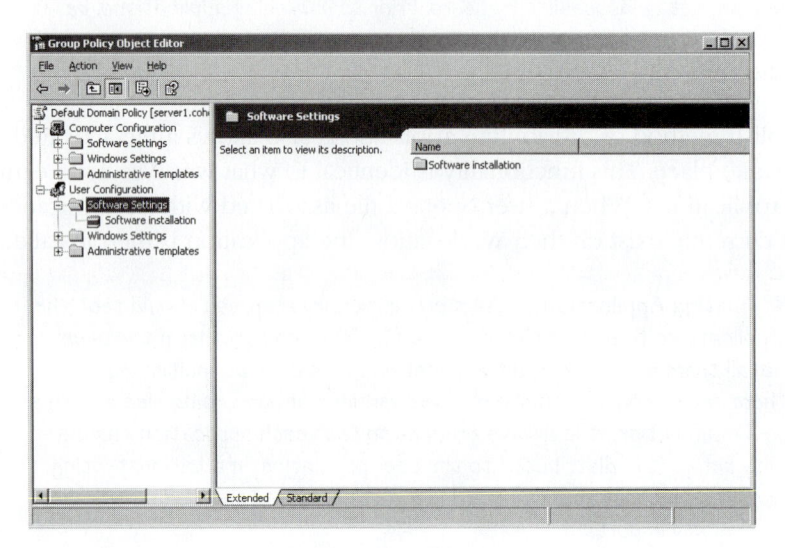

Figure 9-2 Group Policy Object Editor window

2. Right-click the appropriate Software Installation node, and then click Properties.

3. As shown in Figure 9-3, on the General tab of the Software Installation Properties dialog box, type the Uniform Naming Convention (UNC) path (*servername**sharename*) to the software distribution point for the Windows Installer packages (.msi files) in the GPO in the Default Package Location box.

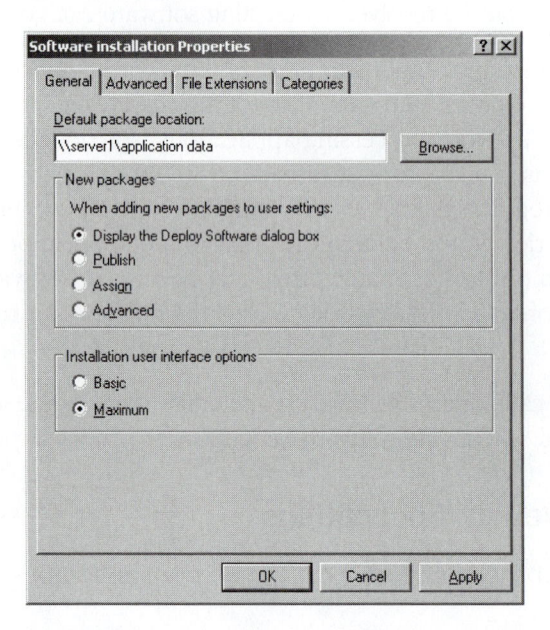

Figure 9-3 General Tab of the Software Installation Properties dialog box

4. In the New Packages section on the General tab, select one of the following:

- **Display The Deploy Software Dialog Box**   This option is used to specify that the Deploy Software dialog box displays when you add new packages to the GPO, allowing you to choose whether to assign, publish, or configure package properties. This is the default setting.

- **Publish**   This option is used to specify that the applications will be published by default with standard package properties when you add new packages to the GPO. Packages can be published only to users, not computers. If this is an installation under the Computer Configuration node of the Group Policy Object Editor console, the Publish choice is unavailable.

- **Assign**   This option is used to specify that the applications will be assigned by default with standard package properties when you add new packages to the GPO. Packages can be assigned to users and computers.

- **Advanced**   This option is used to specify that the Properties dialog box for the package will display when you add new packages to the GPO, allowing you to configure all properties for the package.

5. In the Installation User Interface Options section, select one of the following:

- **Basic**   This option is used to provide only a basic display for users during the installation of all packages in the GPO.

- **Maximum**   This option is used to provide all installation messages and screens for users during the installation of all packages in the GPO.

6. Click the Advanced tab as shown in Figure 9-4, and select any of the following options to apply the options to all packages in the GPO:

- **Uninstall The Applications When They Fall Out Of The Scope Of Management**   This option is used to remove the application when it no longer applies to users or computers.

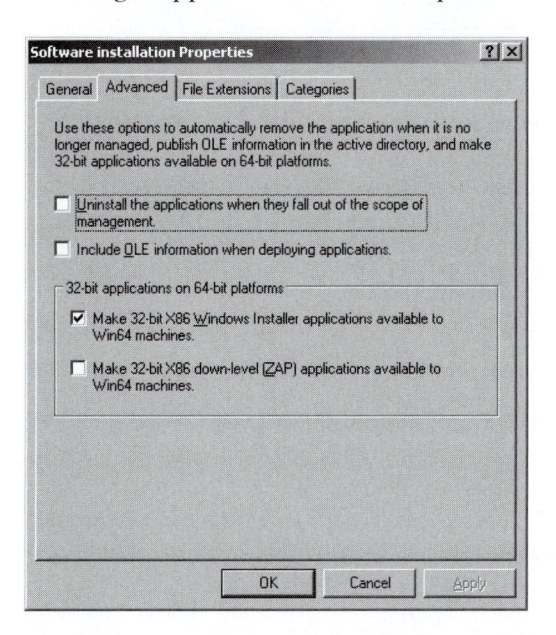

Figure 9-4   Advanced tab of the Software Installation Properties dialog box

- **Include OLE Information When Deploying Applications** This option is used to specify whether to deploy information about Component Object Model (COM) components with the package.

- **Make 32-Bit X86 Windows Installer Applications Available To Win64 Machines** This option is used to specify whether 32-bit Windows Installer Applications (.msi files) can be assigned or published to 64-bit computers.

- **Make 32-Bit X86 Down-Level (ZAP) Applications Available To Win64 Machines** This option is used to specify whether 32-bit application files (.zap files) can be assigned or published to 64-bit computers.

7. Click the File Extensions tab as shown in Figure 9-5, and, from the Select File Extension list, select the file extension for which you want to specify an automatic software installation.

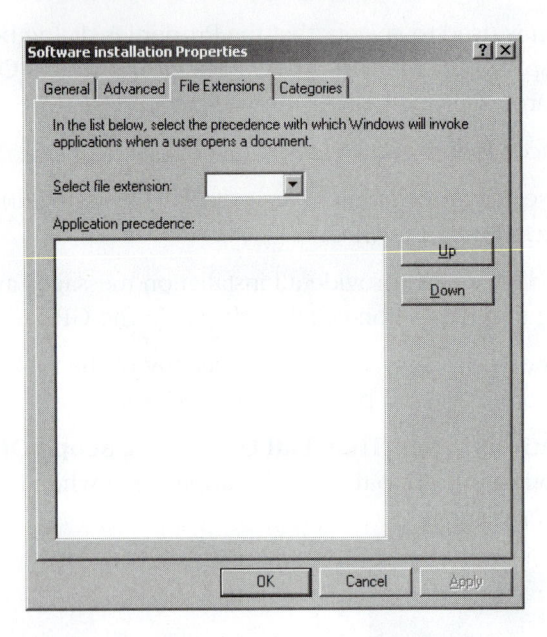

Figure 9-5 File Extensions tab of the Software Installation Properties dialog box

8. In the Application Precedence list box, move the application with the highest precedence to the top of the list using the Up or Down buttons. The application at the top of the list is automatically installed if the user invokes a document with the related filename extension and the application has not yet been installed.

9. Click the Categories tab as shown in Figure 9-6, and then click Add.

10. In the Enter New Category dialog box, type the name of the application category to be used for the domain in the Category box, and click OK.

    NOTE *Application Categories The application categories that you establish are per domain, not per GPO. You need to define them only once for the whole domain.*

11. Click OK.

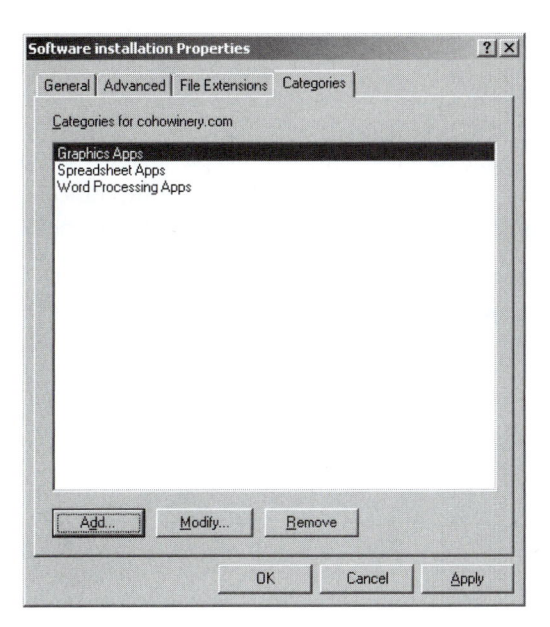

Figure 9-6 The Categories tab of the Software Installation Properties dialog box

NOTE **Uninstalling Software with Group Policy** In rare instances, when applications installed with Software Installation cannot be uninstalled by using Group Policy or Add Or Remove Programs in Control Panel, you can use Msicuu.exe, the Windows Installer Cleanup Utility, or Msizap.exe, the Windows Installer Zapper. These utilities are part of the Windows Support Tools, which you installed in Chapter 2, "Implementing Active Directory." Msicuu is a graphical utility and Msizap is a command-line utility. Msicuu uses Msizap to remove applications. For detailed information about using these commands, refer to Help.

Adding Windows Installer Packages

The next step in allowing for application distribution is to configure Group Policy to associate applications with the GPO. If you selected the default setting from step 4 of the preceding procedure, you will be prompted to specify whether each package is to be assigned or published. The following steps assume the default settings.

▶ **Adding Windows Installer Packages to the GPO**

To add Windows Installer packages to the GPO, complete the following steps:

1. Open Group Policy Object Editor for the GPO you wish to configure. In the Computer Configuration or User Configuration node, open Software Settings.

2. Right-click the Software Installation node, select New, and then click Package.

3. In the Open dialog box, in the File Name list, type the UNC path to the software distribution point for the Windows Installer packages (.msi files), and then click Open. The UNC path is very important here. If you do not use a UNC path to the software distribution point, clients will not be able to find the package files.

4. As shown in the Deploy Software dialog box in Figure 9-7, click one of the following:

   - **Published** This option is used to publish the Windows Installer package to users, without applying modifications to the package. It is only available if the policy was configured under the User Configuration node of Group Policy. Publishing cannot occur in a computer-based policy.

   - **Assigned** This option is used to assign the Windows Installer package to users or computers, without applying modifications to the package.

   - **Advanced** This option is used to set properties for the Windows Installer package, including published or assigned options and modifications.

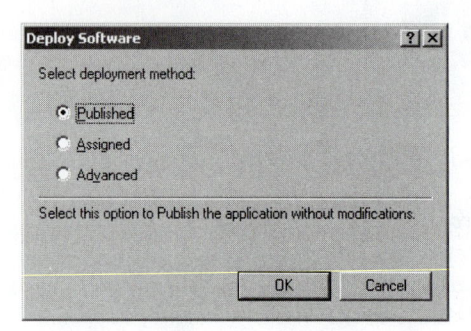

Figure 9-7 Deploy Software dialog box

5. Click OK. The following are the possible results at this point:
   - If you selected Published or Assigned, the Windows Installer package has been successfully added to the GPO and appears in the details pane.
   - If you selected Advanced, the Properties dialog box for the Windows Installer package opens to permit you to set properties for the Windows Installer package, including deployment options and modifications. Setting Windows Installer package properties is covered in the next section.

Setting Windows Installer Package Properties

In the Properties window for each Windows Installer package, additional settings can be associated with the package such as modification or transform (.mst) files and upgrade settings. Modifications to the previously assigned deployment settings can also be made. Figure 9-8 shows the Properties window for a Windows Installer package.

The following list explains the tabs in the package Properties window:

- **General** This tab allows you to change the default name of the package. In addition, a Uniform Resource Locator (URL) can be added to point to a support Web page. Some packages already contain a URL to the support Web page from the manufacturer of the software. Web sites used as support sites can contain valuable user instructions and answers to common questions.

CHAPTER 9: MANAGING SOFTWARE   233

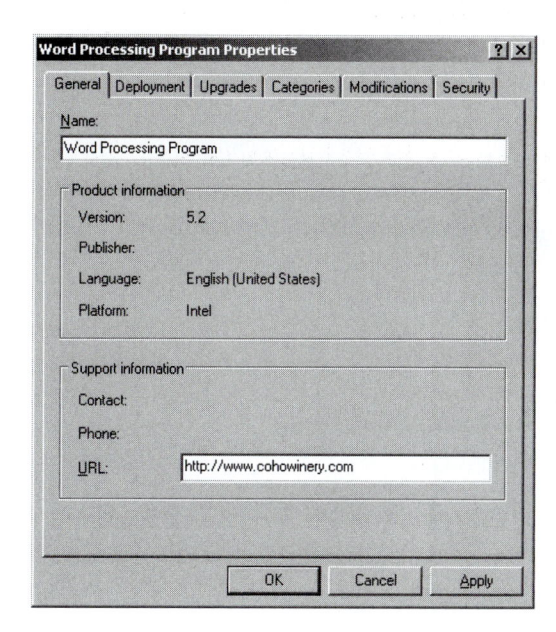

Figure 9-8 Properties window for a Windows Installer package

- **Deployment** As shown in Figure 9-9, this tab contains all of the deployment options discussed previously, including the Deployment Type: Published or Assigned; Deployment Options: Auto-install when the associated document is activated, Uninstall when the application falls out of scope, and Control Panel display selection; and Installation User Interface Options: Basic or Maximum. There is also an Advanced button that contains additional deployment information such as advanced deployment options and diagnostics information.

   NOTE *Assigned versus Published Options   If the package is set to Assigned, the Install This Application At Logon option is available. This option allows the application to be installed immediately, instead of being advertised on the Start menu. If users have slow links between their workstations and the software distribution point, this option should be avoided. The installation can take a lot of time when performed using a slow link.*

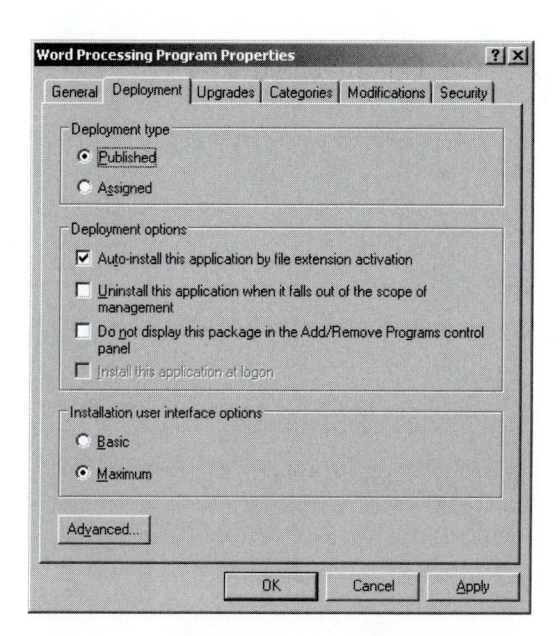

Figure 9-9 Deployment tab on a Windows Installer package Properties dialog box

- **Upgrades** This tab is used to configure any upgrades that will be applied to a package. This tab will not appear on .zap package files. Figure 9-10 shows this tab.

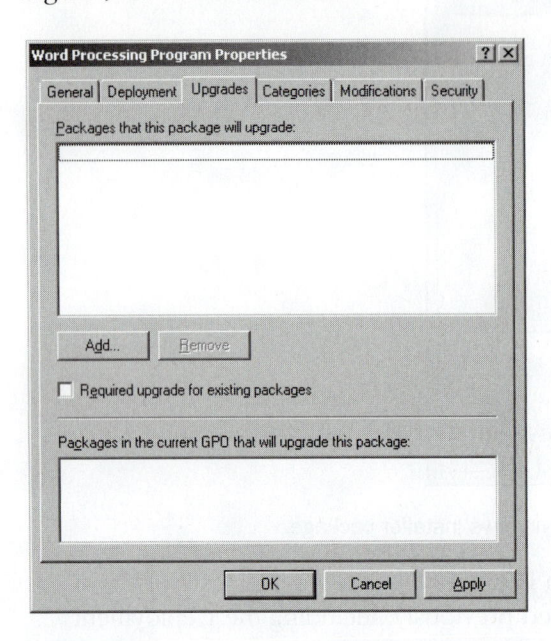

Figure 9-10 Upgrades tab on a Windows Installer package Properties dialog box

- **Categories** As shown in Figure 9-11, this tab is used to configure software categories in the Add/Remove Programs option of Control Panel.

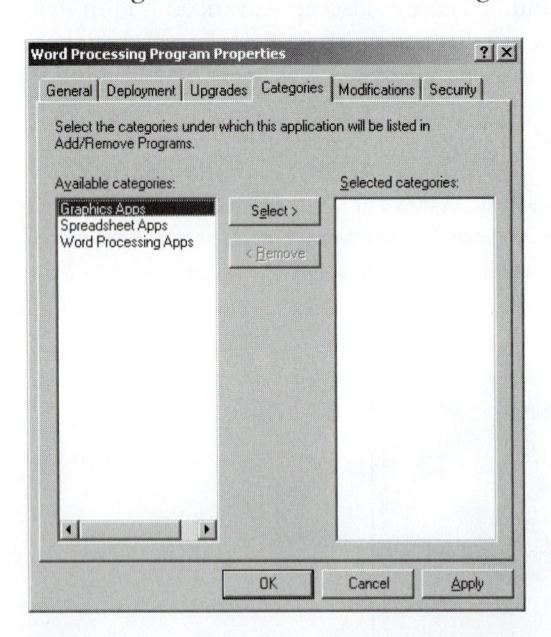

Figure 9-11 Categories tab on a Windows Installer package Properties dialog box

- **Modifications** This tab is used to specify the transform (.mst) files or patch (.msp) files that are to be applied to the package. You can also modify the order in which these files will be applied to the package, as shown in Figure 9-12.

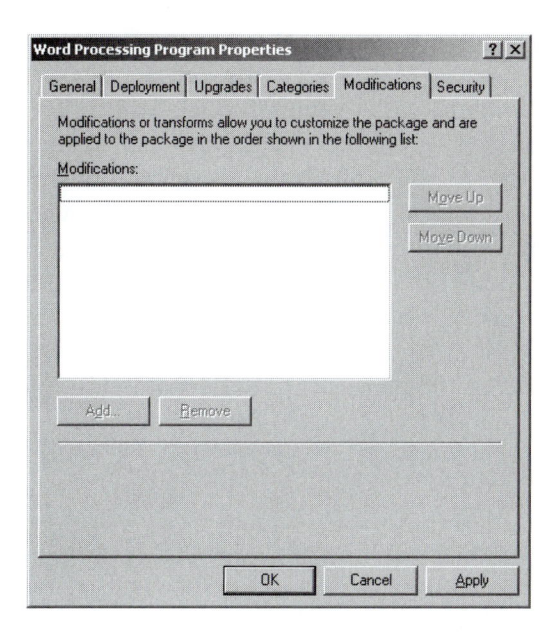

Figure 9-12 Modifications tab on a Windows Installer package Properties dialog box

CAUTION Failing to Complete the Modifications Tab When adding the transform or patch files that you want to apply to an application, be sure you complete all aspects of this tab before clicking OK. When you select OK, the application is assigned or published immediately. If all of the proper configurations have not been made on this tab, you may have to uninstall or upgrade the package in order to make the proper changes.

- **Security** As shown in Figure 9-13, this tab is used to specify who has permissions to install the software using this package.

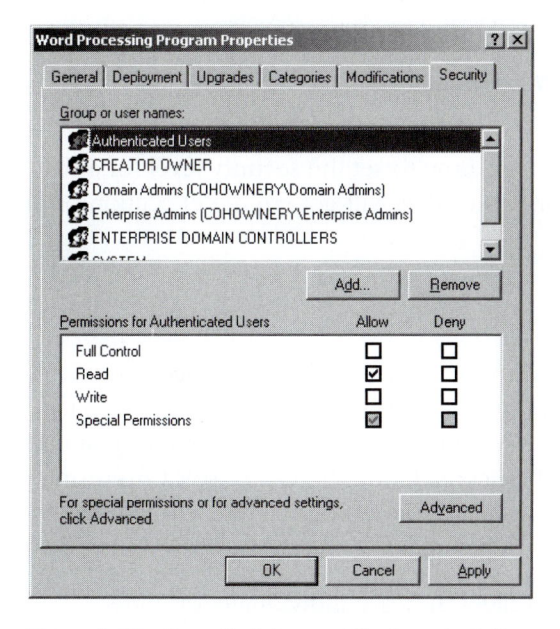

Figure 9-13 Security tab on a Windows Installer package Properties dialog box

SOFTWARE RESTRICTION POLICIES

New to Windows Server 2003 and Windows XP operating systems, software restriction policies give corporations greater control in preventing potentially dangerous applications from running. Software restriction policies are designed to identify software and control its execution. In addition, administrators can control who will be affected by the policies. The Software Restriction Policies node is found in the Windows Settings\Security Settings node of either the User Configuration or the Computer Configuration node of a Group Policy. By default, the Software Restriction Policies folder is empty. As shown in Figure 9-14, when a new policy is defined, two subfolders are created: Security Levels and Additional Rules. The Security Levels folder allows you to define the default behavior from which all rules will be created. The Additional Rules folder is where the criteria for each executable program is defined.

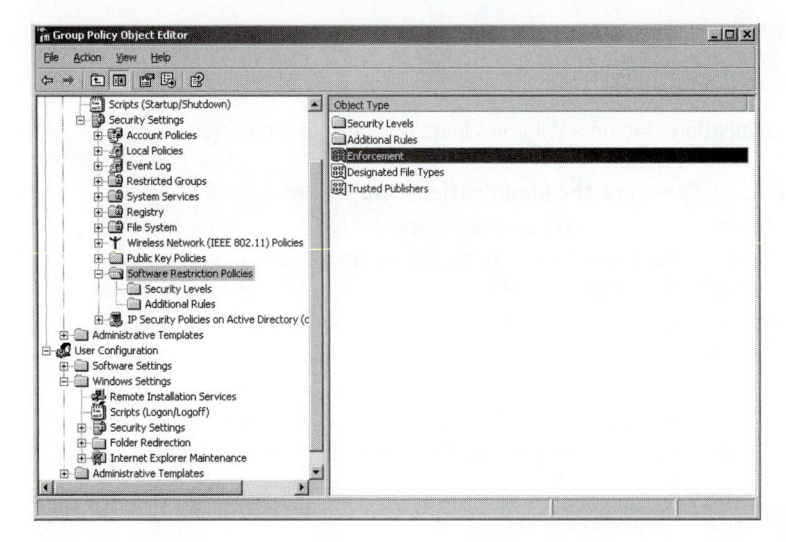

Figure 9-14 Computer Configuration\Windows Settings\Security Settings\Software Restriction Policies folder

In the following sections, we will learn how to set the security level for a software restriction policy and how to define rules that will govern the execution of program files.

Default Security Level

Prior to creating any rules that govern the restriction or allowance of executable files, it is important to understand how the rules work by default. If a policy does not enforce restrictions, executable files run based on the permissions that users or groups have in the file system. When considering the use of software restriction policies, you must determine your approach to enforcing restrictions. The two basic strategies for enforcing restrictions are:

- Allow all applications to run, unless they are individually excluded.
- Deny all applications from running, unless they are individually allowed.

The approach you take depends on the needs of your particular organization. By default, the Software Restriction Policies area has an Unrestricted value in the Default Security Level setting.

For example, consider that, in a high-security environment, you may wish to allow only specified applications to run. In this case, you would set the Default Security Level to Disallowed. By contrast, in a less secure network, you may wish to allow all executables to run, unless you have specified otherwise. This would require you to leave the Default Security Level as Unrestricted. In this case, you would have to create a rule to identify an application before you could disable it. These rules will be discussed in a subsequent section.

The Default Security Level can be modified to reflect the Disallowed setting. Because the Disallowed setting assumes that all programs will be denied, unless there is a specific rule permitting them to run, this setting can cause administrative headaches if not thoroughly tested. All applications you wish to run should be tested to ensure that they will function properly.

▶ **Modifying the Default Security Level Setting**

To modify the Default Security Level setting to reflect the Disallowed setting, complete the following steps:

1. In the Group Policy Object Editor window for the desired policy, expand the Software Restriction Policies node from either the Computer Configuration \Windows Settings\Security Settings or User Configuration\Windows Settings\Security Settings node. If a software restriction policy is not already defined, right-click Software Restriction Policies, and select New Software Restriction Policies.

2. In the details pane, double-click Security Levels. Note the check mark on the Unrestricted icon, which is the default setting.

3. Right-click the security level that you want to set as the default, and then click Set As Default. When changing the default settings to Disallowed, the dialog box shown in Figure 9-15 is displayed.

To view the Default Security Level for your domain's Software Restriction Policies, do Exercise 9-2 now.

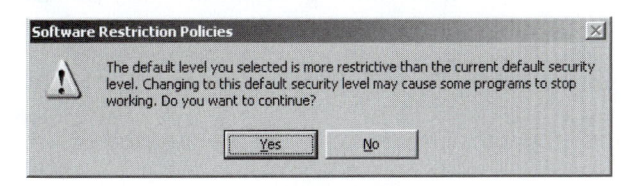

Figure 9-15 Software Restrictions Policies Default Security Level Warning dialog box

Software Restriction Rules

The functionality of software restriction policies is dependent on the rules that are defined to identify software, followed by the rules that govern its usage. When a new software restriction policy is created, the Additional Rules subfolder is displayed. This folder allows you to create rules that specify the conditions under which programs can be executed or denied. The rules that are applied can override the Default Security Level setting when necessary. There are four types of rules that can be used to govern programs. Each of these will be explained in the following sections.

Hash Rule
A **hash** is a series of bytes with a fixed length that uniquely identify a program or file. A hash value is generated by a formula that makes it nearly impossible for another program to have the same hash. A hash is computed by a **hash algorithm**, which in effect creates a fingerprint of the file. If a **hash rule** is used and a user attempts to run a program affected by the rule, the hash value of the executable file is checked. If the hash value of the executable file matches the hash value of the executable file governed by a software restriction policy, the policy settings will apply. Therefore, by using a hash rule on an application executable, you can prevent the application from running. Since the hash value is based on the file itself, the file can be moved from one location to another and still be affected by the hash rule. If the file is altered in any way, the rules in the software restriction policy can be bypassed.

When using hash rules, the following limitations should be observed:

- Software restriction policies affect only the files whose hashed values were created within the software restriction policy.

- If the file is altered in any way, the rules in the software restriction policy can be bypassed.

- Only file types listed in the Designated File Types list are affected by hash rules.

    MORE INFO Hash Algorithms   *Securing data is a top priority of today's administrators. Understanding how hashing works is important foundational information in security planning. Information that is helpful to understanding hash and signature algorithms is located on the Microsoft Developer Network (MSDN) site at the following link: http://msdn.microsoft.com/library/default.asp?url= /library/en-us/security/security/hash_and_signature_algorithms.asp.*

Certificate Rule
A **certificate rule** uses the signing certificate of an application. Certificate rules can be used to allow software from a trusted source to run or disallow software that does not come from a trusted source from running. Certificate rules can also be used to run programs in disallowed areas of the operating system.

The following limitations apply to certificate rules:

- Only file types listed in the Designated File Types list are affected by certificate rules.

- For the certificate rule to function, you must enable the System settings: Use Certificate Rules on Windows Executables For Software Restriction Policies located in Computer Configuration\Windows Settings\Security Settings\Local Policies\Security Options.

- Certificate rules do not apply to files with an extension of .exe or .dll. Instead, they apply only to scripts and Windows Installer packages.

Path Rule

A **path rule** identifies software by specifying the directory path where the application is stored in the file system. Path rules can be used to create an exception rule to allow an application to execute when the Default Security Level for software restriction policies is set to Disallowed, or they can be used to disallow an application from executing when the Default Security Level for software restriction policies is set to Unrestricted.

Path rules can specify either a location in the file system directory to application files or a registry path setting. Registry path rules provide assurance that the application executables will be found. For example, suppose an administrator used a path rule to define a file system path for an application. In this case, if the application were moved from its original file system path to a new location, such as during a restructuring of your network, the original path specified by the path rule would no longer be valid. If the rule specified that the application does not function, except if located in a particular path, the program would be allowed to run from its new path. This could cause a significant security breach opportunity if the program references confidential information. In contrast, if a path rule is defined using a registry key location, any change to the location of the application files will not affect the outcome of the rule. This is because when an application is relocated, the registry key that points to the application's files is updated automatically.

By default, four path rules that allow operating system files to run are located in the Additional Rules folder as shown in Figure 9-16. Note the use of variables such as the percent sign (%) and the asterisk symbol (*). Paths that are specified here support the use of common variables such as: %userprofile%, %windir%, %appdata%, %programfiles%, or %temp%.

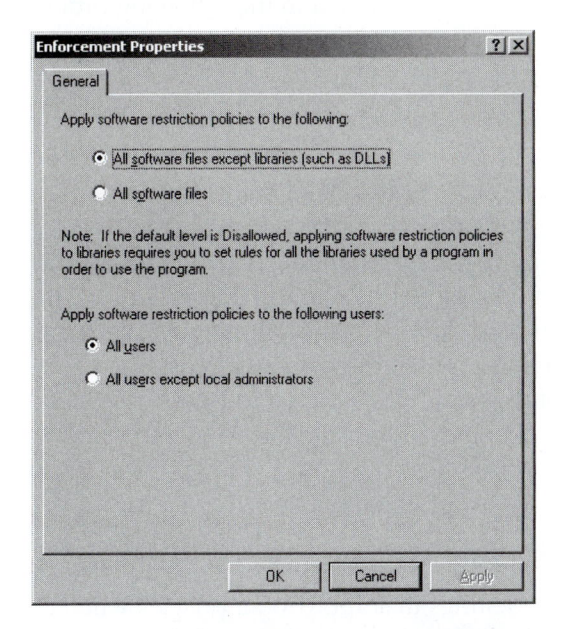

Figure 9-16 Software Restriction Policies Enforcement Properties window

CAUTION **Deleting or Modifying Additional Rules Folder Paths** Deletion or modification of the default rules specified in the Additional Rules folder may cause you to lock all users, including yourself, out of the system. Changes to these rules should be performed only by advanced administrators who have researched and tested the effects of the changes prior to implementation.

NOTE **Preventing the Execution of Programs Attached to E-Mail** Using a path rule that points to the file system directory where your e-mail program stores attached files can prevent users from being able to execute attached programs. This is one method of thwarting viruses that are spread using executables attached to e-mail.

Internet Zone Rule

Internet zone rules apply only to Windows Installer packages that attempt to install from a specified zone such as a local computer, local intranet, trusted sites, restricted sites, and the Internet. This type of rule can be applied to allow only Windows Installer packages to be installed if they come from a trusted area of the network. For example, an Internet zone rule could restrict Windows Installer packages from being installed using the Internet.

Using Multiple Rule Types

A software restriction policy can be defined using multiple rule types to allow and disallow the execution of programs. Using multiple rule types, it is possible to have a variety of security levels. For example, you may wish to specify a path rule that disallows programs to run from the \\Server1\Accounting shared folder and a path rule that allows programs to run from the \\Server1\Application shared folder. You can also choose to incorporate certificate rules and hash rules into your policy. When implementing multiple rule types, rules are applied in the following order:

1. Hash rules
2. Certificate rules
3. Internet zone rules
4. Path rules

When a conflict occurs between rule types such as a hash rule and a path rule, the hash rule prevails because it is higher in the order of preference. If a conflict occurs between two rules of the same type and the same identification settings, such as two path rules that identify software from the same directory, the most restrictive setting will apply. In this case, if one of the path rules were set to Unrestricted and the other to Disallowed, the policy would enforce the Disallowed setting.

Additional Options

Directly under the Software Restriction Policies folder, three specific properties can be configured to provide additional settings that apply to all policies when implemented. The Enforcement, Designated File Types, and Trusted Publishers properties are described in the following sections.

Enforcement

As shown in Figure 9-16, Enforcement properties allow you to determine whether the policies apply to all files or whether library files such as Dynamic Link Library (DLL) are excluded. Excluding DLLs is the default. This is the most practical method of enforcement. For example, if the Default Security Level for the policy is set to Disallowed and the Enforcement properties are set to All Software Files, you would have to create a rule that would allow each and every DLL to be checked before the program is either allowed or denied. By contrast, excluding DLL files by using the default Enforcement property would not require an administrator to define individual rules for each DLL file.

As shown in Figure 9-16, the Enforcement property allows you to specify a global setting to enforce software restriction policies to all files. The Enforcement property also allows an administrator to specify a global setting to enforce software restriction policies to all users, with the exception of the local administrators, who would remain unaffected. For example, when a software restriction policy is used to disallow the execution of administrative utilities located in a particular directory, setting the Enforcement properties to apply to all users, except administrators, would allow administrators to use the recommended RunAs program to access needed administration tools.

Designated File Types

As shown in Figure 9-17, the Designated File Types properties within the Software Restriction Policies folder are used to specify file types that are considered executable. File types that are designated as executable or program files will be shared by all rules, although you can specify a list for a computer policy that is different from one that is specified for a user policy.

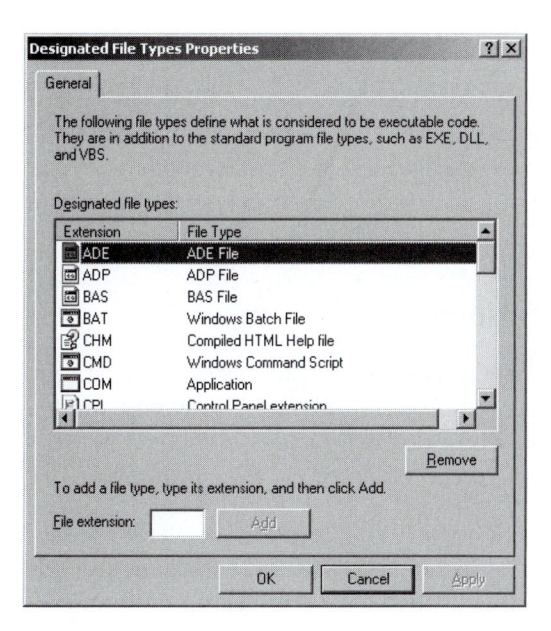

Figure 9-17 Software Restriction Policies Designated File Types Properties window

Trusted Publishers

The Trusted Publishers properties allow an administrator to control how certificate rules are handled. As shown in Figure 9-18, in the Properties dialog box for Trusted Publishers, the first setting allows you to determine which users are allowed to decide on trusted certificate sources. By default, local computer administrators have the right to specify trusted publishers on the local computer and enterprise administrators have the right to specify trusted publishers in an OU. From a security standpoint, in a high-security network, users should not be allowed to determine the sources from which certificates can be obtained.

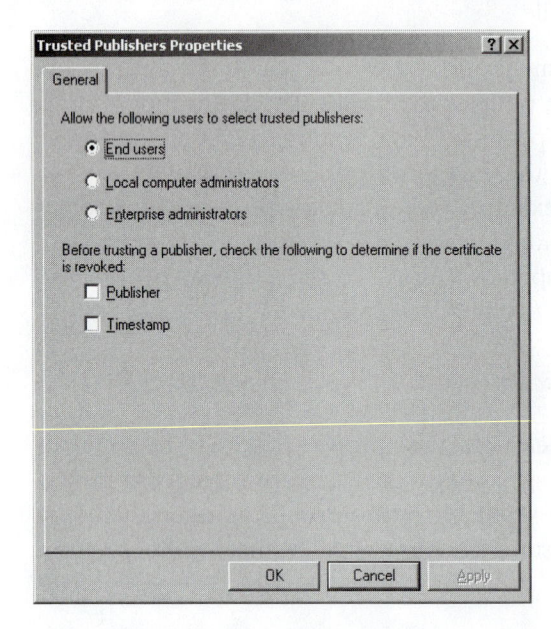

Figure 9-18 Software Restriction Policies Trusted Publishers Properties window

In addition, the Trusted Publisher Properties dialog box also lets you decide if you wish to verify that a certificate has not been revoked. If a certificate has been revoked, the user should not be allowed to gain access to network resources. You have the option of checking either the Publisher or the Timestamp of the certificate to determine if it has been revoked.

Implementation Recommendations

Software restriction policies can be an asset to your organization's security strategy when they are understood and implemented properly. Planning how you want to use software restriction policies is your best defense in preventing problems. Microsoft has several recommendations that can help you to plan and implement software restriction policies, including the following:

- Software restriction policies should be used in conjunction with standard access control permissions. Combining these two security features allows you to have tighter control over program usage.

- The Disallowed Default Security Level should be used cautiously since all applications will be restricted, unless explicitly allowed.

- If policies that cause undesirable restrictions on a workstation are applied, reboot the computer in Safe mode. Software restriction policies cannot be applied in Safe mode. Rebooting in Safe mode is a temporary solution, since the policies remain in effect until they are modified or removed.

- When editing software restriction policies, the policy should be disabled so that a partially complete policy does not cause undesirable results on a computer. Once the policy modifications have been made, the policy can be reenabled and refreshed.

- Creating a separate GPO for software restriction policies allows you to disable or remove them without affecting other policy settings.

- Test all policies before deploying them to the users. Very restrictive policies can cause problems with files that are required in order for the operating system to function properly.

MORE INFO **Implementing Software Restriction Policies** Microsoft Knowledge Base article number 324036 outlines all of the required steps and outcomes for implementing a software restriction policy. This article can be accessed at http://support.microsoft.com/default.aspx?scid=kb;en-us;324036.

SUMMARY

- Group Policy can be used to deploy new software on your network and remove or repair software originally deployed by a GPO from your network. This functionality is provided by the Windows Installer service within the Software Installation extension of either the User Configuration\Software Settings or Computer Configuration\Software Settings node.

- There are three types of package files that are used in conjunction with the Windows Installer service. They include .msi files for standard software installation, .mst files for customized software installation, and .msp files for patching .msi files at the time of deployment. All pertinent files must reside in the same file system directory.

- .zap files can be written to allow non–Windows Installer–compliant applications to be deployed. .zap files do not support automatic repair, customized installations, or automatic software removal. In addition, these files must be published.

- A shared folder named a software distribution point must be created to store application installation and package files that are to be deployed using Group Policy. This is best implemented with Microsoft distributed file system (Dfs) for redundancy and accessibility reasons. Users must have the NTFS Read permission to this folder for software installation policies to function.

- Software to be deployed using Group Policy can either be Assigned or Published. Assigning software using the User Configuration node of a Group Policy allows the application to be installed when the user accesses the program using the Start menu or an associated file. Assigning software can also be performed using the Computer Configuration node of a Group Policy, which forces the application to be installed during computer startup. Publishing an application allows the application to be available through Add Or Remove Programs in Control Panel. In addition, published applications can be divided into domain-wide software categories for ease of use.

- Software restriction policies are new to Windows Server 2003 and allow the executable code of software to be identified and either allowed or disallowed on the network.

- The two Default Security Levels within software restriction policies are Unrestricted, which means all applications function based on user permissions, and Disallowed, which means all applications are denied execution regardless of the user permissions.

- There are four rule types that can be defined within a software restriction policy. They include in order of precedence, hash, certificate, Internet zone, and path rules. The security level set on a specific rule supercedes the Default Security Level of the policy.

- Enforcement properties within software restriction policies allow the administrator to control users affected by the policy. Administrators can be excluded from the application of the policy so that it does not hamper their administrative capabilities.

- Certificate rules require enabling the System settings: Use Certificate Rules on Windows Executables for Software Restriction Policies located in Computer Configuration\Windows Settings\Security Settings\Local Policies \Security Options.

- Path rules can point to either a file system directory location or a registry path location. The registry path location is the more secure option of the two choices since the registry key location changes automatically if the software is reinstalled. In contrast, if a file system directory is blocked for executables, the program can still be run from an alternate location if it is moved or copied there, allowing the possibility of a security breach.

EXERCISES

Exercise 9-1: Using Msiexec to Deploy Software Applications and Patches

To learn the syntax for deploying software from the command line, complete the following steps:

1. From the Start menu, select Help And Support to open the Help And Support Center For Windows Server 2003.
2. In the Search field, type **Windows Installer**, and press Enter.
3. In the Search Results display, double-click to select Msiexec: command-line reference.
4. In the right window pane, click the plus sign (+) to the left of To Install Or Configure A Product. This will expand the syntax and parameters for installing and configuring a product using msiexec.exe at the command line.
5. Continue exploring the options for Msiexec by expanding the plus sign (+) next to each option. You can print the output of this Help screen by clicking the Print icon above the right window pane.

   QUESTION Based on what you have learned in this exercise, what would be the correct syntax for advertising the C:\SharedApps\WPapp.msi to all users and applying the C:\SharedApps\WPapp.mst transform to it when it is installed?

6. Close the Help And Support Center.

Exercise 9-2: Viewing the Default Security Level

To view the current Default Security Level for software restriction policies, complete the following steps:

1. In the Group Policy Object Editor window for the desired policy, expand the Software Restriction Policies node from either the Computer Configuration\Windows Settings\Security Settings or User Configuration \Windows Settings\Security Settings node. If a software

restriction policy is not already defined, right-click Software Restriction Policies, and select New Software Restriction Policies.

2. In the details pane, double-click Security Levels. Note the check mark on the Unrestricted icon; this is the default setting.

3. Double-click the Unrestricted icon to open the Unrestricted Properties window.

   QUESTION   What does the description for this property indicate?

   QUESTION   In your own words, what does the message here mean?

4. Click Cancel to close the Unrestricted Properties window.

5. Right-click in the left window pane on Software Restriction Policies and select Delete Software Restriction Policies. Click Yes in the Confirmation Of Deletion dialog box.

6. Close Group Policy Object Editor.

REVIEW QUESTIONS

1. Which of the following rule types apply only to Windows Installer packages?

    a. Hash rules

    b. Certificate rules

    c. Internet zone rules

    d. Path rules

2. Which file type is used by Windows Installer?

    a. .inf

    b. .bat

    c. .msf

    d. .msi

3. As part of your efforts to deploy all new applications using Group Policy, you discover that several of the applications you wish to deploy do not include the proper package files. What are your options?

4. What are the limitations of the solution you provided in question 3?

5. Your company has just purchased 200 new workstations that need to be deployed to user desktops as soon as possible. At a recent departmental meeting, it was suggested that, rather than installing all applications on each workstation, users should be responsible for installing their own programs. What feature in Windows Server 2003 will allow users to choose and install necessary programs to their computers?

6. List the order of precedence from highest to lowest for software restriction policy rules.

7. In an effort to thwart e-mail viruses on your network, you want to prevent users from running executable files in e-mail attachments. Explain how you would restrict this activity and list any issues that may affect your solution.

8. What two Default Security Levels can be used with a software restriction policy?

9. You are the administrator for a Windows Server 2003 domain. Your company has just purchased a new application that will be used by all employees to create forms. You want to make sure that this application is installed the next time users log on to the network. Explain the steps you would follow to make this happen.

10. Using the same scenario as question 9, is it possible to have the programs install automatically when the computer restarts, as opposed to when a user logs on?

CASE SCENARIOS

Scenario 9-1: Planning Group Policy Software Deployments

Your company, a healthcare organization, is currently working towards compliance with new government standards on patient confidentiality. Your IT department has decided that using software restriction policies in conjunction with standard user access permissions will help to fulfill the necessary security requirements. You are preparing an implementation plan that is based on user needs and security requirements. Users should not be able to access any programs with the exception of those that are pertinent to their jobs. In addition, the user needs within the organization are as follows:

- Users only need access to e-mail and a patient database.
- The patient database has its own built-in security access system that is configured for each user based on their needs within the program.
- All user accounts are located in containers based on their office location.

In addition, the following points should be considered in your implementation plan:

- Software restriction policy settings should not affect settings that are already in place within existing GPOs. If problems arise with restriction policies, they should be easy to rectify, without affecting other security areas.
- Administrator accounts should not be affected by software restrictions.
- Other applications should not be affected by any of the restrictions.

List the key points that should be part of your implementation plan based on the information provided here.

Scenario 9-2: Consulting with Wide World Importers

You have been asked by Max Benson, Chief Executive Officer (CEO) of Wide World Importers, to advise the company on the software deployment issues they are facing. Wide World Importers is an import/export company handling primarily clothing and textile products. They have offices in New York, New York; San Diego, California; and Fort Lauderdale, Florida. Wide World's network is configured as a single Active Directory domain with sites and OUs for each location. Below each top-level OU is a second layer of OUs representing the functional areas of Shipping, Finance, and Marketing. The users and client computers are distributed as shown in Table 9-1.

Table 9-1 **Wide World Importers Network Structure**

Office/OU	Users	Computers	Operating Systems Used
NY/Shipping	15	8	Windows 2000 Professional
NY/Finance	60	60	Windows 2000 Professional and Windows XP Professional
NY/Marketing	175	185	Windows 2000 Professional and Windows XP Professional
CA/Shipping	55	40	Windows 2000 Professional and Microsoft Windows NT version 4.0 Workstation
CA/Finance	110	110	Windows XP Professional
CA/Marketing	210	210	Windows 2000 Professional and Windows XP Professional
FL/Shipping	25	15	Windows NT version 4.0 Workstation
FL/Finance	20	20	Windows 2000 Professional
FL/Marketing	140	150	Windows 2000 Professional and Windows XP Professional

The California and New York offices are connected by a dedicated T-1 line. There are dedicated 256-Kbps fractional T-1 lines connecting the Florida office both to the California and New York offices. Several of the Marketing users have mobile computers, and a portion of their time is spent traveling the world. Access to the main network is accomplished by dialing in to a local Internet service provider (ISP), and then establishing a Layer Two Tunneling Protocol (L2TP) virtual private network (VPN) to the California office. There are three domain controllers and one file server at each location. The wide area network (WAN) links are used heavily during the day, but Wide World does not plan to upgrade them any time soon. It is important that the software deployment strategy you suggest does not adversely affect the WAN links during business hours.

Max has indicated that he wants more control over software deployment and wants to leverage his investment in Windows Server 2003. The main software requirements of the company include Office XP for all users, a third-party program used by Marketing, an application used by Finance for billing and accounting, and a proprietary shipping application developed for Wide World Importers. While all users utilize Office XP, they don't all use the same applications. Many users utilize only Outlook and Word, while others also make use of Access and PowerPoint. Still others use Excel on a daily basis.

Given the concerns of Wide World Importers as outlined above, answer the following questions:

1. Utilizing GPO for software deployment, how can you configure the network in a manner that will not negatively impact the business by saturating the WAN links during deployment?

2. With respect to the marketing, finance, and shipping applications, what are some of the options and considerations when deciding how to deploy these applications?

3. How do you recommend resolving the issue that many users utilize different parts of the Office XP suite of applications?

4. A small number of the client systems are running Windows NT version 4.0 Workstation. How would you advise Wide World Importers regarding software installation for these systems?

5. The shipping application is a proprietary application that does not have an .msi file associated with it. How would you recommend using Group Policy to deploy this application to the Shipping department?

CHAPTER 10
PLANNING A GROUP POLICY MANAGEMENT AND IMPLEMENTATION STRATEGY

Upon completion of this chapter, you will be able to:

- Filter the scope of a GPO using permissions and Windows Management Instrumentation (WMI) filters.
- Describe Group Policy Management Console, its features, and benefits.
- Use Group Policy Management Console (GPMC) to manage GPOs.
- Use RSoP and GPResult to determine and troubleshoot policy settings.
- Use RSoP and Group Policy Management to simulate group policy results.
- Delegate control of a GPO.
- Understand and implement group policy planning guidelines.

This chapter focuses on expanding your knowledge of group policy. Specifically, you will learn how to better plan and manage group policies. In addition to other management tools, we will discuss **Group Policy Management Console (GPMC)**, a new tool in Windows Server 2003 that can assist you in planning, implementing, and troubleshooting group policies. As you most likely have realized by now, group policy is a powerful security tool that can be an administrative benefit when properly used and administered. It is important to be familiar with and have a working ability to analyze and obtain information on how policy settings are applied. As we discussed in previous chapters, the policy application process can be intricate. When multiple policies are being applied to a computer and to a user, it is important to understand which policy settings will be in effect upon policy processing completion. Although we have discussed methods such as Block Policy Inheritance and No Override to alter the flow of group policies within the Active Directory structure, there are several other methods that can be used to filter policy application. These methods will be discussed in this chapter. In addition to defining policy filtering methods, you will learn how to use various tools to assist you in understanding the final effective policy settings for a user or computer and from which GPO the settings originated. Finally, we will discuss the key points to be considered when planning an effective group policy structure.

FILTERING GROUP POLICY'S SCOPE

By default, group policy settings will apply to all child objects within the domain, site, or OU to which they are linked. In addition, the settings will be inherited down through the Active Directory structure unless policy inheritance has been blocked. Using the Block Policy Inheritance policy setting, you can prevent policy settings from applying to all child objects at the current level and all subordinate levels. Although the Block Policy Inheritance setting is useful in some circumstances, it may be necessary to have a policy apply only when certain conditions exist, or only to a certain group of people. To meet the need of refined control over the application of group policies, there are two additional filtering methods that can be used. They include the following:

- **Permissions** This method uses the Security tab of the GPO to determine user and group account access to the policy.
- **WMI Filters** This method uses filters written in the WMI Query Language (WQL), which is similar to structured query language (SQL).

Each of these methods is discussed further in the next sections.

Group Policy Permissions

Permissions can be defined to refine GPOs to include or exclude the application of settings to certain users, groups, or computers. For example, consider a group policy that prevents users from accessing a command prompt and also prohibits access to Control Panel. When applied to general users, the restrictive nature of the policy may be appropriate. However, when applied to administrators it may hinder the ability to perform job responsibilities such as troubleshooting and making configuration changes. Group policy permissions can be implemented to allow a policy to be applied to some users without applying to others.

As shown in Figure 10-1, the Security tab on a GPO allows you to select who can read or make changes to the policy. By default, the Authenticated Users group has the Read and Apply group policy ACE permissions set to Allow. These two permissions are required for policy settings to take effect on a user or group account. Although administrators have Full Control permissions by default, they, too, are members of the Authenticated Users special identity group. They will be affected by the policy settings applied through the policy. To prevent restrictive policies from applying to administrators or other accounts for which they are not intended, you have two options. These options include the following:

- Remove the Allow setting from both the Read and Apply group policy ACEs for the specific group.
- Set the Apply group policy ACE to Deny.

Setting the Apply group policy ACE to Deny for a specific group can also impact users who are members of more than one group. The Deny setting will supercede any Allow setting that is granted to a user through membership to another group. It is important to make sure you know to which groups the affected users belong.

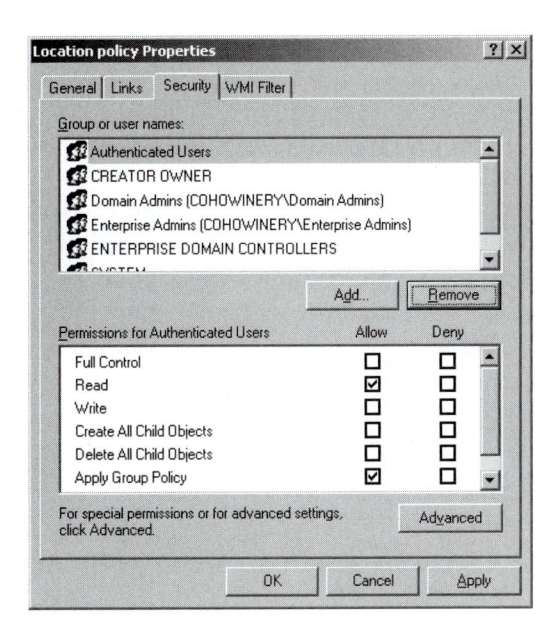

CHAPTER 10: PLANNING A GROUP POLICY MANAGEMENT AND IMPLEMENTATION STRATEGY 253

Figure 10-1 Security tab of a Group Policy Object

▶ **Using Permissions to Filter a GPO**

The following steps outline how to set a GPO's permissions so that the GPO will not be applied to users in the Administrators group.

1. Open the Properties dialog box of the GPO for which you wish to modify the permissions.

2. Select the Security tab from the Properties window. If the Administrators group is not listed in the Group Or User Names window, click Add and type **Administrators** in the Enter Object Names To Select box. Click OK.

3. Make sure that Administrators is selected and click the Deny check box for the Apply group policy permission.

4. Click OK. You will be presented with the dialog box shown in Figure 10-2. Read the dialog box and click Yes to continue.

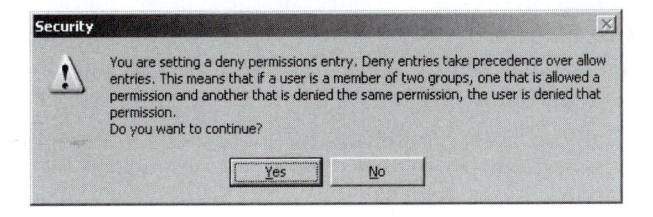

Figure 10-2 Security dialog box displayed when setting Deny on the Apply group policy permission

5. Click OK to close the Properties dialog box for the GPO.

   NOTE *Group Policy Permissions* *It is important to note that group policy permission settings apply to the entire policy. There is no way to set permissions for individual policy settings.*

WMI Filters

Windows Management Instrumentation (WMI) is a component of the Microsoft Windows operating system that provides management information and control in an enterprise environment. It allows administrators to create queries based on hardware, software, operating systems, and services. These queries can be used to either gather data, or, as in the case of GPOs, determine where they will be applied. WMI filters can be used to allow you to control which users or computers will be affected by a GPO based on defined criteria. For example, a WMI filter can be created for a software installation GPO so that only computers that have enough free space on the drive and a fast enough processor to run the application will receive the application. The filter is evaluated at the time the policy is processed. The following list details the key points that should be considered when using WMI filters:

- At least one domain controller running Windows Server 2003 must be present to use WMI filters.
- Filters will only be evaluated on Windows XP Professional or Windows Server 2003 computers. Windows 2000-based computers will ignore WMI filters.
- All filter criteria must have an outcome of true in order for the GPO to be applied. Any criteria with an outcome of false after evaluation will negate the application of the GPO.
- Only one WMI filter can be created per GPO. If multiple requirements are necessary, it is necessary to create multiple GPOs.
- Once created, a WMI filter can be linked to multiple GPOs.

> **NOTE** **Domain Upgrades and WMI Filters** WMI filters can also be used on a Windows 2000 domain where the ADPrep with the /domainprep option has been performed. The /domainprep and /forestprep options will be discussed in further detail in Chapter 12, "Upgrading and Migrating to Windows Server 2003."

Now that you understand the key points regarding the functionality of WMI filters, it is important that you also have examples that illustrate the type of queries that can be performed using WMI filters. Since WMI essentially evaluates data from a destination computer and determines if that data matches the criteria within the filter, administrators can use WMI filters to apply group policies discriminately based on this information. Table 10-1 lists examples of query types that might be useful for determining policy application rules.

Table 10-1 **WMI Filter Examples**

Target Computer	Sample WMI Filter String
All computers that are running Windows XP Professional	`Select * from Win32_OperatingSystem where Caption = "Microsoft Windows XP Professional"`
All computers that have more than 10MB of available drive space on a C: NTFS partition	`Select * from Win32_LogicalDisk WHERE Name= "C:" AND DriveType = 3 AND FreeSpace > 10485760 AND FileSystem = "NTFS"`
All computers that have a modem installed on them	`Select * from Win32_POTSModem Where Name = " MyModem"`

It is important not to overuse WMI filters. As a tool for deploying GPOs to the appropriate users and computers, they are very powerful. However, it is important to consider the performance impact that they will have on the startup and logon processes. WMI filter evaluation creates an additional impact on performance due to the time that it takes to evaluate the criteria. Combining WMI filter evaluation and actual policy application increases the time it takes to deliver a working environment to the user.

WMI filters can be created or modified using either Group Policy Management Console (GPMC) or as illustrated in the next steps. GPMC will be discussed later in this chapter.

▶ **Creating a WMI filter on a GPO**

To create a WMI filter on a GPO, complete the following steps:

1. In the Active Directory Users And Computers console, right-click the domain or organizational unit for which you want to set group policy and a WMI filter. Select Properties.

2. In the Properties dialog box, select the group policy tab. Select or create the policy for which you wish to apply a WMI filter.

3. Click the Properties button in the group policy Properties window and select the WMI Filter tab.

4. Click This Filter and then click the Browse/Manage button.

5. In the Manage WMI Filters dialog box, click the Advanced button.

6. Click New to clear the Filter Name, Description, and Queries fields.

7. Enter a name and a description for the new filter.

8. Enter the desired query information in the Queries section.

9. Click Save and then click OK.

Figure 10-3 shows a completed Manage WMI Filters dialog box.

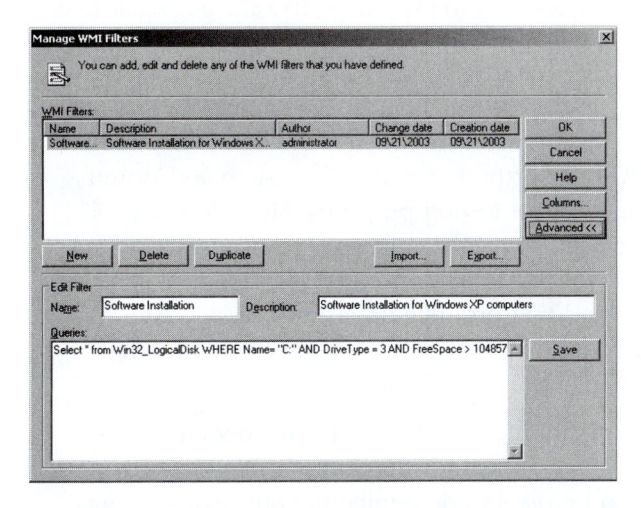

Figure 10-3   Completed Manage WMI Filters dialog box for a GPO

> **MORE INFO**   **WMI Filter Definition**   More information on WMI filter definition can be located on the Microsoft Developer Network (MSDN) Web site at http://msdn.microsoft.com/library/default.asp?url=/library/en-us/wmisdk/wmi/using_wmi.asp.

INTRODUCTION TO GROUP POLICY MANAGEMENT CONSOLE (GPMC)

Group Policy Management Console (GPMC) is a new tool available for managing Windows Server 2003 and Windows 2000 Active Directory domains. GPMC provides a single access point to all aspects of group policy that are spread across other tools such as Active Directory Users And Computers, Active Directory Sites And Services, Resultant Set Of Policy (RSoP), and Group Policy Object Editor. GPMC runs on any Windows Server 2003 or Windows XP Professional with Service Pack 1 (SP1).

This simplified user interface allows administrators to have a single point of administration for creating and modifying group policies, in addition to the following:

- Importing and copying GPO settings to and from the file system. This functionality works within a domain, across domains, or across forests. The Import Settings feature allows settings to be brought from a file system GPO into an existing GPO. The copy feature allows you to copy settings from an existing GPO to a new GPO. Links to the GPO are not modified during an import or copy operation. Table 10-2 details the differences between Import and Copy within GPMC.

Table 10-2 **GPMC Copy versus Import Operation**

Copy	Import
Source: An existing GPO within Active Directory.	Source: Any GPO that was backed up and stored in the file system.
Destination: Creates a new GPO in Active Directory. This new GPO will have a unique GUID.	Destination: Erases the existing settings of an existing GPO in Active Directory.
ACL: Can use the default ACL for new GPOs or copy the ACL from the source GPO.	ACL: Not modified in the destination GPO.
Required Permissions: The right to create GPOs in the target location in addition to Read access to the source GPO is required.	Required Permissions: Read permission to the source GPO and edit rights to the destination GPO.

- Backup and restoration of GPOs is available in GPMC. The Backup feature of GPMC allows a GPO to be exported to the file system and stored for disaster recovery purposes or for testing purposes. Multiple versions of the same GPO can be backed up to the same file system directory. The Restore feature allows a specific GPO to be restored to a prior state. If multiple settings are modified that produce undesirable results, the Restore feature provides a contingency solution. It restores all attributes, settings, ACLs, GUIDs, and links to any WMI filters.

- RSoP functionality integration that includes Group Policy Modeling and Group Policy Results. RSoP is a query engine that looks at GPOs and then reports on its findings. It can be used to determine the effective settings of a user or a computer based on the combination of the local, site, domain, domain controller, and OU policies. RSoP was originally created as a separate MMC snap-in. The two modes, planning and logging, are renamed in GPMC to Group Policy Modeling and Group Policy Results. We will discuss RSoP in further detail later in this chapter.

- Hypertext Markup Language (HTML) reports that allow read-only views of GPO settings and Resultant Set Of Policy (RSoP) information. This information is easily acquired and easy to save or print for documentation or analysis purposes.

- Searching for GPOs based on name, permissions, WMI filter, GUID, or policy extensions set in the GPOs.

- Scripting capabilities for all tasks that are part of the GPMC tool except scripting for individual GPO settings. There are over 30 sample scripts available when GPMC is installed. The sample scripts are installed in the \Program Files\GPMC\Scripts folder on the computer where the GPMC tool is installed.

Installing GPMC

GPMC is available for download at *http://www.microsoft.com/downloads*. Entering a search for *GPMC* will yield appropriate results to locate the gpmc.msi file. Once downloaded, it can be deployed using group policy if desired, or installed directly. Upon installation, the management of group policy will change noticeably to reflect the new tool. For example, the group policy tab for the Properties of a site, domain, or OU will appear as shown in Figure 10-4 with a notification to the existence of Group Policy Management and a button to launch the new tool.

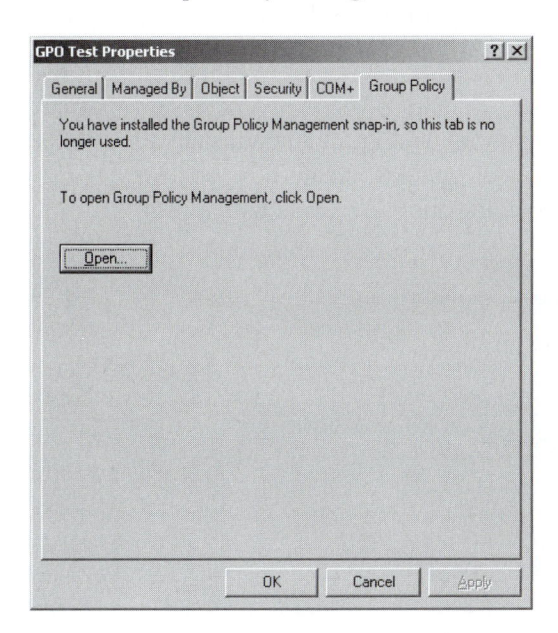

Figure 10-4 Group policy tab of an OU after the installation of GPMC

In addition to the primary capabilities listed previously and the new management interface, GPMC provides a simplified method of delegating the management of GPOs. We will discuss delegation of GPOs in addition to the remaining GPO topics within the context of this new management tool.

Navigating with Group Policy Management

Group Policy Management can be accessed by attempting to use the group policy tab on a site, domain, or OU using the Open button as shown in Figure 10-4, or it can be located in the Administrative Tools folder of the Start menu.

Figure 10-5 illustrates the default view of Group Policy Management when it is launched from the Administrative Tools folder.

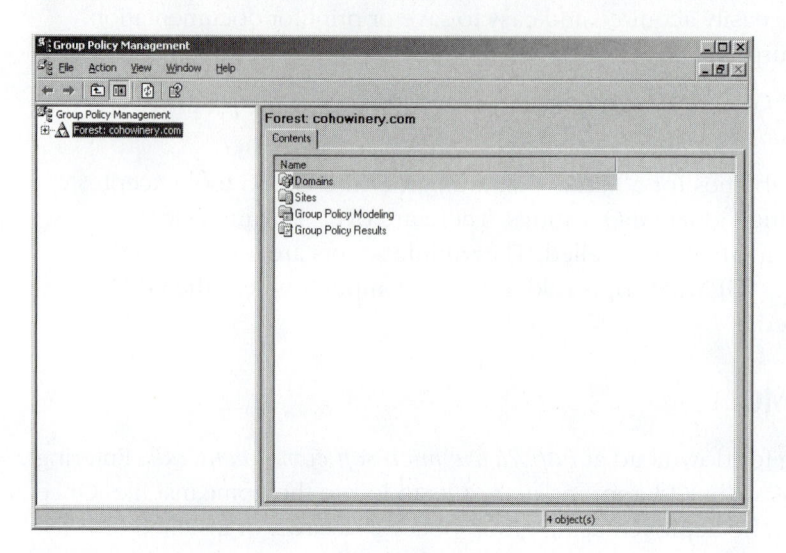

Figure 10-5 Group Policy Management window

Expanding the Forest node in the left console pane will allow you to see the subnodes, which include: Domains, Sites, Group Policy Modeling, and Group Policy Results. When you expand the node that refers to a specific site, domain, or OU, you will see three main tabs in the right console pane. These tabs are as follows:

- **Linked Group Policy Objects** As shown in Figure 10-6, this tab allows an administrator to change the order of policies, create new policies, edit existing policies, create policy links, and view and change the enabled status.

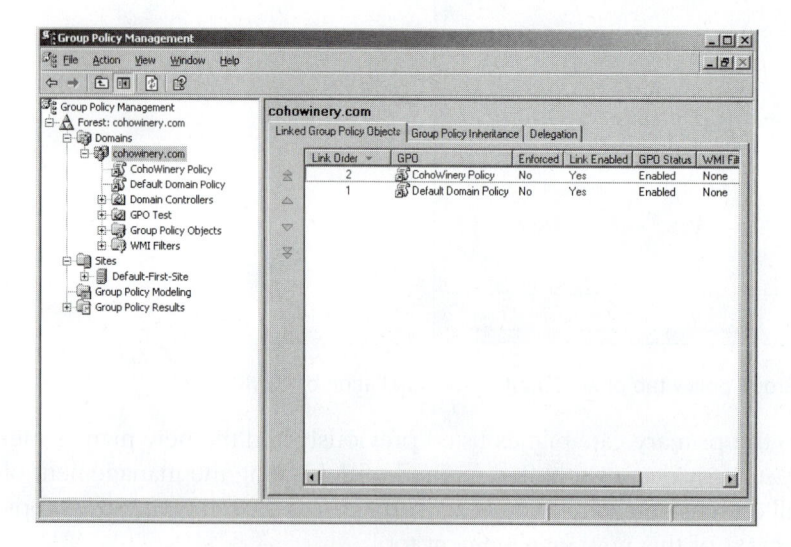

Figure 10-6 Group Policy Management Linked Group Policy Objects tab

- **Group Policy Inheritance** As shown in Figure 10-7, this tab shows the order of precedence for the policies set on this container.

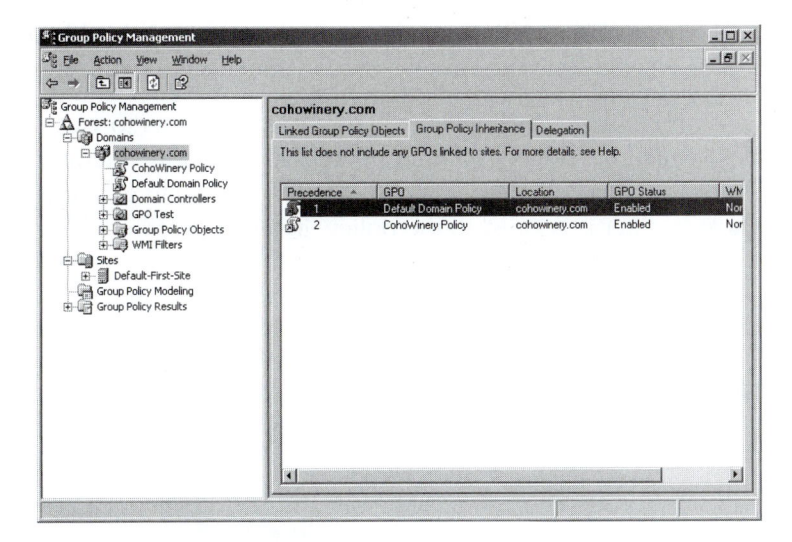

CHAPTER 10: PLANNING A GROUP POLICY MANAGEMENT AND IMPLEMENTATION STRATEGY

Figure 10-7 Group Policy Management Group Policy Inheritance tab

- **Delegation** This tab shows which groups and users have permission to link, perform modeling analyses, or read group policy results information. Modeling is the same as planning mode using RSoP. Reading results data is the same as logging mode using RSoP. RSoP will be discussed later in this chapter. Also located on this tab is an Advanced button that allows administrators to have access to the group policy's Security tab that was available from the Properties window of the group policy prior to installation of GPMC. Figure 10-8 shows the Delegation tab discussed here.

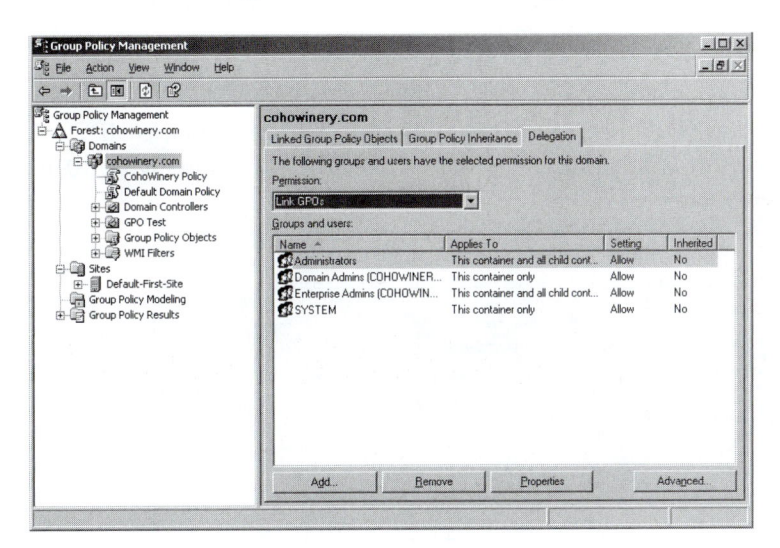

Figure 10-8 Group Policy Management Delegation tab

Managing a Specific GPO

As illustrated previously, Group Policy Management allows administrators to create and modify policies from the container on which they are linked. Additionally, all aspects of each individual policy, including the scope of its application, filtering methods, enabled or disabled status, effective settings, and delegation of application and management, can be managed using Group Policy Management. The tabbed display interface is a logically organized method that is easy to navigate and make changes from. The following list explains and illustrates the features available on each tab when a GPO is selected in the Group Policy Management interface.

- **Scope** As shown in Figure 10-9, this tab allows administrators to view the locations to which the policy is linked. In addition, security filtering using permissions and WMI are also available for viewing, editing, or creating. When a WMI filter is applied to the policy, it will appear in the list with an Open button that will allow modification of the filter. If a WMI filter is not applied to the policy, the button will allow a new one to be created or linked to the GPO.

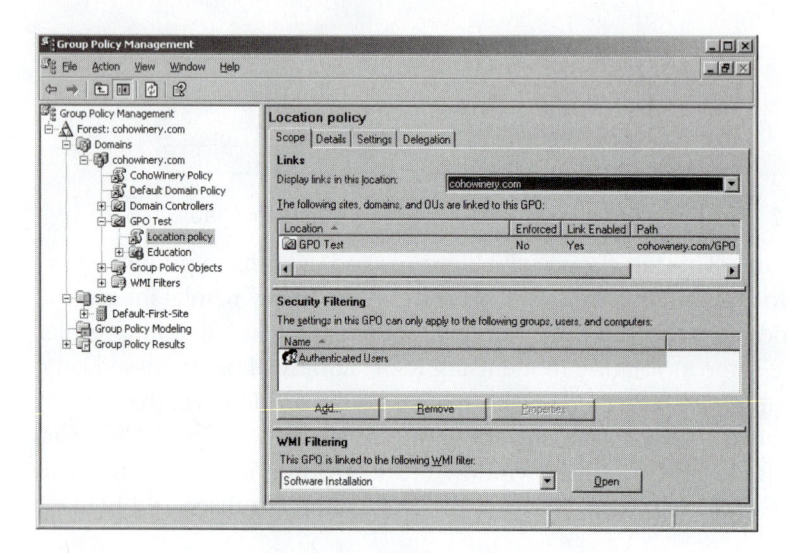

Figure 10-9 Group Policy Management GPO Scope tab

- **Details** This tab allows the GPO to be either enabled or disabled. In addition, it displays read-only information that includes the owner, GUID, creation date, and last modification date. This tab is shown in Figure 10-10.

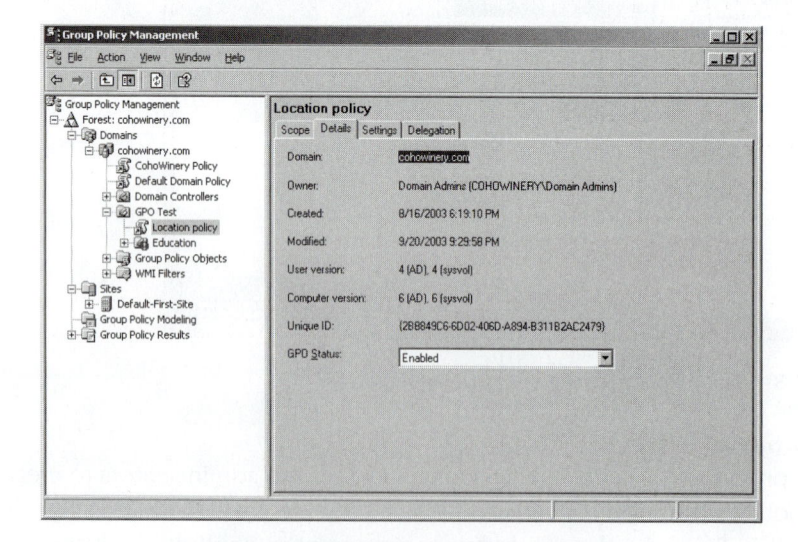

Figure 10-10 Group Policy Management GPO Details tab

- **Settings** As shown in Figure 10-11, when this tab is activated, an HTML report is generated that allows administrators to view settings areas within the GPO that have values other than the original default values. Links on the right side of the report allow detailed information to be displayed or hidden. Right-clicking within this view allows administrators to print or save the report.

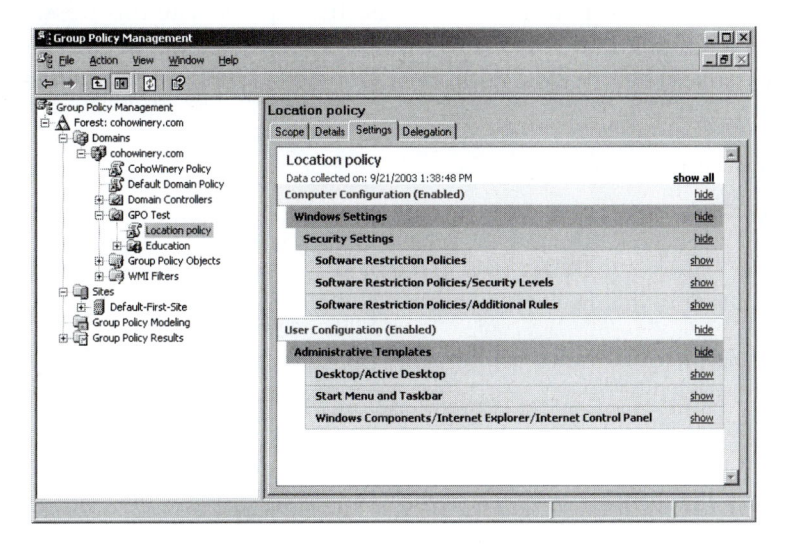

Figure 10-11 Group Policy Management GPO Settings tab

- **Delegation** Figure 10-12, like the previously discussed Delegation tab for a container object, lists the users and groups that have access to this GPO and the permissions that apply to them. The Advanced button allows access to the Security tab that was present on a GPO prior to the installation of GPMC.

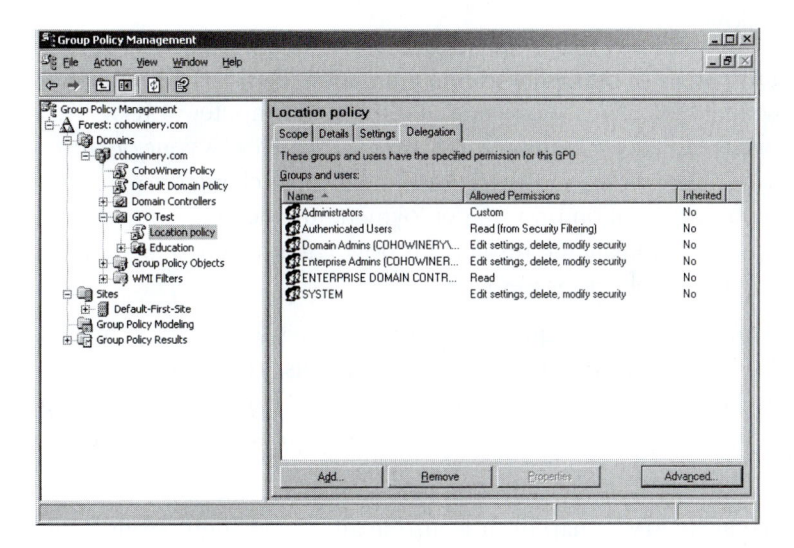

Figure 10-12 Group Policy Management GPO Delegation tab

To practice navigating policies using GPMC, do Exercise 10-1 now.

Now that you have a clearer picture of the Group Policy Management tool and its interface, we will discuss several policy management techniques and how to accomplish them using this new tool.

Determining and Troubleshooting Effective Policy Settings

Resultant Set Of Policies (RSoP) is the sum of the policies applied to a user or computer after all filters, security group permissions, and inheritance settings such as Block Policy Inheritance and No Override. As the application of group policies gets more complex within your Active Directory structure, it can become difficult to know what the final policy settings will be when all processing is complete. In addition, it may be difficult to trace the origin of a particular outcome due to policy inheritance, policy links, and permission settings. To help alleviate this possibly daunting task of determining where policy settings came from and what the results of all cumulative policies will be, Microsoft provides several tools. They include the following:

- Resultant Set Of Policy Wizard
- Group Policy Results and Group Policy Modeling components of Group Policy Management
- GPResult command line tool

Each of these tools provides value in assisting with policy planning and troubleshooting. However, each has a different level of functionality. We will discuss these tools in the next sections.

Resultant Set Of Policy Wizard

The Resultant Set Of Policy Wizard is provided in Windows Server 2003 to assist administrators in determining the effects of policies on users and computers. In addition to assisting in debugging and reporting on existing policies, RSoP allows administrators to simulate policy effects prior to implementing them on the production network.

There are two modes within RSoP that allow the previous functionality. These modes are as follows:

- **Planning mode**   This mode allows administrators to simulate the effect of policy settings prior to implementing them on a computer or user. This mode is beneficial when planning for growth or changes to your organization. You can use planning mode to test the effects of changes to group policy on your organization prior to deployment. In addition, you can use planning mode to simulate the results of a slow link on a GPO in addition to simulating the loopback process.
- **Logging mode**   This mode queries existing policies in the hierarchy that are linked to sites, domains, and organizational units. This mode is useful for documenting and understanding how combined policies are affecting users and computers. The results are returned in an MMC window that can be saved for later reference.

RSoP is available as an MMC snap-in. It is also available through Group Policy Management. In Group Policy Management, the functionalities of planning and logging are renamed respectively to Group Policy Modeling and Group Policy Results. We will learn each method of obtaining RSoP information beginning with the Resultant Set Of Policy MMC snap-in.

As shown in Figure 10-13, in the Resultant Set Of Policy snap-in you must generate data that will serve your query needs. Using the Action menu to generate the data, as suggested in Figure 10-13, will launch the RSoP Wizard. The RSoP Wizard will allow you to specify the extent of your query after determining the mode.

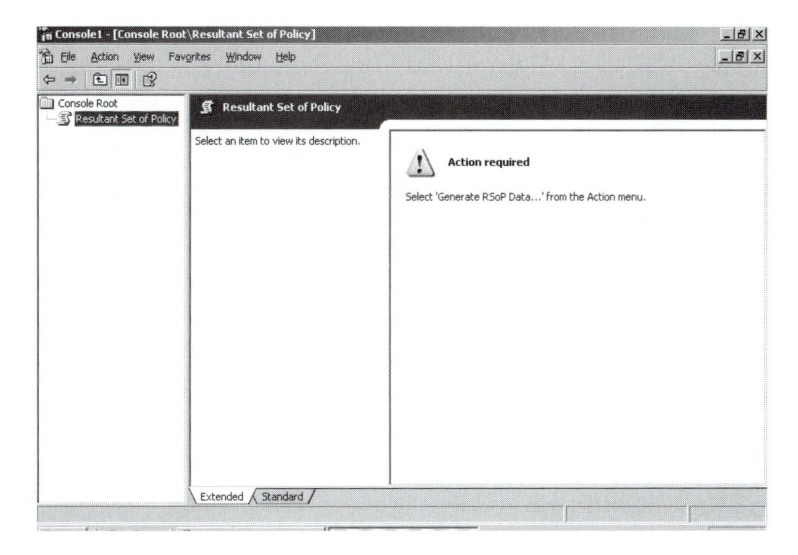

Figure 10-13 RSoP MMC initial window

RSoP uses information that is part of the **Common Information Management Object Model (CIMOM)** database. The CIMOM database is used through WMI and contains information that is gathered when a computer starts and becomes part of the network. This information includes hardware, Group Policy Software Installation Settings, Internet Explorer Maintenance settings, Scripts, Folder Redirection settings, and Security settings. When RSoP is started in either planning or logging mode, information in the CIMOM database is used to assist in producing the desired reports.

▶ **Creating an RSoP Planning Mode Report**

To create an RSoP Planning mode report, complete the following steps:

1. Open a Command Prompt window and type **mmc**. From the File menu select Add/Remove Snap-in and click the Add button.

2. Select the Resultant Set Of Policy snap-in from the Add Standalone Snap-in windows, click Add, and then click Close.

3. Click OK to finish creating the new console window.

4. In the left console pane, select Resultant Set Of Policy.

5. From the Action menu, select Generate RSoP Data to launch the RSoP Wizard. Click Next.

6. In the Mode selection page, select Planning Mode and click Next to continue.

7. In the User And Computer Selection page, complete the appropriate fields to select the user or computer for which you wish to simulate policy settings. Click Next to proceed.

8. In the Advanced Simulation Options page, you may choose to simulate your policy with additional conditions such as slow links and loopback processing. The settings in this window are optional. The Loopback processing option is only available if you chose to simulate settings for a user and computer. Click Next to continue.

9. On the User Security Groups page, you can choose to simulate the effect that changing the user's security group memberships would have. The settings on this page are optional. Click Next to continue.

10. On the Computer Security Groups page, you can simulate changes to the computer's security groups. The settings on this page are optional. Click Next to continue.

11. On the WMI Filters For Users page, select any filters that you would like to include in your simulation. The page settings here are optional. Click Next to continue.

12. On the WMI Filters For Computers page, select any filters that you would like to include in your simulation. The page settings here are optional. Click Next to continue.

13. On the Summary Of Selections page, review your simulation query information, change the domain controller on which you wish to process the simulation if necessary, and click Next to generate the report.

14. Click Finish to close the wizard.

15. The results of your query will be displayed in an MMC window that looks similar to a Group Policy Object Editor window. The MMC can be saved with the results of the query.

▶ **Creating an RSoP Logging Mode Report**

To create an RSoP Logging mode report, complete the following steps:

1. Open a Command Prompt window and type **mmc**. From the File menu, select Add/Remove Snap-in and click the Add button.

2. Select the Resultant Set Of Policy snap-in from the Add Standalone Snap-in windows, click Add, and then click Close.

3. Click OK to finish creating the new console window.

4. In the left console pane, select Resultant Set Of Policy.

5. From the Action menu, select Generate RSoP Data to launch the RSoP Wizard. Click Next.

6. From the Mode Selection page, select Logging Mode and click Next to continue.

7. On the Computer Selection page, you can either select This Computer or select Another Computer and type the name of the computer. If you are not sure of the computer name, you can click Browse to find the computer for which you wish to perform the query. The other option on this page is to click the check box for Do Not Display Policy Settings For The Selected Computer In The Results Display. This will eliminate the computer policy settings from the results window. Click Next to continue.

8. On the User Selection page, select the appropriate bullet for the user for which you wish to display query results. If you chose a computer in step 7 and wish to not have user policy settings displayed in the final results, you can click the check box for Do Not Display User Policy Settings In The Results. Click Next to continue.

9. On the Summary Of Selections page, verify your desired query information, click the check box to show error information, and click Next to begin the analysis. Click Finish to close the wizard.

10. The MMC window will display the results of your policy results request. You can save the MMC window for future access if desired.

> **NOTE** **Required Permissions to Perform an RSoP Query** To create an RSoP query for an existing computer or user, you must be logged on to the local computer as a user, be a member of the local Administrators, Domain Administrators, or Enterprise Administrator group, or have permission to generate an RSoP for the domain or OU in which the user and computer accounts are contained. If the RSoP query includes site GPOs that cross domain boundaries in the same forest, you must be logged on as an Enterprise Administrator.

The results that are displayed for the RSoP query look very similar to the information available when editing or creating a GPO using Group Policy Object Editor. However, only the settings that have been altered from the default will appear. Changes to a policy will not be reflected unless the RSoP query is run again after a GPO has been refreshed by a computer restart, user logon, or through the use of gpupdate.exe.

Using Group Policy Results and Group Policy Modeling

In effect, the same information that is gathered and reported using the Resultant Set Of Policy snap-in can be gathered and reported using the Group Policy Management utility. In fact, it is even simpler to use the Group Policy Management utility to obtain information than to use the Resultant Set Of Policy snap-in. Individual settings that affect the user are easy to find, and multiple queries can be created and stored within one interface. In order to view query results using the RSoP MMC snap-in, it is necessary to save each individual console window. You must run multiple instances of the RSoP MMC snap-in in order to compare results. Using the Group Policy Management tool, you can have multiple queries available within the same interface for comparison purposes. In addition, the interface allows administrators to save the reports for future reference and print them directly from the HTML window pane. This section will demonstrate how to use the Group Policy Modeling and Group Policy Results features of Group Policy Management to obtain RSoP information.

Group Policy Modeling

Group Policy Modeling, referred to as *Planning mode* using the Resultant Set Of Policy snap-in, is used to simulate the effect of a policy on the user environment.

▶ **Creating a Query Using Group Policy Management**

To create a query, complete the following steps using Group Policy Management:

1. From the Administrative Tools folder on the Start menu, open Group Policy Management and browse to the forest or domain in which you want to create a Group Policy Modeling query.

2. Right-click Group Policy Modeling and then click Group Policy Modeling Wizard.

266 CHAPTER 10: PLANNING A GROUP POLICY MANAGEMENT AND IMPLEMENTATION STRATEGY

3. On the Welcome To The Group Policy Modeling Wizard page, click Next.

4. Complete the remaining pages filling in the information that will build the appropriate simulation criteria. These remaining pages are the same as you completed using the Resultant Set Of Policy MMC in Planning mode.

The report that is generated contains three tabs to organize and display important information about the query. These tabs are explained and illustrated next.

- **Summary tab** This tab in the newly created Group Policy Modeling query report will show a summary of information collected during the simulation process. Figure 10-14 shows an example of a Summary report.

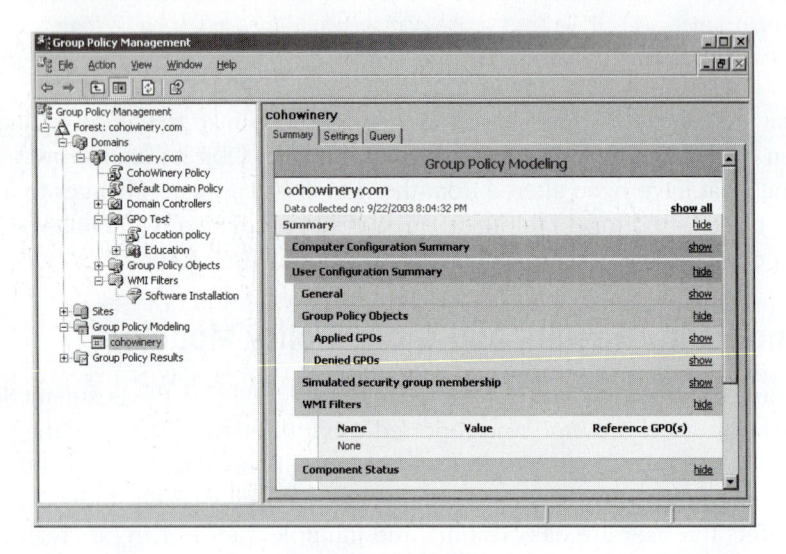

Figure 10-14 Group Policy Modeling Summary tab

- **Settings tab** Figure 10-15 illustrates the Settings tab that is available in the query report window. This tab provides comprehensive information that includes individual policy settings areas and the effects each would have in a live deployment. Using the Show All link in the top right corner of the display will expand the contents of the report. This report can be printed or saved by right-clicking in the display window area and selecting the desired outcome.

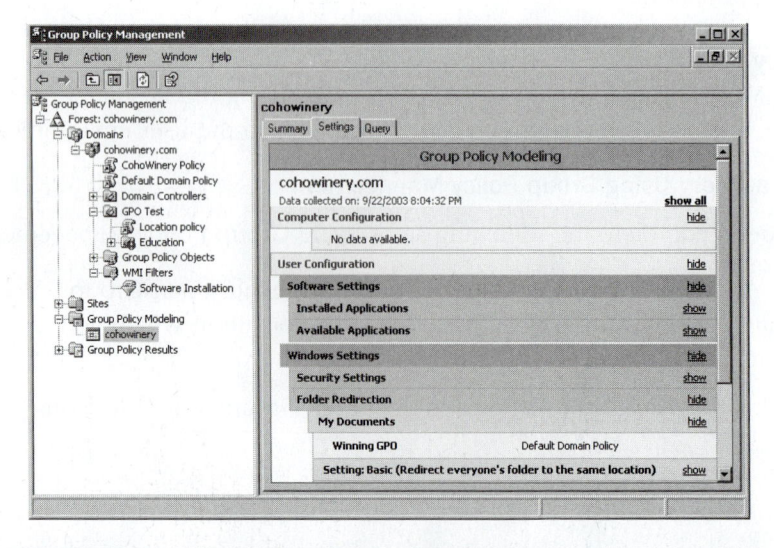

Figure 10-15 Group Policy Modeling Settings tab

CHAPTER 10: PLANNING A GROUP POLICY MANAGEMENT AND IMPLEMENTATION STRATEGY

- **Query tab** The Query tab shown in Figure 10-16 shows the criteria from which the modeling query was performed. This information can be helpful when comparing multiple modeling scenarios during the planning phase of your group policy structure.

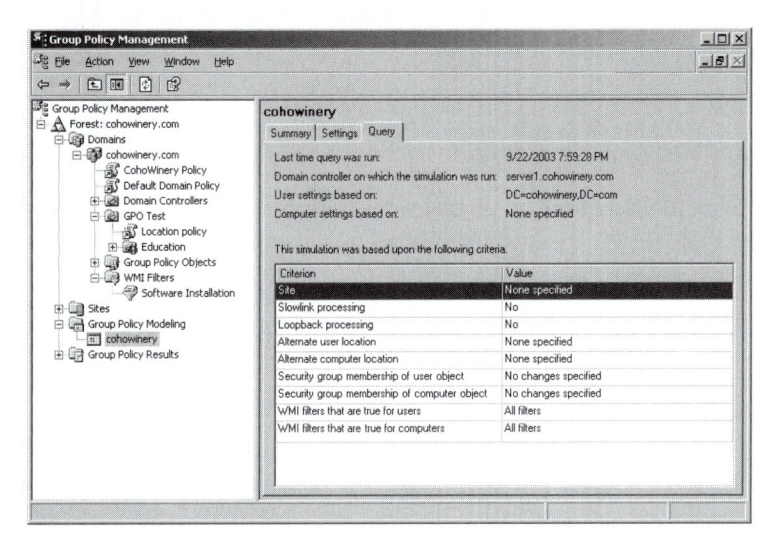

Figure 10-16 Group Policy Modeling Query tab

▶ **Viewing Query Report Information**

After creating a query report and viewing the initial information in the tabs, you can display details regarding the specific RSoP settings that would take place if the policy were implemented. To view this information, complete the following steps:

1. From the Administrative Tools folder on the Start Menu, open Group Policy Management and browse to the forest or domain from which you want to view query results.

2. Open the Group Policy Modeling node. Right-click on the query you wish to view and click on Advanced View. As shown in Figure 10-17, the Resultant Set Of Policy window is opened and individual settings that will affect the user or computer that was part of the modeling criteria will be available. Only settings that have been modified beyond the original policy results will be displayed here.

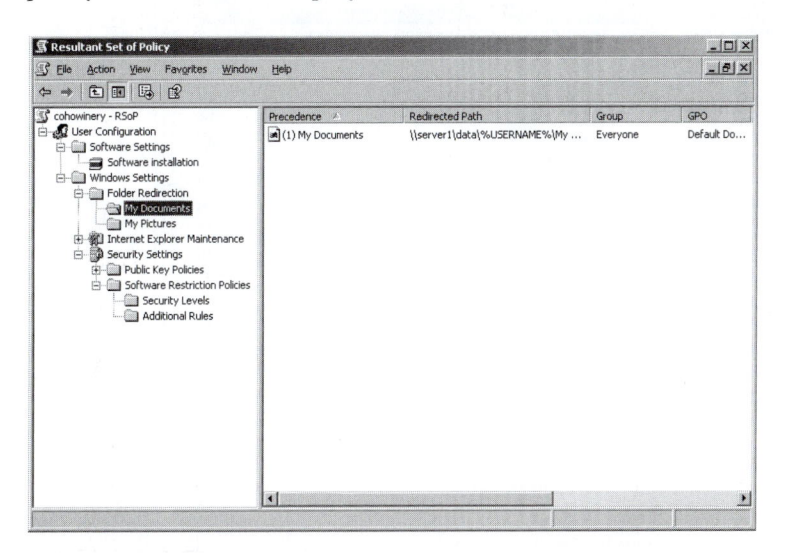

Figure 10-17 Group Policy Modeling Advanced View Resultant Set Of Policy window

Group Policy Results

The Group Policy Results feature in Group Policy Management is equivalent to Logging mode within the RSoP MMC snap-in. Rather than simulating policy effects like the Group Policy Modeling Wizard, Group Policy Results obtains RSoP information from the client computer to show the actual effects that policies have on the client computer and user environment.

▶ **Creating a Group Policy Results Query**

To create a Group Policy Results query, complete the following steps:

1. In Group Policy Management, navigate to and right-click Group Policy Results. Select Group Policy Results Wizard. On the Welcome To Group Policy Results Wizard page, click Next.

2. On the Computer Selection page, select the current computer or click Browse to select another computer. Click Next to continue.

3. On the User Selection page, select the current user or specify another user for which you wish to obtain policy results and click Next.

4. On the Summary Of Selections page, verify your criteria and click Next.

5. Click Finish to close the Completing The Group Policy Results Wizard page.

6. As was true with the Group Policy Modeling Wizard, the report that is generated based on the Group Policy Results criteria includes three tabs. These tabs are explained and illustrated next.

- **Summary tab**   As shown in Figure 10-18, the Summary tab gives an overall summary of the applied policy settings. Note the highlighted triangle with the exclamation point on it. This indicates that some part of the policy processing did not take place. Expanding the link associated with this policy setting provides details and explanations for what happened during processing. Figure 10-19 shows an example of an expanded policy area that was emphasized with the yellow warning triangle.

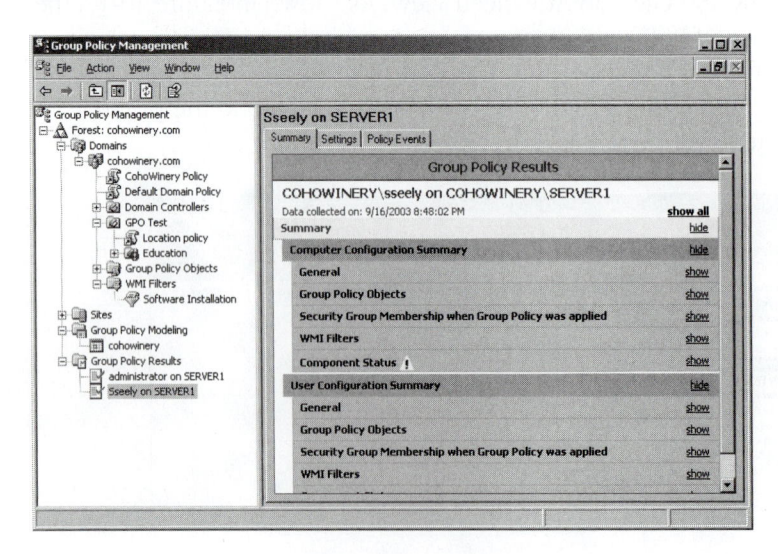

Figure 10-18   Group Policy Results Summary tab

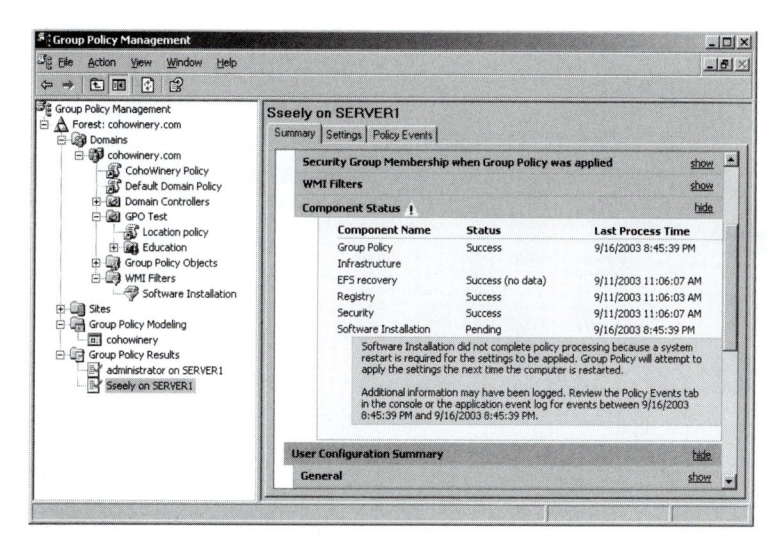

CHAPTER 10: PLANNING A GROUP POLICY MANAGEMENT AND IMPLEMENTATION STRATEGY 269

Figure 10-19 Group Policy Results Summary tab with expanded warning triangle

- **Settings tab** Figure 10-20 illustrates the Settings tab that is available in the query report window. This tab provides comprehensive information that includes individual policy settings areas and their resulting effects. Using the Show All link in the top right corner of the display will expand the contents of the report. This report can be printed or saved by right-clicking in the display window area and selecting the desired outcome.

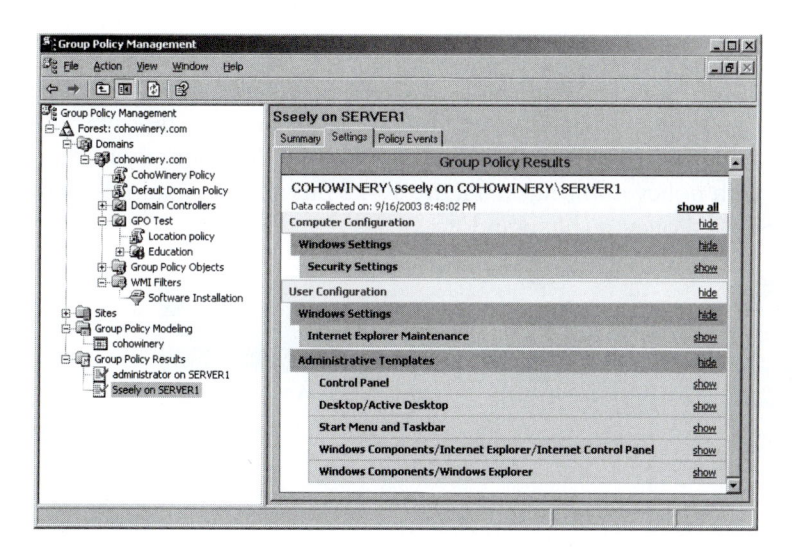

Figure 10-20 Group Policy Results Settings tab

- **Policy Events tab** Shown in Figure 10-21, this tab collects all policy-related events and stores them in one convenient location. The information provided here can be extremely valuable in troubleshooting policy application and consolidating group policy events that are directly related to the queried objects. Double-clicking on any item on this tab will open and display the Event Properties window providing additional information.

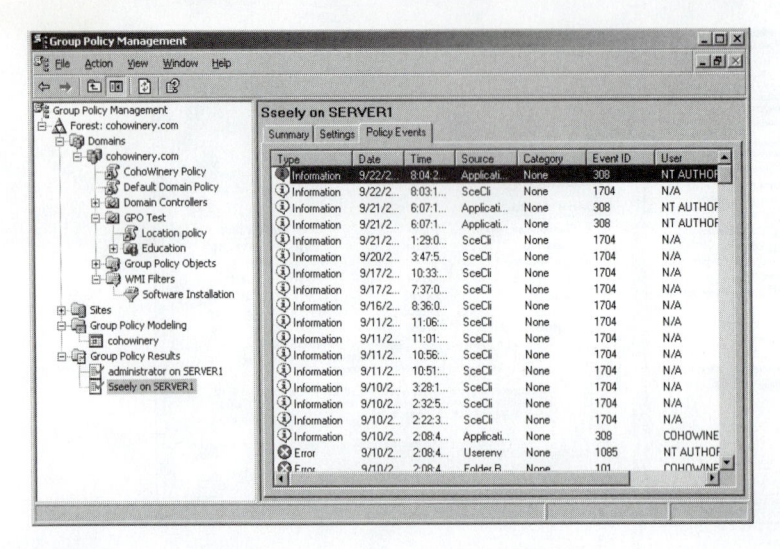

Figure 10-21 Group Policy Results Policy Events tab

In addition to having all of the previously discussed tabs available, the individual policy settings can be seen in the Resultant Set Of Policy results window.

▶ **Opening the Resultant Set Of Policy Results Window**

To open the Resultant Set Of Policy results window, complete the following steps:

1. Open Group Policy Management and browse to locate the Group Policy Results query you wish to view. Right-click the desired query.

2. Click Advanced View. The Resultant Set Of Policy results window will display and you can navigate through the applied settings. The same yellow warning triangle will appear on the parent node where there was a problem with policy application. Figure 10-22 provides an example of a Resultant Set Of Policy results window.

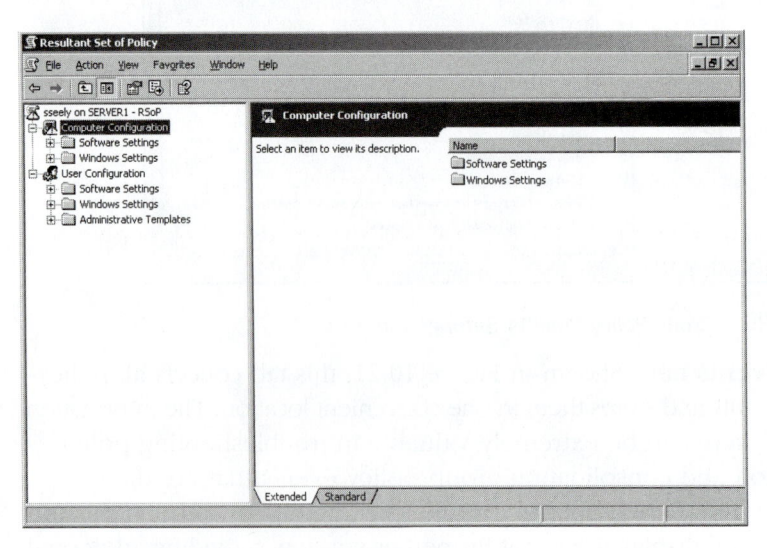

Figure 10-22 Resultant Set Of Policy for Group Policy Results query

▶ Getting More Information About an Error

You can obtain additional information on an error by completing the following steps:

1. Right-click the node with the yellow warning triangle displayed and click Properties.

2. Click the Error Information tab. Figure 10-23 shows the output of this tab. Note that the error information is similar to what was shown on the Summary tab of the original report.

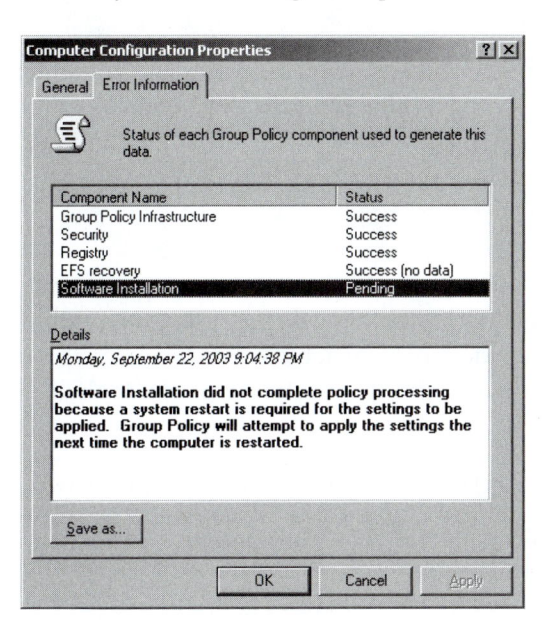

Figure 10-23 Error Information tab from Resultant Set Of Policy node with warning triangle

Using GPResult

Although not quite as easy to read as the Group Policy Results information that can be obtained using GPMC, **GPResult** is a command line tool that allows you to create and display an RSoP query from the command line. It provides comprehensive information about the operating system, the user, and the computer. Information included in a GPResult query includes the following:

- The last time a group policy was applied and the domain controller responsible for its application
- A complete list of applied GPOs
- Applied registry settings
- Redirected folders
- Information on assigned and published applications
- Disk quota information
- IP security settings
- Scripts

GPResult uses syntax to obtain information from the previous list that is similar to the syntax of other command line utilities. This syntax consists of the command followed by switches that enable flexibility in defining the output. The following examples list the syntax necessary to obtain a variety of RSoP information outputs for the user Sseely.

To obtain RSoP information on computer and user policies that will affect Sseely, type the following command from a command line:

```
gpresult /user sseely
```

To narrow the results of the previous command to include only the computer policy information that will affect Sseely, modify the previous command string to include the /scope option. The following example illustrates the required command to do this:

```
gpresult /user sseely /scope computer
```

If you are logged on with a standard user account, you need to supply administrative credentials in order to allow GPResult to function. The following example modifies the command string to include the /u switch to specify a user account with administrative privileges. In addition, the /p switch is used to supply the password for the user account.

```
gpresult /u cohowinery.com/Admin01 /p MSPr3ss#1 /user sseely /scope computer
```

To practice using GPResult, do Exercise 10-2 now.

Although not quite as broad in its capabilities, GPResult provides a valuable method of obtaining information efficiently.

Delegating Group Policy Administrative Control

Like other administrative tasks, you might find it helpful to delegate the ability to manage GPOs to other administrators within your organization. The concept of control delegation is not much different from delegating control of an OU. Using GPMC, you can delegate individual group policy tasks such as creating, linking, and editing a GPO. Prior to the availability of GPMC, it was necessary to have a solid understanding of the individual permissions that were required to perform tasks. GPMC is an interface that simplifies the delegation of specific GPO management tasks by providing the administrator with a task-based delegation method rather than the cumbersome permissions-based method that required a deep knowledge of low-level permissions. group policy delegation includes tasks such as:

- Creation of GPOs
- Permissions on GPOs
- Linking of GPOs to Active Directory sites, domains, domain controllers, or OUs
- Use of Group Policy Modeling and Group Policy Results
- Creation of WMI filters
- WMI permissions

In the next sections, you will learn how to use GPMC to delegate the previously listed administrative tasks.

Delegating GPO Creation

The Group Policy Creator Owners group by default has the permission to create new GPOs. This can be delegated to other groups and users by either adding those groups or users to the Group Policy Creator Owner group, or by using GPMC to explicitly grant the group or user permission to create a GPO. As shown in Figure 10-24, the Delegation tab located under the Group Policy Objects extension in GPMC shows groups that have permission to create GPOs. You have the ability from this tab to add new users or groups to the list of those able to create new GPOs. In addition, you can use the Properties button to modify the membership list of groups that already have delegation permissions.

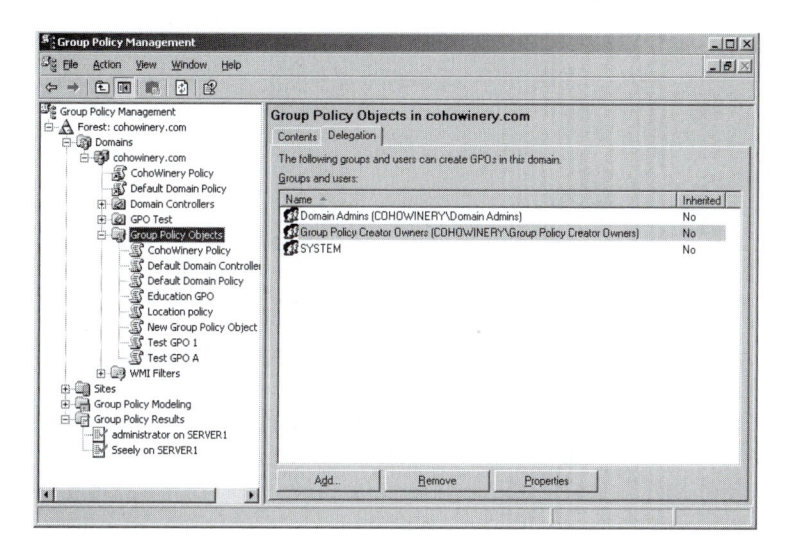

Figure 10-24   Group Policy Objects extension of Group Policy Management

Delegating Permissions to an Individual GPO

Before GPMC was created, administrators had to be aware of the individual permissions and the required combinations to allow delegation of individual GPO permissions. GPMC combines individual permissions that are required to perform specific GPO tasks into categories. These categories and the combined permissions that are implied by them are detailed in Table 10-3.

Table 10-3   GPMC Individual GPO Permissions

Allowed Permissions Category	Underlying Permissions and Effects
Read	Allows Read Access on the GPO
Edit settings	Includes Read, Write, Create Child Objects, and Delete Child Objects
Edit, delete, and modify security	Includes Read, Write, Create Child Objects, Delete Child Objects, Delete, Modify Permissions, and Modify Owner. Implies Full Control without the Apply group policy permission being set.
Read (from Security Filtering)	An automatic setting that appears when a user has Read and Apply group policy permission to the GPO.
Custom	These permissions include those set individually using the ACL editor for the GPO. The ACL editor is invoked by using the Advanced button and shows the Security tab contents for the GPO.

To delegate individual GPO permissions, use the Delegation tab after selecting a specific GPO in Group Policy Management. This tab is shown in Figure 10-25.

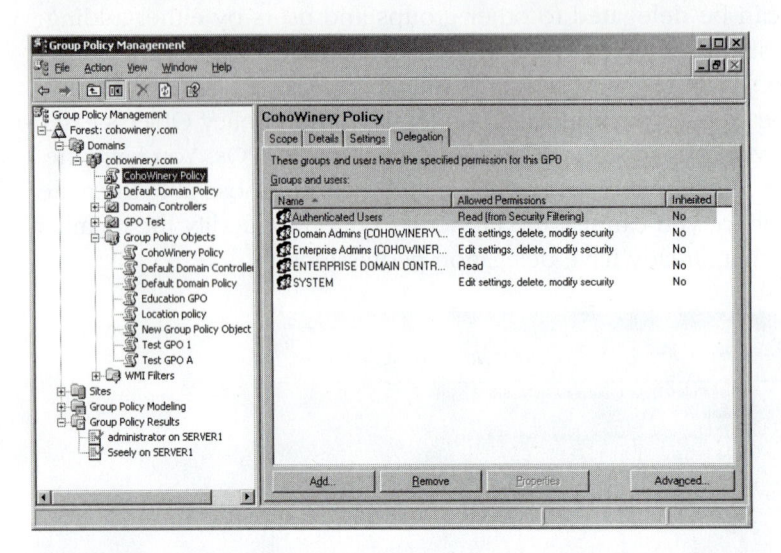

Figure 10-25　Delegation tab on a specific group policy

Delegating Linking, Group Policy Modeling, and Group Policy Results

The ability to link GPOs to sites, domains, domain controllers, and OUs, in addition to using Group Policy Modeling and Group Policy Results within GPMC, are available on the Delegation tab of the specific container for which you want to use them. As shown in Figure 10-26, the Delegation tab contains a drop-down box that allows you to select the permission that you wish to view or modify. For example, if you wish to delegate the ability to use the Group Policy Modeling feature to a sub-administrator, you can select the Perform Group Policy Modeling Analyses option from the Permission drop-down box. The contents of the Groups And Users window will change to reflect the permissions for this task. Using the Add button allows you to add users and groups to the list. Using the Advanced button allows you to view the security settings for the affected container.

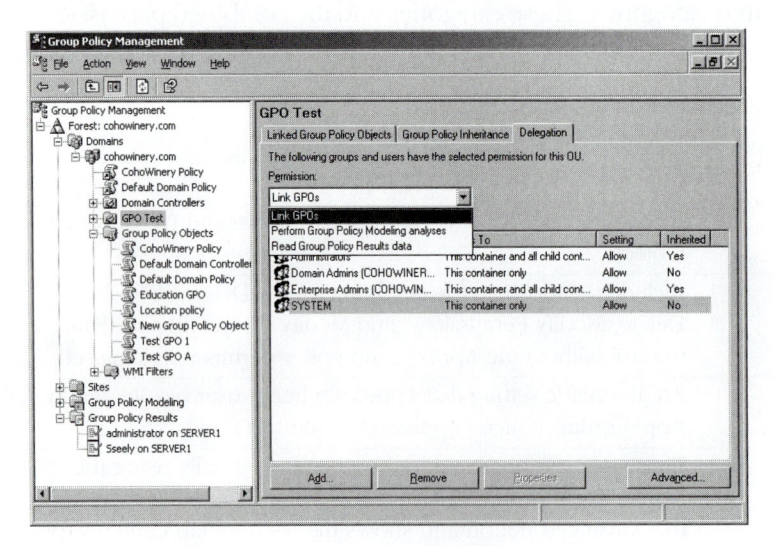

Figure 10-26　Delegation tab on a specific container

Delegating WMI Filter Creation

Permissions to create WMI filters can only be granted to Domain Admins. Permissions can be delegated using the Delegation tab of the WMI Filters setting located subordinate to the domain node in GPMC as shown in Figure 10-27. The two levels of permissions that can be delegated include the following:

- **Creator Owner**   This permission allows administrators to create a new WMI filter and modify only filters that they own. Administrators given this permission cannot modify WMI filters created by other administrators. By default, Group Policy Creator Owners have the Creator Owner permissions.

- **Full Control**   This permission grants the administrator all capabilities for all filters in the domain, regardless of who created them. By default, Domain Admins and Enterprise Admins have Full Control.

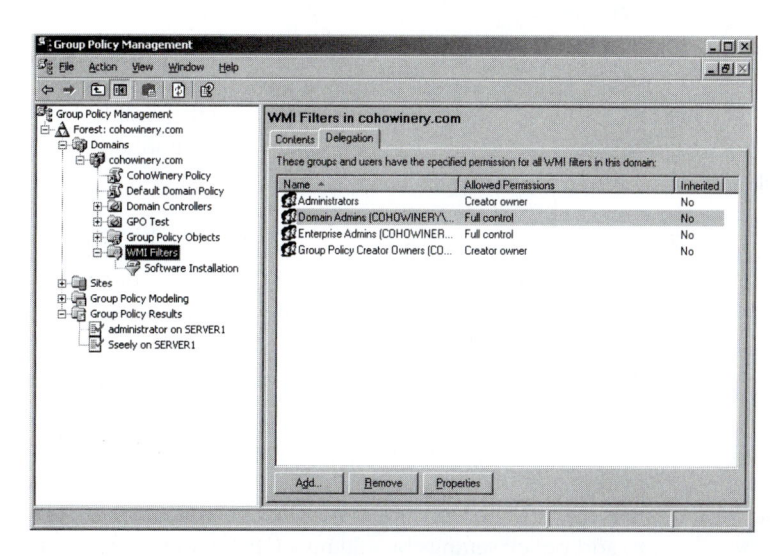

Figure 10-27   Delegation tab for the WMI Filters extension of Group Policy Management

In addition to delegating control over all WMI filters for a domain, individual filters can be delegated by expanding the desired filter and using its Delegation tab. When delegating permission of an individual WMI filter, Edit and Full Control are the two available levels.

> **NOTE**   **Default Read Access Permission to WMI Filters**   All users, by default, have Read access to all WMI filters. This permission cannot be removed or revoked. If the Read permission could be revoked, policy processing on the client could fail. Therefore, the capability to remove this permission does not exist.

> **MORE INFO**   **Group Policy Management Console**   Microsoft has several downloadable documents to assist you in learning more about GPMCs benefits and features. You can learn more about GPMC and download specific information at http://www.microsoft.com/windowsserver2003/gpmc/default.mspx.

PLANNING GROUP POLICY INTEGRATION

When planning to deploy group policies within your organization, you need to consider how group policy will integrate with your Active Directory infrastructure. As we have discussed throughout the last several chapters of this text, group policy is a powerful tool that can enhance the security and management capabilities of your network while increasing your network's ROI. Planning your group policy structure carefully will help alleviate potential problems when your network expands and also when you need to troubleshoot policy-related problems. Table 10-4 provides you with a comprehensive reference of planning guidelines. Each major heading is following by some simple guidelines and supporting rationale for following them.

Table 10-4 Group Policy Guidelines

Guideline	Rationale
Planning	
Create policies at the highest level possible in the Active Directory hierarchy, keeping the settings in this policy as broad as possible.	Policy inheritance will allow settings to flow down the hierarchy. Creating a policy with settings that will be common to all users can be applied and will inherit throughout the structure.
Limit the number of GPOs that are created.	When you create a GPO that needs to be duplicated to other containers, link the original GPO to the other containers. You will avoid the possibility of errors caused by manual duplication of settings. In addition, the less GPOs that you have to worry about updating, the easier your administration will be.
Create specialized GPOs for policies that need to be applied for specific reasons.	Implementing additional GPOs on appropriate OUs to increase security restrictions or install software will allow these settings to only affect those users. It is much easier to add policy settings by adding a GPO than to take away policy settings that were invoked at a parent container.
Disable unnecessary setting areas of each policy.	Disabling unused portions of group policy such as user or computer configuration settings will increase policy processing during startup and logon.
Inheritance	
Only use No Override, Block Policy Inheritance, and security filtering methods sparingly.	A good plan should not make use of too many blocking features. It is easier to begin with fewer restrictions higher in the structure than to try to filter settings that you do not want to affect users further down the hierarchy. Managing and troubleshooting too many filters can be difficult, especially as your organization grows.
Planning Site Policies	
GPOs should be applied to sites when the settings need to apply to all computers and users located in the site.	A GPO that is linked to a site will apply to all users and computers located in that site regardless of their domain membership. GPOs created in a site should be created in the domain with the most domain controllers. Regardless of the origin of the user or computer, a domain controller within the site where the GPO is linked will be contacted first.

(continued)

Table 10-4 **Group Policy Guidelines**

Guideline	Rationale
Planning Administration of GPOs	
Determine which administrators will have policy delegation roles.	Deciding who will perform certain tasks and responsibilities associated with group policy administration will allow you to have better control over troubleshooting, auditing, and reporting prior to the implementation of these policies.
Implementation Planning	
Testing policy settings.	Creating a plan for testing the results of your group policy implementation plan will alleviate the possibility of problems that might create insecurities and accessibility problems. Testing can include actual deployment in a test environment, or it can include a comprehensive simulation plan using Group Policy Modeling.
Documenting the plan.	Good documentation serves multiple purposes that include building a case for improvements and documenting baseline information for troubleshooting purposes. Each policy should be documented in its entirety. This information should include the name, purpose, settings, links to containers, and special settings and permissions that are in use.

RESTORING DEFAULT POLICY SETTINGS

There are two policies that are available by default when a Windows Server 2003 domain is installed. They include the Default Domain Policy and the Default Domain Controller Policy. If you are implementing changes to your policy structure and would like to revert these policies to their original settings, you can use the Dcgpofix utility to do so. The Dcgpofix command-line utility can be found in the C:\Windows\Repair folder on a Windows Server 2003 server. It must be run by a user account with Administrator privileges. Use this utility with caution because it will remove any policy settings applied after the initial installation. At the command line, you can specify to reset the Default Domain Policy, the Default Domain Controller Policy, or both. If the desired target is not specified, Dcgpofix will reset both policies. For example, the required syntax for using Dcgpofix to reset the Default Domain Policy is as follows:

```
dcgpofix /target:domain
```

The required syntax for using Dcgpofix to reset the Default Domain Controller Policy is as follows:

```
dcgpofix /target:dc
```

> **MORE INFO**   **Additional Information on Dcgpofix**   *Specific information on using Dcgpofix and its requirements and limitations can be found at http://www.microsoft.com/technet/treeview/default.asp?url=/technet/prodtechnol/windowsserver2003/proddocs/entserver/dcgpofix.asp.*

SUMMARY

- Application of group policies can be filtered by using Block Policy Inheritance, No Override, permissions, and WMI filters.
- WMI filters allow administrative control over group policy implementation based on criteria that is defined in the filter. After evaluation, all filter criteria must return a value of true for the policy to be applied. Any criteria that return a value of false after evaluation will prevent the policy from being applied.
- Only one WMI filter can be applied to each GPO.
- GPMC can be used to manage all aspects of group policy, including the following: creation, linking, editing, reporting, modeling, backup, restore, copying, importing, and scripting.
- Determining effective group policies can be accomplished using RSoP, GPMC, or GPResult.
- RSoP is an MMC snap-in that has two modes: Planning and Logging. Planning mode allows administrators to simulate policy settings prior to their deployment. Logging mode reports on the results of existing policies.
- Delegating administrative control of group policy management tasks is an important feature when planning a decentralized administrative approach. GPMC is a comprehensive tool that simplifies delegation of all aspects of policy management.
- When planning your GPO infrastructure, use the guidelines presented in this chapter for reference of key concepts.

EXERCISES

Exercise 10-1: Navigating with GPMC

To familiarize yourself with GPMC and how to navigate through this utility, complete the following steps:

1. Open GPMC from the Administrative Tools folder on the Start menu.
2. In the left console pane, expand the Forest node, followed by the Domains node.
3. Click to select the node that refers to your domain name.

    QUESTION What tabs are available in the right console pane?

4. In the left console pane, select the Default Domain Policy.

    QUESTION What tabs are now available in the right console pane for this policy?

5. Click on the Settings tab in the right console pane.

    QUESTION What type of information is presented here?

6. In the left console pane, expand the Group Policy Objects node.

    QUESTION What policies are listed here?

7. Close GPMC.

Exercise 10-2: Using GPResult

To understand the required syntax and options for the GPResult command line utility, complete the following steps:

1. Open a Command Prompt window, type **gpresult /?** and press ENTER. This will display the Help screen for the command.

2. At the prompt, type **gpresult** and press ENTER. What information is output for you after issuing this command?

3. To redirect the output of the gpresult command to a file named MyPol.txt, type **gpresult >MyPol.txt**. The text file will be created and placed in the directory from which you executed the gpresult command.

4. Using Microsoft's security guidelines that suggest not to perform your daily work logged on as Administrator, you need to find policy information being applied to a computer elsewhere on the network. The following information is required to build the correct syntax for GPResult:

   - Domain = contoso.com
   - Administrator account = Administrator
   - Administrator password = MSPr3ss#1
   - Target computer IP address = 192.168.10.201

5. Use the GPResult Help screen output from step 1 and write the necessary syntax to obtain the desired information. This command is not intended to function in the current environment. This step helps to understand the syntax of the command.

6. Close the Command Prompt window.

REVIEW QUESTIONS

1. You are planning the deployment of several new policies at different levels within your organization. Prior to deploying these new policies, you want to ensure they will not adversely affect other policy settings. What can you do to ensure that all policy settings will work together to provide the desired solution?

2. After deploying several new restrictive policies, you are unable to access Control Panel from your workstation, even though you are logged on as Administrator. You suspect that the policy settings are forcing this behavior. What can you do so that the restrictive policy settings will not affect your Administrator account?

3. During a recent training session, you learned about WMI filters. Upon returning to your office and exploring your group policy structure, you implement a filter for a software deployment policy so that the software will be deployed only to computers that have enough drive space and memory. The software deploys to all computers that meet the criteria with the exception of those running Microsoft Windows 98 and Microsoft Windows 2000 Professional. Why is the software not being deployed to these computers even though they have the appropriate drive space and memory availability?

4. What operating systems will support the installation of GPMC?

5. What is the difference between the import and the copy features that are available in GPMC?

6. As the administrator for a newly installed Windows Server 2003 network, you would like to use GPMC to plan and manage your entire GPO structure. Where should you look for this tool?

7. Once GPMC is installed, what changes will you see in the existing tools such as Active Directory Users And Computers?

CASE SCENARIO

Scenario 10-1: Planning GPOs for Tailspin Toys

Tailspin Toys is running a single Windows Server 2003 Active Directory domain with multiple OUs configured for each of their 12 locations. There is an administrator located at each location that is responsible for managing GPOs and user accounts. You are the enterprise administrator responsible for planning the infrastructure. For each challenge listed below, document your options and be prepared to share them with other students.

1. Administrators located at each location should be able to create new GPOs and edit any that they have created. They should not be able to change or delete any GPOs that they have not created. What are your options for providing this functionality?

2. Users in each location are currently all in one OU. There are certain group policies that should only apply to users in some departments and not others. What options should you consider that will allow for group policies to only be applied to the necessary users?

3. Although you have created a domain-wide policy that enforces restrictions on administrative tools, you do not want those settings to apply to users for which you have delegated administrative permissions on each location's OU. What are your options to solve this?

CHAPTER 11
ACTIVE DIRECTORY MAINTENANCE, TROUBLESHOOTING, AND DISASTER RECOVERY

Upon completion of this chapter, you will be able to:

- Define procedures used for Active Directory backup and restore.
- Use the Backup And Restore Wizard to back up and restore the Active Directory database.
- Understand and explain the primary, normal, and authoritative restore processes.
- Explain the **defragmentation** process and understand the differences between an offline and an online defragmentation.
- Implement guidelines and procedures for monitoring Active Directory.
- Use System Monitor and Event Viewer to monitor Active Directory and File Replication services.
- Configure alerts using System Monitor.
- Differentiate and choose the appropriate tools for diagnosing Active Directory problems.

After successfully implementing a Microsoft Windows Server 2003 environment, it is important to implement maintenance procedures to keep it running smoothly. A solid monitoring and maintenance plan can anticipate and prevent potential problems. Troubleshooting problems after they occur is preventable when maintenance and monitoring procedures are in place to help alert of possible issues and proactively manage the environment. This chapter covers guidelines for monitoring and maintaining Active Directory directory service. It also covers how to use the necessary tools to monitor, maintain, and troubleshoot Active Directory. Finally, it covers the appropriate methods for backing up, restoring, and defragmenting the Active Directory database.

MAINTAINING ACTIVE DIRECTORY

Active Directory is a database with its own database engine named the **Extensible Storage Engine (ESE)**. The ESE is responsible for managing changes to the Active Directory database. Changes are referred to as **transactions**. Transactions can contain more than one change, such as the addition of a new object and the modification of an existing object's properties. As requests for the creation or modification of database objects are made, the ESE carries the requests through the following process:

1. Active Directory writes the transaction to a transaction buffer located in memory on the server.

2. Active Directory writes the transaction to the Transaction log file. The default log file is named edb.log. The log file allows the transaction to be stored until it can be written to the actual database. A Transaction log file has a default size of 10 MB. When the default edb.log file is full, it is renamed to include a sequential number as a suffix, such as edb1.log. When the edb.log file reaches its 10-MB capacity, it is renamed to edb$x$.log, where x is replaced with the next sequential number.

3. Active Directory writes the transaction from the transaction buffer to the database. As discussed in Chapter 1, "Overview of Active Directory," the Active Directory database file name is ntds.dit.

4. Active Directory compares the database with the change to the edb$x$.log file from step 2 to ensure that the transaction written matches the log file transaction.

5. Active Directory updates the edb.chk checkpoint file. The checkpoint file is used as a reference for database information that is written to disk. In a case where Active Directory needs to be recovered from a failure, the checkpoint file is used as a starting point. It contains references to the point in the log file from which a recovery must take place.

The caching shown in step 1, in addition to the logging discussed in step 2, allows Active Directory to process multiple additional transactions before writing them to the database. When transactions are written to the database, it is more efficient to write multiple simultaneous transactions stored in the log file than to write each transaction individually.

As is true with any database, modifications and changes to the Active Directory database can affect database performance and data integrity. As modifications are made to the database, **fragmentation** can occur. Fragmentation refers to the condition of a disk when data from the database is divided into pieces scattered across the disk. As the database becomes more and more fragmented, searches for database information slow down and performance deteriorates. In addition, the potential exists for database corruption. There is a process named defragmentation that is used to rearrange the information, making it easier to find during access requests and searches. Defragmentation is the process of taking fragmented database pieces and rearranging them contiguously to make the entire database more efficient. Depending on the method used, the size of the database can be reduced, making room for additional objects. Active Directory has two defragmentation methods: online defragmentation and offline defragmentation. These are explained next.

- **Online Defragmentation**   Online defragmentation is an automatic process that occurs during the **garbage collection** process. The garbage collection process runs by default every 12 hours on all domain controllers in the forest. When the garbage collection process begins, it removes all tombstones from the database. A **tombstone** is what is left of an object that has been deleted. Deleted objects are not completely removed from the Active Directory database. They are marked for deletion. Tombstone objects have a lifetime of 60 days, by default. When the lifetime expires, the objects are permanently deleted during the garbage collection process. Additional free space is reclaimed during the garbage collection process through the deletion of tombstone objects and unnecessary log files. The advantage of an online defragmentation is that it occurs automatically and does not require the server to be offline to run. An online defragmentation does not reduce the actual size of the Active Directory database.

- **Offline Defragmentation**   Offline defragmentation is a manual process that defragments the Active Directory database in addition to reducing its size. Performing an offline defragmentation is not considered a regular maintenance task. You should only perform an offline defragmentation if you need to recover a significant amount of disk space. For example, if your domain controller no longer provides global catalog services in a forest, you may want to recover the disk space that once held the global catalog information. As its name suggests, offline defragmentation requires that the server is taken offline so that the Active Directory database is closed and not in use. The server must be restarted in Directory Services Restore mode and the ntdsutil.exe command line utility is used to perform the offline defragmentation.

The following tasks should be performed prior to running an offline defragmentation:

- Perform a **System State backup**. This procedure backs up the current Active Directory database. Backup is discussed later in this chapter.
- Create a folder to temporarily store the compacted database.
- Check to ensure that you have free space equivalent to the size of the current database, plus at least an additional 15 percent. This ensures that there is enough space for temporary storage during the defragmentation process in addition to space for the newly compacted database.

▶ Performing Offline Defragmentation

To perform an offline defragmentation, complete the following steps:

1. Restart your domain controller and press F8 after the BIOS information is displayed.

2. Select Directory Services Restore Mode (Windows Server 2003 domain controllers only) and press ENTER.

3. Select the Windows Server 2003 operating system and press ENTER. Your computer is running in Safe mode.

4. Log on to Windows Server 2003 with the local Administrator account. This account is the account defined in the local computer database, not the Domain Administrator account.

5. From the Run dialog box on the Start menu, type **cmd** to open a Command Prompt window.

6. Type **ntdsutil** and press ENTER.

7. Type **files** and press ENTER.

8. At the files prompt, type the following command, replacing *drive:* and *directory* with the destination path for the compacted database:

   ```
   compact to drive:\directory
   ```

9. Press ENTER to initiate the creation of a new ntds.dit file in the specified directory.

   NOTE *Directory Paths with Spaces* *When specifying a path that contains spaces at the command line, enclose the entire path in quotes. For example, if the destination path is D:\New Database, the path should be typed at the command line as "D:\New Database."*

10. Type **quit**, and press ENTER to exit the Ntdsutil utility. Type **quit** again. This returns you to the Command Prompt window.

11. Copy the new ntds.dit file from the directory you specified in step 8 to the current Active Directory database path, which by default is C:\Windows\Ntds.

12. Restart your domain controller.

Next, we discuss the benefits of moving the database to a new location and the procedures for doing so.

Moving the Active Directory Database

When you choose to move the database, the rationale for doing so is usually driven by a need for additional disk space. The working database file system location must be updated in the registry—Ntdsutil does this automatically. If you are low on disk space on the drive where the original Active Directory database is stored, you can move the database to a different drive that has sufficient space for the current database. The difference in the outcome between the procedure for compacting the database as discussed previously, and the procedure for moving the database, is that when you move the database, you must ensure that the registry keys used to provide the Active Directory database location are updated. If the registry keys that point to the file system location of Active Directory are not updated, Active Directory is not able to start. When the database is compacted as discussed previously, it is compacted to a new location. On completion, it is moved to the working database location. The registry keys pointing to the path in the file system for the working database do not change.

Moving the database and the associated log files requires two separate move procedures. These procedures are discussed next.

▶ **Moving the Active Directory Database and Log Files**

To move the Active Directory database and log files, complete the following steps:

1. As a precaution, perform a System State backup. This procedure backs up the current Active Directory database. Backup is discussed later in this chapter.

2. Restart your domain controller and press F8 after the BIOS information is displayed.

3. Select Directory Services Restore mode (Windows Server 2003 domain controllers only) and press ENTER.

4. Select the Windows Server 2003 operating system and press ENTER. Your computer is running in Safe mode.

5. Log on to Windows Server 2003 with the local Administrator account. This account is the account defined in the local computer database, not the Domain Administrator account.

6. From the Run dialog box on the Start menu, type **cmd** to open a Command Prompt window.

7. Type **ntdsutil** and press ENTER.

8. Type **files** and press ENTER.

9. At the files prompt, type the following command, replacing *drive:* and *directory* with the destination path where you will move the database:

   ```
   move DB to drive:\directory
   ```

10. Press ENTER to move the database to the new location.

11. To move the Transaction log files, at the files prompt, type the following command:

    ```
    move logs to drive:\directory
    ```

12. Press ENTER to complete the command. Twice, type **quit** and press ENTER to exit the Ntdsutil utility and command line.

13. Restart the domain controller.

After the database has been moved, you will need to perform a backup of System State data to ensure that in a failure, you can restore the database to the correct path. System State data and backup procedures will be covered later in this chapter.

BACKING UP ACTIVE DIRECTORY

One of the most essential functions of an administrator is ensuring that data and operating system information is backed up in case of a failure. Procedures that include the frequency of backups in addition to the type of information that needs to be backed up should be planned and implemented in every organization. Depending on the number of servers in your organization, your plan may vary.

For example, if you have only one domain controller in your environment that services logons and stores data, then you must back up this computer frequently in case of a failure. In another scenario that includes one domain controller and several member servers that are storing data and delivering applications, the domain controller's Active Directory database should be backed up frequently, while the data stored on each member server is backed up separately. Although backing up data is extremely important, this section covers the procedures necessary to back up Active Directory. Without a backup of Active Directory, if your domain controller fails, users are not able to access shared resources and it is necessary to rebuild the database manually.

When you back up System State data, you include the Active Directory. The System State data includes operating system–specific information that is needed for installed services and operating system components to function. When you back up System State data, it is backed up in its entirety; it is not possible to back up only certain elements of it. Dependency relationships exist between many of the components. The contents of the System State data vary depending on the operating system and components installed. On a domain controller, System State data includes the following:

- **Active Directory database** This database includes the current database file, NTDS.dit. If the database is not moved, the file is located in the C:\Windows\Ntds folder.

- **Sysvol shared folder** This folder structure contains Group Policy templates and logon scripts.

- **Registry** This database contains information about the domain controller's computer configuration, including hardware settings.

- **System startup files** These files include the boot files and system files required to start Windows Server 2003. Without these files, the domain controller does not start properly.

- **Component Object Model (COM+) Class Registration database** This database contains information about COM+ applications.

- **Certificate Services database** This database is only present if the domain controller has Certificate Services installed and configured.

- **Cluster service information** This component is present if the server is part of a cluster on your Windows Server 2003 network. A cluster is a group of servers that contain the same services and are presented to users as a single system. Clustering improves scalability, availability, and manageability of your network.

    NOTE *System State Data* *System State data can only be backed up from a local computer. You cannot backup the System State data located on a remote computer. You must be a member of the local Administrators, Backup Operators, or Domain Admins group to backup System State data.*

Active Directory can be backed up by using the graphical user interface (GUI) or command line tools that are provided in Windows Server 2003. The GUI tool is named the Backup Or Restore Wizard. The command line tool is named

Ntbackup.exe. This section covers using the Backup Or Restore Wizard. The next section provides an overview of the necessary procedures for backing up Active Directory.

Preparing to Back Up Active Directory

The following is a list of pre-backup tasks that should be completed prior to beginning your backup procedure:

- Check to ensure the target media device to which you back up is listed in the Windows Server 2003 hardware compatibility list (HCL) or Windows Server Catalog Web site.

- Ensure that your backup device is attached to a computer on the network and is turned on. If you are backing up to tape, you must attach the tape device to the computer on which you run Backup.

- Check to ensure the medium is loaded in the media device. For example, if you are using a tape drive, ensure that a tape is loaded in the tape drive.

   NOTE **Windows Server 2003 Hardware Compatibility List (HCL)** *For a list of Windows Server 2003 hardware and software components that are compatible, consult the Windows Server Catalog Web site located at: http://www.microsoft.com /windows/catalog/server/.*

▶ **Backing Up Active Directory**

To back up Active Directory, complete the following steps:

1. Log on to your domain as Administrator. On the Start menu, point to All Programs, Accessories, System Tools, and select Backup.

2. On the Welcome To The Backup Or Restore Wizard page, click Next.

3. On the Backup Or Restore page, select Backup Files And Settings, and then click Next, as shown in Figure 11-1.

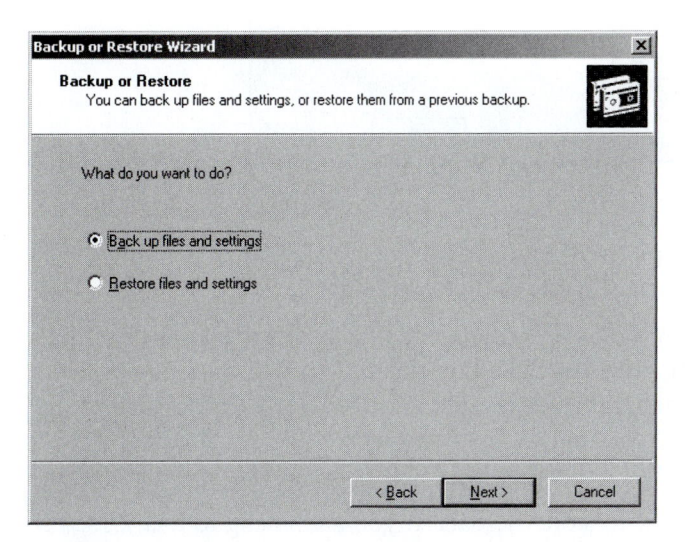

Figure 11-1   Backup Or Restore page

4. On the What To Back Up page, as shown in Figure 11-2, select Let Me Choose What To Back Up, and then click Next.

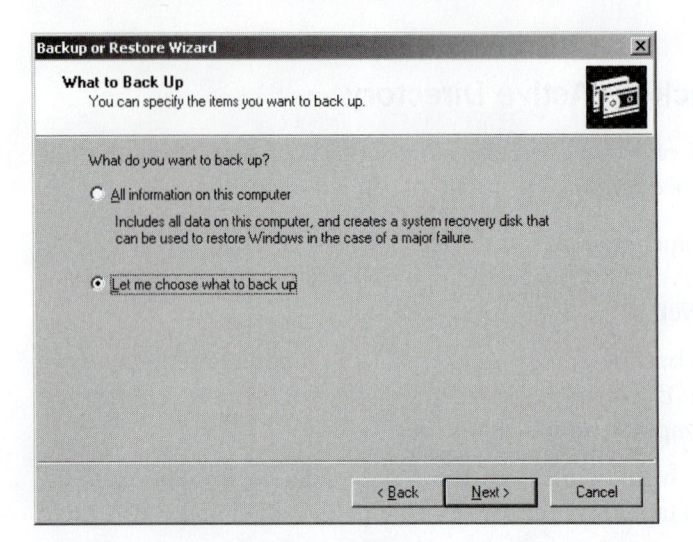

Figure 11-2 What To Back Up page

5. On the Items To Back Up page, as shown in Figure 11-3, expand the My Computer item, and then select System State. Click Next.

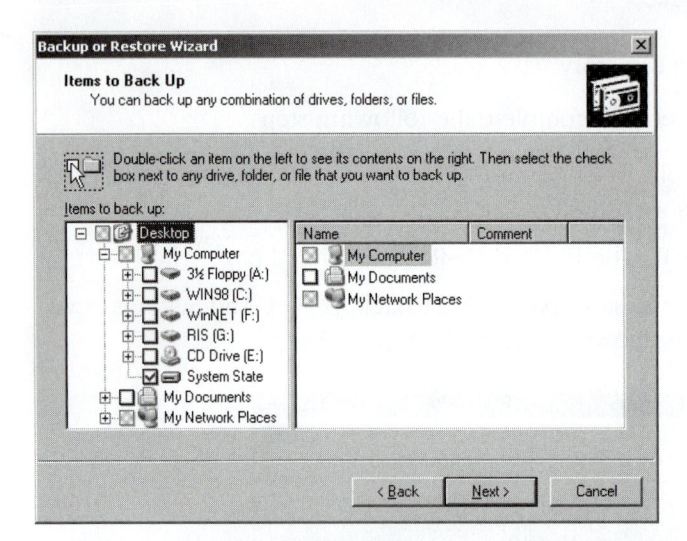

Figure 11-3 Items To Back Up page

6. On the Backup Type, Destination, And Name page, as shown in Figure 11-4, complete the following steps:

   a. Select Tape in the Select The Backup Type list if you are using a tape medium; otherwise, this box defaults to File. Using a file as your target medium assumes that you back up to a location within the existing file system such as an alternate physical drive.

   b. In the Choose A Place To Save Your Backup list, choose the location where you want to store the data. If you are saving to a tape, select the tape name. If you are saving to a file, browse to the path for the backup file location.

CHAPTER 11: ACTIVE DIRECTORY MAINTENANCE, TROUBLESHOOTING, AND DISASTER RECOVERY 289

    c. In the Type A Name For This Backup box, enter a descriptive name for the backup.

    d. Click Next.

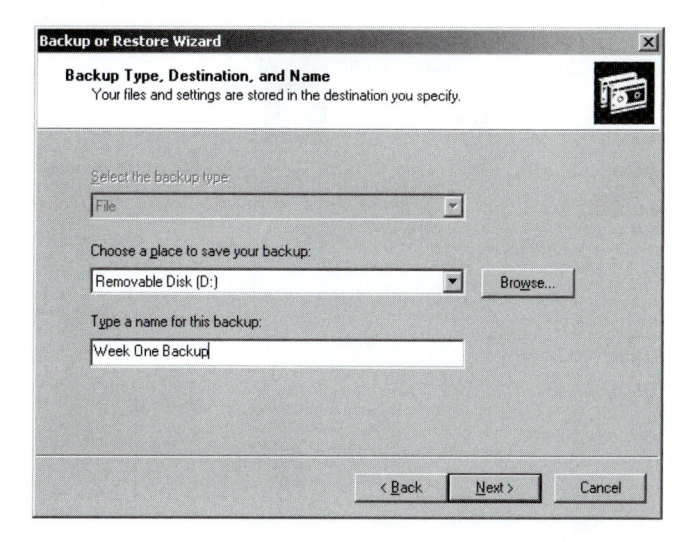

Figure 11-4   Backup Type, Destination, And Name page

7. On the Completing The Backup Or Restore Wizard page, click Advanced. This allows you to set additional parameters for your backup, such as verification, hardware compressions, and labels.

8. On the Type Of Backup page, as shown in Figure 11-5, select Normal as the backup type used for this backup job. Normal is the only backup type supported by Active Directory. Click Next.

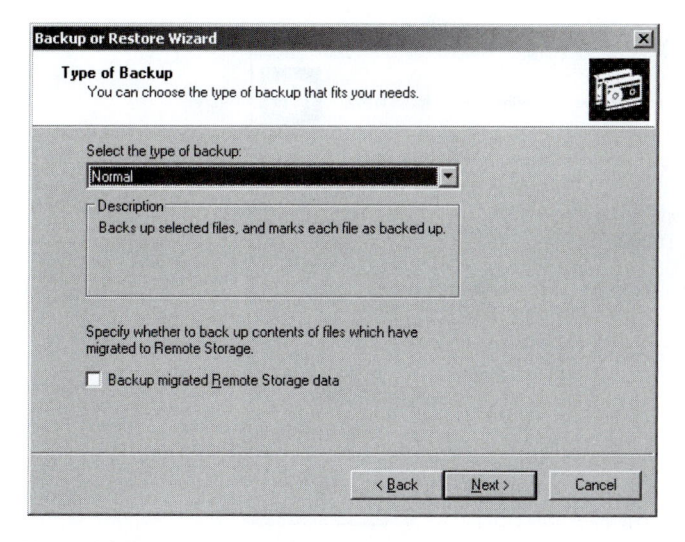

Figure 11-5   Type Of Backup page

9. On the How To Back Up page, as shown in Figure 11-6, select the Verify Data After Backup check box. This option causes the backup process to take longer, but it confirms that files are correctly backed up. If you are using a tape device and it supports hardware compression, select the Use Hardware Compression, If Available check box to enable hardware

compression. Do not select the Disable Volume Shadow Copy check box. By default, Windows Backup creates a volume shadow copy of your data to create an accurate copy of the contents of the hard drive, including open files or files in use by the system. Click Next.

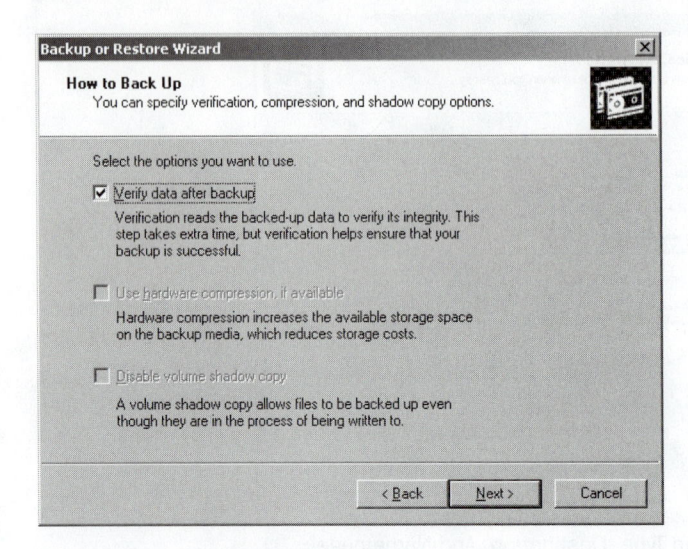

Figure 11-6 How To Back Up page

10. On the Backup Options page, as shown in Figure 11-7, select the Replace The Existing Backups option, then select the Allow Only The Owner And The Administrator Access To The Backup Data And To Any Backups Appended To This Medium check box. This action saves only the most recent copy of Active Directory and allows you to restrict who can gain access to the completed backup file or tape. Click Next.

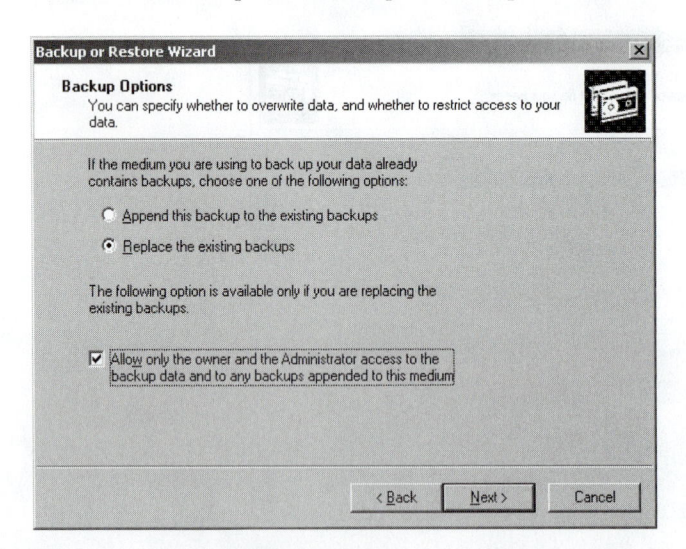

Figure 11-7 Backup Options page

11. On the When To Back Up page, as shown in Figure 11-8, select Now. Click Next.

12. On the Completing The Backup Or Restore Wizard page, click Finish to start the backup operation.

13. The Backup Progress window shows the progress of the backup.

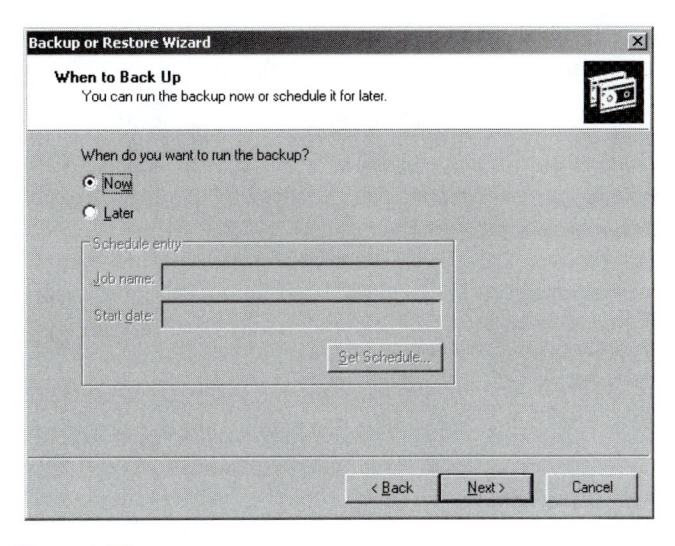

CHAPTER 11: ACTIVE DIRECTORY MAINTENANCE, TROUBLESHOOTING, AND DISASTER RECOVERY   291

Figure 11-8   When To Back Up page

14. When the backup operation is complete, the Backup Progress window, as shown in Figure 11-9, shows that the backup is complete. You can click the Report button to see a report about the backup operation, as shown in Figure 11-10. The report is stored on the hard disk of the computer on which you are running the backup.

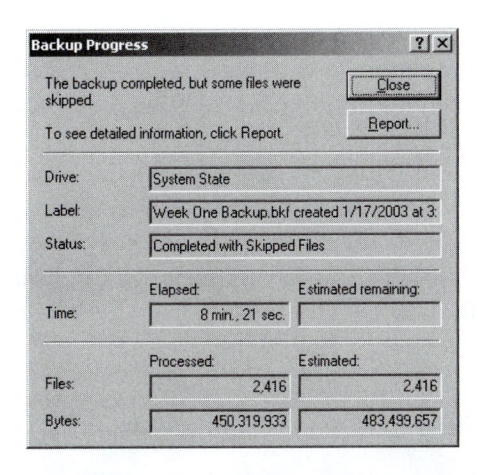

Figure 11-9   Backup Progress window showing completed backup

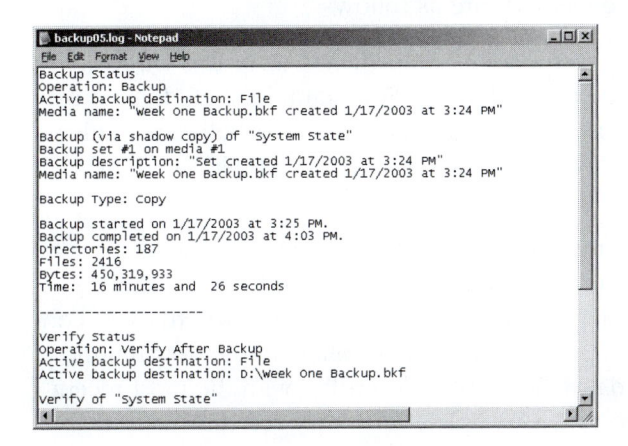

Figure 11-10   Backup operation report

15. Close the report when you have finished viewing it and then click Close to exit the backup operation.

   NOTE **Backing Up All Disks** To backup all information on the computer, including System State data and file system data, on the What To Back Up page, click the check box for All Information On This Computer. It is necessary to backup the entire drive in order to recover fully from a failure.

   NOTE **Using Ntbackup** Information on using the Ntbackup command line tool can be obtained in the Windows Server 2003 Help And Support Center. The Help And Support Center can be accessed directly from the Start menu. Using Ntbackup as the keyword in the Search window of this tool returns results specific to the command line tool.

RESTORING ACTIVE DIRECTORY

Windows Server 2003 offers the ability to restore the Active Directory database if necessary. Depending on your environment and the situation from which you need to recover, you have a couple of options for restoring the Active Directory database to a domain controller. These restoration methods are discussed next.

Using the Replication Process

As covered in Chapter 3, "Working with Active Directory Sites," when there are multiple domain controllers in a domain, the Active Directory database is replicated within each domain controller. This replication ensures availability, accessibility, and fault tolerance. Fault tolerance is used in the replication process when one of the domain controllers experiences a hardware or software failure. For example, if one of the domain controllers fails and requires a clean installation of the operating system, you can reinstall Active Directory as you normally would through the Dcpromo tool. Once this is finished, you can allow normal replication to repopulate the domain controller with database information from the other domain controllers.

Backup Utility Restoration Options

The Backup utility allows several different restoration methods depending on the goals for your restore. These methods are as follows:

- **Primary restore** This method is required when all Active Directory information is lost for the entire domain. For example, if all domain controllers fail, or if there was only one domain controller before the failure, you need to perform a primary restore in order to rebuild the domain from a recent backup.

- **Normal restore** This method restores the Active Directory database to its state before the backup. This method can be used when you want to restore a single domain controller to a point in time when it was considered good. If there are other domain controllers in the domain, the replication process updates the domain controller with the most recent information after the restore is complete. You may see this method also referred to as a non-authoritative restore.

Using Ntdsutil

In addition to the two methods provided by the Backup utility, the Ntdsutil command line utility allows you to perform an **authoritative restore**. An authoritative restore cannot be performed using any other Windows Server 2003 tool. This method is used with the normal restore to allow certain database information to be marked as authoritative, or most current, so that the replication process will not overwrite this data. This type of restore is helpful in correcting administrative mistakes that have been replicated to all domain controllers in the domain. For example, if an organizational unit (OU) that contains multiple users is mistakenly deleted, that deletion replicates to all domain controllers, causing users in that OU to no longer exist. Using an authoritative restore, you can obtain a backup from a date prior to the errant deletion and mark the OU as current. When the OU is restored, it is replicated to the rest of the domain, allowing you to recover the user accounts it originally contained.

In addition to the ability to assist with performing an authoritative restore, the Ntdsutil tool offers the ability to assist with other Active Directory repairs. The following list includes several of these important options:

- **Ntdsutil files** Allows you to move, recover, and compact the Active Directory database
- **Ntdsutil semantic database analysis** Allows you to verify and repair the Active Directory database
- **Ntdsutil metadata cleanup** Allows you to remove objects such as domains, naming contexts, and servers from the Active Directory database

> **CAUTION** Tombstone Lifetime and Restoration of Active Directory Active Directory cannot be restored from a backup that is older than the tombstone lifetime of 60 days, by default. Domain controllers only keep track of deleted objects for the duration of the tombstone lifetime. If your backup is older than the tombstone lifetime, you lose any changes that you made to the database since this backup.

Performing a Primary Restore

When a catastrophic event affecting all your domain controllers requires an entire domain to be restored, you should perform a primary restore on the first domain controller in a domain and a normal restore on the remaining domain controllers. A primary restore is also the appropriate action to take when a standalone domain controller requires restoration.

▶ **Performing a Primary Restore**

To perform a primary restore, complete the following steps:

1. Restart your domain controller and press F8 after the BIOS information is displayed.
2. Select Directory Services Restore Mode (Windows Server 2003 domain controllers only) and press ENTER.

3. Select the Windows Server 2003 operating system and press ENTER. Your computer is running in Safe mode.

4. Log on to Windows Server 2003 with the local Administrator account. This account is the account defined in the local computer database, not the Domain Administrator account.

5. On the Start menu, point to All Programs, Accessories, System Tools, and select Backup.

6. On the Welcome To The Backup Or Restore Wizard page, click the Advanced Mode button.

7. On the Welcome To Backup Utility Advanced Mode page, select the Restore And Manage Media tab. Select what you want to restore, and then click Start Restore.

8. In the Warning dialog box, click OK.

9. In the Confirm Restore dialog box, click Advanced.

10. In the Advanced Restore Options dialog box, click When Restoring Replicated Data Sets, Mark the Restored Data As The Primary Data For All Replicas, and then click OK twice. This option should only be selected when you want to restore the first replica set to the network and ensures that all File Replication Service (FRS) data is replicated to other servers.

11. In the Restore Progress dialog box, click Close.

12. In the Backup Utility dialog box, click Yes.

13. When finished, close all open applications and restart your server normally. All information from the restore process is replicated to all other domain controllers on the network.

Performing a Normal Restore

Upon completion of the previous steps in a domain environment, you can use a normal restore on the remaining domain controllers within the domain. Using this option restores Active Directory objects with their original Update Sequence Number (USN). Any other domain controller with a higher USN for a particular object overwrites the object during the replication interval in order to ensure that all domain controllers have the most recent object information.

▶ Performing a Normal Restore

To perform a normal restore of Active Directory, complete the following steps:

1. Restart your domain controller and press F8 after the BIOS information is displayed.

2. Select Directory Services Restore Mode (Windows Server 2003 domain controllers only) and press ENTER.

3. Select the Windows Server 2003 operating system and press ENTER. Your computer is running in Safe mode.

4. Log on to Windows Server 2003 with the local Administrator account. This account is the account defined in the local computer database, not the Domain Administrator account.

5. On the Start menu, point to All Programs, Accessories, System Tools, and select Backup.

6. On the Welcome To The Backup Or Restore Wizard page, click Next.

7. On the Backup Or Restore page, click Restore Files And Settings.

8. Under Items To Restore on the What To Restore Page, expand the list to locate System State data. Click on the check box to select System State data and then click Next. When you restore the System State data, the System State data located on your computer is overwritten by the Backup utility. This includes any System State data that does not pertain to Active Directory, such as registry settings and other configurations. You need to reconfigure these items after your restore process is complete.

9. On the Completing The Backup Or Restore Wizard page, click Finish.

10. Click OK in the Warning dialog box.

11. Click Close in the Restore Progress dialog box.

12. Click Yes in the Backup Utility dialog box.

NOTE *Frequent Backups to System State Data* Backing up your System State data frequently can help you to avoid losing changes that occur after the last backup. It is a good practice to back up System State data after any major configuration changes so that the changes are not lost if a restoration is necessary.

Performing an Authoritative Restore

As previously stated, an authoritative restore requires the use of the Ntdsutil tool instead of the Backup Or Restore Wizard.

▶ **Performing an Authoritative Restore**

To perform an authoritative restore, complete the following steps:

1. Restart your domain controller and press F8 after the BIOS information is displayed.

2. Select Directory Services Restore Mode (Windows Server 2003 domain controllers only) and press ENTER.

3. Select the Windows Server 2003 operating system and press ENTER. Your computer is running in Safe mode.

4. Log on to Windows Server 2003 with the local Administrator account. This account is the account defined in the local computer database, not the Domain Administrator account.

5. On the Start menu, select Run. Type **ntdsutil** and press ENTER.

6. At the Ntdsutil prompt, type **authoritative restore** and press ENTER.

7. At the Authoritative Restore prompt, you have several options depending on your desired outcome. These options include:

- Authoritatively restore the entire database. To restore the entire database, type the following at the Ntdsutil prompt and press ENTER when done:

   ```
   restore database
   ```

- Authoritatively restore a portion or subtree of the directory. For example, to perform an authoritative restore of an OU named Marketing for the east.cohowinery.com domain, type the following at the Ntdsutil prompt and press ENTER when done:

   ```
   restore subtree OU=Marketing,DC=east,DC=cohowinery,DC=com
   ```

   The authoritative restore opens the ntds.dit file, increases version numbers, counts the records that need updating, verifies the number of records updated, and reports completion.

8. Type **quit** and press ENTER to exit the Ntdsutil utility and close the Command Prompt window.

9. Restart the domain controller in Normal mode. When the restored domain controller is online and connected to the network, normal replication synchronizes the restored domain controller with any changes from the additional domain controllers that were not overwritten by the authoritative restore. Replication also propagates the authoritatively restored objects to other domain controllers in the forest. The deleted objects that were marked as authoritative are replicated from the restored domain controller to the additional domain controllers. Because the restored objects have the same object globally unique identifier (GUID) and object SID, security remains intact, and object dependencies are maintained.

10. Ensure the integrity of the computer's Group Policy by performing one of the following:

- If you authoritatively restored the entire Active Directory database, copy the Sysvol directory to the alternate location over the existing one after the Sysvol share is published.

- If you authoritatively restored specific Active Directory objects, copy only the policy folders identified by the GUID corresponding to the restored policy objects from the alternate location after the Sysvol share is published. Then, copy them over the existing ones.

When authoritatively restoring either the entire Active Directory database or selected objects, it is important that you copy the Sysvol share and policy data from the alternate location *after* the Sysvol share is published. If the computer is in a replicated domain, it may take several minutes before the Sysvol share is published because it needs to synchronize with its replication partners. If all computers in the domain are authoritatively restored and restarted at the same time, then each will be waiting indefinitely to synchronize with each other. In this case, restore one of the domain controllers first so that its Sysvol share can be published, then restore the other computers by using the normal restore option.

MONITORING ACTIVE DIRECTORY AND FILE REPLICATION SERVICES

Monitoring the Active Directory service is an important part of network administration. Monitoring allows you to take a proactive approach to network management. By raising the awareness of possible network problems before they occur, you have better control over the impact of these problems. Creating a monitoring plan can help you to flag processes or configuration issues that may initially be minor before they turn into something potentially catastrophic to your network. For example, monitoring the disk space use on the drive that holds the ntds.dit file and discovering that you are low on available disk space can lead you to resolve this situation before all the free space is used.

Monitoring Active Directory can provide the following benefits:

- Early alerts to potential problems
- Improved system reliability
- Fewer support calls to the helpdesk
- Improved system performance

Now that you understand the importance of monitoring, it is necessary for you to understand several of the important items to consider when developing your monitoring plan. In addition, you need to know which tools are available to assist you in monitoring. The next sections cover how to collect and find information related to Active Directory errors and warnings by using Event Viewer and System Monitor. Additionally, the monitoring of the File Replication Service (FRS) and its importance to the health of your Windows Server 2003 network is discussed.

Understanding Event Logs

Windows Server 2003 uses Event Viewer to record system events that take place, such as security, application, and directory service events. Active Directory–related events are recorded in the Directory Service log. The Directory Service log is created when Active Directory is installed. It logs informational events such as service start and stop messages, errors, and warnings. This log should be the first place you look when you suspect a problem with Active Directory. Figure 11-11 shows the Directory Service log on a Windows Server 2003 computer.

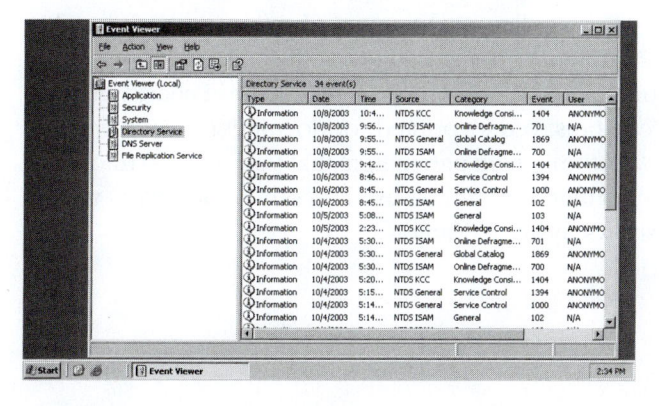

Figure 11-11   Event Viewer Directory Service log

In addition to the Directory Service log, the FRS log should also be monitored for errors and warnings. FRS is the service that is used to maintain the consistency of Active Directory information throughout the forest. FRS replicates the Sysvol folder structure throughout domain controllers. If FRS is not functioning, your Active Directory database does not replicate properly, causing potential problems. Figure 11-12 shows the File Replication Service log on a Windows Server 2003 computer.

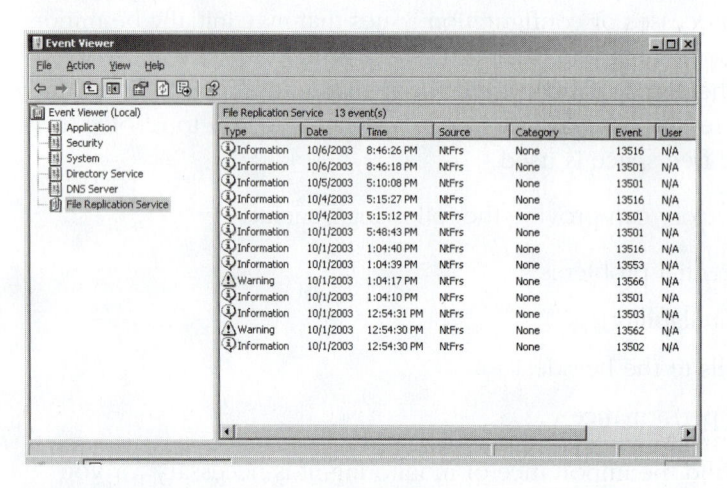

Figure 11-12 Event Viewer File Replication Service log

Since Event Viewer shows logs for both informational messages and error messages, it is important to monitor for some basic events that can provide indications of overall system health. In the *type* field of any of the log files in Event Viewer, you should monitor and filter on events that indicate a warning or stop error. A warning is indicated by a yellow triangle with an exclamation mark, and a stop error is indicated by a red circle with an X on it. The event details will provide additional information that pertains to possible reasons for the entry in addition to resources that can provide possible solutions.

Using System Monitor

System Monitor is a tool that is located within the Performance Monitor console. This tool is based on the Performance Monitor tool designed for Microsoft Windows NT version 4.0 networks and should not be confused with the System Monitor tool that is part of the Windows 98 operating system. System Monitor in Windows Server 2003 allows you to collect real-time information on your local computer or from a specific computer to which you have permissions. This information can be viewed in a number of different formats that include charts, graphs, and histograms. The reports can be saved or printed for documentation purposes. System Monitor allows you to customize the parameters that you want to track and store them in an MMC snap-in so that they can be used on other computers within your network. Figure 11-13 shows System Monitor.

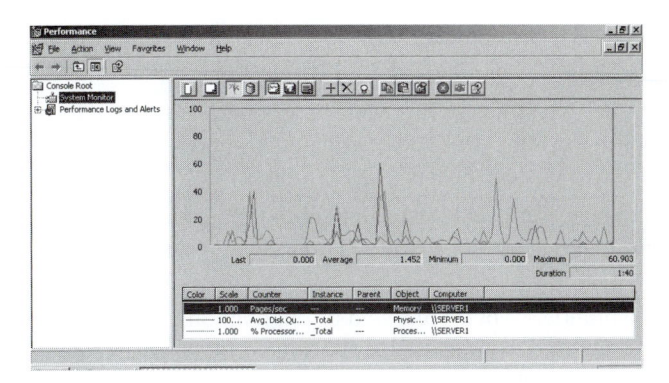

CHAPTER 11: ACTIVE DIRECTORY MAINTENANCE, TROUBLESHOOTING, AND DISASTER RECOVERY

Figure 11-13 System Monitor in the Performance console

▶ Opening System Monitor

To open System Monitor, complete the following steps:

1. On the Start menu, point to Administrative Tools and click Performance.
2. In the left window pane, click System Monitor.

Before you can effectively use System Monitor, you need to understand how to configure it so that you can obtain the desired information. System Monitor uses categories to organize the items that can be monitored. These categories are referred to as **performance objects**. Performance objects contain performance counters that are associated with the category that you want to monitor. **Performance counters** are the specific processes or events that you want to track. For example, on the NTDS performance object, the DRA Inbound Bytes Compressed counter will monitor the size of compressed data that was replicated from other sites. As shown in Figure 11-14, an explanation can be obtained for each counter to assist you in choosing the most appropriate counters for your environment.

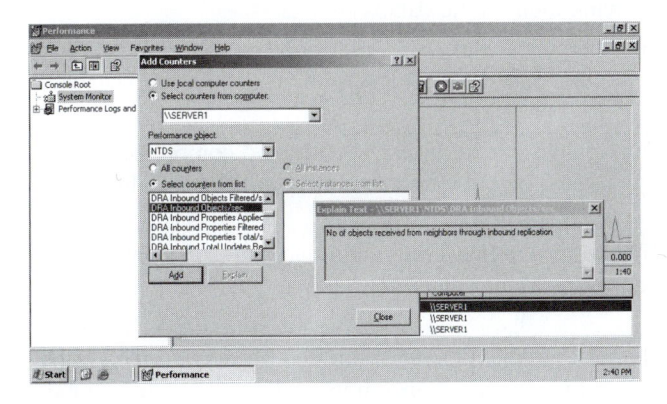

Figure 11-14 System Monitor performance counter explanation

The NTDS performance object contains over 120 performance counters that pertain to Active Directory. It is important for you to determine which of these counters suit your purposes. Table 11-1 provides you with a breakdown of the counters that you should consider adding to your basic monitoring plan.

Table 11-1 Basic NTDS Performance Object Counters

Counter	Description
DRA Inbound Bytes Compressed (Between Sites, After Compression)/Sec	The compressed size, in bytes, of inbound compressed replication data. This is the size after compression, from Directory System Agents [DSAs] in other sites.
DRA Inbound Bytes Compressed (Between Sites, Before Compression)/Sec	The original size, in bytes, of inbound compressed replication data. This is the size before compression, from DSAs in other sites.
DRA Inbound Bytes Not Compressed (Within Site)/Sec	The number of bytes received through inbound replication that were not compressed at the source from other DSAs in the same site.
DRA Inbound Bytes Total/Sec	The total number of bytes received through replication per second. It is the sum of the number of uncompressed bytes and the number of compressed bytes.
DRA Inbound Full Sync Objects Remaining	The number of objects remaining until the full synchronization process is completed, or set.
DRA Inbound Objects/Sec	The number of objects received, per second, from replication partners through inbound replication.
DRA Inbound Objects Applied/Sec	The rate per second at which replication updates are received from replication partners and applied by the local directory service. This count excludes changes that are received but not applied, such as when the change is already present. This indicates how much replication update activity is occurring on the server due to changes generated on other servers.
DRA Inbound Object Updates Remaining in Packet	The number of object updates received in the current directory replication update packet that have not yet been applied to the local server. This tells you when the monitored server is receiving changes and taking a long time applying them to the database.
DRA Outbound Bytes Compressed (Between Sites, After Compression)/Sec	The compressed size, in bytes, of outbound compressed replication data, after compression, from DSAs in other sites.
DRA Outbound Bytes Compressed (Between Sites, Before Compression)/Sec	The original size, in bytes, of outbound compressed replication data, before compression, from DSAs in other sites.
DRA Outbound Bytes Not Compressed (Within Site)/Sec	The number of bytes replicated that were not compressed from DSAs in the same site.
DRA Outbound Bytes Total/Sec	The total number of bytes replicated per second. This is the sum of the number of uncompressed bytes and the number of compressed bytes.
DRA Pending Replication Synchronizations	The number of directory synchronizations that are queued for this server but not yet processed. This helps in determining replication backlog. The larger the number, the larger the backlog.
DRA Sync Requests Made	The number of synchronization requests made to replication partners.
DS Directory Reads/Sec	The number of directory reads per second.

(continued)

CHAPTER 11: ACTIVE DIRECTORY MAINTENANCE, TROUBLESHOOTING, AND DISASTER RECOVERY

Table 11-1 Basic NTDS Performance Object Counters

Counter	Description
DS Directory Writes/Sec	The number of directory writes per second.
DS Search Suboperations/Sec	Number of search sub-operations per second. One search operation is made up of many sub-operations. A sub-operation roughly corresponds to an object the search causes the DS to consider.
Kerberos Authentications	The number of times per second that clients use a ticket to this domain controller to authenticate to this domain controller.
LDAP Client Sessions	The number of connected LDAP client sessions.
LDAP Searches/Sec	The number of search operations per second performed by LDAP clients.
NTLM Authentications	The number of Windows NT LAN Manager (NTLM) authentications per second serviced by this domain controller.

> **MORE INFO** *Active Directory Performance Counters* The Microsoft Developer Network (MSDN) Web site has more information about performance counters and their uses. This information is located at http://msdn.microsoft.com/library/default.asp?url=/library/en-us/counter/counters1_hxde.asp.

Understanding that FRS is important to the proper functioning of Active Directory, you should include counters that allow you to monitor its health. The FileReplicaConn and FileReplicaSet performance objects contain the counters that monitor FRS. The FileReplicaConn object shows statistics on the health of the replica connections to distributed file system (DFS) roots. DFS is used to distribute file system information across multiple servers for fault tolerance and load balancing. When DFS is implemented, it allows users to access a logical drive that points to a physical location that is transparent to them. The FileReplicaSet object shows performance statistics for the replica set stored on the monitored server. Table 11-2 shows the important FileReplicaSet counters that you should consider adding to your basic monitoring plan.

Table 11-2 Basic FileReplicaSet Object Counters

Counter	Description
Change Orders Received	Number of change notifications received from inbound partners.
Change Orders Sent	Number of change notifications sent out to outbound partners.
File Installed	Number of replicated files installed locally.
KB Of Staging Space Free	Amount of free space in the staging directory used by FRS to temporarily store files before they are replicated. The default staging space is 660 MB.
KB Of Staging Space In Use	Amount of space in the staging directory currently in use. If the staging directory runs out of space, then replication stops.
Packets Received	Number of FRS data or remote procedure calls (RPCs) received by FRS.

(continued)

CHAPTER 11: ACTIVE DIRECTORY MAINTENANCE, TROUBLESHOOTING, AND DISASTER RECOVERY

Table 11-2   Basic FileReplicaSet Object Counters

Counter	Description
Packets Sent	Number of FRS data and control packets sent to all outbound partners associated with this replica set member.
USN Records Accepted	Number of records that are accepted for replication. Replication is triggered by entries written to the NTFS change journal. FRS reads each file close record from the journal and determines whether to replicate the file or not. An accepted record generates a change order, which is then sent out. A high value on this counter, about one every five seconds, indicates a lot of replication traffic. This can cause replication latency.

NOTE   Command Line Utility to Monitor FRS   You can use the Ntfrsutl command line utility, which is included with Windows Support Tools, to monitor the FRS on local and remote computers. You can even configure Ntfrsutl to poll the FRS service at specific intervals. To learn more about the capabilities of Ntfrsutl, run the **ntfrsutl /?** command from a Command Prompt window.

▶ **Adding Performance Counters and Display Options**

Once you have determined the counters you want to monitor, you must add them to the System Monitor console. To add performance counters and display options to your System Monitor console, complete the following steps:

1. In your System Monitor console window, click the plus sign (+) on the System Monitor menu bar. The Add Counters dialog box opens.

2. In the Add Counters dialog box, select the computer from which you want to obtain data. If you select Use Local Computer Counters, data is collected from the local computer. If you choose Select Counters From Computer, you can use either an IP address, or the UNC name of the computer for which you want to collect data. Figure 11-15 shows the Add Counters dialog box.

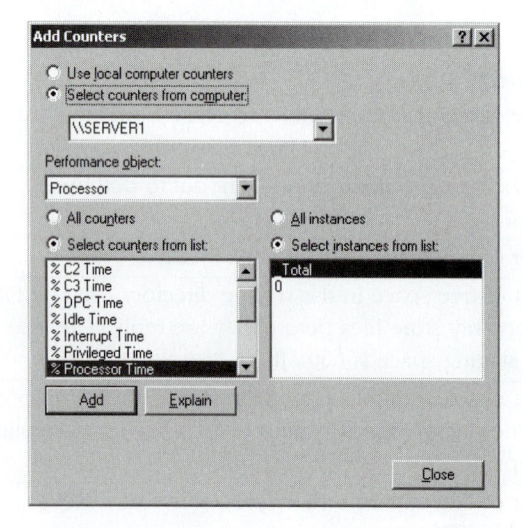

Figure 11-15   System Monitor Add Counters dialog box

3. In the Performance Object list, select the performance object you want to monitor. For example, to monitor Active Directory, select the NTDS object.

4. Select the counters you want to monitor. If you want to monitor all counters, select the All Counters button. If you want to monitor only particular counters, click the Select Counters From List button and select the individual counters you want to monitor. You can select multiple counters by holding the CTRL key and clicking on the counters.

5. Click the Add button.

6. When you are finished adding counters, click Close. The chosen counters appear in the lower part of System Monitor. Each counter is represented by a different color.

7. On the toolbar, you can change the display output to reflect graph, histogram, or report display by choosing the appropriate tool. It is easiest to use a graph format if you are monitoring performance over extended periods of time. Reports and histograms only reflect the most recent values and averages, and may not reflect the information you need for long-term reporting.

You may also want to set additional parameters such as the interval of time between data collections. To set additional parameters, you must modify the System Monitor Properties settings. Figure 11-16 shows the General tab of the System Monitor Properties dialog box from which you can modify these options.

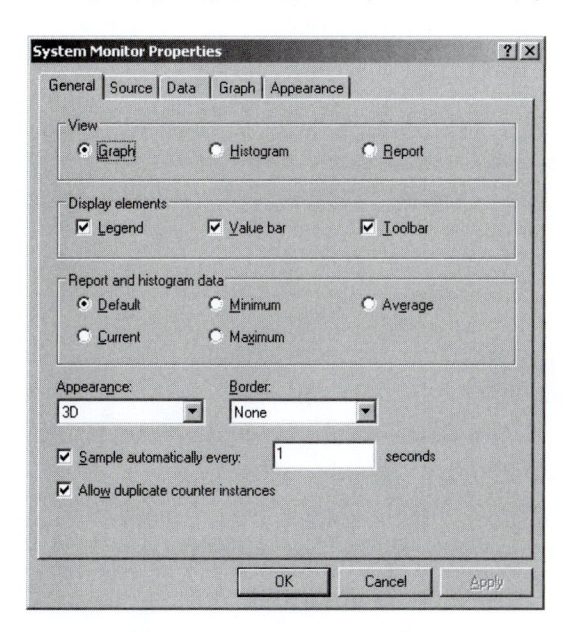

Figure 11-16   System Monitor Properties General tab

Configuring Alerts

Although you can set counters to assist you in monitoring your network through System Monitor, it is impossible to expect that counters are constantly monitored. Generally, System Monitor reports are examined and perhaps used for documentation.

System Monitor allows an administrator to set alerts that are triggered when a counter exceeds or falls below a certain threshold. For example, you may want to have an alert set that notifies a particular user and also writes a warning event to the Application log when the disk space on the volume containing the Active Directory database falls below 50 megabytes (MB). This allows immediate attention to be devoted to resolving a potentially critical event prior to any negative impact. As you configure alerts in System Monitor, limit your alerts to only items that require immediate attention. Unnecessary alerts defeat the purpose of the tool and may be considered more of a burden than they're worth.

▶ **Configuring an Alert Using System Monitor**

To configure an alert using System Monitor, complete the following steps:

1. Click Start, point to Administrative Tools, and then click Performance.
2. Double-click Performance Logs And Alerts and then click Alerts. Existing alerts are listed in the details pane. A green icon indicates that the alerts are running; a red icon indicates alerts are stopped.
3. Right-click a blank area of the details pane and click New Alert Settings.
4. In the New Alert Settings dialog box, in the Name box, type the name of the alert, and then click OK.
5. In the General tab of the dialog box for the alert, type a comment to describe the alert in the Comment box, and then click Add.
6. In the Add Counters dialog box, choose the computer for which you want to create an alert.

   NOTE **Alert Creation Options** *To create an alert on the computer on which the Performance Logs And Alerts service runs, click Use Local Computer Counters. To create an alert on a specific computer, regardless of where the service is run, click Select Counters From Computer and specify the name of the computer.*

7. In the Performance Object list, select NTDS.
8. Select the counters you want to monitor and then click Add.
9. Click Close when you have finished selecting counters to monitor for the alert.
10. In the General tab, specify Under or Over in the Alert When The Value Is box. In the Limit box, specify the value that should trigger the alert.
11. In the Sample Data Every section, specify the amount and the unit of measure for the update interval in the Interval box and the Units box, respectively.
12. In the Action tab of the dialog box for the alert, select an option for when an alert is triggered, as described in Table 11-3.

13. In the Schedule tab of the dialog box for the alert, configure the options as shown for counter logs.
14. Click OK.

Table 11-3 **Options in the Action Tab**

Option	Description
Log An Entry In The Application Event Log	Creates an entry that is visible in the Application log in Event Viewer
Send A Network Message To	Triggers the Messenger service to send a message to the specified computer
Start Performance Data Log	Runs a specified counter log when an alert occurs
Run This Program	Triggers the service to create a process and run a specified program when an alert occurs
Command Line Arguments	Triggers the service to copy specified command line arguments when the Run This Program option is used

The next section covers several key points to remember when troubleshooting Active Directory functionality and replication.

DIAGNOSING AND TROUBLESHOOTING ACTIVE DIRECTORY

After you collect information through your monitoring process, you must have an understanding of the tools and techniques used to further investigate a potential problem. For example, the logs available in Event Viewer only record critical events and errors in the Directory Service log. In some cases, by the time the error is recorded, the problem may be serious. To assist you with obtaining more detailed information in the event logs, you can set the event logs to record diagnostic information specific to Active Directory–related processes. Configuring Active Directory diagnostic event logging requires that you edit the registry. The following key contains the additional areas that can be logged into the Directory Service log:

`HKEY_LOCAL_MACHINE\SYSTEM\CurrentControlSet\Services\NTDS\Diagnostics`

If you decide to configure any of these additional processes for logging in Event Viewer, then consider increasing the size of the log files. Additional entries may cause your logs to fill up faster than you originally anticipated, and therefore you need to make adjustments so that data is not overwritten when the log fills up. In addition, when you increase monitoring, it can impact performance. You should monitor only items that you suspect might be causing problems.

> **MORE INFO** **Diagnostic Event Logging** For more information about configuring Diagnostic Event Logging, see Microsoft Knowledge Base Article 314980, "HOW TO: Configure Active Directory Diagnostic Event Logging in Windows 2000."

> **CAUTION** **Editing the Registry** Editing the registry can be a risky process and should only be attempted by experienced administrators. Mistakes made during registry editing can cause irreversible damage to your operating system.

In addition to monitoring Event Viewer and System Monitor, many of the tools mentioned previously in this textbook are helpful in diagnosing and troubleshooting Active Directory–related problems. Table 11-4 lists these tools and how they can assist in diagnosing problems in Active Directory.

Table 11-4 Active Directory Diagnostic Tools

Tool	Description
Dcdiag	This Windows Support tool can analyze the state of the domain controllers in the forest or enterprise and report any problems to assist in troubleshooting.
Dsastat	This Windows Support tool can compare directory information on domain controllers and detect differences.
Replmon	This Windows Support tool can display replication topology, monitor replication status, including group policies, and force replication events and knowledge consistency checker (KCC) recalculation. This tool has a graphical user interface (GUI).
Repadmin	This Windows Support tool can check replication consistency between replication partners, monitor replication status, display replication metadata, and force replication events and knowledge consistency checker (KCC) recalculation.
Netdom	This Windows Support tool can manage and verify trusts, join computers to domains, and verify replication ability and permissions between partners.
Ntfrsutl	This Windows Support tool can list the active replica sets in a domain, in addition to displaying FRS memory, configuration and display of the ID table, and the inbound log or outbound log for a computer hosting FRS.
Netdiag	This Windows Support tool can be used to diagnose and troubleshoot connectivity and client issues. It has a wide range of capabilities that include domain controller discovery, DNS, Kerberos, and IPSec. Using the /fix switch, it can be used to correct DNS entries and GUIDs on domain controllers.
ADSIEdit	This graphic Windows Support tool can be used to verify the current functional level and perform low-level Active Directory editing. It provides a means to add, delete, and edit Active Directory objects.
LDP	This graphic support tool provides a much more detailed method of adding, removing, searching, and modifying the Active Directory database.
Kerbtray	This downloadable tool is used to display ticket information for a computer running the Kerberos protocol.
Nltest	This tool is typically used to verify trusts and check replication. This tool was originally created for Windows NT version 4.0.
DSAcls	This command line tool can be used to display or modify permissions of an Active Directory object. In effect, it is equivalent to the Security tab of an object.

SYSTEM SERVICES

Depending on the type of server, either a domain controller or member server, you want to be aware of services that are required for Active Directory functionality. Because there are security threats in the computing world, many companies are increasing their security. They increase security partly by disabling services that are unnecessary within their specific environments. The information presented here is intended for Active Directory functionality on a domain controller. It is important to note that if you plan to add additional services or other applications such as Microsoft Exchange, you must become familiar with their dependencies. The most difficult part of securing your system by disabling services is in understanding which services are needed for basic functionality. Table 11-5 lists the base services that are required on a domain controller running Windows 2000, or higher.

To view and understand the services on your domain controller, do Exercise 11-1 now.

Table 11-5   Domain Controller Required Services

Service	Description
Distributed File System	This service is required for the Active Directory Sysvol share.
File Replication	This service is needed for file replication between domain controllers.
Intersite Messaging	This service is needed for Active Directory replication.
Kerberos Key Distribution Center	This service is required to allow users to log on using the Kerberos protocol.
Remote Procedure Call (RPC) Locator	This service allows the domain controller to provide RPC name service.
DNS Server	This service is required if Active Directory–integrated DNS is in use.
Netlogon	This service is responsible for maintaining a secure channel between clients or domain controllers connected to this domain controller.
Windows Time	This service provides time synchronization for all clients and servers within the domain.

SUMMARY

- Active Directory has two defragmentation methods: online defragmentation and offline defragmentation. Online defragmentation is an automatic process triggered by the garbage collection process. Offline defragmentation is a manual process that requires the server to be restarted in Directory Services Restore mode. The ntdsutil.exe command line utility is used to perform the offline defragmentation.

- The Active Directory database can be moved to a new location should you decide that there is a need to relocate it due to space limitations. This is accomplished with the ntdsutil.exe command line utility.

- When you backup Active Directory, you need to include the System State data. The System State data includes operating system–specific information that is needed for installed services and operating system components to function.

- In the event of a domain controller failure, there are three restore options in Windows Server 2003. They include: primary, normal, and authoritative. The primary restore method is required when all Active Directory information is lost for the entire domain. The normal restore method restores the Active Directory database to its state before the backup. After a normal restore, replication of more recent object information from other domain controllers is used to update the database to match all other domain controllers. An authoritative restore uses the Ntdsutil command line utility and allows you to mark records that supercede any existing records during replication.

- Active Directory cannot be restored from a backup that is older than the default tombstone lifetime of 60 days. Domain controllers keep track of deleted objects only for the duration of the tombstone lifetime.

- When monitoring the health of Active Directory, you can examine the Directory Service log to obtain information. The Directory Service log is created when Active Directory is installed. By default, it logs informational events such as service start and stop messages, errors, and warnings. Additional diagnostic logging can be achieved by modifying the registry.

- System Monitor in Windows Server 2003 allows you to collect real-time information on your local computer or from a specific computer to which you have permissions. This information can be viewed in a number of different formats that include charts, graphs, and histograms.

- System Monitor uses performance objects, or categories, and performance counters to organize performance information. Performance counters are the specific processes to monitor. There are many counters available, therefore it is important to carefully plan to use only the helpful counters.

- In addition to using the FileReplicaSet counters, you can use the Ntfrsutl command line utility, which is included in the Windows Support Tools, to monitor the FRS on local and remote computers.

- As part of your effort to secure your domain environment, you should be aware of the required services for Active Directory functionality. Several of the base required services include Net Logon, File Replication, Distributed File System, Intersite Messaging, Kerberos Key Distribution Center, Remote Procedure Call (RPC) Locator, and Windows Time. If the domain controller is providing DNS, then DNS should be enabled as well.

EXERCISE

Exercise 11-1: Viewing System Services

To view and understand the services currently running on your domain controller, complete the following steps:

1. Open the Services tool from the Administrative Tools folder.
2. Locate the services listed in Table 11-5 and note their current status and startup type on a separate sheet of paper.
3. Of the additional services that are listed as Started, list several additional services and provide a brief description of what they do.
4. Select several of the services from the list you created in steps 2 and 3 and locate them within the Services tool. Double-click on each service and select the Dependencies tab.

   QUESTION What type of information is provided on this tab?

5. After reviewing several services from step 4, can you find any similarities in dependencies? If so, note them and be prepared to share your findings with your class.
6. Close the Services tool.

REVIEW QUESTIONS

1. Which Active Directory performance-monitoring tool should you use first to locate the causes of a problem with Active Directory?
2. What is the difference between a performance object and a performance counter?
3. What is the function of an alert?
4. You are the network administrator for a small legal firm that is using a single-server Windows Server 2003 network. You are preparing to back up your server for the first time and you need to ensure that the Active Directory database, in addition to the Certificate Services database, is backed up. What type of backup will you need to perform?
5. Describe a normal restore, when you might use it, and the tool that you must understand to perform it.
6. Describe an authoritative restore, when you might use it, and the tool that you must understand to perform it.

7. Which method of restore should you use if a domain controller has completely failed?

8. As part of your weekly monitoring review, you discover that the disk that holds the Sysvol volume is extremely low on space. You recently removed the global catalog role that was originally assigned to this server in hopes of recovering some of the space. It seems that you need to find another solution for your low drive space problem. You determine that until you upgrade the server, you have no other location to which you can move the Active Directory database and Sysvol contents. What can you do to try to recover some of the space?

CASE SCENARIO

Scenario 11-1: Consulting for Margie's Travel

You are a computer consultant for Margie Shoop, the owner of Margie's Travel. Margie has a single Active Directory domain structure with the domain margiestravel.com. Margie has travel agencies worldwide, at 50 locations in 7 countries. All locations are connected to a satellite array. Margie has signed a 10-year contract to provide satellite access to her 500 locations. Connectivity to the satellite array varies from 57 Kbps to 128 Kbps. Although her locations vary greatly in the number of computer and user accounts, each location with more than 15 users has its own domain controller, global catalog server, and DNS server, all typically configured on the same computer. There are nine sites in the margiestravel.com Active Directory infrastructure.

Given this information about Margie's Travel, answer the following questions:

1. You discuss performance monitoring with Margie. During your conversation, you learn no one has ever used System Monitor to check the performance of her domain controllers. Margie wants to know why anyone would even bother. What do you say to her?

2. Margie tells you that some of her domain controllers have multiple hard disks. She tells you that the additional physical hard disks are not being used. She wants to know if they can be used in some way to improve the performance of Active Directory. What would you tell her?

3. Margie says that her local domain controllers operate slowly sometimes. She theorizes that this could be due to the other domain controllers synchronizing information with her local domain controllers. What could you monitor to help solve Margie's problem?

4. Margie sends you to Cairo, Egypt, to troubleshoot a few domain controllers in her Egypt location. You find some event messages concerning replication events, but you would like to see more detailed information than what is in the log now. What can you do?

CHAPTER 12
UPGRADING AND MIGRATING TO WINDOWS SERVER 2003

Upon completion of this chapter, you will be able to:

- Understand the difference between a **migration** and an **upgrade**.
- Define the upgrade and migration paths available.
- Understand the required steps to upgrade or migrate from Microsoft Windows NT Server 4.0 to Microsoft Windows Server 2003.
- Associate migration tools that are available with the tasks they can be used to perform.
- Explain the difference between an interforest migration and an intraforest migration.
- Explain the process and recommended order for upgrading Windows NT 4.0 domains.
- Explain the necessary security privileges for migrating between two forests.
- Explain the necessary requirements for migrating sIDHistory information to the target domain.

This chapter introduces the key planning decisions and tasks that are necessary during an upgrade or migration to Windows Server 2003. It covers the required procedures for upgrading and migrating from either Microsoft Windows NT 4.0 or Microsoft Windows 2000 domains to a Microsoft Windows Server 2003 forest. This chapter is not intended to be a comprehensive guide, but is rather an introduction and reference for understanding the upgrade and migration processes.

REASONS TO UPGRADE OR MIGRATE

When a company makes the decision to transition from one operating system version to another, it is a decision that requires careful planning. Chapter 1, "Overview of Active Directory," contains explanations of many new features that are only available in Windows Server 2003. When an organization's network is upgraded, these features can be used. There are three paths that can be taken to transition a company network to a Windows Server 2003 environment. They include the following:

- Performing an upgrade
- Performing a migration
- Performing a clean installation

A clean installation means installing the new operating system on a newly formatted drive and freshly configuring all new services such as Active Directory and DNS.

The terms "upgrade" and "migrate" can be confusing and are often used interchangeably when they have not been properly defined. However, these two methods are distinctly different from one another. The difference between them determines the approach that is taken to plan and implement the new operating system. Transitioning to Windows Server 2003 sometimes employs both of these methods in order to obtain the desired structure for the new network. Upgrade and migration are defined as follows:

- **Upgrade** An upgrade, sometimes referred to as an in-place upgrade, assumes that you are satisfied with the domain structure of the existing network. The term *in-place* means that the existing hardware is compatible with the new operating system and that the upgrade is performed directly on that computer. In addition, an upgrade also assumes that the source operating system has been checked for upgradeability to the new operating system. After upgrading the servers, the physical structure of the old network remains intact. In other words, the upgrade of a network with 20 domains results in the same 20 domains with users and resources remaining in the same locations as they were originally. In a Windows NT 4.0 upgrade to Windows Server 2003, the Windows NT 4.0 domains become Windows Server 2003 functional level domains only after all domains have been upgraded. The version of the original operating system dictates the required procedures for upgrading to the new operating system version.

- **Migration** The migration process involves the restructuring of the logical network. For example, when a company network running Windows NT 4.0 includes many domains joined by trust relationships, it may be wise to plan a new structure that consolidates domains to ease administration and improve accessibility. Several different approaches exist for simplifying the domain structure through the migration process. Many migrations consist of the upgrade to a new domain followed by the migration of existing domains to the newly created structure. The version of the original operating system impacts the required procedures and final outcome of the migration.

> **NOTE** **Supported Upgrade Paths** An important part of planning includes ensuring the source domain operating system can be upgraded to Windows Server 2003. If you plan to upgrade from an operating system version prior to Windows Server 2003, you can consult a supported upgrade paths table located in the Windows Server 2003 documentation at http://www.microsoft.com /windowsserver2003/evaluation/whyupgrade/supportedpaths.mspx.

MIGRATING AND UPGRADING WINDOWS NT 4.0 TO WINDOWS SERVER 2003

When transitioning from a Windows NT 4.0 network to a Windows Server 2003 environment, the procedure is likely a hybrid approach that consists of both upgrade and migration procedures. You may perform an in-place upgrade on some servers while restructuring and migrating other servers to consolidate domains.

Small to medium-sized organizations that are currently running Windows NT 4.0 can take advantage of Active Directory features by upgrading their environment to the Standard Edition, Enterprise Edition, or Datacenter Edition of Windows Server 2003. When performing an upgrade of a Windows NT 4.0 domain to a Windows Server 2003 Active Directory environment, the existing server hardware can be used if it meets the Windows Server 2003 system requirements. Alternatively, new server hardware can be introduced.

Upgrading a Windows NT 4.0 domain to Windows Server 2003 Active Directory involves the following steps:

- Preparing to upgrade
- Upgrading the PDC
- Upgrading any additional domain controllers
- Completing post-upgrade tasks

The following sections cover each of these steps.

> **NOTE** **Consolidating Multiple Windows NT 4.0 Domains** If you are consolidating multiple Windows NT 4.0 domains into a single Active Directory domain by using a restructuring tool such as the Active Directory Migration Tool (ADMT), see "Migrating from Microsoft Windows NT Server 4.0 to Windows Server 2003" on the Web at http://www.microsoft.com/reskit.

Preparing to Upgrade

The preparation phase of upgrading Windows NT Server 4.0 to Windows Server 2003 should include the following tasks:

- **Document the existing environment.** This can be accomplished either manually or by using a network discovery tool such as Visio Network AutoDiscovery. Documentation of the existing domain structure, services, and resources assist you in planning and flagging potential difficulties that may occur.

- **Back up your Windows NT 4.0 domain data.** A solid backup of your existing Primary Domain Controllers (PDCs) and backup domain controllers (BDCs) is a best practice for disaster recovery in the event you need to restore your network to Windows NT Server 4.0.

- **Identify the current versions of Windows NT Server 4.0.** In order for the upgrade process to function, Windows NT 4.0 servers must be running Service Pack 5 or later.

- **Assess hardware requirements.** You must ensure that the servers you intend to upgrade contain the appropriate hardware requirements to run the new operating system. You should ensure that there is ample free disk space to hold the Active Directory database and log files. The Winnt32.exe command line tool can be used to identify any potential upgrade problems, such as inadequate hardware resources or compatibility problems.

To identify potential upgrade problems, use the `winnt32 /checkupgradeonly` command located in the I386 directory on your installation media. For example, if your installation source is the Windows Server 2003 operating system CD in the D drive, select Run from the Start menu and type the following command:

```
D:\I386>winnt32 /checkupgradeonly
```

It can take a few minutes for the Microsoft Windows Upgrade Advisor screen to appear. The report generated by the Microsoft Windows Upgrade Advisor assists you in identifying incompatibilities. Reported problems such as incompatible hardware issues and insufficient disk space requirements must be resolved before proceeding with the upgrade.

- **Delegate the DNS zone for the new Windows Server 2003 domain.** To configure the DNS zone for the single domain forest, the DNS administrator of your existing DNS infrastructure delegates the zone that matches the name of the new Windows Server 2003 domain to the DNS servers that are running on the domain controllers in the single domain forest. The delegation that occurs in this step references the first Windows Server 2003–based domain controller, which does not currently exist. The DNS service is installed and configured on the first Windows Server 2003–based domain controller in a later step. However, it is important to add this record before you install Active Directory on the PDC, because the Active Directory Installation Wizard uses the record to configure the new DNS zone that Active Directory uses.

▶ **To delegate the DNS zone for the Windows Server 2003 domain, complete the following steps:**

1. Create a name server (NS) resource record in the parent zone. Use the full DNS name of the domain controller, as follows:

   `forest_root_domain IN NS domain_controller_name`

2. Create a host address (A) resource record in the parent zone. Use the full DNS name of the domain controller, as follows:

   `domain_controller_name IN A domain_controller_ip_address`

For example, Fabrikam's PDC name is SEA-FAB-DC01, and its IP address is 172.16.12.2. During the Active Directory installation, Fabrikam installs the DNS Server service on this domain controller. In preparation for that step, the DNS administrator for Fabrikam created the following DNS resource records in the parent zone, fabrikam.com:

```
fabricorp IN NS SEA-FAB-DC01.fabricorp.fabrikam.com
SEA-FAB-DC01.fabricorp.fabrikam.com IN A 172.16.12.2
```

> **NOTE** **Delegating the DNS zone for Windows Server 2003** If you do not have a DNS infrastructure, or if your DNS services are provided by an ISP, you do not need to complete this step.

- **Relocate the LAN Manager Replication (LMRepl) file replication service.** The Windows Server 2003 File Replication Service (FRS) replaces LMRepl from Windows NT Server 4.0. In Windows NT Server 4.0, the LMRepl service is responsible for replicating the NetLogon share containing logon scripts and profiles. The LMRepl service can be configured on both member servers and domain controllers in the Windows NT 4.0 environment. In Windows Server 2003, the Sysvol shared folder contains information that was previously supported by LMRepl in Windows NT Server 4.0. Because the LMRepl service is no longer supported in Windows Server 2003, it is necessary to ensure that the logon scripts and profiles once supported by this service are available after the upgrade to Windows Server 2003. In addition, if you plan to upgrade the Windows NT 4.0 servers over time, you must ensure that the LMRepl service is maintained for servers that continue to run Windows NT Server 4.0. In order to maintain the replication of files in the NetLogon shared folder in the Windows NT 4.0 network, upgrade all servers that are hosting import directories before you upgrade the server that is hosting the export directory.

    > **NOTE** **LMRepl Replication Server** Windows NT 4.0 Server contains both an import and an export directory as part of the NetLogon shared folder structure. The export directory is considered the main replication directory. The contents of the export directory are replicated to all servers containing an import directory. To determine whether the PDC is hosting the export directory, open Server Manager, select the PDC, click Computer from the menu bar, and then click Properties. Click Replication and verify that Export Directories is selected.

If the PDC you want to upgrade is hosting the export directory, you can do one of the following:

- Promote a BDC that meets the Windows Server 2003 domain controller hardware requirements to become the new PDC and demote the existing PDC to serve as a BDC hosting the export server.

- Reconfigure the LMRepl export server on a BDC and remove it from the PDC.

    > **NOTE** **Testing LMRepl** To ensure that LMRepl continues to function, it should be tested. Steps to verify LMRepl's functionality can be found at http://www.microsoft.com/technet/treeview/default.asp?url=/technet/prodtechnol/windowsserver2003/proddocs/deployguide/dssbe_upnt_dknr.asp.

CAUTION *Upgrading More Than One Microsoft Windows NT 4.0 Server* It is important to upgrade the designated LMRepl export server last in order to maintain replication with other servers.

- **Add a Windows Server 2003 member server to the Windows NT 4.0 domain.** Although this step is not required, it is a recommended procedure. Installing a Windows Server 2003 member server into an existing Windows NT 4.0 domain produces no problems for the existing network. However, it does provide a quick and easy second domain controller on the completion of the first Windows Server 2003 domain controller upgrade. After the initial Windows NT 4.0 PDC is upgraded to Windows Server 2003, the member server can be promoted to a second domain controller by installing Active Directory. This provides fault tolerance for the new Active Directory domain.

NOTE *Preventing Changes to the Windows NT 4.0 domain* It is important to ensure that after you complete updates and replicate them to the BDC, no new changes to the domain take place. Changes that take place prior to the upgrade of the PDC to Windows Server 2003 are not part of the offline BDC that is used in the event a recovery is necessary. For more information on this, see Micro-soft Knowledge Base article 326209, "HOW TO: Upgrade a Windows NT 4.0-Based PDC to a Windows Server 2003-Based Domain Controller."

NOTE *Remote Access Service Migration* If Remote Access Service (RAS) or Routing and Remote Access Service (RRAS) is running on the PDC, a BDC, or a member server running Windows NT 4.0, you should migrate the service before you upgrade the operating system on that server. If you do not, you will have to reduce the security of your domain controllers once the domain is installed, as described in Microsoft Knowledge Base articles 325363, 254311, and 240855.

Upgrading the PDC

When you are finished with all of the preparatory tasks, you are ready to upgrade the PDC to Windows Server 2003. The two approaches that can be taken with regard to the domain structure outcome include either a single-domain strategy or a multi-domain strategy. These are explained in the next sections.

A Single-Domain Strategy

A single-domain strategy typically begins with an in-place upgrade of the PDC in the largest account domain. In Windows NT 4.0, domains are usually separated into account and resource domains. Account domains contain the user accounts that provide logon capabilities. The resource domains contain the resources such as printers that users need to access for productivity. This upgraded domain becomes the forest root of the new Windows Server 2003 forest.

Figure 12-1 shows a Windows NT 4.0 network for A. Datum Corporation that contains two account domains and one resource domain. In this particular instance, the PDC in the Acct_DomainB domain should be upgraded first based on the fact that there are more users in the domain than in the Acct_DomainA domain.

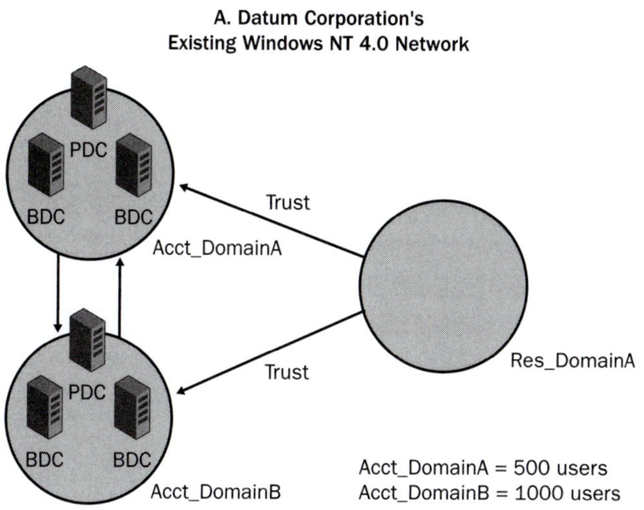

Figure 12-1 A. Datum Corporation's Windows NT 4.0 Network

When the PDC in Acct_DomainB is upgraded to Windows Server 2003, the functional level for the upgraded forest should be set to Windows Server 2003 interim until all domains have been upgraded or migrated to the new structure.

During the operating system upgrade, the computer restarts three times. After you upgrade the operating system on a Windows NT 4.0 domain controller to Windows Server 2003, the computer is in an intermediate state. The computer is no longer a Windows NT 4.0–based domain controller, and it is not a Windows Server 2003–based member server or domain controller until Active Directory is installed. After the computer restarts for the last time, the Active Directory Installation Wizard appears so that you can complete the domain upgrade. The Active Directory Installation Wizard creates the Active Directory database and moves objects from the Windows NT 4.0 Security Accounts Manager (SAM) to the Active Directory database. In addition, on the first domain controller in a new domain, the wizard completes the following tasks:

- Prompts the administrator to verify the installation and configuration of the DNS Server service.

- Configures DNS recursive name resolution forwarding by adding the IP addresses of the existing entries for Preferred DNS Server and Alternate DNS server to the list of DNS Servers on the Forwarders tab of the Properties sheet for the domain controller.

- Configures DNS recursive name resolution by root hints by adding the root hints that are configured on the Preferred DNS server to the list of DNS Servers on the Root Hints tab of the Properties sheet for the domain controller.

- Configures the Preferred DNS Server to point to the DNS server that is running locally on the domain controller, and configures the Alternate DNS Server to point to the closest DNS server.

- Creates two application directory partitions that are used by DNS. The DomainDnsZones application directory partition holds domain-wide DNS data, and the ForestDnsZones application directory partition holds forest-wide DNS data.

- Prompts the administrator to select the forest functional level. This should be set to Windows Server 2003 interim. When performing an upgrade, only two functional levels are available during the upgrade process: Windows Server 2003 interim and Windows 2000. Setting the forest functional level to Windows Server 2003 interim enables Windows NT 4.0 servers to co-exist until they can be upgraded.

When you complete the Active Directory Installation Wizard, verify that all information on the Summary page is accurate. After the Active Directory Installation Wizard finishes, you are prompted to restart the computer. The installation is not complete until the computer restarts. The newly upgraded Windows Server 2003 domain controller holds the PDC emulator FSMO role. The PDC emulator role allows the remaining BDCs in the domain to view the Active Directory database as if it is the same as the Windows NT 4.0 original SAM database.

Once the initial domain controller processes are complete, you can continue upgrading or retiring the remaining BDCs from the same domain until all desired domain controllers are upgraded. Figure 12-2 illustrates the A. Datum Corporation's new domain structure for the servers from the Acct_DomainB domain.

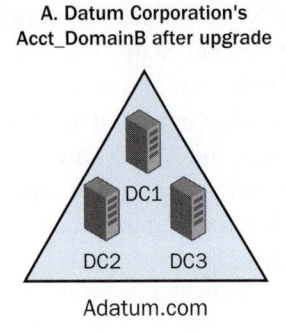

Figure 12-2   A. Datum Corporation's Windows Server 2003 domain

Migrating External Domains   In order to end up with a single domain structure for A. Datum Corporation, the externally trusted domains named Acct_DomainA and Res_DomainA must be migrated into the new forest root domain using **Active Directory Migration Tool (ADMT)**. ADMT is a migration tool that can be used to migrate users, groups, and computers from one domain to another. When migrating from either Windows NT 4.0 Server or Windows 2000, two types of domain migration can be used: interforest migration and intraforest migration. These migration types are described in the following sections.

Interforest   The term **interforest migration** is used to define the migration of objects across domain and forest boundaries. For example, migrating from Windows NT Server 4.0 is always considered an interforest migration because Windows NT 4.0 domains cannot be part of a Windows 2000 or Windows Server 2003 Active Directory forest. Interforest migrations clone objects in the target domain.

Cloning means that the objects are copied rather than moved. The accounts are mirrored in the target domain and the sIDHistory attribute of the migrated object allows accessibility to resources allowed in the source domain to remain intact. Cloning provides a safety net in case of an emergency when you need to restore the original domain structure. Table 12-1 defines the tools available for performing interforest migration tasks.

Table 12-1 Interforest Migration Tools

Utility	Description
Active Directory Migration Tool (ADMT)	ADMT is a Microsoft Management Console (MMC) snap-in that provides graphical support in the form of wizards to automate migration tasks such as moving users, groups, and computers between or within forests, migrating trusts, and performing security translation.
ClonePrincipal	Used to clone user and group accounts from a Windows NT 4.0 or Windows 2000 source domain in a separate forest to a native mode Windows 2000 or Windows Server 2003 target domain.
Netdom	Used to move computer accounts from a Windows NT 4.0 or Windows 2000 source domain to a Windows 2000 or Windows Server 2003 target domain.
	Netdom is also used to re-create trusts, typically in migration scenarios between the target domains and any domains trusted by or trusting the source domain.

Intraforest The term **intraforest migration** is used to define the migration of objects from domains within the existing forest. This method is used when a restructure of the logical network is desired, but all objects are part of the same forest. For example, an intraforest migration does not include migrations that involve Windows NT Server 4.0. Only Windows 2000 or other Windows Server 2003 domains can be restructured using an intraforest migration. This method is destructive because the source object no longer exists after the objects are moved. Table 12-2 defines the tools available to perform an intraforest migration.

Table 12-2 Intraforest Migration Tools

Utility	Description
Active Directory Migration Tool (ADMT)	ADMT is a Microsoft Management Console (MMC) snap-in that provides graphical support in the form of wizards to automate migration tasks such as moving users, groups, and computers between or within forests, migrating trusts, and performing security translation.
Movetree	Used for moving users, groups, and organizational units (OUs) between Windows 2000 or Windows Server 2003 domains in the same forest.
Netdom	Used to move computer accounts from a Windows NT 4.0 or Windows 2000 source domain to a Windows 2000 or Windows Server 2003 target domain.
	Netdom is also used to re-create trusts, typically in migration scenarios between the target domains and any domains trusted by or trusting the source domain.

ADMT provides a tool that simplifies and supports many of the common migration tasks. ADMT includes wizards that automate migration tasks such as copying users, groups, and service accounts, moving computers, migrating trusts, and performing security translation. Security translation replaces the access control entries (ACEs) on resource ACLs so that security identifiers (SIDs) from the source domain are replaced with the migrated users' new SIDs in the target domain. The process of copying domain user accounts and computer accounts from different source domains to a single target domain is referred to as restructuring.

When you use ADMT to restructure Windows NT 4.0 domains, ADMT copies the accounts that are migrated, so that when the accounts are created in the target domain, they continue to exist in the source domain. The primary security identifiers (SIDs) for the accounts can be migrated to the sIDHistory in the target domain.

In addition, it can be used to analyze the migration outcome before and after the actual process has taken place. Figure 12-3 illustrates that the migrated domains can be placed in OUs of the Windows Server 2003 domain structure.

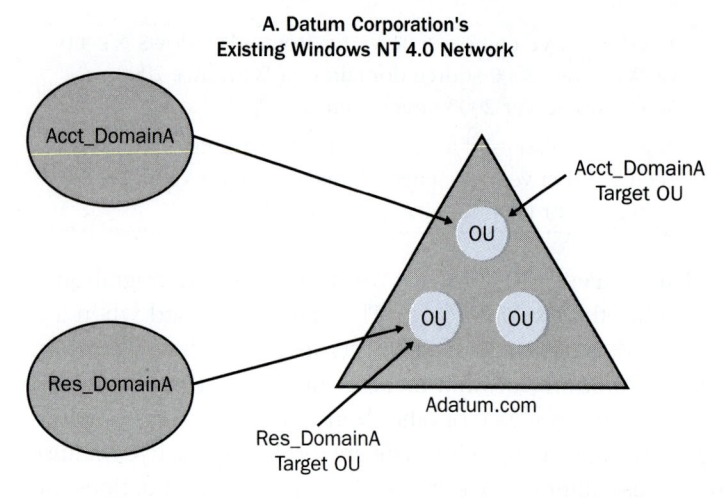

Figure 12-3 A. Datum Corporation's Windows Server 2003 domain with external domains migrated to OUs

> **NOTE Locating ADMT** ADMT is located on the Windows Server 2003 operating system CD as an .msi file named admigration.msi in the \i386\admt directory. ADMT can also be downloaded from Microsoft's web site at http://www.microsoft.com/downloads/details.aspx?familyid=788975b1-5849-4707-9817-8c9773c25c6c&displaylang=en.

Before using ADMT to migrate the remaining domains to Windows Server 2003, the following verifications must be done:

- Ensure that the ADMT tool is run from the server holding the PDC emulator role in the Windows Server 2003 target domain. The target domain is the domain to which you want to migrate objects.

- Ensure that the source domain, the domain containing the objects to be migrated, is running Windows NT Server 4.0 with Service Pack 4 or later.

- Ensure that the target Windows Server 2003 domain has the functional level set to Windows 2000 native. Prior to the migration, you must raise the functional level. In the upgrade process described previously for the first domain, you set the domain functional level to Windows 2000 mixed in order to maintain communication with the BDCs until they upgrade.

Performing ADMT Preparation Tasks   Before running ADMT, you must prepare both the source and the target domains by completing several tasks. These tasks are required domain and security configurations that allow ADMT to function. The ADMT preparation tasks include the following:

- Configure manual trusts between the source domain and the target domain. The source domain must trust the target domain and the target domain must trust the source domain.

- The Domain Admins global group in the source domain must be added to the Administrators local group in the target domain. In addition, the Domain Admins global group in the target domain must be added to the Administrators local group in the source domain. This will allow you to successfully run ADMT and perform the migration.

- A new local group in the source domain named *SourceDomain*$$$ must be created. This group must be left empty. For example, if the domain name is Fabrikam, the new local group will be called Fabrikam$$$.

- Auditing of success and failure for user and group management should be configured in the source domain. Auditing of the success and failure for Audit account management in the target domain should be configured as part of the Default Domain Controllers Policy.

- On the PDC in the source domain, open the registry editor and complete the following:

    a. Navigate to the following key:

    ```
    HKEY_LOCAL_MACHINE\System\CurrentControlSet\Control\LSA registry key
    ```

    b. Add the following value:

    ```
    TcpipClientSupport:REG_DWORD:0x1
    ```

CAUTION   Editing the Registry   Using Registry Editor can be risky. If edits are incorrect, serious problems may result in the necessity to reinstall the operating system.

NOTE   Configuring Migration Tasks Automatically   Configuring the previously described local group, auditing, and registry modification can be performed automatically by using the User Migration Wizard in Test mode within ADMT.

MORE INFO   Detailed ADMT Information   Detailed information and procedures for ADMT can be located in the Windows Server 2003 product documentation. The documentation can be found at http://www.microsoft.com/technet/treeview/default.asp?url=/technet/prodtechnol/windowsserver2003/support/Default.asp.

A Multi-Domain Strategy

A multi-domain strategy is the second strategy that can be used to upgrade the A. Datum Corporation's Windows NT 4.0 network to Windows Server 2003. The structure of the upgraded network in this scenario is that all domains remain separate domains, but they are part of a single-forest structure with parent/child domains. The goals of the organization for this multi-domain strategy are usually administration-based. If the company wants to maintain separate domains based on any business concern, such as delegated domain administration, this strategy might be best.

Procedures for Multi-Domain Strategy Figure 12-4 shows the A. Datum Corporation network in a multi-domain strategy after migration. Notice that there is a forest root from which all domains become children. The forest root domain is typically empty and contains a new Windows Server 2003 environment.

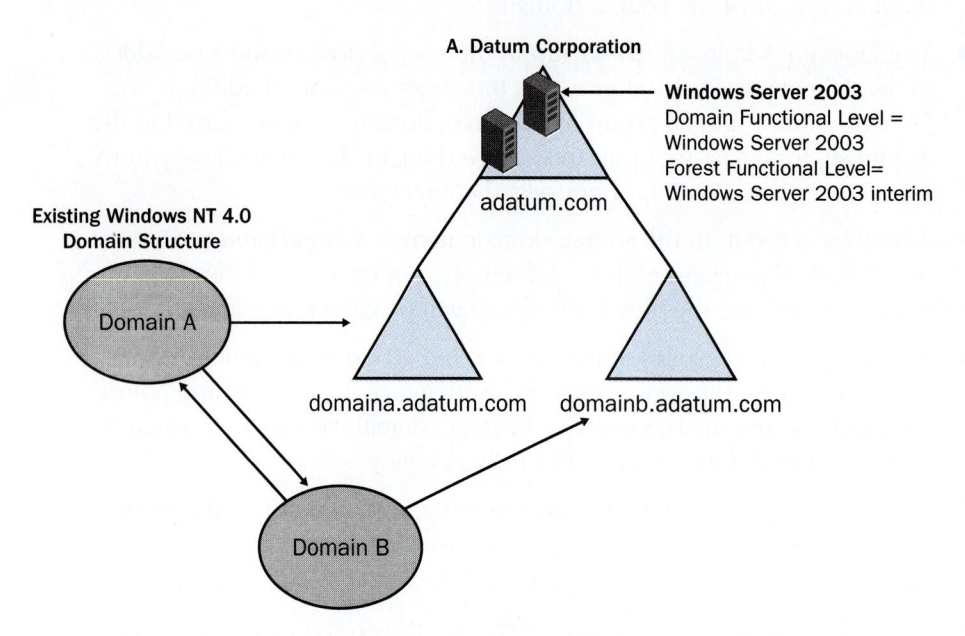

Figure 12-4 A. Datum Corporation's Windows Server 2003 domain using a multi-domain strategy

The tasks required to complete the migration from multiple Windows NT 4.0 domains to a Windows Server 2003 multi-domain forest are as follows:

- **Install a new Windows Server 2003 empty forest root domain** The first domain controller must have Active Directory installed on it as the forest root domain. This should be a new server, not one that has been upgraded from your Windows NT 4.0 domain.

- **Modify the domain and forest functional levels** The domain functional level must be set to either Windows 2000 native or Windows Server 2003. This can be accomplished by using Active Directory Domains And Trusts. As you may recall, the Windows Server 2003 domain functional level does not provide accessibility for Windows 2000 or earlier domain controllers. The step assumes you have no intentions of maintaining functionality for prior operating system versions. The forest functional level must be set to Windows Server 2003 interim. Because you previously performed a new installation of Active Directory, setting the forest functional level to Windows Server 2003 interim is not available by default within a graphical user interface (GUI) such as Active Directory Domains And Trusts. You must use either the Adsiedit.msc tool or the Ldp.exe command-line tool.

MORE INFO Using ADSIEdit and LDP To Modify Functional Levels *The Windows Server 2003 Deployment Kit offers detailed information on how to modify functional levels using Adsiedit.msc and Ldp.exe. The deployment kit can be found at http://www.microsoft.com/downloads/details.aspx?familyid=6cde6ee7-5df1-4394-92ed-2147c3a9ebbe&displaylang=en.*

- **Create delegation entries in DNS for PDCs** As discussed earlier in this chapter, the delegation entries will provide a pre-defined pointer that will be used when Active Directory is installed.

- **Upgrade Windows NT 4.0 PDC** When you upgrade a domain's existing PDC to Windows Server 2003, you must install Active Directory and create this new domain as a child of the empty root domain. This domain is automatically set to Windows Server 2003 interim functional level because the forest functional level was previously set to Windows Server 2003 interim. The Active Directory Installation Wizard automatically notices the DNS delegation and prompts to install DNS locally. When accepted, DNS creates the default application partition for the storage of DNS data. In order for this to occur, you must be logged on as a member of the Enterprise Admins group.

- **Create delegation entries for BDCs and upgrade them** Continue upgrading the BDCs for the child domain.

- **Raise domain to Windows Server 2003 functional level** When all BDCs have been upgraded, raise the functional level of the upgraded domain to Windows Server 2003.

- **Repeat process for additional domains** Continue upgrading additional Windows NT 4.0 domains to Windows Server 2003 by following the same process of first upgrading the PDC and creating a child domain. Each domain that is created should be analyzed to ensure a separate domain is justified. If a separate domain is not warranted, the users and resources can be migrated to an existing domain using ADMT, as described above.

- **Advance forest functional level** After all domains are either upgraded or migrated, and if you want to take full advantage of Windows Server 2003, raise the forest functional level to Windows Server 2003.

MORE INFO Additional Resource for Upgrading from Windows NT Server 4.0 *For more information and detailed procedures, download the "Migrating from Windows NT Server 4.0 to Windows Server 2003" guide located at http://www.microsoft.com/downloads/details.aspx?displaylang=en&familyid=e92cf6a0-76f0-4e25-8de0-19544062a6e6.*

MIGRATING AND UPGRADING WINDOWS 2000 TO WINDOWS SERVER 2003

When performing an upgrade of a Windows 2000 environment to Windows Server 2003, the process is much smoother due to the shared architecture and compatibility of Active Directory between these versions. In a Windows 2000 upgrade scenario, the process does not necessarily include a forest, domain, or OU restructuring unless there is a business reason to change the existing infrastructure. Windows Server 2003 domain controllers can be integrated into the existing Windows 2000 domain as Flexible Single Master Operations (FSMO) role holders or even global catalog servers. New Windows Server 2003 servers can be deployed and become part of the existing infrastructure seamlessly. Once you have determined that you want the entire Windows 2000 infrastructure to be upgraded, you must prepare the existing Windows 2000 domain to accept and accommodate the new features of Windows Server 2003. This includes extending the schema for existing objects and new objects. In addition, it includes hardening the default security for the network. Hardening the security means that the security becomes stronger by taking actions such as removing the Everyone built-in group, which is equivalent to the Authenticated Users group in Windows Server 2003.

Preparing for a Windows 2000 Upgrade

Adprep.exe is the tool that makes all of the necessary changes to transition from Windows 2000 to Windows Server 2003. There are two steps to take to prepare for an upgrade. These include:

- **Preparing the forest** This is accomplished by running Adprep.exe with the /forestprep switch. The adprep /forestprep command must be run on the schema operations master within the domain. You must be logged on as a member of the Schema Admin and Enterprise Admin groups, or you must have the appropriate authority. This forest preparation task extends the schema to include the necessary components for Windows Server 2003. It has little effect on Windows 2000 domain controllers. If domain controllers are running Service Pack 3 or later, there is no affect. If domain controllers are running Service Pack 2, the effects are negligible. When this task is complete, the following container is created:

    ```
    CN=Windows2003Update,CN=ForestUpdates,CN=Configuration,
    DC=<forest_root_domain>,DC=<tld>
    ```

    In the previous example, <forest_root_domain> is replaced with the domain name of the forest root and <tld> refers to the top-level domain. For example, using fabrikam.com as the forest root name, the newly created container is as follows:

    ```
    CN=Windows2003Update,CN=ForestUpdates,CN=Configuration,DC=fabrikam,DC=com
    ```

- **Preparing the domain** This is accomplished by running Adprep.exe with the /domainprep switch. The adprep /domainprep command does not run if the forestprep changes do not exist. This command must be run on the infrastructure master of each domain in the forest. In order to use this command, you must be logged on as a user with domain administrator privileges. The domain preparation process creates several new objects in the Active Directory database and extends the ACLs of several objects so that new features such as Resultant Set of Policies (RSoP) and security changes function properly. When this task is complete, the following container is created in Active Directory:

`CN=Windows2003Update,CN=DomainUpdates,CN=System,DC=<domain>,DC=<tld>`

In the previous example, <domain> is replaced with the proper domain name and <tld> refers to the top-level domain. For example, using fabrikam.com as the domain name, the newly created container is as follows:

`CN=Windows2003Update,CN=DomainUpdates,CN=System,DC=fabrikam,DC=com`

> **NOTE** **Adprep Log Files** Adprep creates a log file that can be used to troubleshoot and document changes made to the Active Directory database. This log file can be found in the following folder:
>
> `systemroot\System32\Debug\Adprep\Logs`

Upgrading to Windows Server 2003

Once the preparation steps are complete, you can proceed to upgrading or joining Windows Server 2003 domain controllers to the domain. There are two methods that can be used to introduce the first Windows Server 2003 computer. They include:

- Upgrade an existing Windows 2000 domain controller or Windows NT 4.0 PDC.
- Install Windows Server 2003 as a member server and run the Active Directory Installation Wizard.

Required User Rights

If you choose to upgrade an existing Windows 2000 domain controller, you must ensure that you have the appropriate rights to perform an upgrade of the operating system. The following rights are required for the user account that performs the upgrade:

- Back up files and directories
- Modify firmware environment values
- Restore files and directories
- Shut down the system

Although the previously listed rights are rights associated by default with the Administrators group, you can verify the rights by using the Local Security Settings MMC snap-in with the Group Policy Object Editor on the Windows 2000 computer.

> **MORE INFO** **Verifying User Rights for the Upgrade** Microsoft Knowledge Base Article 323042, "Required User Rights for the Upgrade from Windows 2000 to Windows Server 2003," provides you with detailed steps on how to verify the necessary user rights for performing an upgrade to Windows Server 2003.

Depending on the desired logical structure for the final network, you can continue upgrading the remaining domains and domain controllers or you can opt to restructure the network to reflect consolidation. The decision to consolidate domains is to be made before the actual process takes place. As part of the planning process, you must ensure that you determine which domains to upgrade and which to migrate before you begin any actual procedures. Migrating from Windows 2000 to Windows Server 2003 is discussed in the next section.

> **MORE INFO** **Upgrading Windows 2000 to Windows Server 2003** Microsoft Knowledge Base Article 325379, "How to Upgrade Windows 2000 Domain Controllers to Windows Server 2003," provides detailed preparation and procedures for upgrading Windows 2000 to Windows Server 2003.

Migrating from Windows 2000 to Windows Server 2003

The migration procedure for Windows 2000 to Windows Server 2003 requires the use of ADMT, as discussed earlier in this chapter. Migration using ADMT allows administrators to maintain user access to resources while domains are being restructured. When migrating from Windows 2000, the migration is considered an interforest migration if you plan to migrate domains from separate forests. However, if you intend to migrate domains within the same forest structure in order to relocate users or resources, a Windows 2000 migration is considered an intraforest migration.

The following sections provide an overview of the migration process using ADMT and assume that you are performing an interforest migration.

Migration Prerequisites

In order for ADMT to function, you must ensure that the following security guidelines are met:

- The user account performing the migration must have Administrator rights in the source domain.
- The user account performing the migration must have Administrator rights on each computer object that you migrate.
- The user account performing the migration must have Administrator rights on each computer for which you translate security from the source domain to the target domain.
- The user account performing the migration must have domain administrator privileges in both the source and target domains.
- Each computer you want to migrate must have the administrative shares C$ and Admin$.
- You must ensure that the source domain trusts the target domain. It is optional that you create a second trust requiring the target domain to trust the source.

ADMT can be configured to migrate sIDHistory by ensuring the following tasks are completed:

- Creation of a new empty local group in the source domain called *Source-Domain$$$*.
- Auditing for success and failure of Audit account management on both domains in the Default Domain Controllers Policy.
- Modification of the registry on the PDC emulator in the source domain to include access to the SAM. This involves the following steps in the Registry Editor:
    - Navigate to the following key:

    `HKEY_LOCAL_MACHINE\System\CurrentControlSet\Control\LSA registry key`

    - Add the following value:

    `TcpipClientSupport:REG_DWORD:0x1`

NOTE **Configuring Migration Tasks Automatically** *Configuring the previously described local group, auditing, and registry modification can be performed automatically by using the User Migration Wizard in Test mode within ADMT. You may be prompted to restart the computer when using this feature.*

Administrators should have a solid migration plan in place before beginning the actual process. It is important to not only be aware of the tools that are available to assist you in performing a migration, but also perform a practice migration in a test environment before performing it live. There are many considerations, such as application compatibility, that should be thoroughly tested before the migration is complete. Management generally does not favorably view interruptions in network service that occur because of poor planning.

MORE INFO **Additional Information on ADMT and Password Migration**
Microsoft Knowledge Base Article 326480, "How to Use Active Directory Migration Tool Version 2 to Migrate from Windows 2000 to Windows Server 2003," provides steps on how to enable interforest password migration.

SUMMARY

- The two main methods used to transition from a previous Windows-based operating system to Windows Server 2003 include upgrade and migration. Whether you choose to upgrade or migrate depends on your existing environment, hardware requirements, and the goals for your new network environment.

- Preparing to upgrade a network includes tasks such as documentation of the existing environment, backup of the existing data, and identification of existing versions and service packs. In addition, you should delegate the DNS zone for the new Windows Server 2003 domain so that the Active Directory Installation Wizard can use the new record to configure the new DNS zone. If the source domain is Windows NT 4.0–based, you must ensure the LMRepl file replication service is maintained for any servers that continue to run Windows NT Server 4.0.

- When upgrading Windows NT Server 4.0 to Windows Server 2003, the domain functional level is automatically set to Windows Server 2003 mixed. This allows any remaining Windows NT 4.0 BDCs in the domain to view the Active Directory domain as if it is a Windows NT 4.0 SAM database.

- Migrations from either Windows NT Server 4.0 or Windows 2000 can be categorized as either interforest or intraforest migrations. Windows NT Server 4.0 migrations are, by default, interforest migrations.

- Interforest migrations can be facilitated through the use of ADMT, ClonePrincipal, and Netdom. Interforest migrations are considered nondestructive since the original objects are maintained. A cross-forest trust must be established in order to migrate between two separate forests.

- Intraforest migrations can be facilitated through the use of ADMT, Movetree, and Netdom. Intraforest migrations are considered destructive since the original objects are destroyed during the migration process.

- The functional level of the Windows Server 2003 target domain should be set to Windows 2000 native in order to migrate from either Windows NT Server 4.0 or Windows 2000.

- ADMT preparation tasks include ensuring appropriate administrative privileges in the source and target domains. In addition, a new source domain local group must be created and named *SourceDomain*$$$. The auditing should be properly configured, and the registry should be modified to accommodate access to the database.

- When upgrading from Windows 2000, the Adprep command line utility is used to prepare the forest and domain for the new Windows Server 2003 Active Directory modifications. The changes include extension of the schema and creation of additional objects and attributes.

- Each computer object that you want to migrate must have the C$ and Admin$ administrative shares.

- ADMT can be configured to migrate sIDHistory and passwords in Windows Server 2003.
- When all migration steps are complete, the forest should be advanced to Windows Server 2003 in order to allow for full functionality of the new network environment.

REVIEW QUESTIONS

1. What are the preparation steps necessary to prepare for the upgrade of Windows NT Server 4.0 to Windows Server 2003?
2. What tools can be used to assist in performing an interforest migration?
3. What tools can be used to assist in performing an intraforest migration?
4. If you are planning to migrate sIDHistory for a Windows 2000 to Windows Server 2003 migration, what steps do you need to take for this to function?
5. What is the difference between Movetree and ClonePrincipal?
6. From where can you obtain ADMT?
7. What type of trust should you create in order to migrate users and computers from a different forest to a local one?
8. From which computer in a Windows 2000 domain should the adprep /domainprep and adprep /forestprep commands be run?

CASE SCENARIO

Scenario 12-1: Restructuring Wingtip Toys

You are a consultant for Wingtip Toys and have been asked to assist in planning and implementing Windows Server 2003 across the entire company over the next several months. The current configuration consists of two Microsoft Windows NT 4.0 domains and a Windows 2000 domain that has a forest root name of wingtiptoys.com. The main office is located in Dallas, Texas, where the forest root domain resides. This Windows 2000 domain has two child domains named for their respective locations as newyork.wingtiptoys.com and sanfran.wingtiptoys.com. There is also an additional Windows 2000 domain located at a remote location in Kansas City that currently has no connectivity to other locations. The Windows NT 4.0 domains each have one PDC and two BDCs. All servers have Service Pack 2 installed.

You have the task of developing a plan that includes restructuring the network to consolidate to one domain with a forest root of wingtiptoys.com. The following questions help you to develop your plan:

1. The New York and San Francisco locations can remain as they are, but both locations must have all servers upgraded to Windows Server 2003. What Windows 2000 domain do you upgrade to Windows Server 2003 first?

2. What must you do before you run the upgrade from the installation media for Windows Server 2003 on the first Windows 2000 domain controller?

3. The Kansas City facility is closing. The users are relocated either to New York or to San Francisco. The data and all user accounts must be transferred from the existing domain to the new domain structure. Where in the Active Directory structure do you put the Kansas City users and what tool do you use to get them there?

4. You must take what considerations into account for the upgrade of the Windows NT 4.0 domains?

5. If you find that the BDC within one of the Windows NT 4.0 domains is the best candidate for the first upgrade procedure, what must you do to upgrade this server first?

6. When you finish upgrading and migrating all of the desired domain controllers, what must you do to take advantage of Windows Server 2003 features such as Universal Group Membership Caching?

APPENDIX A
DNS OVERVIEW

NAME RESOLUTION

Name resolution is an essential function on all Transmission Control Protocol/Internet Protocol (TCP/IP) networks. When you design a network infrastructure, you need to determine names for your computers and how those names will be resolved into IP addresses. As with IP addressing, the names you choose for your computers will be affected by your network's interaction with the Internet and by the applications that the computers run.

What Is Name Resolution?

TCP/IP communication is based on IP addresses. Every IP datagram transmitted by a TCP/IP computer contains a source IP address that identifies the sending computer, and a destination IP address that identifies the receiving computer. Routers use the network identifiers in the IP addresses to forward the datagrams to the appropriate locations, eventually getting them to their final destinations.

It is burdensome to remember the 32-bit IP addresses that are associated with Web sites, file system shares, and e-mail addresses, so it is common practice to assign friendly names to these resources. Friendly names are a convenience for people—they do not change how computers use TCP/IP to communicate among themselves. When you use a name instead of an address in an application, the computer must convert the name into the proper IP address before initiating communication with the target computer. This name-to-address conversion is called *name resolution*. For example, when you type the name of an Internet server in your Web browser, the browser must resolve that name into an IP address. Once the computer has the address of the Internet server, it can send its first message through TCP/IP, requesting access to the resource that you specified in the browser.

The Domain Name System (DNS) is the name resolution mechanism computers use for all Internet communications and for private networks that use the Active Directory directory services included with Microsoft Windows Server 2003 and Windows 2000. The names that you associate with the Internet, such as the names of Internet servers in Uniform Resource Locators (URLs) and the domain names in e-mail addresses, are part of the DNS namespace and are resolvable by DNS name servers. Windows Server 2003 includes its own DNS server that you can deploy on your private network.

> **NOTE** **DNS and Active Directory** *Active Directory is also based on DNS. The names you assign to computers on an Active Directory network can be resolved by DNS servers. To enable DNS resolution, you must deploy a DNS server on your own network.*

The Windows operating systems prior to Windows 2000 used NetBIOS names to identify the computers on the network. The NetBIOS name of a computer running Windows is the name you assign to it during the operating system installation. Windows includes several name resolution mechanisms for NetBIOS names, including Windows Internet Naming Service (WINS). Starting with Windows 2000, Windows operating system releases rely on Active Directory and DNS instead of NetBIOS names. However, all Windows versions still include a WINS client, and Windows Server 2003 and Windows 2000 Server still include the WINS server so they can interact with computers on the network running previous operating systems.

What Is a Host Name?

The processes by which friendly names are associated with IP addresses and the mechanisms used to perform name resolution have evolved over the years. When the Internet was established in 1969 as an experimental wide area network (WAN) named ARPANET by the United States Defense Advanced Research Project Agency (ARPA), system administrators assigned single-word friendly names to their computers. These friendly names, *host names*, represented the computer's IP address in applications and other references. Today, the term *host* refers to any device on a TCP/IP network that has an IP address.

Resolving Host Names

One method of resolving host names into IP addresses is by using a *host table*. A host table is a text file named hosts that contains a list of host names and their equivalent IP addresses, similar to the following list:

```
172.16.94.97    server1     # source server
10.25.63.10     client23    # x client host
127.0.0.1       localhost
```

The host table consists of three columns, which list the following, from left to right:

- **IP addresses**   The IP address of a particular system on the network.
- **Host names**   The host name associated with the IP address in the first column.
- **Comments**   The computer ignores everything after the # symbol when it scans the host table. Administrators use this space to add comments, such as a description of the system that the IP address and host name in the first two columns represent.

When an application encounters a reference to a host name, it consults the computer's hosts file, searches for the name, and reads the IP address associated with that name. Every computer that uses TCP/IP contains a host table. The advantage of using a host table for name resolution is that resolution is simple and fast. Because the table is stored on the computer's local drive, no network communication is required. You can modify the host table on your Windows computer and use it to resolve frequently used host names. On a computer running Windows 2000, the table is named hosts, and it is located in the *%systemroot%*\system32\drivers\etc folder. You can modify the file by adding entries using any text editor, such as Notepad.exe, in Windows 2000.

The disadvantages of host tables as a general-purpose name resolution mechanism outweigh their advantages. In the early days of ARPANET, the entire network consisted of a few dozen computers. The operators of those computers each chose their own host name. The host table was small and easily maintained, with the network's users informally notifying each other of new names to be added to their tables. As the network grew, ARPANET's administrators decided to create a central registry for the host names. The Network Information Center (NIC) at Stanford Research Institute (SRI) in Menlo Park, California, was chosen to maintain the master hosts file for all of the computers on ARPANET. System administrators all over the network sent their new host names, which they chose themselves, to SRI, and SRI added them to the master host table. Network users then downloaded the latest version of the hosts file periodically and copied it to their systems.

The process of adding entries to the host table, obtaining latest versions, and copying them to computers gradually became burdensome as the network continued to grow. The number of additions to the master host table increased, making it difficult for SRI to keep up with the changes, and the number of users downloading the file created an excessive amount of network traffic. Name conflicts also became a problem because users assigned host names to their computers without checking to see whether another computer already used the same name.

Today, it is easy to see why the use of host tables for name resolution was only a temporary solution. A single host table listing the names and IP addresses of all the computers on the Internet would be colossal and would change thousands of times per second. A more efficient solution, such as the Domain Name System (DNS) became necessary as the Internet evolved.

THE DOMAIN NAME SYSTEM (DNS)

Maintaining an extensive list of IP addresses and hosts requires a distributed database, one that avoids the maintenance and traffic problems inherent in a single data store. One objective of the ARPANET project was to create a means for administrators to assign host names to their computers without duplicating the names of other systems. Another objective was to store those names in a database that was distributed among servers all over the network, to avoid creating a traffic bottleneck or a single point of failure and to standardize a system for host naming and accessing electronic mailboxes. DNS was developed to meet these goals.

At its core, the DNS is still a list of names and their IP addresses, but instead of storing all the information in one place, the DNS distributes it among servers all over the Internet. The DNS consists of three elements:

- **The DNS namespace**   A specification for a tree-structured namespace in which each branch of the tree identifies a *domain*. Each domain contains an information set that consists of host names, IP addresses, and other information. Query operations are attempts to retrieve specific information from a particular information set.

- **Name servers** Applications running on server computers that maintain information about the domain tree structure and contain authoritative information about specific areas of that structure. The application is capable of responding to queries for information about the areas for which it is the authority, and it also has pointers to other name servers that enable it to access information about any other area of the tree.

- **Resolvers** Client programs that generate requests for DNS information and send them to name servers for fulfillment. A resolver has direct access to at least one name server and can also process referrals to direct its queries to other name servers when necessary.

In its most basic form, the DNS name-resolution process consists of a resolver submitting a name resolution request to its designated DNS server. If the server does not possess authoritative information about the requested name, it forwards the request to another DNS server on the network. The second server generates a response containing the IP address of the requested name and returns it to the first server. The first server relays the information to the resolver. In practice, however, the DNS name resolution process can be considerably more complex.

What Is a Domain?

For the DNS to function, the namespace must be divided in a way that distributes it among many servers. Servers also must be able to locate the authoritative source for a particular name. To accomplish these goals, the developers of the DNS created the concept of the domain. A *domain* is an administrative entity that consists of a group of hosts that are usually computers. The DNS namespace consists of a hierarchy of domains, and each domain has DNS name servers that are responsible for supplying information about the hosts in that domain. The designated name servers for a particular domain are the authoritative source of information about that domain. When a DNS server is the authoritative source for a domain, it possesses information about the hosts in that domain, which it stores in the form of resource records.

NOTE Domain Meanings In the context of DNS, the term *domain* has a different meaning than it has in Active Directory. A Windows Server 2003 domain is a grouping of Windows computers and devices that are administered as a unit. In DNS, a domain is a group of hosts, and possibly subdomains, that represent a part of the DNS namespace.

Resource Records

The *resource record* is the fundamental data storage unit in all DNS servers. When DNS clients and servers exchange name and address information, they do so in the form of resource records. The most basic common resource record is the Host (A) resource record, which consists of the host name and its IP address. However, DNS servers can also store other types of resource records, some of which are described in the following sections.

Start of Authority (SOA) The SOA resource record identifies which name server is the authoritative source of information for data within this domain. The first record in the zone database file must be an SOA record. In the Windows Server 2003 DNS server, SOA records are created automatically with default values when you create a new zone. Later, you can modify the individual field values as needed.

Unlike most resource records, SOA records contain a variety of fields, most of which are used for name server maintenance operations. Table A-1 lists these fields using the name designated in the Windows Server 2003 DNS console interface as well as by the field name specified in the DNS standard (in parentheses).

Table A-1 DNS Console Interface SOA Record Fields

DNS Fields	Description
Serial Number (Serial)	Contains a version number for the original copy of the zone.
Primary Server (Mname)	Contains the fully qualified domain name (FQDN) of the DNS name server that is the primary source of data for the zone.
Responsible Person (Rname)	Contains the name of the mailbox belonging to the person responsible for the administration of the zone.
Refresh Interval (Refresh)	Specifies the time interval in seconds at which secondary master name servers must verify the accuracy of their data.
Retry Interval (Retry)	Specifies the time interval in seconds at which secondary master name servers will retry their zone transfer operations after an initial transfer failure.
Expires After (Expire)	Specifies the time interval after which a secondary master name server will remove records from its zone database file when they are not successfully refreshed by a zone transfer.
Minimum (Default) TTL (Minimum)	Specifies the lower end of the range of Time-To-Live (TTL) values supplied with every resource record furnished by the zone. A server receiving resource records from this zone saves them in its cache for a period of time between this minimum field value and a maximum value specified in the TTL field of the resource record itself.

Name Server (NS) The NS resource record identifies the name server that is the authority for the particular zone or domain. This resource record consists of a single Nsdname field containing the name of a DNS name server. Microsoft DNS Server creates NS resource records by default in every new zone. When you create subdomains and delegate them into different zones, NS records enable the name server to refer queries to the authoritative name server for a subdomain.

Host (A) The A resource record is the fundamental data unit of the DNS. This resource record has a single Address field that contains the IP address associated with the system identified in the Name field. Host resource records provide the name-to-IP-address mappings that DNS name servers use to perform name resolution.

> **NOTE** Host Records and IPv6 The Host (A) resource record is intended for use with 32-bit IP version 4 (IPv4) addresses only. To map a DNS name to a 128-bit IP version 6 (IPv6) address, DNS uses a different resource record, called IPv6 Host (AAAA).

Alias (CNAME) The Canonical Name (CNAME) resource record is used to specify an alias, or alternative name, for the system specified in the Name field. The resource record contains a single Cname field that holds another name in the standard DNS naming format. You create CNAME resource records to use more than one name to point to a single IP address. For example, you can host a File Transfer Protocol (FTP) server such as ftp.adatum.com and a Web server such as www.adatum.com on the same computer by creating an A record in the adatum.com domain for the host name www and a CNAME record equating the host name ftp with the A record for www.

Host Information (HINFO) The HINFO resource record contains two fields, called CPU and OS, which contain values identifying the processor type and operating system used by the listed host. You can use this record type as a low-cost resource tracking tool.

Mail Exchanger (MX) A secondary but crucial function of the DNS is the direction of e-mail messages to the appropriate mail server. Although the DNS standards define a variety of obsolete and experimental resource records devoted to e-mail functions, the resource record in general use for e-mail transmission is the MX record. This resource record contains two fields, called Preference and Exchange. The Preference field contains an integer value that indicates the relative priority of this resource record compared to others of the same type and class in the same domain. The lower the value, the higher the priority. The Exchange field contains the name of a computer that is capable of acting as an e-mail server for the domain specified in the Name field.

Pointer (PTR) The PTR resource record is the functional opposite of the A record, providing an IP-address-to-name mapping for the system identified in the Name field using the in-addr.arpa domain name. The PTR resource record contains a single Ptrname field, which contains the FQDN of the system identified by the IP address in the Name field. When you create the appropriate reverse lookup zone on your DNS Server, you can create PTR resource records automatically with your A records.

Service (SRV) The service resource (SRV) record enables clients to locate servers that are providing a particular service. Windows 2000 Active Directory clients rely on the SRV record to locate the domain controllers they need to validate logon requests.

Understanding Domain Hierarchy Levels

The hierarchical nature of the DNS domain namespace makes it possible for any DNS server on the Internet to use a minimum number of queries to locate the authoritative source for any domain name. This efficiency is possible because the domains at each level are responsible for maintaining information about the domains at the next lower level. Each level of the DNS domain hierarchy has name servers that are responsible for the individual domains at that level.

At the top of the domain hierarchy are the *root name servers*, which are the highest level DNS servers in the entire namespace. They maintain information about the top-level domains. All DNS name server implementations are preconfigured with the IP addresses of the root name servers because these servers are the ultimate source for all DNS information. When a computer attempts to resolve a DNS name, it begins at the top of the namespace hierarchy with the root name servers and works its way down through the levels until it reaches the authoritative server for the domain in which the name is located.

Just beneath the root name servers are the top-level domains. There are seven main top-level domains in the DNS namespace:

- com
- net
- org
- edu
- mil
- gov
- int

> **NOTE** **Other Top-Level Domains** Other top-level domains include two-letter international domain names representing most of the countries in the world, such as *it* for Italy and *de* for Germany (Deutschland). Internet entrepreneurs have also promoted a number of newer top-level domains, such as biz and info, which have yet to see widespread commercial use.

The top two levels of the DNS hierarchy, the root and the top-level domains, are represented by servers that exist primarily to respond to queries for information about other domains. There are no hosts in the root or top-level domains, except for the name servers themselves. For example, there is no DNS name consisting of only a host and a top-level domain, such as www.com. The root name servers respond to millions of requests by sending the addresses of the authoritative servers for the top-level domains, and the top-level domain servers do the same for the second-level domains.

Each top-level domain has its own collection of second-level domains. Individuals and organizations can purchase these domains. For example, the second-level domain adatum.com belongs to a company that purchased the name from one of the many Internet registrars that sell domain names to consumers. For an annual fee, you can buy the rights to a second-level domain.

To use the domain name, you must supply the registrar with the IP addresses of the DNS servers that will be the authoritative sources for information about this domain. The administrators of the top-level domain servers then create resource records pointing to these authoritative sources, so that any DNS server for the com top-level domain receiving a request to resolve a name in the adatum.com domain can reply with the addresses of the adatum.com servers.

> **NOTE** **Domains and DNS Servers** To create authoritative sources for your Internet domain, you can deploy your own DNS servers. A DNS server can use Windows Server 2003 or another operating system. Alternatively, you can pay to use your ISP's DNS servers. If you decide to host an Internet domain on your own DNS servers, those servers must be accessible from the Internet and therefore must have registered IP addresses.

Once you buy the rights to a second-level domain, you can create as many hosts as you want in that domain, by creating new resource records on the authoritative servers. You can also create as many additional domain levels as you want. For example, you can create the subdomains sales.adatum.com and marketing.adatum.com, and then populate each of these subdomains with hosts, such as www.sales.adatum.com and ftp.marketing.adatum.com. The only limitations on the subdomains and hosts you can create in your second-level domain are that each domain name can be no more than 63 characters long and that the total FQDN, including the trailing period, can be no more than 255 characters long. For the convenience of users and administrators, most domain names do not approach these limitations.

Understanding the DNS Name Resolution Process

The resolution of a DNS name on the Internet proceeds as follows:

1. An application running on the client computer has a name to resolve and passes it to the DNS resolver running on that system. The resolver generates a DNS name resolution request message and transmits it to the DNS server address specified in its TCP/IP configuration.

2. On receiving the request, the client's DNS server checks its own database and cache for the requested name. If the server has no information about the requested name, it forwards the request message to one of the root name servers on the Internet. In processing the request, the root name server reads only the top-level domain of the requested name and generates a reply message containing the IP address of an authoritative server for that top-level domain. The root name server then transmits the reply back to the client's DNS server.

3. The client's DNS server now has the IP address of an authoritative server for the requested name's top-level domain, so it transmits the same name resolution request to that top-level domain server. The top-level domain server reads only the second-level domain of the requested name and generates a reply containing the IP address of an authoritative server for that second-level domain. The top-level server then transmits the reply to the client's DNS server.

4. The client's DNS server now has the IP address of an authoritative server for the second-level domain that contains the requested host. The client's DNS server forwards the name resolution request to that second-level domain server. The second-level domain server reads the host in the requested name and transmits a reply containing the A resource record for that host back to the client's DNS server.

5. The client's DNS server receives the A resource record from the second-level domain server and forwards it to the resolver on the client computer. The resolver then supplies the IP address associated with the requested name to the original application. After the original application receives the requested name, direct communication between the client and the intended destination can begin.

Speeding Up the DNS Process

The name resolution process described earlier might seem incredibly long and tedious, but it actually proceeds very quickly. DNS mechanisms such as combined DNS servers and name caching help to shorten the process.

Combined DNS Servers You just saw the process of resolving the top-level and second-level domain names rendered as a series of steps, but it doesn't always happen in this way. The most commonly used top-level domains, such as com, net, and org, are hosted by the root name servers. This hosting eliminates one entire referral from the name resolution process.

Name Caching The other mechanism that speeds up the DNS name resolution process is name caching. Most DNS server implementations maintain a cache of information they receive from other DNS servers. When a server has information about a requested FQDN in its cache, it responds directly using the cached information instead of sending a referral to another server. Therefore, if you have a DNS server on your network that successfully resolves the name www.adatum.com for a client by contacting the authoritative server for the adatum.com domain, a second user trying to access the same host a few minutes later receives an immediate reply from the local DNS server's cache. Subsequent queries do not repeat the entire referral process, but instead use the locally cached data. Caching is a critical part of the DNS because it reduces the amount of network traffic generated by the name resolution process and reduces the burden on the root name and top-level domain servers.

Referrals and Queries

The process by which one DNS server sends a name resolution request to another DNS server is called a *referral*. Referrals are essential to the DNS name resolution process. The DNS client is not involved in the name resolution process at all, except for sending one query and receiving one reply. The client's DNS server might have to send referrals to several servers before it reaches the one that has the information it needs.

DNS servers recognize two types of name resolution requests:

- **Recursive query** In a *recursive query*, the DNS server receiving the name resolution request takes full responsibility for resolving the name. If the server possesses information about the requested name, it replies immediately to the requestor. If the server has no information about the name, it sends referrals to other DNS servers until it obtains the information it needs. TCP/IP client resolvers always send recursive queries to their designated DNS servers.

- **Iterative query** In an *iterative query*, the server that receives the name resolution request immediately responds to the requester with the best information it possesses. This information can be cached or authoritative, and it can be a resource record containing a fully resolved name or a reference to another DNS server. DNS servers use iterative queries when communicating with each other. It would be improper to configure one DNS server to send a recursive query to another DNS server.

Reverse Name Resolution

Sometimes a computer needs to convert an IP address into a DNS name. This conversion process is known as *reverse name resolution*. Because the domain hierarchy is separated into domain names, there is no practical way to resolve an IP address into a name using iterative queries. You could forward the reverse name resolution request to every DNS server on the Internet in search of the requested address, but that would be impractical.

The developers of the DNS created a special domain called in-addr.arpa that is specifically designed for reverse name resolution. The in-addr.arpa second-level domain contains four additional levels of subdomains, with each level consisting of subdomains that are named using the numerals 0 to 255. For example, beneath in-addr.arpa are 256 third-level domains, which have names ranging from 0.in-addr.arpa to 255.in-addr.arpa. Each of the 256 third-level domains can have 256 fourth-level domains below it, numbered from 0 to 255. This is also true of each fourth-level domain, which can have 256 fifth-level domains, numbered from 0 to 255, and each fifth-level domain, which can have up to 256 hosts in it, numbered from 0 to 255.

Using this hierarchy of subdomains, it is possible to express the first three bytes of an IP address as a DNS domain name and to create a resource record named for the fourth byte in the appropriate fifth-level domain. For example, to resolve the IP address 192.168.89.34 into a name, a DNS server locates a domain named 89.168.192.in-addr.arpa and reads the contents of a special type of resource record called 34 in that domain. Address-to-name mappings use a special type of resource record called a Pointer (PTR).

> **NOTE** **Reverse Lookup Domains** In the in-addr.arpa domain, the IP address is reversed in the domain name because IP addresses have the least pertinent bit (the host identifier) on the right. In DNS FQDNs, the host name is on the left.

Using Active Directory

If you plan to run Active Directory on your network, you must have at least one DNS server on the network that supports the SRV resource record, such as the DNS Server service in Windows Server 2003. Computers on the network running Windows 2000 and later use DNS to locate Active Directory domain controllers. To support Active Directory clients, it is not necessary for the DNS server to have a registered IP address or an Internet domain name.

> **NOTE** **SRV Resource Records** The SRV resource record was not part of the original DNS standards; it is a relatively recent development. As a result, you might encounter DNS server implementations that do not support this record type. Before you deploy an Active Directory network, ensure that your DNS servers support RFC 2052. For more information on RFC 2052, see, "A DNS RR for Specifying the Location of Services (DNS SRV)," published by the Internet Engineering Task Force (IETF).

Combining Internal and External Domains

When you design a DNS namespace that includes both internal and external domains, you can use the following strategies:

- Use the same domain name internally and externally.

- Create separate and unrelated internal and external domains.
- Make the internal domain a subdomain of the external domain.

These options are discussed in the following sections.

Using the Same Domain Name

Using the same domain name for your internal and external namespaces is a practice Microsoft strongly discourages. When you create an internal domain and an external domain with the same name, you make it possible for a computer in the internal network to have the same DNS name as a computer on the external network. This duplication wreaks havoc with the name resolution process. (You could make this arrangement work by copying all the zone data from your external DNS servers to your internal DNS servers, but the extra administrative difficulties make this a less than ideal solution.)

Using Separate Domain Names

When you use different domain names for your internal and external networks, you eliminate the potential name resolution conflicts that result from using the same domain name for both networks. However, this solution requires you to register two domain names and to maintain two separate DNS namespaces. The different domain names can also be a potential source of confusion to users who have to distinguish between internal and external resources.

Using a Subdomain

The solution that Microsoft recommends for combining internal and external networks is to register a single Internet domain name and use it for external resources, and then create a subdomain beneath the domain name and use it for your internal network. For example, you can register the name adatum.com and use that domain for your external servers, and then you can create a subdomain named int.adatum.com for your internal network. If you must create additional subdomains, you can create fourth-level domains beneath int for the internal network and additional third-level domains beneath adatum for the external network.

This solution makes it impossible to create duplicate FQDNs and lets you delegate authority across the internal and external domains, which simplifies the DNS administration process. In addition, you register and pay for only one Internet domain name, not two.

Creating an Internal Root

When you use the Windows Server 2003 DNS server with the namespace configurations previously described, your network's namespace is technically part of the Internet DNS namespace, even if your private network computers are not accessible from the Internet. All your DNS servers use the root of the Internet DNS as the ultimate source of information about any part of the namespace. When a client on your network sends a name resolution request to one of your DNS servers and the server has no information about the name, it begins the referral process by sending an iterative query to one of the root name servers on the Internet.

If you have a large enterprise network with an extensive namespace, you can create your own internal root by creating a private root zone on one of your Windows

Server 2003 DNS servers. This causes the DNS servers on your network to send their iterative queries to your internal root name server rather than to the Internet root name server. The name resolution process speeds up because DNS traffic is kept inside the enterprise.

> **PLANNING** **When to Use an Internal Root** Creating an internal root is advisable when the majority of your clients do not need frequent access to resources outside your private namespace. If your clients access the Internet through a proxy server, you can configure the proxy to perform name resolutions by accessing the Internet DNS namespace instead of the private one. If your clients require access to the Internet but do not go through a proxy server, you should not create an internal root.

Understanding DNS Server Types

You can deploy Windows Server 2003 DNS servers in a number of configurations, depending on your infrastructure design and your users' needs.

Using Caching-Only Servers

It is not essential for a DNS server to be the authoritative source for a domain. In its default configuration, a Windows Server 2003 DNS server can resolve Internet DNS names for clients immediately after its installation. A DNS server that contains no zones and hosts no domains is called a *caching-only server*. If you have Internet clients on your network but do not have a registered domain name and are not using Active Directory, you can deploy caching-only servers that provide Internet name resolution services for your clients.

> **NOTE** **Windows DNS Server Defaults** The Windows Server 2003 DNS server comes configured with the names and IP addresses of the root name servers on the Internet. It can resolve any Internet DNS name using the procedure described earlier in this chapter. As the server performs client name resolutions, it builds up a cache of DNS information, just like any other DNS server, and begins to satisfy some name resolution requests using information in the cache.

In some instances, you might want to use some caching-only servers on your network even if you are hosting domains. For example, if you want to install a DNS server at a branch office for the purpose of Internet name resolution, you are not required to host a part of your namespace there. You can install a caching-only server in the remote location and configure it to forward all name resolution requests for your company domains to a DNS server at the home office. The caching-only server resolves all Internet DNS names directly.

Using Forwarders

A *forwarder* is a DNS server that receives queries from other DNS servers that are explicitly configured to send them. With Windows Server 2003 DNS servers, the forwarder requires no special configuration. However, you must configure the other DNS servers to send queries to the forwarder.

You can use forwarders in a variety of ways to regulate the flow of DNS traffic on your network. As explained earlier, a DNS server that receives recursive queries from clients frequently has to issue numerous iterative queries to other DNS servers on the Internet to resolve names, generating a significant amount of traffic on the network's Internet connection. You can use forwarders to redirect this Internet traffic in several scenarios.

For example, suppose a branch office is connected to your corporate headquarters using a T-1 leased line, and the branch office's Internet connection is a slower, shared dial-up modem. In this case, you can configure the DNS server at the branch office to use the DNS server at headquarters as a forwarder. The recursive queries generated by the clients at the branch office then travel over the T-1 to the forwarder at headquarters, which resolves the names and returns the results to the branch office DNS server. The clients at the branch office can then use the resolved names to connect directly to Internet servers over the dial-up connection. No DNS traffic passes over the branch office's Internet connection.

You can also use forwarders to limit the number of servers that transmit name resolution queries through the firewall to the Internet. If you have five DNS servers on your network that provide both internal and Internet name resolution services, you have five points where your network is vulnerable to attacks from the Internet. By configuring four of the DNS servers to send their Internet queries to the fifth server, you have only one point of vulnerability.

Chaining Forwarders A DNS server that functions as a forwarder can also forward its queries to another forwarder. To combine the two scenarios described in the previous section, you can configure your branch office servers to forward name resolution requests to various DNS servers at headquarters, and then have the headquarters servers forward all Internet queries to the one server that transmits through the firewall.

Using Conditional Forwarding One new feature in Windows Server 2003 is the ability to configure the DNS server to forward queries conditionally, based on the domain specified in the name resolution request. By default, the forwarder addresses you specify in the Forwarders tab in a DNS server's Properties dialog box apply to all other DNS domains. However, when you click New and specify a different domain, you can supply different forwarder addresses so that requests for names in that domain are sent to different servers.

As an example of conditional forwarding, suppose a network uses a variety of registered domain names, including contoso.com. When a client tries to resolve a name in the contoso.com domain and sends a query to a DNS server that is not an authoritative source for that domain, the server normally must resolve the name in the usual manner, by first querying one of the root name servers on the Internet. However, using conditional forwarding, you can configure the client's DNS server to forward all queries for the contoso.com domain directly to the authoritative server for that domain, which is on the company network. This keeps all the DNS traffic on the private network, speeding up name resolution and conserving the company's Internet bandwidth.

You can also use conditional forwarding to minimize the network traffic that internal name resolution generates by configuring each of your DNS servers to forward queries directly to the authoritative servers for their respective domains. This practice is an improvement even over creating an internal root, because there is no need for the servers to query the root name server to determine the addresses of the authoritative servers for a particular domain.

There are two main drawbacks to using conditional forwarding extensively on a large enterprise network. These drawbacks are the amount of administrative effort needed to configure all the DNS servers with forwarder addresses for all the domains in the namespace and the static nature of the forwarding configuration. If your network is expanding rapidly and you are frequently adding or moving DNS servers, the extra effort required to continually reconfigure the forwarder addresses can outweigh the potential savings in network traffic.

Creating Zones

A *zone* is an administrative entity on a DNS server that represents a discrete portion of the DNS namespace. Administrators typically divide the DNS namespace into zones to store them on different servers and to delegate their administration to different people. Zones always consist of entire domains or subdomains. You can create a zone that contains multiple domains only when those domains are contiguous in the DNS namespace. For example, you can create a zone containing a parent domain and its child because they are directly connected, but you cannot create a zone containing two child domains without their common parent because the two children are not directly connected.

You can also divide the DNS namespace into multiple zones and host them on a single DNS server, although there is usually no compelling reason to do so. The DNS server in Windows Server 2003 can support as many as 200,000 zones on a single server. (It is hard to imagine what scenario would require that many zones.) In most cases, an administrator creates multiple zones on a server and then delegates most of them to other servers. These servers, in turn, become responsible for hosting zones.

Understanding Zone Types

Every zone consists of a zone database that contains the resource records for the domains in that zone. The DNS server in Windows Server 2003 supports three zone types that specify where the server stores the zone database and what kind of information it contains. These zone types are as follows:

- **Primary zone** A primary zone contains the master copy of the zone database, in which administrators make all changes to the zone's resource records. If the Store The Zone In Active Directory (Available Only If DNS Server Is A Domain Controller) check box is cleared, the server creates a primary master zone database file on the local drive. This is a simple text file that is compliant with most non-Windows DNS server implementations. Otherwise, the database is stored in the Active Directory database.

- **Secondary zone** A secondary zone, a duplicate of a primary zone on another server, contains a backup copy of the primary master zone database file, stored as an identical text file on the server's local drive. You cannot modify the resource records in a secondary zone manually. You can only update them by replicating the primary master zone database file using a process called a zone transfer. You should always create at least one secondary zone for each file-based primary zone in your namespace, to provide fault tolerance and to balance the DNS traffic load.

- **Stub zone**   A stub zone is a copy of a primary zone that contains SOA and NS resource records, plus the Host (A) resource records that identify the authoritative servers for the zone. The stub zone forwards or refers requests. When you create a stub zone, you configure it with the IP address of the server that hosts the primary zone from which the stub zone was created. When the server hosting the stub zone receives a query for a name in that zone, it either forwards the request to the host of the zone or replies with a referral to that host, depending on whether the query is recursive or iterative.

You can use each of these zone types to create forward lookup zones or reverse lookup zones. Forward lookup zones contain name-to-address mappings, and reverse lookup zones contain address-to-name mappings. If you want a DNS server to perform name and address resolutions for a particular domain, you must create both forward and reverse lookup zones containing that domain, using the domain name for the forward lookup zone and an in-addr.arpa domain for the reverse lookup zone.

Using File-Based Zones

When you create primary and secondary zones, you must configure zone transfers from the primary zone to the secondary zones to keep them updated. In a *zone transfer*, the server hosting the primary zone copies the primary master zone database file to the secondary zone to make their resource records identical. This enables the secondary zone to perform authoritative name resolutions for the domains in the zone, just as the primary does. You can configure zone transfers to occur when you modify the contents of the primary master zone database file or at regular intervals.

Full Zone Transfers   When you add a new DNS server to the network and configure it as a new secondary master name server for an existing zone, the server performs a *full zone transfer (AXFR)* to obtain a full copy of all resource records for the zone. Then, at specified times, the DNS server hosting the primary zone transmits the database file to all the servers hosting secondary copies of that zone. File-based zone transfers use a technique in which the servers transmit the zone database file either in its native form or compressed.

Incremental Zone Transfers   Some DNS server implementations also use the full transfer method when the zone requires updating after changes are made to the primary zone database file. However, the Windows Server 2003 DNS Server also supports *incremental zone transfer (IXFR)*, which is a revised DNS zone transfer process for intermediate changes. IXFR is defined by an additional DNS standard for replicating DNS zones. For more information about the standard, see RFC 1995, "Incremental Zone Transfer in DNS." This zone transfer method provides a more efficient way of propagating zone changes and updates. In earlier DNS implementations, requests for an update of zone data require a full transfer of the entire zone database using an AXFR query. With incremental transfers, DNS servers use an

IXFR query. IXFR enables the secondary master name server to pull only the zone changes that are required to synchronize its copy of the zone with its source—either a primary master or another secondary master copy of the zone maintained by another DNS server.

With IXFR zone transfers, the servers first determine the differences between the source and replicated versions of the zone. If the zones are identified as being the same version—as indicated by the Serial field in the SOA resource record of each zone—no transfer occurs. If the serial number for the zone at the primary master server is greater than the serial number at the requesting secondary master server, the primary master performs a transfer of only the changes made for each incremental version of the zone. For an IXFR query to succeed and an incremental transfer to occur, the primary master name server for the zone must keep a history of incremental zone changes to use when answering these queries. The incremental transfer process requires substantially less traffic on a network, and zone transfers are completed much faster.

> **NOTE** Creating Secondary Zones A Windows Server 2003 DNS server can host both primary and secondary zones on the same server. You don't have to install additional servers just to create secondary zones. You can configure each of your DNS servers to host a primary zone and then create secondary zones on each server for one or more of the primary zones on other servers. Each primary zone can have multiple secondary zones located on servers throughout the network. This provides fault tolerance and prevents all the traffic for a single zone from flooding a single LAN.

In addition to occurring because of a manual initiation, a zone transfer occurs during any of the following scenarios:

- When you start the DNS Server service on the secondary master name server for a zone
- When the refresh interval time expires for the zone
- When changes are made to a primary master name server that is configured with a notify list

Zone transfers are always initiated by the secondary master server for a zone and are sent to the DNS server configured as its master server. This master server can be any other DNS name server that hosts the zone, either a primary master server or another secondary master server. When the master server receives the request for the zone, it can reply with either a partial or a full transfer of the zone.

Zone transfers between servers follow an ordered process, which varies depending on whether a zone has been previously replicated, or if the servers are performing an initial replication of a new zone.

Using Active Directory–Integrated Zones

When you are running the DNS Server service on a computer that is an Active Directory domain controller and you select the Store The Zone In Active Directory (Available Only If DNS Server Is A Domain Controller) check box when creating a zone using the New Zone Wizard, the server does not create a zone database file.

Instead, it stores the DNS resource records for the zone in the Active Directory database. Storing the DNS database in Active Directory provides a number of advantages, including ease of administration, conservation of network bandwidth, and increased security.

In Active Directory–integrated zones, the zone database is replicated to other domain controllers along with all other Active Directory data. Active Directory uses a multi-master replication system so that copies of the database are updated on all domain controllers in the domain. You can modify the DNS resource records on any domain controller hosting a copy of the zone database. Active Directory updates all of the other domain controllers. Creating secondary zones or manually configuring zone transfers is not necessary because Active Directory performs all database replication activities.

By default, Windows Server 2003 replicates the database for a primary zone stored in Active Directory to all the other domain controllers running the DNS server in the Active Directory domain where the primary zone is located. You can also modify the scope of zone database replication to keep copies on all domain controllers throughout the enterprise or on all domain controllers in the Active Directory domain, whether or not they are running the DNS server. If all of your domain controllers are running Windows Server 2003, you can also create a custom replication scope that copies the zone database to the domain controllers that you specify.

Active Directory conserves network bandwidth by replicating only the DNS data that has changed since the last replication and by compressing the data before transmitting it over the network. The zone replications also use the full security capabilities of Active Directory, which are considerably more robust than those of file-based zone transfers.

Because Windows Server 2003 replicates the Active Directory database to other domain controllers, creating secondary zones is not a prerequisite for replication. Indeed, you cannot create an Active Directory–integrated secondary zone. However, you can create a file-based secondary zone from an Active Directory–integrated primary zone, and there are occasions when you might want to create a secondary zone. For example, if no other domain controllers are running DNS in the Active Directory domain, there are no other domain controllers in the domain, or your other DNS servers are not running Windows Server 2003, it might be necessary to create a file-based secondary zone instead of relying on Active Directory replication. If you do this, you must manually configure the DNS servers to perform zone transfers in the normal manner.

> **MORE INFO** For more information on implementing and supporting DNS in a Windows Server 2003 environment, consult the *Windows Server 2003 Deployment Kit: Deploying Network Services* guide. In addition, the *Planning, Implementing, and Maintaining a Windows Server 2003 Active Directory Infrastructure* textbook provides additional details on DNS.

GLOSSARY

AAS   *See* application advertisement script.

access control lists (ACLs)   ACLs contain a list of all users or groups in the form of an Access Control Entry (ACE) that have access to the object or file. In addition, each listed item includes the associated permissions or rights that have been granted to the object.

access token   A data structure that contains the security identifier (SID) for a security principal, SIDs for the groups to which the security principal belongs, and a list of the security principal's privileges (also named user rights) on the local computer.

ACL   *See* access control lists.

Active Directory Installation Wizard   This is the tool used to install or remove Active Directory services from a Windows Server 2003 machine. It can be started from the command prompt by typing **dcpromo** or by accessing the Manage Your Server Web page.

Active Directory Migration Tool (ADMT)   A Microsoft Management Console (MMC) snap-in that provides graphical support, in the form of wizards, to automate migration tasks such as moving users, groups, and computers between or within forests; migrating trust; and performing security translation.

administrative templates   Built-in templates that provide predefined registry-based policy settings that can be used to configure computer and user accounts within Active Directory. These templates are based on Unicode text files with a .adm extension. Windows Server 2003 administrative template settings are based on five .adm files that are included with the operating system.

Adprep.exe   The command-line tool used to prepare a Windows 2000 forest and domain for an upgrade to Windows Server 2003. Adprep /forestprep runs on the schema master FSMO role holder. Adprep /domainprep runs on the infrastructure master FSMO role holder on the domain. Adprep /domainprep does not function if the changes performed by adprep /forestprep are not completed.

aging and scavenging   The process that can be used by Windows Server 2003 DNS to clean up the DNS database when resource records are no longer required. By default, it is disabled.

anonymous logon group   A special identity group that was listed as the member of the Everyone group prior to Windows Server 2003. Anonymous users do not have to supply a username and password during logon.

application advertisement script (AAS)   A script that uses Software Installation, which is an extension of Group Policy, to assign programs to groups of users. The programs appear on the users' desktops when they log on.

application directory partitions   Application partitions are new to Windows Server 2003 and can store any hierarchy of objects with the exception of security principal objects such as users or computers. The information in this partition can be configured to replicate to any domain controller in the forest, even if the chosen domain controllers are not all in the same domain. Application directory partitions allow controlled replication of DNS information. They are created by default when DNS is installed during Active Directory installation.

application partition   A new partition to Windows Server 2003 that allows information to be replicated to administratively chosen domain controllers. An example of information that is commonly stored in an application partition is DNS data. Application partitions allow control over the scope and placement of information to be replicated.

asynchronous processing   This type of processing allows scripts or policies to be run at the same time, without waiting for others to complete.

audit policy A policy that determines the security events to be reported to the network administrator. Settings for this policy are defined in Computer Configurations/Windows Settings/Security Settings/Local Policy/Audit Policy.

authentication The process for verifying that an entity or object is who or what it claims to be. Examples include confirming the source and integrity of information such as verifying a digital signature or verifying the identity of a user or computer.

authoritative restore In Windows Backup, this is a type of restore operation performed on an Active Directory domain controller in which the objects in the restored directory are treated as authoritative, replacing through replication all existing copies of those objects.

backup domain controller (BDC) A domain controller running Windows NT Server 4.0 or earlier that receives a read-only copy of the directory database for the domain. This directory database contains all account and security information for the domain.

batch files An ASCII (unformatted text) file that contains one or more operating system commands. A batch program's file name has a .cmd or .bat extension. When you type the file name at the command prompt along with the path to the file, or when the batch program is called from another program, its commands are processed sequentially. Batch programs are also named batch files.

BDC See backup domain controller.

Block Policy Inheritance A container setting that prevents policies of parent containers from being applied at this level. This setting does not prevent policies set as No Override from being applied.

bridgehead server The server at each site responsible for compressing, decompressing, sending, and receiving Active Directory domain replication traffic between sites.

built-in group accounts The default security groups installed with the operating system. Built-in groups have been granted useful collections of rights and built-in abilities. In most cases, built-in groups provide all the capabilities needed by a particular user. For example, if a domain user account belongs to the built-in Administrators group, logging on with that account gives a user administrative capability over the domain and the domain servers. To provide a needed set of capabilities to a user account, assign it to the appropriate built-in group.

built-in user accounts The default security accounts installed with the operating system. Built-in users have been granted useful collections of rights and built-in abilities.

CA See enterprise certificate authority.

certificate rule A software restriction rule that requires a digital certificate in order to allow the execution of the designated program.

child domains Subdomains of a parent directory structure. When Active Directory is installed on a domain controller in an existing domain, selecting the child domain automatically creates the trust paths between the parent and child domains and also appends the parent domain name.

CIMOM See Common Information Management Object Model.

ClonePrincipal A command line utility used to clone user and group accounts from a Microsoft Windows NT 4.0 or Microsoft Windows 2000 source domain in a separate forest to a native mode Windows 2000 or Windows Server 2003 target domain.

Comma-Separated Value Directory Exchange (CSVDE) A command line utility for the purpose of importing or exporting Active Directory objects. CSVDE uses a text file written using comma-separated values (CSV). The file must contain a header record that defines the attributes to be imported or exported. It can be created in any text editor and must be saved with a .csv extension.

Common Information Management Object Model (CIMOM) This database is commonly referred to as the WMI database and contains information that is gathered when a computer logs on to the network. (*See also* Windows Management Instrumentation.)

configuration container Contains application information stored in Active Directory such as Site information and distributed application information.

Glossary

configuration partition The Active Directory partition that contains the replication topology for the entire forest in addition to any other configuration data. Configuration partition information is replicated to all domain controllers in the forest.

connection object The name given to the link between domain controllers that replicate with one another in a site.

container object An object such as a domain or an organizational unit that is used to organize other objects.

convergence The point in time at which all domain controllers have identical Active Directory information achieved through replication.

cross-forest trust A one-way trust that is established between forest root domains to provide resource access in each forest.

CSVDE *See* Comma-Separated Value Directory Exchange.

default domain controllers policy This policy is linked to the Domain Controllers container and affects all domain controllers within this container. As domain controllers are added to the domain, they are automatically placed in this container and are affected by any settings applied with this policy.

default domain policy One of two policies installed when Active Directory is installed. This policy is linked to the domain, and settings in it affect all users and computers in the domain.

Default-First-Site-Name The name given to the first site created in Active Directory Sites And Services upon the creation of an Active Directory forest.

defragmentation This is the process of rewriting parts of a file to contiguous sectors on a hard disk to increase the speed of access and retrieval. In Active Directory, defragmentation rearranges how the data is written in the directory database file to compact it.

delegation of administration The process of assigning permission to a user who will be able to manage an organizational unit (OU) and all of the resources it contains.

Delegation Of Control Wizard The Active Directory tool that is used to assign responsibility for management and administration of a portion of the Active Directory database to another user or group.

denial-of-service attack (DoS) An attack in which an attacker exploits a weakness or a design limitation of a network service to overload or halt the service, so that the service is not available for use. This type of attack is typically started to prevent other users from using a network service such as a Web server or a file server.

DHCP *See* dynamic host configuration protocol.

directory partition Directory partitions are divisions of the Active Directory database that allow forest and domain information to be separated. The separation of the database facilitates replication of necessary forest or domain information to the appropriate destination. The Active Directory database is divided into four partitions that include the schema, configuration, domain, and application partitions.

disk quotas A policy setting that allows administrators to define the amount of storage space that is allocated to users across the system.

distinguished name (DN) The full name of an object that includes all hierarchical containers leading up to the root domain. The distinguished name begins with the object's common name and appends each succeeding parent container object reflecting the object's location in the Active Directory structure.

distribution groups A group that is used solely for e-mail distribution and one that is not security-enabled. Distribution groups cannot be listed in discretionary access control lists (DACLs) used to define permissions on resources and objects. Distribution groups can be used only with e-mail applications such as Microsoft Exchange to send e-mail to collections of users. If you do not need a group for security purposes, create a distribution group instead of a security group.

DNS *See* domain name system.

domain A grouping of objects in Active Directory that can be managed together. A domain can function as a security boundary for access to resources such as computers, printers, servers, applications, and file systems.

domain controller A computer running Windows Server 2003 that has Active Directory installed on it. Domain controllers maintain a read/write database of all users, resources, and security on the network. Domain controllers are also used to authenticate users by verifying their logon credentials with the corresponding Active Directory object's properties.

domain family Consists of a parent domain and all child domains within the same contiguous namespace. For example, cohowinery.com, north.cohowinery.com, and south.cohowinery.com are all part of the same domain family.

domain local group A security or distribution group that can contain universal groups, global groups, and accounts from any domain in the domain tree or forest. A domain local group can also contain other domain local groups from its own domain. Rights and permissions can be assigned only at the domain containing the group.

domain name system (DNS) The service that is responsible for resolving computer host names and domain names to TCP/IP addresses or vice versa. It is also used by Active Directory to locate servers and other services that provide services to the client machines.

domain naming master A domain controller that holds the domain naming master role in Active Directory. This role controls the addition and removal of domains in the Active Directory forest. This role can be assigned only to one domain controller in the forest.

domain partition The Active Directory partition that contains all objects and attribute values associated with the local domain. All domain controllers within the domain replicate this information. The information is not replicated to domain controllers in other domains.

domain user accounts User accounts that are created on a domain controller within an Active Directory domain. Domain user accounts are the central security point for network and resource access. In order to gain access to domain resources, you must have a valid domain user account.

DoS *See* denial-of-service attack.

dsadd A command line utility that allows Active Directory objects to be created, deleted, viewed, or modified from a command prompt. Dsadd can be used in conjunction with other scripting tools to provide automation of these tasks.

dynamic host configuration protocol (DHCP) A TCP/IP service protocol that offers dynamic leased configuration of host IP addresses and distributes other configuration parameters to eligible network clients. DHCP provides safe, reliable, and simple TCP/IP network configuration, helps prevent address conflicts, and helps conserve the use of client IP addresses on the network.

enrollment agent certificate Enrollment agent certificates are used to generate a smart card for users in the organization. An enrollment agent certificate is created by an enterprise CA.

enterprise certificate authority (CA) An entity responsible for establishing and vouching for the authenticity of public keys belonging to users (end entities) or other certification authorities. Activities of a certification authority can include binding public keys to distinguished names through signed certificates, managing certificate serial numbers, and certificate revocation. In Windows Server 2003, an enterprise CA can issue certificates only within the Windows Server 2003 forest to which it is a member.

ESE *See* Extensible Storage Engine.

Extensible Storage Engine (ESE) The Extensible Storage Engine component is a database storage engine used for a variety of operating system components, including Active Directory.

external trust A trust that is established between domains in separate forests. This is more specific than the cross-forest trust because resource access can be achieved only between the domains.

fault tolerance The ability to recover from a failure. Fault-tolerant systems allow network operations to continue after a failure occurs, whether it is hardware or software related.

flexible single master operations role holder (FSMO) A Windows Server 2003 domain controller that has been assigned a special role in the functionality of Active Directory. The roles are separated into per-forest and per-domain roles that include Primary Domain Controller (PDC) emulator, schema master, domain-naming master, Relative Identifier (RID) master, and infrastructure master.

folder redirection A policy that allows administrators to redirect local computer folders stored in the Documents And Settings directory to a designated target location. Folders can be redirected to a network location or to an alternate location on the local computer.

forest The highest container in Active Directory. The forest contains contiguously named trees. All domain trees in a forest share a common configuration, schema, and global catalog.

forest root domain The forest root domain is the first domain established in the Active Directory structure.

forward lookup zones The zone created in DNS to provide DNS name to IP address mappings. Forward lookup zones are used to resolve service and resource location queries.

FQDN *See* fully qualified domain name.

fragmentation This is the scattering of parts of the same disk file over different areas of the disk. Fragmentation occurs as files on a disk are deleted and new files are added. It slows disk access and degrades the overall performance of disk operations, although usually not severely.

FSMO *See* flexible single master operations role holder.

fully qualified domain name (FQDN) This is the complete DNS name used to reference a host's location in the DNS structure; for example, server1.south .cohowinery.com. The FQDN includes the final 'dot' at the end of the naming string.

garbage collection The garbage collection process is a process that runs by default every 12 hours on all domain controllers in the forest. When the garbage collection process begins, it removes all tombstones from the database. Additional free space is reclaimed during the garbage collection process through the deletion of tombstone objects and unnecessary log files.

global catalog A domain controller that contains a partial replica of every domain in Active Directory. In other words, a global catalog holds a replica of every object in Active Directory, but with a limited number of each object's attributes. The global catalog stores those attributes most frequently used in search operations (such as a user's first and last names) and those attributes required to locate a full replica of the object. The Active Directory replication system builds the global catalog automatically. The attributes replicated into the global catalog include a base set defined by Microsoft. Administrators can specify additional properties to meet the needs of their installation.

global group A security or distribution group that can have users, groups, and computers from its own domain as members. Global security groups can be granted rights and permissions on resources in any domain in the forest.

globally unique identifier (GUID) A 128-bit or 16-byte value generated from the unique identifier on a device, the current date and time, and a sequence number.

GPC *See* Group Policy container.

GPMC *See* Group Policy Management Console.

GPO *See* Group Policy Object.

GPResult This command line tool will query and display RSoP information. It provides a fast and efficient method of gathering and displaying effective policy settings.

GPT *See* Group Policy template.

group A collection of users, computers, contacts, and other groups. Groups can be used as security or as e-mail distribution collections. Distribution groups are used only for e-mail. Security groups are used both to grant access to resources and as e-mail distribution lists.

Group Policy The infrastructure within the Active Directory directory service that enables directory-based change and configuration management of user and computer settings, including security and user data. You use Group Policy to define configurations for groups of users and computers. With Group Policy, you can specify policy settings for registry-based policies, security, software installation, scripts, folder redirection, remote installation services, and Internet Explorer maintenance. The Group Policy settings that you create are contained in a Group Policy Object (GPO). By associating a GPO with selected Active Directory system containers—sites, domains, and organizational units (OUs)—you can apply the GPO's policy settings to the users and computers in those Active Directory containers.

Group Policy container (GPC) An Active Directory container that stores properties of the GPO. This container can be viewed by using the Advanced Features View setting in Active Directory Users And Computers. GPCs are named according to the globally unique identifier (GUID) given to the Group Policy when it is created. Each GPC is represented by its GUID name in the System\Policies container within the Active Directory structure.

Group Policy Management Console (GPMC) The Group Policy Management Console (GPMC) integrates the Group Policy functionality provided by the Active Directory Users And Computers, Active Directory Sites And Services, Resultant Set Of Policy, ACL Editor, and Delegation Wizard tools into a single console. Core Group Policy tasks can be accomplished without the use of these separate tools. GPMC is available as a free download.

Group Policy Object (GPO) A collection of Group Policy settings. GPOs are essentially the documents created by the Group Policy snap-in, a Windows utility. GPOs are stored at the domain level and they affect users and computers contained in sites, domains, and OUs. In addition, each Windows computer has exactly one group of settings stored locally, called the local GPO.

Group Policy Object Editor A tool used to create and edit GPOs, it can be opened using Microsoft Management Console (MMC) or by choosing Edit or New from the Group Policy tab of the Properties window on an Active Directory site, domain, or organizational object.

Group Policy template (GPT) A GUID-named folder that stores policy settings such as security settings and script files. It is located in the Policies sub-folder of the Sysvol volume within an Active Directory domain.

GUID *See* globally unique identifier.

hash A fixed-size result that is obtained by applying a one-way mathematical function, sometimes named a hash algorithm, to an arbitrary amount of data. If there is a change in the input data, the hash changes. The hash can be used in many operations, including authentication and digital signing. A hash is also named a message digest.

hash algorithm An algorithm that produces a hash value of some piece of data such as a message or session key. With a good hash algorithm, changes in the input data can change every bit in the resulting hash value. For this reason, hashes are useful in detecting any modification in a data object such as a message. Furthermore, a good hash algorithm makes it computationally infeasible to construct two independent inputs that have the same hash. Typical hash algorithms include Message Digest versions, 2, 4, and 5 (MD2, MD4, and MD5), and SHA1. It can also be named a hash function.

hash rule Used within a software restriction policy to identify specific software based on a hash of the software.

header record The first line in a text file that is used to import users into the Active Directory database. This record contains valid attributes from the schema. The order of the header record defines the order for each data record within the file.

high capacity When used to refer to a server or domain controller, this machine has a greater processing ability, relative to the other domain controllers available. A high-capacity server generally has a faster central processing unit (CPU), more memory, and faster network access.

highly available When used to refer to a server or domain controller, this machine is centrally located if possible and contains additional hardware, such as a redundant array of independent disks (RAID) controller. RAID allows a server to keep functioning even if one of the drives in the array experiences a failure.

ICANN *See* Internet Corporation for Assigned Names and Numbers.

infrastructure master A domain controller that holds the infrastructure master role in an Active Directory domain. The infrastructure master updates group-to-user references whenever a group membership changes and replicates the changes across the domain. There can be only one infrastructure master per domain in an Active Directory forest.

inheritance A mechanism that allows a given access control entry (ACE) to be copied from the container where it was applied to all children of the container. Inheritance can be combined with delegation to grant administrative rights to a whole subtree of the directory in a single update operation.

interforest migration The migration of users and computers between two separate forests. A cross-forest trust must be created for objects to be migrated across forest boundaries.

Internet Corporation for Assigned Names and Numbers (ICANN) A nonprofit organization responsible for IP address space allocation, protocol parameter assignment, domain name system management, and root server system management functions.

Internet zone rule Used within a software restriction policy to identify software based on the zone of the Internet from which the software is downloaded.

intersite replication The process of replicating Active Directory information from one site to another.

intraforest migration The migration of users and computers within the same forest structure. This type of migration can be used to refer to a restructure of existing forest objects.

intrasite replication The process of replicating Active Directory information between domain controllers within a site.

IP address For Internet Protocol version 4 (IPv4), a 32-bit address used to identify a node on an IP internetwork. Each node on the IP internetwork must be assigned a unique IP address, which is made up of the network ID plus a unique host ID. This address is typically represented with the decimal value of each octet separated by a period, for example, 192.168.7.27. In Windows 2003, you can configure the IP address statically or dynamically through DHCP. For Internet Protocol version 6 (IPv6), an identifier that is assigned at the IPv6 layer to an interface or a set of interfaces and that can be used as the source or destination of IPv6 packets.

KCC *See* knowledge consistency checker.

Kerberos The main security authentication mechanism used by Windows Server 2003. Developed by the Massachusetts Institute of Technology, it uses a ticket system to create keys that identify users to the network.

knowledge consistency checker (KCC) The service responsible for setting up replication connections between sites. It works in conjunction with the ISTG.

latency The amount of time or delay it takes to replicate information throughout the network.

LDAP *See* Lightweight Directory Access Protocol.

LDAP Data Interchange Format Directory Exchange (LDIFDE) A command line utility used to create, modify, and delete Active Directory objects. LDIFDE uses a line-separated file format that can be created in any text editor.

LDIFDE *See* LDAP Data Interchange Format Directory Exchange.

Lightweight Directory Access Protocol (LDAP) The standard directory access protocol for Active Directory that is defined by RFC 1777. It facilitates access and management of objects in Active Directory.

local group account A group that can be granted permission to resources on the local computer. This group is stored in the local security database of the computer in which it is created and it cannot be centrally managed.

local Group Policy Object *See* Group Policy Object (GPO).

local user account A user account that resides in the database of the local computer. This account provides access only to the local computer and does not by default have access to domain resources.

loopback setting A Group Policy setting that forces the computer policy to be reapplied after all user policies have been applied. When set to Enabled, this setting has two options, Merge and Replace. Merge appends the computer policy settings after the user policy settings have been applied, making changes to some, but not necessarily all settings. Replace overwrites all conflicting user policy settings with the computer policy settings.

Lost and Found container A container used for orphaned objects. Orphaned objects are objects for which the parent container has been deleted.

Microsoft Management Console (MMC) An extensible tool that can be used to customize management functions. It has many snap-ins that can be added to create a customized management tool for all levels of administrators.

migration The term used to describe moving or copying Active Directory objects from a source domain to a new location. A migration is typically part of a network restructuring and is used to organize resources and accounts to better serve the corporate security or accessibility goals.

MMC *See* Microsoft Management Console.

Movetree.exe A command line tool used to move objects in Active Directory.

.msi file An installation database file that provides information needed to install software using a Group Policy. .msi files are included with all applications that are certified to run on Windows Server 2003.

.msp file A database file that provides service pack or patch information for an .msi file. This file must be located in the same directory as the .msi file that it will update.

.mst file A transform file that contains information for modifying the .msi file from which it originated. Transform files are used to customize the installation of an application. This file must be located in the same directory as the .msi files that it will update.

multi-master replication Windows Server 2003 domain controllers contain read/write copies of the Active Directory database. When a change takes place in the Active Directory database, the change is copied to all domain controllers in the domain. Because each domain controller has the authority to write changes to the database and replicate those changes to all other domain controllers, a Windows Server 2003 domain is said to be a multi-master domain.

naming standards document A document that is usually created in the planning stages to outline how objects will be named in Active Directory. This document includes standards that define the number and type of characters permitted in an object's name. Examples should also be included to further illustrate the standard.

nesting The term used to describe the process of placing group objects on the membership list of other group objects. Nesting simplifies the assignment of permissions to resources when used properly.

NetBIOS name The naming mechanism that was used to refer to a computer or domain in earlier versions of Windows. It consists of a 15-character name and a sixteenth character that references a service. It usually matches the DNS name.

No Override A Group Policy setting that can be enabled to force policies settings to apply to the associated container and all sub-containers. No Override cannot be blocked at any level in the hierarchy.

node A folder or subfolder that is part of a hierarchical structure. In this textbook, the term node is used to refer to a folder or hierarchy within a Group Policy setting structure.

nonlocal Group Policy Object *See* Group Policy Object (GPO).

normal restore In Windows Backup, this is a type of restore that can be used when you want to restore a single domain controller to a point in time when it was considered good. If there are other domain controllers in the domain, the replication process will update the restored domain controller with the most recent information after the restore is complete. This is also referred to as a non-authoritative restore.

object An element in Active Directory that refers to a resource. Objects can be either container objects or leaf objects. Containers are used to organize resources for security or organizational purposes while leaf objects refer to the end-node resources such as users, computers, and printers.

object attributes Properties of an object class that help to define the object. For example, a user object contains attributes such as password, logon name, home directory, and so on. The schema defines the attributes that belong to each object class.

object class A type of object that is found in Active Directory. Examples of existing object classes include users, groups, and computers. Each object class includes attributes that hold values specific to the class type.

offline defragmentation This is a manual process that defragments the Active Directory database and reduces its size. Offline defragmentation should be performed only when you need to recover a significant amount of disk space. In this process, the server is taken offline so that the Active Directory database is closed and not in use. The server must be restarted in Directory Services Restore mode and the Ntdsutil.exe command line utility is used to perform the offline defragmentation.

offline files A policy setting that allows files to be made available when a network connection is not present. Offline files work well with mobile computers. When combined with folder redirection, offline files allow changes to be made to files locally and redirected to a network drive when it becomes available.

one-way trust A trust that extends only in one direction. For example, if DomainA trusts DomainB, DomainB can access resources in DomainA; however, the reverse is not true.

online defragmentation This is an automatic process that occurs during the Garbage Collection process. The advantage of an online defragmentation is that it occurs automatically and does not require the server to be offline to run. An online defragmentation does not reduce the actual size of the Active Directory database.

Operations master A domain controller that has been assigned Active Directory operations that are single master--that is, operations that are not permitted to occur at different places in the network at the same time. Some single-master operations include schema modification, domain naming, and the relative identifier (RID) allocator.

organizational unit (OU) A container class within the Active Directory structure used to organize resources according to the logical structure of a company. OUs will accept Group Policy assignments; container objects will not.

parent/child relationships An object that resides directly above another object within the same namespace is considered a parent. A child object is contained within a parent object. For example, if folderB is contained within folderA, folderA is the parent and folderB is the child. When multiple containments exist, a parent can also be a child; for example, folderC is contained in folderB, and folderB is inside folderA.

path rule Used within a software restriction policy to identify software based on the location in which the software is stored. A path can be designated to point to the file system or to a location in the registry.

PC/SC *See* personal computer/smart card.

PDC emulator A domain controller that has been assigned the PDC emulator master operations role in an Active Directory domain. The PDC emulator provides access for downlevel computers that do not have the directory services client installed. In addition, it provides backward compatibility for Windows NT BDCs by replicating Active Directory objects changes to them. In a Windows 2000 or Windows Server 2003 domain, it also provides time synchronization and password replication for passwords that have recently changed. There can be only one domain controller assigned the PDC emulator role in each domain.

performance alert This is a feature that detects when a predefined counter value rises above or falls below the configured threshold and notifies a user by means of the Messenger service.

performance counter In System Monitor, this data item is associated with a performance object. For each counter selected, System Monitor presents a value corresponding to a particular aspect of the performance that is defined for the performance object.

performance objects In System Monitor, this is a logical collection of counters that is associated with a resource or service that can be monitored.

personal computer/smart card (PC/SC) A removable device such as a credit-card type or USB device that is used to store authentication information for users to gain access to network resources. Smart cards provide a higher level of security for authentication due to the cryptography and use of PKI.

personal identification number (PIN) A combination of digits used as a kind of password to gain access to a resource. Smart cards require that a PIN is established for the smart card to be successfully read.

PIN *See* personal identification number.

PKI *See* public key infrastructure.

pointer (PTR) record A record created in the reverse lookup zone of DNS that points to a host (A) address record in a forward lookup zone.

primary restore In Windows Backup, this method is required when all Active Directory information is lost for the entire domain. For example, if all domain controllers fail, or if there is only one domain controller before the failure, you need to perform a primary restore in order to rebuild the domain from a recent backup.

public key infrastructure (PKI) A system of digital certificates, certification authorities, and other registration authorities that verify and authenticate the validity of each party involved in an electronic transaction. Standards for PKI are still evolving, even though they are being widely implemented as a necessary element of electronic commerce.

RAID *See* redundant array of independent disks.

realm trust A trust that is established between a non-Windows platform that uses Kerberos for authentication. These are one-way trusts by default.

redundant array of independent disks (RAID) A method used to standardize and categorize levels of fault tolerance with regard to disk systems. The levels range from 0 to 5, with RAID 5 providing the highest level of fault tolerance. As implemented in Windows Server 2003, RAID levels 0, 1, and 5 are available.

relative distinguished name Refers to the object's name and does not include hierarchical containers within the domain structure. (*See also* distinguished name for further information.)

remote procedure call (RPC) over Internet Protocol (IP) RPC over IP is the most common intersite transport protocol.

replica ring The logical connection between domain controllers within a site that exchange Active Directory information.

replication The process of copying updated information from a data store or file system on a source computer to a matching data store or file system on one or more destination computers to synchronize the data. In Active Directory, replication synchronizes schema, configuration, application, and domain directory partitions between domain controllers.

replication topology Defines the path used by replication traffic.

Resultant Set Of Policies (RSoP) A feature that simplifies Group Policy implementation and troubleshooting. RSoP has two modes: logging mode and planning mode. Logging mode determines the resultant effect of policy settings that have been applied to an existing user and computer based on a site, domain, and OU. Planning mode simulates the resultant effect of policy settings that are applied to a user and a computer.

return on investment (ROI) A measurement of the amount of time it takes to receive the payback on the network or a specific product. In the case of Windows Server 2003, a good example is measured in saved administrative resources. Group policies provide an opportunity for ROI since they save administrators from having to travel between sites in order to implement changes to the user environment.

reverse lookup zones A zone created in DNS to provide IP address to DNS name resolution. It is not required but can be helpful in troubleshooting.

RID master A domain controller that has been assigned the RID FSMO role in an Active Directory domain. The RID master is responsible for assigning pools of identifiers to domain controllers for use during object creation. There can be only one domain controller assigned the RID master role in each domain.

role seizure A technique used only when there is a catastrophic failure of a domain controller holding a FSMO role. Seizing a role can be defined as a forced, permanent transfer. This procedure assumes that you cannot restore the domain controller that previously held the role.

role transfer A technique used to move a FSMO role from one domain controller to another. Transfers can be done as a management technique to provide improved performance or when a domain controller will be taken offline for maintenance.

Run As A program used to establish a second logon session using a different set of user credentials. Run As is typically used to perform administrative tasks, while maintaining a primary logon as a standard user.

schema Defines the available object types (object classes) and their attributes within the Active Directory database.

schema master A domain controller that has been assigned the schema FSMO role in an Active Directory forest. The schema master is the domain controller from which all schema modifications and queries take place. There can be only one domain controller assigned the schema master operations role in any forest.

schema partition Contains the rules for creating objects and object attributes. This partition is replicated to all domain controllers within the Active Directory forest.

SDLC *See* System Development Life Cycle.

secondary logon service The service that allows a second session to be activated using a different set of credentials. This service is required by the Run As program.

security group A group that can be listed in DACLs used to define permissions on resources and objects. A security group can also be used as an e-mail entity. Sending an e-mail message to the group sends the message to all the members of the group.

security identifier (SID) A variable length identifier that is assigned to every object in the Active Directory database. Internal processes always refer to an object's SID rather than the object name.

shortcut trust A manually created trust that allows child domains in separate trees to communicate more efficiently by eliminating the tree-walking of a trust path.

SID *See* security identifier.

Simple Mail Transport Protocol (SMTP) A transport protocol used for intersite replication traffic. It requires configuration of a certificate authority (CA) and is limited to replicating global catalog, schema, and configuration context information.

single-master operations *See* operations master.

site Consists of one or more well-connected IP subnets. A site should contain only subnets connected by fast and reliable links. Commonly interpreted as LAN connectivity.

site link A logical transitive connection between two or more sites that mirrors the network links and allows replication to occur.

site link bridge The linking of more than two sites for replication using the same transport. It mimics the routed network environment.

smart card A credit card-sized device that is used with an access code to enable certificate-based authentication and single sign-on to the enterprise. Smart cards securely store certificates, public and private keys, passwords, and other types of personal information. A smart card reader attached to the computer reads the smart card.

SMTP *See* Simple Mail Transport Protocol.

software categories Used with published applications to group available application choices within the Add and Remove Programs option of Control Panel.

software distribution point A shared folder that contains all of the files necessary to allow an application to be installed from across the network.

software restriction policy A collection of policy settings that define what software can run on a computer based on the Default Security Level for a Group Policy Object (GPO). Exceptions to the Default Security Level can then be defined by certificate rules, hash rules, path rules, registry path rules, and Internet zone rules.

special identity groups These groups are not visible in Active Directory Users And Computers (MMC snap-in). Their membership lists are automatically populated by the operating system depending on their use. They are usually used to represent a class of users or the system itself. They cannot be modified or deleted. However, if assigned to a resource, they can be removed from that resource if deemed necessary, for example, the Everyone group.

strong passwords Strong passwords are a combination of a required password length, password history, character types, and minimum password age.

subnet object Logically represents the physical subnets of the network infrastructure. Sites are linked to the subnets they will service.

synchronous processing This type of processing allows an entire script or policy to be run completely before initiating another.

System Development Life Cycle (SDLC) A structured process used to develop information systems software, projects, or components that includes the analysis, design, implementation, and maintenance phases.

System Monitor This is a tool that is located within the Performance Monitor console that allows collection of real-time information on your local computer or from a specific computer to which you have permissions. This information can be viewed in a number of different formats that include charts, graphs, and histograms.

System State data In Windows Backup, this is a collection of system-specific data maintained by the operating system that must be backed up as a unit. It is not a backup of the entire system. The System State data includes the registry, COM+ Class Registration database, system files, boot files, and files under Windows File Protection. For a certificate server, the System State data also includes the Certificate Services database. If the server is a domain controller, the System State data also includes the Active Directory database and the Sysvol directory. If the server is a node in a cluster, it includes the Cluster database information. The IIS Metabase is included if Internet Information Services (IIS) is installed.

Sysvol folder The folder used to store replication data such as logon scripts and profiles. It requires an NTFS partition.

TCO *See* total cost of ownership.

timestamp An attribute set on an object to indicate when it was last updated. Timestamps are used to assist in the resolution of conflicts during replication. If a change was made to an attribute of the same object, the timestamp can help determine which object is the most up-to-date.

timestamp token-style card A smart card that resembles a key and uses a USB port for access to the computer system.

tombstone A tombstone includes references or portions left of an Active Directory object that has been deleted.

total cost of ownership (TCO) A measurement of the total amount of money a network implementation, software, or hardware component costs to implement and maintain throughout its lifetime of use.

transactions In Active Directory, database changes are referred to as transactions. Transactions can contain more than one change, such as the addition of a new object and the modification of an existing object's properties.

transform file A file that consists of instructions to modify or customize a program such as an .msi file during installation.

transitive trust A trust relationship that allows a child domain to trust another child domain because of their common relationship to a parent domain; for example, if A trusts B and B trusts C, then A trusts C.

tree A collection of related domains that share a contiguous name and two-way transitive trusts.

tree-walking The process of using the parent/child trust paths to locate resources within a forest.

unicodePwd attribute The password stored in Active Directory on a user object. This attribute can be written under restricted conditions, but it cannot be read. The attribute can only be modified; it cannot be added on object creation or queried by a search. To modify this attribute, the client must have a 128-bit Secure Sockets Layer (SSL) connection to the server. For this connection to be possible, the server must possess a server certificate for a 128-bit RSA connection, the client must trust the certificate authority (CA) that generated the server certificate, and both client and server must be capable of 128-bit encryption.

Uniform Resource Locator (URL) The global address of a location on the Internet or on an intranet. It includes the protocol, the domain name, and the exact location of a resource. For example: http://www.microsoft.com.

universal group A security or distribution group that can be used anywhere in the domain tree or forest. A universal group can have members from any Windows domain in the domain tree or forest. It can also include other universal groups, global groups, and accounts from any domain in the domain tree or forest. Rights and permissions must be assigned on a per-domain basis using appropriate domain local groups, but they can be assigned at any domain in the domain tree or forest. Universal groups can be members of domain local groups and other universal groups, but they cannot be members of global groups. Universal groups appear in the global catalog and should contain primarily global groups.

universal group membership caching A new feature in Windows Server 2003 that allows domain controllers to process a logon or resource request without the presence of a global catalog server. The domain controller periodically contacts a global catalog server for universal group membership information. This information is copied to the domain controller.

Update Sequence Number (USN) A number assigned to an object that is incremented by one each time an attribute change occurs. USNs are used in determining the most up to date information.

upgrade Installation of a new operating system version on an existing computer. For example, if a computer is running Windows 2000, and if Windows Server 2003 media is used directly on that computer to update the operating system, then this is referred to as an upgrade.

UPN *See* User Principal Name.

User Principal Name (UPN) A naming format that allows simplification of access to multiple services such as Active Directory and e-mail. A UPN uses the same format that is common to e-mail applications, that is, user@domainname.com.

USN *See* Update Sequence Number.

Windows Installer An extensible software system that manages the installation, addition, and deletion of software components, monitors file resiliency, and maintains basic failure recovery with rollbacks. Windows Installer supports installing and running software from multiple sources, and developers can configure Windows Installer to install custom applications.

Windows Installer Service A component of the Windows operating system that simplifies the application installation process, Windows Installer manages the installation and removal of applications by applying a set of centrally-defined setup rules during the installation process.

Windows Management Instrumentation (WMI) WMI is the Microsoft implementation of Web-Based Enterprise Management (WBEM), an industry initiative to develop a standard technology for accessing management information in an enterprise environment. The WMI infrastructure is a Microsoft Windows operating system component that moves and stores information about managed objects.

Windows Script Host (WSH) A powerful administrative scripting tool that can run scripts created in either VBScript or JScript. WSH allows these scripts to be run from either the Windows desktop using wscript.exe or from a command line using cscript.exe.

WMI *See* Windows Management Instrumentation.

WSH *See* Windows Script Host.

X.500 A set of standards defining a distributed directory service, developed by the International Organization for Standardization (ISO).

.zap file A non-Windows Installer package that can be created in a text editor. A .zap file looks and functions very much like an .ini file. .zap files allow an application that does not contain support for Windows Installer to be installed using Group Policy.

INDEX

A

AAS (application advertisement script), 164
access control entry (ACE), 29, 320
access control lists (ACLs), 8
  controlling access to domain objects, 9
  defined, 6
  hiding objects, 147–148
access tokens, 112, 114
accounts
  administrator account, 112, 113, 145
  attributes for. *See* attributes for creating user accounts
  authentication, 112
  guest, 112, 113
  local, 112
  lockout duration, 187
  as object class, 5
  policy, 185
  security, 140–145
ACE (access control entry), 29, 320
ACL. *See* access control lists (ACLs)
Active Directory
  advanced features, 164, 193
  components, 7
  Domains And Trusts, 49, 102, 146
  features, advances, 164, 193
  implementation. *See* implementation
  Installation Wizard (Dcpromo). *See* installation
  Migration Tool (ADMT). *See* Active Directory Migration Tool (ADMT)
  Object Type page, 151
  overview, 2–26
  Restore mode, 13
  Sites And Services
    creating site structure, 71–73
    enabling universal group membership caching, 87
    Group Policy Management Console (GPMC), 256
    managing Active Directory physical structure, 60
    managing replication, 73–75
    providing information to optimize replication, 11
    viewing Active Directory physical structure, 60
    viewing connection objects, 64
  structure, 171
  Users And Computers
    creating users and groups, 118, 129
    enabling user accounts for Smart Card authentication, 145

    finding Group Policy container using Advanced view, 163
    Group Policy Management Console (GPMC), 256
    starting, with Run As, 146
    verifying delegated permissions, 152
    viewing domain roles, 101
Active Directory Migration Tool (ADMT)
  generally, 318
  preparation tasks, 321, 326
Active Directory schema, 4–6, 102, 125
  modifying, 46–48
administration, delegation of, 8, 14
administrative templates
  defined, 168
  Help, 169
  setting options, 171
administrative tools
  centralized administration and, 2
  folder. *See* Administrative Tools folder
Administrative Tools folder, 11, 43
administrators
  account, 112, 113, 145
  benefits, 161
Admins group
  Domain, 124, 145
  Enterprise, 125, 145
  Schema, 125, 145
ADMT. *See* Active Directory Migration Tool (ADMT)
aging and scavenging, 41
alerts, 303
American National Standards Institute (ANSI) text files vs. Unicode-based text files, 168
Anonymous Logon group, 126
application advertisement script (AAS), 164
application partitions, 10, 39–41
applications
  assignment, 226
  publishing, 226
assignment of user rights, 189, 194
associated privileges, 114
asynchronous processing, 174
attributes, naming, 12, 13
attributes for creating user accounts
  DN, 130
  objectClass, 131
  saMAccountName, 130
  telephoneNumber, 131
  userAccountControl, 131
  userPrincipalName, 131
audit, security. *See* security audit

363

Audit Policy Plan, 193
audits
   directory service access, 193
   event failures, 190
   object access, 190, 193
   privilege use, 190
   process tracking, 190
Authenticated Users group, 252
authentication
   functionality, 188
   generally, 112
   request, 87
autoenrollment
   certificate, 200
   settings, 204
automatic caching, 209
automatic certificate request, 199
automatic trust. *See* trust relationships
auxiliary classes, linking individual objects to, 20

B

backup
   command line utility, authoritative restore, 293
   operators, 194
   restoration options, 292–294
   strategy, 210, 211
backup domain controllers (BDCs), 92
Backup Or Restore Wizard, 287
Backup Utility Restoration Options, 292–294
backwards compatibility, 16, 48
bandwidth
   conservation, 28
   constraints, 86
batch files, 129
BDCs (backup domain controllers), 92
Berkeley Internet Name Domain (BIND), 29
BIND. *See* Berkeley Internet Name Domain (BIND)
Block Policy Inheritance, 175
bridgehead server, 62, 69
built-in
   container, 171
   security group, 120
   user account, 112
business model, Active Directory implementation plan and, 13

C

CA (certification authority), 68, 143
caching
   automatic, 209
   credentials, 86
   manual, 209
   universal group membership, 83–85

catalog, global. *See* global catalogs
centralized configuration, 162
centralized management, 161
certificate trust lists (CTLs), 199
certificates
   autoenrollment, 200
   requests, automatic, 199
   rules. *See* software restriction policies
   service, 286
   trust list (CTL), 199
   trusted root, 184, 199
certification authority (CA), 68, 143
Change Management Process (CMP), 48
child containers
   group policy inheritance and, 8
   group policy object assignment, 175
child domains, 7, 8
child object. *See* objects, child, creation/delegation
CIDR (Classless Inter-Domain Routing), 71
CIMOM (Common Information Management Object Model), 263
Classless Inter-Domain Routing (CIDR), 71
clock synchronization setting, 188
Cluster Service, 286
CMP (Change Management Process), 48
Comma-Separated Value Directory Exchange (CSVDE), 129
Common Information Management Object Model (CIMOM), 263
company model, representation of, 146
compatibility
   backwards, 16, 48
   dialog page, 31
   with Windows NT 4.0, 16
Component Object Model (COM), 230, 286
Conf.adm administrative template, 168
configuration
   centralized, 162
   computer, 167, 172, 226
   node, 165, 185
   partition, 9
   user
      Account policies, 185
      assigning applications, 226
      disabling user or configuration node settings, 214
      Group Policy settings, 167
      policies, processing order of, 172
Configure Your Server Wizard page, 30
confirmation request, 86
connection objects, 63
connectivity tests, 76
contact, as object in organizational unit, 8
container objects, 7
converting group types, 116

domains 365

cost value, 66
Create New Domain page, 32
cross-forest trusts. *See* trust relationships
cryptographic service provider (CSP), 202
CScript.exe, 129
CSP (cryptographic service provider), 202
CSVDE (Comma-Separated Value Directory Exchange), 129
CTLs (certificate trust lists), 199
Current Location OU, 172

D

Database and Log Folders page, 35
DCdiag, 76
Dcpromo tool, 28, 292
Default Domain Controller policy, 165, 175, 277
default groups, 120, 121
Default Security Level, 237
Default-First-Site-Name, 60, 71
DefaultIPSiteLink, 71
defragmentation
  offline, 283
  online, 282
delegated permission, 87, 152
delegation of administration, 8, 14
Delegation Of Control Wizard, 150
denial-of-service attack (DoS), 189
designated file types properties. *See* software restriction policies
desktop environment, 160
DHCP (Dynamic Host Configuration Protocol), 120
diagnostic tools, 306
directory
  functions, naming, 11
  partitions, 9–11, 17, 39
  service
    access, for audit, 193
    log, 195, 297
  systemroot, 35
Directory Services Restore Mode, 30, 37, 283, 285, 293
Directory System Agents (DSAs), 299
disabled setting, 171
disks
  quotas, 210, 212
  space requirement, 28
distinguished name (DN), 12, 92, 130
Distributed File System (DFS), 301
distribution groups, 115
distribution share, 225
DN (distinguished name), 12, 92, 130
DNS. *See* Domain Name System (DNS)
DNS Registration Diagnostics page, 36

domain controllers, 8
  adding with Active Directory Installation Wizard, 28, 31–39
  backup, 92
  defined, 2
  dynamically registering with DNS at startup, 42–43
  failure, single vs. multiple domains, 4
  forest root domain, adding second to, 45
  high capacity, 96–97
  highly available, 96–97
  promoting standalone servers to, 3
  replication, 59–77
  system services, 307
domain local group. *See* domains
domain name page, 34
Domain Name System (DNS)
  described, 12–13
  detection and installation, 36–37
  Dynamic Host Configuration Protocol (DHCP), 120
  Event Log policy, DNS log, 195
  as network client locator service, 15
  server support requirements, 28
domain naming master role, 94
domain partition, 10
domain tree. *See* domains
domain-linked policy, 171
domains
  account, policy for, 185, 186
  child, 7, 8
  components, naming attributes and, 12
  as container objects, 7
  defined, 8
  family, 9
  forest root, 7, 9, 31, 45
  functional level. *See* functional levels
  group policy. *See* group policy
  linked policy, 171
  local group, 116, 127
  mixed mode, 17
  name. *See also* Domain Name System (DNS)
    changing, 18, 20
    fully qualified. *See* Fully Qualified Domain Name (FQDN)
    page, 34
    registration, 33
    standards, 11–13
  naming
    attributes, 12, 13
    master, 93, 99, 102
    standards, 11–13
  as object classes, 5
  objects in, 9
  in organizational units, 9
  parents, 7

domains, *continued*
   replication. *See* domain controllers, replication; replication
   trees
      as container objects, 7
      defined, 9
   user accounts, 112
drag and drop, 153
drive, shared, as object class, 5
Dsadd command, 129, 130
DSAs (Directory System Agents), 299
Dsmove command, 154
Dynamic Host Configuration Protocol (DHCP), 120
dynamic update, 15, 28, 29

E

Education OU, 172–177
EFS (Encrypted File System), 184, 199
e-mail name, consistency with logon name, 13
enabled settings, 171
Encrypted File System (EFS), 184, 199
Enforce User Logon Restrictions, 188
enforcement property. *See* software restriction policies
enrollment agent certificates, 144
enterprise certification authority. *See* certification authority (CA)
enterprise trust list, 184, 199
Event Viewer, 73, 184
events
   failure, 190
   tracking, 189
Everyone group, 126
Exchange. *See* Microsoft Exchange, object naming standards and
Explain tab, 169
Extended tab, 169
Extensible Storage Engine (ESE), 282

F

family, domain, 9
fast link, 11
failure
   auditing event, 190
   planned, 100
fault tolerance, 3, 96
File Replication Service (FRS), 297, 301, 315
FileReplicaConn, 301
FileReplicaSet, 301
firewalls, 69
Flexible Single Master Operation (FSMO), 31, 83, 102–105, 188, 324
folders
   administrative tools folder, 11, 43
   Group Policy Template, structure of, 164
   Intersite Transports, 72

   as leaf object, 7
   redirection, 205
   shared
      as object class, 5
      in organizational unit, 8
   Sysvol structure
      entering location for folder, 35
      GPT folder structure, 164–165
      requirement for installing Active Directory, 28
      restoring Active Directory database, 296
      System State data, 286
forced replication. *See* replication, forced
forest
   as container object, 7
   creating, 33
   defined, 9
   directory partitions and, 9–11
   functional level. *See* functional levels
   migration, interforest, 319, 326
   multiple-tree structure, 11
   root
      domain. *See* domains, forest root
      name, 10
forward lookup zone, 42, 52
FQDN (Fully Qualified Domain Name), 33
fragmentation, 282
FSMO. *See* Flexible Single Master Operation (FSMO)
Full Control, 192
Fully Qualified Domain Name (FQDN), 33
functional levels
   Active Directory implementation plan and, 13
   domain, 15–19, 116, 120
   forest, 15, 19–21, 70, 116
   group scopes and, 120
   interim mode, 18
   native mode domain, 17
   raising domain and forest, 48–49

G

Garbage Collection process, 283
global catalogs, 10, 84, 87, 92, 99, 118
global groups, 117
globally unique identifiers (GUIDs), 6, 92, 163, 296
GPC. *See* Group Policy Container (GPC)
GPMC. *See* Group Policy Management Console (GPMC)
GPResult, 271
GPT. *See* Group Policy Template (GPT)
Gpupdate.exe, 214
group policy
   Block Policy Inheritance, 175
   container, 163
   creator owners, 273
   delegation, 272

domain, 172
generally, 13, 147, 160
guidelines, 276
inheritance, 8, 14, 166
local, 127, 162, 172
loopback, 175
management console. *See* Group Policy Management Console (GPMC)
modeling, 265
nested OU structure and, 8
No Override, 174
nonlocal, 162, 171
object. *See* Group Policy Object (GPO)
processing of, 172
organizational units and, 8, 172
refresh
  interval, 213
  manual, 214
results, 268
settings, 167, 168
site, 172
template. *See* Group Policy Template (GPT)
Group Policy Container (GPC), 163
Group Policy Creator Owners group, 273
Group Policy Management Console (GPMC)
  generally, 255
  individual GPO permissions, 273
  installation of, 257
  navigating with, 257
Group Policy Object (GPO)
  configuring, 228
  generally, 162, 226
  Editor, 166, 168, 231, 256
  local, 162
  nonlocal, 162
  status information, 164
  version information, 164
Group Policy Refresh Interval, 213
Group Policy Results, 268
Group Policy Template (GPT)
  folder structure, 164
  generally, 163
groups
  Anonymous Logon, 126
  Authenticated Users, 252
  converting, 115
  default, 120, 121
  distribution, 115
  domain local, 116, 127
  Everyone, 126
  generally, 114
  global, 117
  implementation plan, 127
  local, 127, 162, 172
  nesting of, 119, 140
  as object classes, 5
  in organizational unit, 8
  policy. *See* group policy
  scopes, 116, 120
  security, 115, 120
  special identity, 125
  types, converting, 115
  universal, 17, 84, 86, 117
guest account, 112, 113
GUIDs (globally unique identifiers), 6, 92, 163, 296

H

hackers, 145
Hardware Compatibility List (HCL), 287
Hash
  algorithm, 238
  rule. *See* software restriction policies
header record, 130
high capacity domain controllers, 96–97
highly available domain controllers, 96–97
hives, registry, 164, 165
HKEY_CURRENT_USER hives, 165
HKEY_LOCAL_MACHINE hives, 164
host names, 14
hotfixes, 223

I

ICANN (Internet Corporation for Assigned Names and Numbers), 33
IETF (Internet Engineering Task Force), 11
implementation
  costs, 161
  group, 127
  planning for, 13
  security audit, 193
  software restriction policy, 242
  System Development LifeCycle (SDLC), 222
incoming trust. *See* trust relationships
InetOrgPerson, 8, 20
infrastructure master, 90, 95, 99
inheritance. *See* group policy
installation
  requirements, 28, 29
  verification, 39
  wizard, 28, 30, 32
interforest migration tools, 319, 326
interim mode. *See* functional levels
Internet Corporation for Assigned Names and Numbers (ICANN), 33
Internet Engineering Task Force (IETF), 11
Internet Protocol (IP), 28, 67
Internet zone rule. *See* software restriction policies
intersite replication, 65
Intersite Topology Generator (ISTG), 65
Intersite Transports folder, 72

intraforest migration tools, 319, 326
intrasite replication, 63
Intres.adm administrative template, 168
IP (Internet Protocol), 28, 67
IP subnet, 11, 60, 65
ISTG (Intersite Topology Generator), 65

K

KCC (Knowledge Consistency Checker), 11, 63
KDC (Key Distribution Center), 188
Kerberos authentication protocol, 22, 93, 188, 189
Key Distribution Center (KDC), 188
Knowledge Consistency Checker (KCC), 11, 63

L

LAN (local area network), 60
LAN Manager Replication (LMRepl), 315
latency, 64, 104
LDAP (Lightweight Directory Access Protocol), 11
LDAP Data Interchange Format Directory Exchange (LDIFDE), 129
LDIFDE (LDAP Data Interchange Format Directory Exchange), 129
leaf objects
  definition, 7
  group policy inheritance and, 8
Lightweight directory access protocol (LDAP), 11
line-separated formats, 131
linked value replication, 20
links. See site links
List Contents permission, 148
LMRepl (LAN Manager Replication), 315
load balancing, 8
local administration permission, 224
local area network (LAN), 60
local groups, 127
Local Security Authority (LSA), 63
local user account, 112, 160
logoff script, 173
logon
  benefits of, 161
  name, consistency with e-mail name, 13
  scripts, 173
lookup zones, 39, 42, 44, 52
loopback setting, 175, 177
Lost and Found container, 91
LSA (Local Security Authority), 63

M

Manage Your Server Web page, 30
management tasks, delegation, 149, 150
manual caching, 209

Manual Replication Paths, 64
manual trust. See trust relationships
Maximum Tolerance value, 188
member servers, 112
membership
  level, 114
  list, 70
Microsoft Exchange, object naming standards and, 12
Microsoft Management Console (MMC), 47, 166
Microsoft Systems Management Server, 115
Microsoft Windows. See individual Windows entries
migration
  of external domains, 318
  of networks, 48
  operating system, 312
  of users, 28
  from Windows 2000, 319, 326
  from Windows NT 4.0, 313
mixed mode, 17, 85
MMC (Microsoft Management Console), 47, 166
monitor replication. See replication
Monitoring Active Directory
  Event Viewer, 297
  System Monitor, 298
movetree.exe, 91
msi file. See Windows Installer Service
msp files. See Windows Installer Service
mst files. See Windows Installer Service
multi-master replication model, 3, 89

N

names. See also naming
  Default-First-Site-Name, 60, 71
  e-mail, 13
  distinguished, 92, 130
  forest root, 10
  host, 14
  Internet Corporation for Assigned Names and Numbers (ICANN), 33
  logon, 13
  space, sharing within domain tree, 9
  unique, 6
naming. See also names
  attributes, 12, 13
  domain. See domains
  of forest roots, 10
  standards, 11–14, 140
natural latency, 104
ndtsutil command, 13
nesting
  of group, 17, 119, 148
  OU structure, 8
NetBios domain name page, 33, 34

Netdom, 53
Netlogon server, 15, 31, 42
network
   backup strategy. *See* backup
   internal and external, 33
   management tools, 159
   Not Configured setting, 171
   security. *See* security
   settings, 159, 171
   topology, 62
New Object-Group dialog box, 118
New Trust Wizard, 51
nodes, 167
Not Configured setting, 171
Nslookup, 43
NT Directory Service (NTDS), 63
NTFS volume, 193, 211
NTDS (NT Directory Service), 63
Ntdsutil, 104

O

Object Identifier (OID), 47
Object Type page, 151
objectClass. *See* attributes for creating user accounts
objects
   access, for audit, 190, 193
   adding to database, 46
   attribute, 4, 6, 20, 29
   child, creation/delegation, 152
   class
      defined, 5
      creating and modifying, 9
      naming attributes for, 12
   connection, 63
   container, 7
   defined, 5
   hiding, 147
   hierarchy, 39
   leaf, 7
   moving of, 153
   naming standards, 11, 12
   in organizational units, 8
   referencing in Active Directory, 12, 13
   restoration of, naming attributes and, 13
   search, facilitation of, 84
   size, 29
   subnet, 65
Offline Files, 208
OID (Object Identifier), 47
one-way trust. *See* trust relationships
operating system compatibility, 31
optional object attributes, 6
organizational units (OUs)
   benefits, 146–148
   creating structure, 148–153
   definition, 7
   moving objects between OUs, 153–154
   order applied in group policies, 172–177
   possible objects contained by, 8
   size in Active Directory database, 29
OU. *See* organizational units (OUs)
outgoing trust. *See* trust relationships

P

Package Creation Application, 224
parent/child relationships, 7, 8
parents. *See also* parent/child relationships
   container, 172
   policy, 175
   structure, 167
partitions
   application, 10, 39–41
   configuration, 9
   directory, defined, 9
   domain, 10
   global catalog, 10
   schema, 9
passwords
   account security. *See* security
   administrator, 113
   Directory Services Restore Mode, 30, 37
   policies, 185
   strategy, planning, 155
   strong, 113, 141, 145
patch files. *See* Windows Installer Service
path rules. *See* software restriction policies
PDC (primary domain controller), 92
Performance Monitor, 298
Performance Object Counters, 299, 303
permissions
   assignment, 115
   default, 36
   delegated, 87, 152
   level, 114
   List Contents permission, 148
   settings, 30
Permissions page, 37
Personal Computer/Smart Card (PC/SC), 143
personal identification number (PIN), 140
planned failures, 100
planning, design components and, 13
policy
   group. *See* group policy
   processing, 174, 214
   registry-based, 160
   removal, 208
   security. *See* security
   settings, user, 177
   site-linked, 171
   software restriction. *See* software restriction policies
Policy Processing Optimization, 214
port 3268, 84, 88
pre-backup tasks, 287

preferential account modification replication, 90
primary domain controller (PDC), 92
primary domain controller (PDC) emulator, 90, 99, 101
printers
   as leaf object, 7
   as object class, 5
   in organizational unit, 8
privileges
   associated, 114
   use for audit, 190
   processing, asynchronous, 174
profiles, user, 174
public key infrastructure (PKI), 143
publishing an application, 226
pyramid OU structure, 148

R

RAID (redundant array of independent disks), 97
RAS (remote access server), 37
redundancy, 3, 4, 8
redundant array of independent disks (RAID), 97
refreshing
   group policy, 214
   replication topology. *See* replication
referencing objects in Active Directory, 12, 13
registration authorities (RAs), 143
registration problems, 76
registry
   entries, 164, 165
   generally, 286
   key, 168
registry-based policy, 160
registry.pol, 164
relative distinguished name, 12
relative identifier (RID) master, 90, 91, 104
remote access server (RAS), 37
remote location, 86
remote procedure calls (RPC), 67
Remove Active Directory page, 32
repackaging of software, 223
Repadmin, 76, 104
replica ring, 59, 63
replication
   directory partitions and, 9
   file replication. *See* File Replication Service (FRS)
   forced, 75
   generally, 3, 59
   of global catalog, 10
   Inter-site Topology Generator (ISTG), 19
   LAN Manager Replication, 315
   linked value, 20
   metadata, 76
   monitor, 75
   multi-master system, 3, 4
   optimizing, 11
   paths, manual, 64
   preferential account modification, 90
   process, 292
   purpose of, 8
   refreshing, 74
   tests, 76
   topology, 9, 11, 62, 74
ReplMon, 76
required object attribute, 6
resource
   access
      Active Directory implementation plan and, 13
      troubleshooting, 8
   location, 4
restoration of objects, 13. *See also* backup
Restore mode, 13
Resultant Set of Policy (RSoP)
   generally, 256, 261
   logging mode report, 264
   planning mode report, 263
   Wizard, 262
retention setting, 184
Return on Investment (ROI), 161
reverse lookup zone, 44
RID master. *See* relative identifier (RID) master
rights assignment, 189, 194
ROI (Return on Investment), 161
role
   holder, 83, 93, 100
   seizure, 100
   transfer, 100
root certificate, trusted, 184, 199
RPC over IP, 67. *See also* remote procedure calls (RPC)
RSoP. *See* Resultant Set of Policy (RSoP)
Rule of 3, 63
Run As program, 145, 241

S

SAM (Security Accounts Manager), 112, 129
saMAccountName. *See* attributes for creating user accounts
scalability, naming standards and, 11
scavenging, 41
schema
   Access Control Lists (ACLs) and, 6
   defined, 5
   master, 93, 98, 102
   modifying, 46
   partition, 9
   redefinition, 20

Schema Management snap-in, 6
schema master role, 94
Scripting Host. *See* Windows Scripting Host (WSH)
scripts
  shutdown, 173
  startup, 173
SDLC. *See* System Development Life Cycle (SDLC)
searching. *See* resource, location
secondary forward lookup zone, 52
Secondary Logon service, 146
security
  of accounts, 140–145
  accounts manager. *See* Security Accounts Manager (SAM)
  Active Directory implementation plan and, 13, 14
  administration
    guidelines, custom, 8
    tools, 2
  administrator account, use of, 112, 113
  audit. *See* security audit
  authority, local. *See* Local Security Authority (LSA)
  certificates, sizing of, 29
  dynamic updates and, 15
  firewall, 69
  forest level, 9
  guest account, 112, 113
  groups, 115, 120
  identifier. *See* Security Identifier (SID)
  level, default, 237
  network, generally, 159
  organizational units and, 8
  options, 189, 195
  password. *See* strong passwords
  Password Policies, 185
  permissions, default, 36
  policies, 184–198
  principle, sizing of, 29
  public key infrastructure (PKI), 143
  settings, 184
    Account Lockout Policies, 186
    Account Policies, 185
    advanced, 194
    Audit Policy. *See* security audit
    Event Log Policy, 195
    IPSec Policy, 184
    Kerberos policy, 188
    Local Policies, 189
    node, 187, 191
    Password Policies, 185
    Public Key Policies, 199
    Registry and File System Policies, 198
    Restricted Groups Policy, 196
    Software Restriction Policies, 204
    System Services Policy, 197
    Wireless Network (IEEE 802.11) Policies, 198
  smart card. *See* smart card authentication
  threats, 85
Security Accounts Manager (SAM), 112, 129
security audit
  account logon event category, 192
  account management category, 192
  implementation of, 193
  logon event category, 192
  planning of, 191
  policy, 189
  policy change category, 192
  setting, 189
  specifying events, 191
  system events category, 192
Security Identifier (SID), 17, 90, 320
security settings. *See* security
seizing an FSMO role, 103, 105
service packs, 223
service resource (SRV) records, 15, 28, 42–44
services, system, 307
shared drives, as object class, 5
shared folder. *See* folders
shutdown scripts, 173
SID (Security Identifier), 17, 90, 320
Simple Mail Transport Protocol (SMTP), 68
single domain networks, 85
single-master operations. *See* Flexible Single Master Operation (FSMO)
site links
  bridge, 69, 72, 73
  generally, 65
  objects
    cost, 66
    frequency, 66
    schedule, 66
  policy. *See* site-linked policy
  transitive, 70
site-linked policy, 171
sites
  as container object, 7
  defined, 11
  link. *See* site links
  topology, 61
Sites And Services snap-in
  creating site structure, 71–73
  enabling universal group membership caching, 87
  Group Policy Management Console (GPMC), 256
  managing Active Directory physical structure, 60
  managing replication, 73–75

Sites And Services snap-in, *continued*
    providing information to optimize
        replication, 11
    viewing Active Directory physical structure,
        60
    viewing connection objects, 64
sizing requirements, 29
smart card authentication, 139, 144, 145
SMTP (Simple Mail Transport Protocol), 68
software categories, 227
software restriction policies
    certificate rule, 238
    designated file types, 241
    enforcement, 241
    generally, 236
    hash rule, 238
    implementation recommendations, 242
    Internet zone rule, 240
    path rule, 239
    security setting, 204
    trusted publishers, 242
Software Settings folder, 168
space requirements, 29
special identity groups, 125
SRV records. *See* service resource (SRV)
        records
standalone servers, 112
startup scripts, 173
strong passwords, 113, 141, 145
subnets. *See also* IP subnet
    mask, 71
    objects, 65
Support Tools, 75
synchronization. *See* time synchronization
synchronous processing, 174
system activities, 189
System Development Life Cycle (SDLC)
    implementation, 222
    maintenance, 222
    planning, 222
    removal, 222
system services, 307
System State
    backup, 283, 285
    data, 286
System.adm administrative template, 168
systemroot directory, 35, 164
Systems Management Server, 115
Sysvol folder, 28, 30,
    backing up System State data, 286
    defined, 35
    ensuring Group Policy integrity after
        backup, 296
    Group Policy Template, 164

T

tattooing, 208
Tasks To Delegate page, 151
TCO (Total Cost of Ownership), 161, 225
TCP/IP (Transmission Control Protocol/
        Internet Protocol), 28, 36, 120
telephoneNumber. *See* attributes for creating
        user accounts
time synchronization, 90, 93, 188
timestamps, 41, 62, 93
token-style cards, 143
tombstones, 283
tools, administrative. *See* administrative tools
Total Cost of Ownership (TCO), 161, 225
tracking events, 189
transactions
    generally, 282
    log file, 28
transfer of
    domain naming master, 103
    FSMO role, 102, 103
    Infrastructure master, 102
    PDC emulator, 102
    RID master, 102
    schema master, 103
transform files. *See* Windows Installer Service
transitive site links, 70
Transmission Control Protocol/Internet
        Protocol (TCP/IP), 28, 36, 120
tree, domain. *See* domains
tree-walking, 22
troubleshooting resource access, 8
trust models. *See* trust relationships
trust relationships
    Active Directory implementation plan and,
        13
    automatic, 52
    cross-forest, 20–24, 50, 85, 117
    external, 51
    incoming, 52
    manual, 52
    models, comparing, 21–23
    one-way, 50
    outgoing, 52
    realm, 51
    revocation, 53
    short-cut, 22, 49
    tree-walking, 22
    two-way, 24, 51
    verification, 52
trusted publishers properties. *See* software
        restriction policies
trusted root certificates, 184, 199
two-way trusts. *See* trust relationships

U

Uniform Naming Convention (UNC), 228
Uniform Resource Locator (URL), 12, 232
unique names, 6
universal groups, 17, 84, 86, 117
unplanned failures, 100
Update Sequence Numbers (USNs), 62, 294
upgrades
   backup, 314
   DNS zone, 314
   documentation, 313
   hardware requirements, 314
   multi-domain strategy, 322
   operating system, 312
   of PDC, 316
   preparation, 313, 314
   required user rights, 325
   single domain strategy, 316
   from Windows 2000, 324
   from Windows NT 4.0, 313
UPN (User Principal Name), 13, 54, 84
URL (Uniform Resource Locator), 12, 232
user
   accounts
      attributes. *See* attributes for creating user accounts
      authentication, 112
      local, 112
      as object class, 5
      types of, 112
   activities, 198
   configurations, 167, 172, 185, 214, 226
   logon/logoff scripts, 173
   as objects in organizational unit, 8
   policy settings, 177
   profiles, 174
   rights assignment, 189, 194
   validations, 174
User Principal Name (UPN), 13, 54, 84
User Rights Assignment, 174
userAccountControl. *See* attributes for creating user accounts
userPrincipalName. *See* attributes for creating user accounts
Users And Computers, Active Directory
   creating users and groups, 118, 129
   enabling user accounts for Smart Card authentication, 145
   finding Group Policy container using Advanced view, 163
   Group Policy Management Console (GPMC), 256
   starting, with Run As, 146
   verifying delegated permissions, 152
   viewing domain roles, 101
USNs (Update Sequence Numbers), 62, 294

V

validations, user, 174

W

WAN (wide area network), 60
well-connected IP subnets, 60
wide area network (WAN), 60
Windows 2000
   compatibility with Windows Server 2003, 16
   native mode, raising domains to prior to migrating to Windows Server 2003, 49, 116
Windows Installer Packages
   generally, 231
   properties, 232
Windows Installer Service, 222
Windows Management Instrumentation (WMI), 254
Windows NT 4.0, compatibility with, 16
Windows Scripting Host (WSH), 129
Windows Server 2003
   Active Directory implementation plan and, 13
   Active Directory installation, 28
   Domain Name System (DNS) and, 12, 15
   transitioning to, 16
   User Principal Names (UPNs) in, 13
Windows Server Catalog, 287
Windows Settings, 168
Windows Support Tools, 104, 230
WMI (Windows Management Instrumentation), 254
WMI Filters, 252
WMI Query Language (WQL), 252
Wmplayer.adm administrative template, 168
WQL (WMI Query Language), 252
WScript.exe, 129
WSH (Windows Scripting Host), 129
Wuau.adm administrative template, 168

X–Z

X.500, 11
zone transfer, 28
zones
   lookup, 39, 42, 44, 52
   scavenging for, 39–41

SYSTEM REQUIREMENTS

To complete the exercises in this textbook, you need to meet the following minimum system requirements:

- Microsoft Windows Server 2003, Enterprise Edition (A 180-day evaluation edition of Windows Server 2003, Enterprise Edition is included on the CD-ROM)
- Microsoft PowerPoint or Microsoft PowerPoint Viewer (PowerPoint Viewer is included on the Supplemental Student CD-ROM)
- Microsoft Word or Microsoft Word Viewer (Word Viewer is included on the Supplemental Student CD-ROM)
- Microsoft Internet Explorer 5.01 or later
- Minimum CPU: 133 MHz for x86-based computers and 733 MHz for Itanium-based computers (733 MHz is recommended)
- Minimum RAM: 128 MB (256 MB is recommended)
- Disk space for setup: 1.5 GB for x86-based computers and 2.0 GB for Itanium-based computers)
- Display monitor capable of 800 x 600 resolution or higher
- CD-ROM drive
- Microsoft mouse or compatible pointing device

UNINSTALL INSTRUCTIONS

The time-limited release of Microsoft Windows Server 2003, Enterprise Edition, will expire 180 days after installation. If you decide to discontinue the use of this software, you will need to reinstall your original operating system. You might need to reformat your drive.